THE
AMERICAN ALPINE
JOURNAL

1988

THE AMERICAN ALPINE CLUB
NEW YORK

ISSN 0065-6925
ISBN 0-930410-33-5

Manufactured in the United States of America

Articles and notes submitted for publication
and other communications relating to

THE AMERICAN ALPINE JOURNAL

should be sent to

THE AMERICAN ALPINE CLUB
113 EAST 90th STREET
NEW YORK, NEW YORK 10128-1589 USA
(212) 722-1628

THE OFFICERS AND BOARD OF DIRECTORS OF
THE AMERICAN ALPINE CLUB
ARE GRATEFUL TO THE FOLLOWING CORPORATIONS
FOR THEIR GENEROUS SUPPORT IN 1987

BACKPACKER MAGAZINE

ADOLPH COORS COMPANY

Friends of

The American Alpine Journal

**THE FOLLOWING PERSONS HAVE MADE CONTRIBUTIONS
IN SUPPORT OF THE CONTINUED PUBLICATION OF
THE AMERICAN ALPINE JOURNAL**

Robert H. Bates

John M. Boyle

Yvon Chouinard

Lydia L. Hall

Andrew Carson Harvard

James F. Henriot

James Dell Morrissey

Joseph E. Murphy, Jr..

William Lowell Putnam

Vincent & Mildred Starzinger

David H. Swanson

Horst Von Hennig

David G. Ward

Frank G. Wells

T. C. Price & Margaret F. Zimmermann

THE AMERICAN ALPINE JOURNAL

VOLUME 30 • ISSUE 62 • 1988

CONTENTS

COVER PHOTO: Cerro Torre, Torre Egger and Torre Standhardt, Patagonia.
Photo by Gino Buscaini

THE AMERICAN ALPINE CLUB

OFFICIALS FOR THE YEAR 1988

The Climb of the Century

RICK SYLVESTER

FOR SEVENTEEN YEARS I'd kept as secret as a blabbermouth like me could an idea for a first ascent in Yosemite Valley. Each year first ascents seem increasingly hard to come by, especially in areas as popular and accessible as Yosemite. Yet this one was strikingly obvious. For all those years I fretted and worried that someone would beat me to it. But I worried even more about doing it myself.

Between September 28 and October 3, Chauncey Parker and I climbed Upper Yosemite Falls Wall. In what some climbers view as an absurd application of Comici's famous dictum about the ideal line being the one where a drop of water falls, Chauncey and I climbed directly in line where the world's third-highest waterfall normally plummets down, varying little to left or right. We climbed it when it was bone-dry. That's what made it possible, something like the exact opposite of the situation where ice *aficionados* wait for conditions and temperatures to make their activity possible.

Surprisingly, dry conditions aren't all that rare. Most years, unless there has been an exceptionally heavy snowpack the preceding winter, Yosemite Creek, and consequently the Falls, dry up. A brief window permitting climbing usually occurs sometime beginning in mid September. In dry 1987, this period was longer, the creek having dried up earlier.

If Chauncey and I had been caught on the wall when the Falls resumed flowing, we would have made mountaineering history. If, for instance, a surprise deluge in the high country started filling the water table, we might have been the principals in a new type of death. Jed Williamson would have had to create a new category for us in his annual *Accidents in North American Mountaineering*. Somehow, that seemed too high a price to pay for fame.

I feel our route was the last great unclimbed line in the continental United States, certainly the last great *most obvious* unclimbed line. In all modesty, I see it as the climb of the century. I hope my fellow climbers will at least grant it was the season's sensation.

Let me clarify this. For certainly longer and harder climbs have been and will be done than Waterfall Wall. But Waterfall Wall was special; it had charisma. It was unique, whereas other routes seem like a variation on a theme. Naturally I exaggerate, though not completely. All first ascents contain an element of mystery, involving as they do the setting of hand and foot where no person has ever been before. But to place oneself in a location where for eons

1

trillions of tons of water have almost continually cascaded down involved more than mystery. It verged on being a mystical experience.

Or I should more accurately say that the *idea* of the climb was mystical. The actual experience involved the usual hard work and suffering, both physical and mental in this case, as we were constantly aware of potential death by water torture. As I mentioned to Chauncey, "I don't mind suffering in the usual way. I just don't want to suffer in any *new* way."

Aside from the fear of dying, I felt certain qualms about going up there. I wondered if our presence might somehow be construed as a desecration or sacrilege. My feelings were akin to the idea that the footprints and high-tech litter left behind on the moon detract from its romance. *Climb of the Century?* Perhaps it might be viewed as the *Crime of the Century*. Well, just so it didn't become the *Death of the Century*.

I had met Chauncey—he went by "Chuck" then—about fifteen years ago when I gave a slide show in Phoenix. We'd shared some desert climbing, including an old aid overhang that enjoyed a brief distinction of being the hardest free pitch in Arizona. This was 5.10c, so I'm obviously talking history.

A chance encounter a winter ago at a local search-and-rescue meeting reunited us. Remarkably, Chauncey still had the same wheels, the same '63 Dodge van he'd had in the desert. Wealth of experience may be the only association climbing bears to riches.

Sunday, September 27. We sorted our gear on the Valley floor and then commenced hiking up the Falls trail with loads so heavy we couldn't straighten up. We bore far more hardware than necessary. It's a bad sign when you can get into your pack only with the help of your partner. It's another bad sign when you hear your partner muttering and groaning to himself all the way up the approach.

After about a vertical thousand feet, we left the trail for the base of Upper Yosemite Falls Wall. That area is one of the natural wonders of the world. Yet, few hikers bound for the top of the Falls trail stray from their appointed rounds. If they did detour from the beaten path, they might marvel at the huge horizontal granite with its many pothole pools created by the action of the falls. We spent our first night there, sleeping poorly due to the crazy buffeting winds which are a strange nightly phenomenon of the Falls Amphitheater. They were to plague us every night.

The next morning we ascended the gully used by *Arrow Chimney, Arrow Direct* and *Tower of Geek* aspirants. That involved a bit of ropework. The grunt section was followed by a scramble left over an exposed but ropeless traverse to the start of the route. We were now a couple of hundred feet above the ground on a beautiful ledge directly in line with the dried-up waterfall. It was my first time back there in seventeen years. I had forgotten what a unique and magnificent place it was.

In 1970, Bugs McKeith, an excellent and popular Scottish climber, tragically later killed in a fall on Mount Assiniboine, and I had done a route, *Vía Sin Agua*, that followed a prominent flake system directly up a few hundred feet before traversing an obvious line left. Reputedly, it had never enjoyed a second ascent. Sometime after that climb, I'd gotten the idea that Bugs and I had skirted the main issue, that of continuing straight up the wall to the Fall's mouth. I started to feel that that was the real climb and line. As a result, the wall had grown to obsess me. Its blankness oppressed me. Fear tormented me. Blankness meant slow progress, and the slower, the more chance of being caught if the waterfall started up (perhaps more accurate: started *down*) again.

The ledge we walked out on to start the climb was the same one I'd always figured John Muir had traversed and subsequently written about. Now, there was a nonspecialist, unlike so many of today's climbers. Were Muir alive today, I'm sure he'd view climbing in its broader context of adventure and exploration. The type of fellow who seeks out the tallest, most wildly swaying tree to ascend during a violent storm is a man after my own heart.

If you sense that I've an axe to grind, you've sensed correctly. I have several in fact. All these years, I had been a bit amazed at the fact that *Vía Sin Agua* had never had a second ascent. Was I mad at this? Perhaps. *Vía Sin Agua* is a great excursion, an excellent itinerary in a unique location with lots of free climbing. There was no reason it shouldn't have had a second ascent. Of course, Bugs and I never expected it to become popular, but not to have a second ascent! Was this because it was perceived as a sort of gimmick climb, possible only when the Falls are dry? No, I actually think my main peeve is different. Many present-day climbers are caught up in the so-called numbers game, climbing solely to push their difficulty level. Who today is going to bother with a 5.8, A3 route? I get caught up in this myself. Pushing limits is worthwhile, but it represents only one of the many potential rewards of climbing. Whatever happened to climbing, even pure rock climbing, for things like the sake of exploration? Yes, I know; the numbers game can be viewed as an exploration of limits, admittedly a very engrossing and stimulating pursuit. But what about old-fashioned exploration, experiencing new territory, the adventure of the unknown, just plain curiosity as a motivating force? (Be careful! Curiosity killed the cat, Sylvester!)

Chauncey set down his load. "Whew, no more load carrying!"

"Yes, only hauling now."

"Well, let's begin suffering."

Chauncey and I reclimbed the pitches Bugs and I had done so long ago. It struck me that it was left to me to make the long-delayed second ascent of at least the first pitches of *Vía Sin Agua*. There was no sign of a bolt I'd placed on the initial pitch which Bugs and I had used for a necessary leftwards pendulum. However, I was surprised to discover one of my pitons at the first belay, Centipede Ledge. That archaeological find left me with strange feelings, although perhaps not so strange as my reactions a few minutes earlier to a 15-foot fall I'd taken. Just after encountering the largest rock frog I'd ever seen on a big wall, I was unexpectedly dropped when a piton behind an expanding flake pulled. To fall on the first 50 feet of a major route was a first for me. On

one of Chauncey's first leads, he suffered a similar fate and matched my fall. We hoped those wouldn't prove symbolic of worse things to come.

If we were looking for bad omens, there seemed no dearth. Just before setting out, I'd alerted John Dill, the Valley's long-time and very capable search-and-rescue technician, as to our plans. When I found John at the search-and-rescue cache, he was recreating the situation which had led to an Austrian's death on El Cap's Nose. He was trying to figure out the subjective errors the climber had made. Bad signs? In the days leading to our climb, an almost unprecedented number of recent climbing accidents had come to my attention. If I were into symbolism or unduly superstitious, I might have put off the climb for yet another year. But I knew that if not then, reputedly the second driest year in recorded Californian history, I might as well forget it.

I'd signed out for the climb. This was a non-mandatory procedure in Yosemite, unlike, for example, a park like the Tetons, where it's a firm regulation. It is the first time I'd signed out for a Valley route in over fifteen years, when it used to be required. I wanted to be sure of covering as best I could any potential liability in case we ended up needing a rescue. I had a gut-feeling worry, the fear that had kept me off the wall all those years, a fear that I was fated. No matter when I went out on that wall, a storm would ensue. No matter how stealthily I snuck up on it, even if I padded my hammer with a handkerchief, as I'd done doubling for Moore playing Bond in the climbing scene climax of *For Your Eyes Only*, the wall would know. The Shadow had nothing over that wall. And even if I had found not one, but two, lucky pennies just before the approach hike, deep down I knew I was doomed. Like many, I shared the deep concern that I'd already gotten away with too much, that maybe this cat had already run through all of his nine lives. At least I couldn't have made it simpler for John. To check on us, he had a clear view right from the porch of his search-and-rescue office. No daily drive down to El Cap Meadows. He only had to stick his neck out the door.

What was it like up there? That might be an unfair question, one Chauncey and I should possibly decline to answer if directly asked. This attitude might stem in part from Kurt Diemberger's classic, the one many climbers, including me, feel bears the most beautiful title in mountaineering literature, *Summits and Secrets*. That suggests, and perhaps rightly so, that there are secrets to be discovered high up. Possibly only those who make the effort, who essentially pay their dues, should be rewarded with the knowledge. So I've toyed with the idea of keeping the secret of Waterfall Wall. But, what the heck. Today I feel in a magnanimous mood and I won't be hard-nosed.

The wall, 1430 feet in height, is monolithic, very blank. Whereas *Vía Sin Agua* followed a natural line, this new route was a typically modern climb, not obvious, subtle, involving the connecting of obscure and thin features. Earlier I had speculated that with *Vía Sin Agua* Bugs and I had avoided the real issue. But of course we couldn't have done Waterfall Wall then, at least not in the current best style. Copperheads hadn't been invented yet. We would have been forced to resort to a lot more bolt drilling, i.e. defacement of the rock. Of course what would that have mattered, except to ourselves, to our own exertion? Judging by the overwhelming popularity of *Vía Sin Agua*, who was going to follow us up Waterfall Wall's more demanding and more dangerous line to discover all the telltale holes, shameful evidence of our opting away from the full challenge, the scary zipper potential?

The climbing was predominantly hard aid, mostly A4. In one pitch we used more hooks and copperheads than I'd used in my whole previous career. Frankly, that had been a record of wimpishness of which I was quite proud. For despite the fact I'd done over thirty big walls including the Big Daddy, as we used to call El Cap, this house-of-cards, hold-your-breath, mental-sweat, more-engineering-than-elegant-ballet-movement climbing is a type I've never particularly relished. Wasn't it Patrick Henry who had exclaimed, "Give me free climbing or give me death." Isn't it the license plate of New Hampshire which contains the state motto "Climb free or die?" I've long preferred the healthy physical sweat of honest free climbing to the mental sweat of hard aid, though I readily admit that the self-control and relaxed mind essential for success is equally true in both disciplines.

Several of my leads—and Chauncey's were as bad or worse—represented the thinnest aid pitches of my life. Dowels, hooks, copperheads, tiny RPs—it was enough to make grown men vomit. On one pitch the only piece I had thought was any good, a #3 Friend, came out before Chauncey reached it jümaring. During one of his leads, Chauncey remarked that it was the first time he had ever felt a sense of security from moving *onto* a hook. Another section he dubbed the "Rolaid Crack" for the relief it, at least temporarily, afforded. Can dowels hold falls? That was a question that had never occurred to me before Waterfall Wall. How can we rely on this stuff? Not to mention, how can I maintain any last vestige of self-respect playing these games now that I'm a parent?

Just before setting off for the Valley, I'd become aware of a unique possibility. A couple of local climbers had acquired the newest wrinkle in the great ethics controversy, a battery-powered Bosch drill. What an inspiration! Perhaps they'd let me borrow or rent it. I mean, of all the potential first ascents and new routes in the world, could there be a single one more than Waterfall Wall with its time-bomb waterfall ticking overhead where its use would be more justified, where the time element was more critical? The Bosch was the perfect solution.

But then my old spoilsport traditionalist conscience broke in! "If you're going to deface the rock, you should pay the price, e.g. hard labor." Believe me, I'm no puritan, but I'd long known that the whole point of climbing, especially in this day and age, was *how*, not *what*. Some might think that the purpose was to get to the Fall's mouth. But they would have been mistaken. It was really *how* we got there. If it was just to get to the top, why should we ever have bothered to leave the tourists and the trail? That's faster anyway. It had begun to seem as if everyone had forgotten Lito's classic essay, *Games Climbers Play*. The Skinner-Watts-Griffith crowd at the first so-called Great Debate in Denver surely seemed illiterate enough on the subject.

Besides, save for the hard work of bolting, what is to keep climbers honest? From the very start of my climbing career, I heard tales of Cro-Magnon specimens who reputedly could bolt more quickly than nail A3 or A4. Perhaps I lamented I had never had the strength to be numbered among their ranks. But with the facility of a Bosch, can anyone assure me that it would be used only where there was no chance for even the thinnest hard aid placements? C'mon, get real.

The very instant I started placing the first bolt in new terrain, in the section we called "The Desert"—dead vertical, hammer stretched overhead—I knew with absolute certainty that not trying to borrow the Bosch had been an unmitigated disaster of uncalculable dimension and sadness. Naturally, later I knew I was dead right not to have taken one along. And the later it becomes, the further in time from the completion of the route, the more faded and dimmed the memory of that exhausting work under the enervating sun, the more certain I become of my chosen path of ethical purity. As it turned out, we used only 20 bolts and dowels for actual progress.

One last word before leaving the subject of style and ethics. That lone bolt I'd placed on *Vía Sin Agua* seventeen years before that was gone still haunted me. Why was it gone? Had the Falls washed it away? If so, how long had it taken? How many years had it been able to withstand the nearly constant bombardment? Or had it fallen victim to the winter ice build-up? Yes, that might be more likely. Wait a minute! Forget about mundane concerns like the ethical purity of arm versus battery-powered drills. We might have a real breakthrough here. We might have the first self-perpetuating big-wall first ascent here. It was one thing when Valley golden boys one-uped the Europeans by having the second clean pitches to preserve as much of the first-ascent flavor as possible. But this, where even the bolts and the dowels get removed, clearly represented a step beyond! So much for subsequent ascents becoming vastly easier due to prior route knowledge and fixed gear. Here, future parties, assuming there would ever be any, would be plagued by doubt and uncertainty as to what they could expect. They might well be faced with the price of the same rigors as the first ascentionists yet for vastly diminished rewards, since they couldn't claim the glory of being first.

All the hard aid meant hard work and that meant slow climbing. That in turn meant more chance of getting caught in a storm and a resultant resurgent waterfall. Like many adventurous endeavors but more so, what this route was all about was calculated risk.

As it turned out, it took six days, exactly double what I'd estimated. I had assured one potential partner who had work commitments that he'd definitely be back in Tahoe after three days. Well, Bill would have lost his job. Three days in a row, Chauncey and I barely made more than a pitch. It was slow going, almost embarrassingly so. But of course there was also our heavy load, much of it unnecessary pitonage as well as the unnatural heat beside the nature of the climbing. We may have been slow, but we hold the record. That was a consoling thought until Pat, one of John Dill's co-workers, remarked after we got down, "You looked like trash up there." So much for swelled heads.

I had the odd pitches and Chauncey, the even. The right-facing flake system of *Vía Sin Agua* turned into the right end of a huge ledge which cut horizontally across the face. This Bugs and I had christened "The Sidewalk." Parts of it were so broad that one could walk unroped without a sense of panic. To gain the ledge required a wiggle through a hole. I'd forgotten how tight it was. The haulsack needed to be unpacked to get its contents through.

The next morning Chauncey started the fourth pitch, the first onto new territory. I could scarcely contain myself. At last, after all those years, after all the planning, hopes, worry and secrecy, it was really happening. Chauncey was traversing into the Eye of the Waterfall, the Headwall, the Desert. His pitch took most of the day and twilight caught me just twenty feet above his belay. A tricky diagonal rappel brought us back to the same bivy as the night before. The way things looked above, it appeared to be the last real ledge and definite feature we would find for a while.

It also brought us an essential piece of luck. Chauncey found a couple of pools in the flake-and-ledge system, one containing clean water, the result of a seemingly impossible spring in the middle of the barren wall. We ended up cutting it pretty close. Perhaps we could have finished if we had run out of water. I'd had to do that years before on the first ascent of *Son of Heart* where my partner and I climbed two-and-a-half days in 100° heat with no food and more important, no water, to finish ten day's effort. I was younger then. On Waterfall Wall, I found myself doing something new, having water relayed up to me in the middle of a lead so I could slake my thirst and wet my dried mouth, the latter as much the result of the tension created by the hard aid as by the heat.

While the leader died a thousand deaths strung out on A4, often requiring five or six hours to progress a single rope-length, the belayer was in a totally different world. Ironically, his problem was boredom. The second had lots of time to meditate on where he'd gone wrong. He had whole days to ruminate on what genetic character fault or sin of an ancestor he must be atoning for. Else, why had he been attracted somehow to this perverse activity, this mind-numbing, body-ravaging, soul-destroying madness, rather than, say, something civilized like golf.

For diversion there were occasional hikers on the Falls trail to look at and shout at. There was also the almost daily party suddenly and dramatically appearing on the skyline near the tip of the Lost Arrow Spire. A twosome would turn up like clockwork almost the exact time each day. Wonderful air shows were put on by the swifts as they zoomed and swooped in the updrafts. Who says animals don't play? One day a rare peregrine falcon put in an appearance. Modern belay devices allow safety without constant pinpoint attention to the rope. That meant the second could even read. Chauncey polished off the entire book I'd taken along. I have mixed feelings about the practice. It's unnerving to be sweating blood and then glance down and see your belayer totally oblivious, lost in literature.

Naturally we had a great view. We could see most of the east end of the Valley. And it, us. We were potentially the best show in town. We could see and be seen by Yosemite Lodge, Camp Curry, the core village area with the market and Visitors' Center, just about all the campgrounds, and even, at one extreme, the west-facing rooms of the luxurious Ahwahnee Hotel and, at the exactly opposite extreme, the Camp 4 parking lot. We should have stuck out like sore thumbs. (Pat's "trash" seems a trifle harsh.) Yet, I've a feeling that fame eluded us. I have the strongest suspicion that virtually no one spotted us up there. We'd probably have to resort to something really drastic, like writing accounts for the *American Alpine Journal*.

The wall's exposure was enhanced by its steepness and blankness. The huge flat granite slab directly below, so much more unfriendly in appearance than the pine carpet at El Cap's base, proved at first a frightening factor for me. Then, after a couple of days, I got used to the vertical world, and my thoughts became disassociated from the ground. Fear turned into contempt. The last two days of the climb I scarcely noticed the exposure. Occasionally I'd glance down in an attempt to give myself a jolt but it hardly worked. Besides, I had more important things on my mind, such as food. Why does your partner's always seem better, not to mention more plentiful?

My attitude toward the sky evolved similarly. The climb had begun, as I'd insisted, under a perfect blue sky. Eight years earlier, two of us had done the hard approach and spent the night near the start of the route, intending to climb it. The next morning, a couple of clouds had appeared and I said, "Let's beat it." Two days later a thin trickle of Falls was flowing again.

On Chauncey's and my second day a cloud build-up began. The next couple of days it started earlier and became greater. The sky changed from blue to downright scary, the clouds showing black bottoms and the smell of water was in the air. As the climb wore on and the debilitating heat continued to beat down oppressively upon us, I found myself, seemingly perversely, wanting clouds, welcoming the relief of shade when they were directly in front of the sun. It wasn't that I didn't care any more. That attitude is mostly true only in cheap literature and bad films. Rather, I was willing to gamble with the odds of potential future death versus the all-too-certain harsh reality of my present discomfort.

By day we sweltered, performing the scary hard climbing without a breath of cooling wind. And the torture continued into the night when we slept fitfully, buffeted about by the continually strong, chilly gusts which regularly arise just after dark only in that amphitheater of Yosemite. It was like the Patagonian express-train winds, jerking at you like a terrier all night long, leaving you too bleary-eyed and sluggish to set out willingly the next morning. It was the worst of two worlds: Yosemite's reflecting oven by day and a high-alpine bivy by night. The wind against Chauncey's water bottle beside his portaledge sounded like someone shaking a martini.

If that weren't enough, things happened on the climb that had never happened to me before. Halfway up we were reduced to one hammer when the handle of Chauncey's split in two, the head flying over his shoulder. We had to relay mine back and forth between leading and seconding. This was facilitated by a third rope, a technique I'd created on *Son of Heart* so that I could still get more gear if I were in the second half of a lead and prone to my characteristic lack of good foresight. I didn't like to dwell on the consequences of losing that last hammer, especially if retreat, i.e. replacing anchors, proved necessary.

At another point I stupidly dropped something. I'd always prided myself on having dropped very little gear during the course of my climbing. But we'd already taken up the practice of sharing Chauncey's portaledge after I dropped my Forrest hammock spreader and spent one of the worst nights ever, squeezed against the hard wall. I hadn't taken a portaledge due to the extra weight, figuring the hammock would be fine for just the couple of ledgeless nights. Wrong, wrong! It's hard to believe how few years ago it was that single-suspension-point hammocks seemed the state-of-the-art cat's meow. As in the case of the Bosch drill, once you know of the existence of something better, suffering seems intolerable.

My first thought was that I'd dropped the drill. The frayed end of the bit of parachute cord that connected it to me dangled from my gear sling. My mind ran riot for a moment, then went numb. "The climb's over; the dream's finished" flashed through my mind before I discovered I still had the drill. It was safely nestled in the bolt sack. It was two hooks that had fallen. If it had been the drill, we would have been stopped cold. And I knew I would never have returned. Repeat all the hard work to get that high? Experience brain death again on all those A4 leads? No way!

Then there was the bizarre. Earlier, just before embarking onto the new territory of the virgin wall, I'd gotten my upper body wedged in space between blocks near the bivy ledge. What might sound funny resulted in pure claustrophobia and trauma. It was difficult to maintain control and fight down the rising paralyzing panic. And if this wasn't enough, halfway up the climb in the middle of one more A4 lead, Chauncey cavalierly announced we were climbing on the wrong rope. Mistakenly, he'd failed to bring along his newest and best one. Instead, our lifeline was one that contained a worrisome sheath fray. I felt it wouldn't be inappropriate if another fifteen years passed before we climbed together again.

On the fifth day, the climbing began going faster as we had a real crack system to work with. But Chauncey's disappointment was keen when it became apparent that we wouldn't reach the top that day but were in for one more night out. The next morning began with another A4 pitch, another "Morning Eye Opener" as we called it, that was hard right off the bivy belay. My nerves were getting a little frayed. Fun was fun, but now we just wanted to finish. I had figured the hard aid was behind us. The capper was having to drill some more, on the last day. It didn't seem fair. Nothing seemed fair any more. When I started to go free off a hook, trying to clamber onto the first decent ledge in days, I couldn't complete the move. I'd forgotten I'd clipped into the hook. I couldn't get a boot back into the *étrier*. I was in danger of ripping back onto the A4. At last the ordeal ended with the consolation of ending on a beautiful ledge. The top looked less than half a pitch away with easier going.

It was Chauncey's lead. My enthusiasm turned to consternation as I kept paying out more and more rope. What was going on? Chauncey finally yelled "Off belay!" when there was no more rope. Just where was the summit? Was this a cruel variation of the old "It's just around the corner" routine? My pitch, the eleventh, was also a full rope-length. But that one was pure enjoyment — well, as much enjoyment as one can experience in that fatigued state. It consisted of moderately difficult free climbing on perfectly clean rock. I could still free-climb; I hadn't forgotten how! I exited from the world of the vertical and found anchors just above the lip of the Falls.

The creek bed was solid bedrock, like a huge trough or the bottom of a pipe. It was a fantastic spot. It was for things like this I'd gotten into climbing. But as we stuffed our gear into packs, we realized it was the end of the day.

I don't think I'd ever been less confident of success on a major route before. I never believed the route was in the bag until we were hiking down. But we didn't appreciate the victory at the time, for the descent was a cruel trial. Despite being devoid of all food and water, our loads were still killing. The ridiculous amount of hardware by itself just about filled them. The trail, mostly cobbled, did not lend itself to any rhythm, and certainly not on a moonless night with a burned-out headlamp. We raced to make it down before the Valley's last restaurant closed. Our appetites were well honed. Not to be able to appease them until the following morning loomed as an unthinkable calamity of tragic proportions. In our state, pain *per se* was no more acute than a pleasure missed or even deferred. Thus, for me the descent was a Bataan death march. And the Four Seasons had closed, but the Loft stayed open an hour later, until ten, and we made it.

A week later I returned to the Valley with my family. On the wall I'd resolved to share this special place with the special people of my life. I wasn't spending enough time with my family. And the kids grow up so fast! There is a danger of losing something more irreplaceable than a first like Waterfall Wall. We hiked up the Falls trail. We left the trail and cross-countried over to the wondrous Falls base area. I explained to Cheyenne and Terray that whereas the rock was smooth from all the water, it was nevertheless nothing like the glacier polish that delighted them along the flanks of Lambert Dome. We explored the huge granite base area, venturing as far as we could without ropes into the gorge below. We dipped in the spring-fed pool. My family gathered garbage—we made it a game—and an article or two we had dropped on the climb, including bits of my broken plastic hammock spreader.

An evening later as we toasted marshmallows around a campfire, it started to drizzle. But it wasn't enough to affect the Yosemite Creek watershed. The Falls remained dry. It was another week and a half before the first real autumn rains came to thirsty California. And the Falls flowed again.

Lukpilla Brakk's Western Edge

PHILIP C. POWERS, *Unaffiliated*

WALKING OUT after our climb of Gasherbrum II was quite a social experience. The Baltoro Glacier had lost its snow and become populated. We found friends to feed us, doctors to mend us and porters a plenty to speed us out. We hurried to Skardu with typical roadhead fever but found little satisfaction: beer, mail and such. The friends who were to climb with me above the Biafo Glacier were still a day's wait and a day's drive away in Rawalpindi.

Tony Jewell, Phil Peabody* and Tom Walter arrived the day before the Gasherbum II boys flew home. They had hitched a ride with a French Chogolisa expedition. This second expedition already promised to be simpler and easier without the logistical nightmares of the higher peaks. Sub-6000-meter goals require no permits and no liaison officers. We had some monetary help from the National Outdoor Leadership School and the advantage of making all the arrangements a second time in 1987. It would be a friendly relaxed trip. After a few days of purchasing, arranging and bouldering, we picked up Greg Collins and Sue Miller at the airport, thus completing our crew. That same day we drove to Dasso, hired porters and managed to inveigle our jeep drivers to continue through a few rough sections to a camp past Biansapa.

The quick pace for Greg and Sue, who just a few days before were teaching in the mountains of Alaska, did not slow till we arrived four days later on July 25 at Base Camp up the Biafo Glacier. Expeditions coming out from the mountains all brought the same news: disappointment, bad weather and deep snow on the high peaks. We experienced the traditional porter problems at Baintha, our destination on the north side of the Biafo. Ahmad, our friend and sardar, never could explain the logic of the strike for higher wages *after* our loads had already arrived intact.

On July 28, in an Alaskan drizzle that became a heavy rain, three of us moved six miles up the Biafo: Sue Miller to get a better look up-glacier, Greg Collins and I to climb the golden western edge of Lukpilla Brakk. The next morning under a clear blue sky, we humped our loads up the lower snow slope, anxious for and intimidated by the spire above. We said goodbye to Sue

---

*Recipient of American Alpine Club Climbing Fellowship Grants.

PLATE I

Photo by Greg Collins

LUKPILLA BRAKK from the West. Bottom several hundred feet are hidden.

while underestimating the number and difficulty of the lower pitches. Though the climbing at the spire's base was not steep, it was seamy and quite hard. Harder still was hauling our heavy bag. Tony Jewell had made it for us and we were convinced that he had added special, hidden rock-grabbers. Dusk brought us to "Sickle Ledge" where we began the first of our major ledge excavations under the roofs and steepening wall above.

We left some rope and gear to lighten the rock-grabbing haulbag-beast and began a cold morning of climbing with no sun till noon. Greg left the ledge via a steep hand crack. The next section widened and steepened in a cold wet corner. Greg was forced to drill the first of two bolts on the route. He pulled up over a body-length roof and was at "Tower Ledge" at over 16,000 feet.

The summer's storminess often granted clear mornings but rarely allowed a full day of fun. We were not climbing so fast that we needed to take a three-hour break, but it was blowing and snowing so hard by the time I reached the ledge that we took one anyhow. Bivy sacks and candy bars. The storm lifted long enough for two more pitches at dusk before retreating to our now nicely gardened ledge.

Melting snow for breakfast was easy. It was four inches deep on our bivy sacks. I won the disconcerting chore of jümaring the lines to retrieve a rope for the descent. Greg's talk of the rope-eating rodent he saw at our high point did not help. We were safely down by noon, leaving four ropes in place. At Baintha that night we were all together again. The storm had forced Tony Jewell, Phil Peabody and Tom Walter off their route on the "Ogre Stump."

We baked, bouldered and chased the local bear around for four days. He loved to eat our kerosene, candy bars and sometimes a butane canister for dessert. Our bear visited us nightly and he became progressively bolder and smarter as our tactics for scaring him became more creative. In the beginning we just threw rocks and yelled. Sue usually slept through these attacks, but one night she woke and threw Greg's walkman. We knew we had trained our bear well when he evaded the 200-pound food barrel Tony tried to drop on his head with an elaborate snare.

With light packs and with the crux pitches fixed, Greg and I reached Tower Ledge early on August 6. Steep rock, tough route-finding and harder climbing soared up above us. We woke to beautiful weather which allowed us a full day of climbing on the best rock we had yet been on. I led through some unbelievably thin flakes while Greg hid behind packs and made a neck shield out of rope. Steep cracks and tiny roofs brought us to a large roof which had worried us from the start. We were able to pass it on an unprotected face to a tiny roof and a mossy aid crack. Here the climbing became more intricate and the route-finding tricky. It was still a long way to "Snow Pillar Ledge."

We expected that the climbing would ease at least a bit at the base of the pillar. Instead, we were in steep aid cracks. When they finally widened, they became too wide to aid and much too icy to be fun. Greg free-climbed this nastiness, mumbling about run-outs and nonexistent tube chocks. He was forced to downclimb or lower twice to retrieve large Friends from below. I was

Tom Walter on the Summit Ridge of "Ogre Stump" above Uzun Brakk Glacier.

mostly concerned with finding comfort at my cold hanging belay by eating a granola bar. Whoosh! A brick-sized rock passed by me, carrying my snack with it. Ice-filled finger cracks in the back of a chimney and a final short moonlit pitch brought us to the big gardenable ledge.

Within minutes of tying-in the next morning, Greg was trying to warm his fingers with the breath from his question, "Who needs coffee when you can stand on tied-off knifeblades first thing in the morning?" I understood his question later when leading past a giant, detached chopping-block flake which woke me up. Above the chopping-block, the climbing was pure fun on excellent granite. Even the 30-foot ice section in Fires was enjoyable: hand-jamming between the icicles. By two P.M. we had reached the first summit of the spire and its amazing bus-sized balanced boulder. Though this summit is two pitches from the true top, the incoming snow and wind of a big new storm made it easy to call the bus-stop the end of our route. We descended to the Snow Pillar Ledge by dark and spent the long stormy night huddled, laughing and happy, under a portaledge fly. At 17,000 feet, there was not enough air under the fly both to breathe and operate the stove at full power.

The snow fell deep again. We rose reluctantly to horrid visibility and packed for the tedious descent. Any smugness I had felt in being healthy while others suffered from "third-world bowels" vanished that morning. Greg engineered the rappels and we were in Base Camp eating Sue's freshly baked cookies that night.

Meanwhile, Tony Jewell and Tom Walter had done an impressive route on a previously unclimbed rock tower that rises from the Uzun Brakk Glacier, two-and-a-half miles south-southwest of the Ogre (Baintha Brakk). We could not find any local name for this 18,000-foot peak, but it has been referred to as the "Ogre Stump." Tony Jewell describes the climb: "We ascended the dominant prow and the southwest side of the peak and took three days to climb it and to rappel off. There were 21 pitches and we rated it VI, 5.10+, A2. The crux, led by Tom Walter, consisted of a huge ice block choking the top of a dihedral two pitches from the summit. With no other option, Tom had to do several layback moves on the edge of the ice to overcome this formidable obstacle."

Before the bear's impact on our rations slowed us down, Greg Collins and Sue Miller made an enjoyable ascent of P 19,100, east of the Biafo Glacier on the south side of the Baintha Lukpar Glacier, opposite Latok II. Tony Jewell and Tom Walter paired up again to reach the top of Gamma Sokha Lumbu by its snowy northwest ridge.

Summary of Statistics:

AREA: Biafo Glacier, Karakoram, Pakistan.

ASCENTS: Lukpilla Brakk, 5380 meters, 17,650 feet; New Route, the Western Edge; Foresummit reached on August 7, 1987 (Collins, Powers); VI, 5.11, A3, 23 pitches.

"Ogre Stump," 5487 meters, 18,000 feet; First Ascent; Southwest Face; August 13, 1987 (Jewell, Walter); VI, 5.10+, A2, 21 pitches.

P 19,100, 5822 meters; August 14, 1987 (Collins, Miller).

Gama Sokha Lumbu, 6282 meters, 20,610 feet, August 23, 1987 (Jewell, Walter).

PLATE 3

Photo by Philip Powers

**Greg Collins leading the 12th pitch
of LUKPILLA BRAKK.**

The Golden Pillar: Spantik

ANTHONY VICTOR SAUNDERS, *North London Mountaineering Club*

IN THE HEART of the Karakoram, in the ancient Mirdom of Nagar, lies a little known mountain. Although the Karakoram Highway passes no more than 20 miles from it, the peak is not visible from the road. Yet, from Nagar the mountain is striking. On the Skardu side of the watershed, the peak is called Spantik*. (This may be a Balti name. I have not been there.) According to some sources, the peak is also known as Yengutz Sar, but this is clearly erroneous as the peak cannot be seen from the Burushaski-speaking Yengutz Har Valley (Valley of the Torrent of the Flour Mills).

The first Westerners to attempt the mountain were the Americans Fanny Bullock Workman and her husband Dr. William Hunter Workman. In 1906, they laboriously climbed the Chogolungma Glacier, taking in the peaks of Chogo and Lungma on the way to the plateau, about 1000 feet below the summit. Their name for the mountain was "Pyramid Peak." The Workmans's effort was not bettered till half a century later when in 1955 West Germans Reiner Diepen, Eduard Reinhardt and Jochen Tietze made a successful ascent by the Chogolungma Glacier, possibly following the route pioneered by the Workmans. The Germans used the name of Spantik.

On the north side of the mountain, a large monolithic pillar catches the evening sun and gives the mountain its Burushaski name, Ghenish Chhish, which means Golden Peak. The Golden Pillar is marble. The rock is crystalline, almost sugary in parts, but generally sound. It is the *coup de grace* of a vertical outcrop of metamorphic limestone, which leapfrogs the glaciers from above the village of Hoppar. Looking out from high on the pillar, we were able to see the cream-yellow rock arcing from glacier to glacier for 15 miles, like a series of rainbows.

The Golden Pillar is the clear, unavoidable challenge of the mountain, soaring from the glacier for 2200 meters. The summit is about 300 meters higher and set back, perhaps, three kilometers from the pillar. We had seen the pillar in 1984 while attempting to climb Bojohagur Duanasir, a 24,045-foot

---

*The name is indeed Balti: *Spang* = grass and *tik* = place. The German linguist Wilhelm Kick, who has studied the place names in the Chogolungma valley, explains that the name apparently came from a grassy slope on the southeast spur of the mountain; the name then was transferred to the peak itself.—*Editor*.

(7329-meter) mountain directly above the Karakoram Highway. We failed to climb the peak alpine-style while Japanese made the first ascent, using five camps and several kilometers of fixed rope. Despite differences in attitudes, when Phil Butler and I met them on Day 10 of our gruelling 14-day climb, they offered us food and had kind words about our effort. The 1984 Bojohagur expedition was a North London Mountaineering Club affair and it was much the same team that, having seen the Golden Pillar in 1984, knew it would have to return. Even though Golden Peak was on the horizon, it was clear that something remarkable, even very nasty, decorated its north face.

In England, further enquiries revealed little of the mountain's history. From Poland the encyclopedic Zbigniew Kowalewski sent us photographs taken from Kunyang Chhish. Nazir Sabir, Doug Scott and Tadeusz Piotrowki (who perished during the awful summer of 1986) all kindly donated "front-on" prints, which all but persuaded us to cancel. At the same time we began to compare the pillar to the Walker Spur, just a little higher, and perhaps a bit harder. During 1986, the team jelled. It was to consist of Bojohagurites Phil Butler, Mick Fowler, Dr. John English and me, with two new members, Liz Allen and Bruce Craig. Mick's father George Fowler, our liaison officer Dr. Iqbal Ahmed and our Nagari cook Rajab Zawat completed the expedition.

We established Base Camp at 4000 meters at a place known to locals as Suja Bassa on July 14. The march from the roadhead at Hoppar had taken five days, though it could easily have been done in three. The porters originally wanted to take six, but we compromised on five and a goat. (It is "traditional" for expeditions to give their porters a goat.) Visitors to this region should note that the daily rate of pay is not excessive, but the "traditional" day stages can be as short as one-and-a-half hours. This makes Nagar the most expensive region in the Karakoram for expeditions. We found the Hoppar men honorable. Having struck a bargain, they invariably stuck to it.

We made a dump of gear at 4500 meters two hours above Base, directly across the small Golden Pillar Glacier from the base of the pillar. From there we could see that the pillar was divided into four sections. First, a 400-meter pinnacle, the First Tower, barred access to the long serpentine snow arête. The arête ended in a small step which led to the third section, a tiny hanging glacier. The fourth part was the point of the exercise, a 1200-meter wall, a great spear thrust into the sky.

On July 19, Fowler and I made a preliminary reconnaissance of the approaches to the pillar. It took three days to reach the hanging glacier. Meanwhile English and Allen made a start on the Descent Ridge. They were stopped by deep snow and indifferent weather, but not before they had climbed the initial 400-meter Prominence, a sort of pyramidal tower. Butler and Craig inspected the Yengutz Pass, which had not, so far as we knew, been crossed. This initial flurry of activity was followed by attempts on the pillar or on the ridge which failed in appalling weather.

On the evening of August 5, Fowler and I walked to the gear dump, knowing it was our last chance to try the route. Fowler, a Civil Servant, was

PLATE 4

Photo by A.V. Saunders

The Golden Pillar—SPANTIK.

due back at his desk on the 23rd in 18 days' time. If we allowed ten days for the climb, he would just make it. We had packed and repacked after lunch, shouldered the enormous loads and wordlessly began to walk. The weather was variable in the extreme. There was even a minor snowstorm while we climbed.

During that night, we climbed the 1000 meters to the hanging glacier and spent the remainder of the 6th praying for good weather. On Day 2, we were fortunate and by starting at four A.M. were able to climb ten pitches of slabs and walls to reach the Amphitheater by five P.M. It was important to get there as there would have been no possibility of finding a bivouac ledge on the slabs.

We had thought, when we started, that the main difficulty of this day would be the little walls which crossed the slabs and a larger wall which barred access to the Amphitheater. In fact, we found the reverse was true. There was no ice on the rock, and the blank-surfaced slabs offered precarious climbing with no protection. The walls, however, contained cracks which could be cleaned of snow to hold the occasional runner.

On Day 3, the weather was not so kind. We stopped at midday for a brew which became a bivouac, as it began to snow heavily. We had climbed out of the Amphitheater by a system of steep chimneys and grooves. This was one of the few parts of the route we had not been able to examine with binoculars and so from a route-finding point of view, we had passed one of the two cruxes. This day also included some of the most technically demanding climbing. The first pitch out of the Amphitheater was a groove with an overhanging section. Mick managed to place two wobbly pegs above his head and then began to swear loudly and forcibly. He could not, it seems, clip into the pegs because the sling was stuck under his hood. The belay was on black shale and Mick was grinning like a cat with two tails as he pointed to the shale chimney that continued in the direction we wanted to climb. It looked as if it were coated in inches of thick, inviting ice, but it was deceiving. The pitch was horrible: verglas on shale fragments.

Although it snowed overnight, the next morning brought visibility, if not clear skies. As the mists receded, we recognized the features that would act as landmarks. It was enough to go on with. We began to follow lines on the right wall of the pillar. By midday, we reached a large flat ledge, the top of a giant jammed block. There we made tea and relaxed until it occurred to us to look up. We were completely surrounded by overhangs. Fowler led an aid pitch to gain the lowest of a series of ramps. The lower ramps led to a shield, which was the other area of uncertainty for us. From Base Camp there had appeared to be no line around this feature, but a hidden chimney revealed itself at the end of the ramp. Because it was blank-sided and there was no belay at the top, I had to belay Mick by wedging my body across the chimney and asking him not to fall.

I do not remember having a more miserable bivouac than the one we had that night. We were benighted and there was no ledge, nor even the possibility of cutting one on the thin ice. We used the tent as a hanging bag, inside of

which Mick spent the night in his harness, while I stood in my rucksack. It snowed all night.

The 3:30 alarm was greeted with relief. It was Day 5. Looking up we could see the final ramps. When we reached them, they looked easy, but as we climbed, the truth dawned on us. They were covered with a layer of powder snow which, when swept off, revealed blank rock. We could place no runners and the side wall pushed you off balance. We had 100-foot run-outs and lots, and lots of fear. These ramps in turn led to the final vertical book-shaped corner under an ear-shaped sérac. Mick made short work of the difficulties, banging in the pegs with care. (I had asked him not to disturb the sérac above us.) And then we found the snow leading to the plateau so deep that we began to have horrible thoughts of being forced down the way we had come up.

Day 6 was our summit day. At six A.M. we started from the tent, leaving behind all but our clothes and a stove. At 12:45 we stood on top of the Golden Peak. It was August 11. We could see Bojohagur, Batura, Diran, Trivor and other large peaks, but from Kunyang Chhish black clouds were invading the sky. The storm overtook us within the hour. First the electric shocks. We hid, trying to bury ourselves and our axes in the snow. The high winds swept in from the south. We had fears for the tent. We could imagine it flying down to Base Camp. The winds brought drifting snow and a white-out. Our tracks disappeared. We were high on the plateau, surrounded by precipices. After a bit of experimentation, we found that on all fours we could feel the softness of the slope where our tracks had been filled in and so we crawled down toward the tent.

By the morning of Day 7, the weather had regained its composure. It was clear and frigid. Below us a sea of clouds filled the valleys. It was worrying because we could not see where to leave the plateau to find the Descent Ridge. During the climb, we had noted a tongue of the plateau stretching out over the ridge. On this tongue lay some ice blocks, which we referred to as the "Crumbs." After three worrisome hours of crossing the high plateau, with its crevasses large enough to swallow a battleship, we arrived at the top of an icefall. There below us were the Crumbs. The valley fog was receding and the tongue was revealed, but where on the edge of the tongue was the descent? We knew that if we picked the wrong spot, not only would we miss the ridge, but we would also be abseiling over large séracs into space.

In the icefall we made our very first snow bollard abseils, but they led to the tongue, where we found the Crumbs were 40 feet high. Guessing that the ridge would be near the tip of the tongue, we pitched the tent and waited for the mist to clear down to the valley. We made a brew and dozed, mentally tired and needing to get down. At 5:30 P.M., it did clear. We had no *dead-men* for snow belays. We dug a large hole in the soft plateau. I got as deep into the hole as possible and so we had a *live-man* belay. Mick gingerly stepped toward the edge, got on his stomach and crawled towards it. It was an easy cornice. He descended a few feet before coming back to the belay.

"Well, Mick, how is it?"

PLATE 5

Photo by A.V. Saunders

The Ear Sérac on the Golden Pillar.

PLATE 6

Photo by A.V. Saunders

Fowler on the Amphitheater on the Golden Pillar.

"You try," was all he said.

I looked over the edge of the cornice and saw the Descent Ridge snaking down to the Prominence. Surely we were going to survive this climb. Already I had begun to debate the value of it all. What is the point of mountaineering? It seemed to me in that moment that the nature of the goal did not matter. Are we driven to reach goals but can learn no lessons from them? There is no pot of gold, only the rainbow.

"I suppose it's because we live in an achievement-oriented society," I said to Mick. He looked at me as if I had just announced I was stark staring mad.

In the tent we discussed our plans if we could get down safely. Over to the north, I could see the Yengutz Har Pass. I decided that after a few days' rest I would try with the others to cross that pass. Fowler said that if we could get down the next day, he would walk out to Hoppar the following day, take a jeep and bus to Gilgit and hope to catch his plane to London from Islamabad on Sunday.

"Why the great rush?" I asked.

"Because it means by Monday the 16th I shall have parked those Civil Service shoes under that Civil Service desk and saved a whole week of annual leave. Know what I mean, Vic?" He tapped the side of his nose.

Iqbal, Butler, Craig and I did eventually complete the traverse of the pass. It took us four hard days for the round-trip, much longer than anticipated. We had made the mistake of selling our rope in Hispar and then descending the Hispar Gorge on the wrong bank. We found ourselves soloing across difficult rock-climbing ground without a rope above roaring Hispar River. The other three showed great patience, waiting for me, tired and emaciated.

As for Fowler, I don't know where he got the energy, but he caught the flight. By Monday morning, 9:30 sharp, those Civil Service shoes were under that Civil Service desk.

Summary of Statistics:

AREA: Western Karakoram, Pakistan

NEW ROUTE: Spantik or Ghenish Chhish, 7027 meters, 23,055 feet, Northwest Pillar, Summit reached on August 11, 1987 (Fowler, Saunders). (Fifth ascent of the peak.)

PERSONNEL: Anthony Victor Saunders, leader, Elizabeth Allen, Philip Butler, Bruce Craig, Dr. John English, Michael Fowler, George Fowler, liaison officer Dr. Iqbal Ahmed.

Makalu

GLENN PORZAK

PORTING ONE OF the lowest success
ratios (20%) of any of the world's fourteen 8000-meter peaks, Makalu has been
a true nemesis for the American Himalayan climber. At 27,825 feet, the fifth
highest mountain in the world has been the objective of no less than ten
American expeditions or expeditions with an American presence. Yet, prior to
1987, only one American, John Roskelley, had reached its summit.

It was against this backdrop that our team of nine Colorado climbers and
four Sherpas set out in March of 1987 to challenge the Great Black
One—so-called because of the mountain's distinctive band of dark granite.
Located on the border of Nepal and Tibet approximately 12 miles east of
Mount Everest, Makalu would more than live up to its reputation as one of the
more difficult 8000ers.

The nucleus of our team consisted of six members of the successful 1983
American expedition to 26,398-foot Shishapangma. They were John Cooley,
Ed Ramey and Sandy Read, and summitters Mike Browning, Chris Pizzo and
I. In addition, the group included Dave Herrick, Dr. Stefan Goldberg and Gary
Neptune. Pizzo had reached the summit of Everest in 1981 and Neptune in
1983. Finally, we also had the good fortune to employ four topnotch high
altitude porters: Lhakpa Dorje (the Sardar), Sherpa Lhakpa Nuru, who had
previously climbed to 8100 meters on Makalu with Reinhold Messner, Sherpa
Dawa Nuru, and Motilal, a Gurung from the Makalu region.

From Kathmandu, we began our journey to Base Camp by flying east 100
air miles to Tumlingtar, a small village situated on the Arun River at less than
1500 feet. After rounding up enough porters to carry our 130 loads, we were
on our way.

Over the next three days we gradually ascended the lowland forests,
traversed terraced fields of flooded rice paddies, and meandered along forested
ridges covered with tropical vegetation. After camping by the picturesque
village of Num, on the fourth day we descended more than 3000 vertical feet
to cross the Arun River, only to immediately regain every inch of lost altitude
by climbing to the village of Sedua on the opposite mountainside. The next day
the terrain became more rugged as we fought our way through dense, almost
jungle-type terrain infested with leeches, until we eventually reached the
village of Tashigaon. Located at 7000 feet, the dozen or so log and stone
houses of this settlement would be the last signs of any permanent habitation
that we would see for the next two months.

29

After enduring a day-long strike and switching to porters who were better equipped to handle higher altitudes, the real adventure began. Less than an hour out of Tashigaon, the path steepened. Up we climbed through thick bamboo and then rhododendron forests, until on the afternoon of the seventh day we encountered deep snow at 10,000 feet. We were at the base of Shipton's Pass, the logistical nightmare of virtually every expedition to the Makalu region. Rising to 13,400 feet, this rugged and storm-swept pass is snow-covered most of the year. While numerous expeditions have had to spend many days ferrying loads over it, the gods were to smile kindly upon us. Despite turbulent weather and snows over six feet deep, we got all of our loads across in just two days.

From the top of Shipton's Pass, we descended 4500 vertical feet to the Barun River which is fed by Makalu's northwestern and southern glaciers. For the next three days we journeyed through perhaps the most remote and spectacular mountain terrain I have ever seen. With the valley floor consisting of lush tundra and rushing streams, flanked by sheer rock walls and countless waterfalls plunging thousands of feet, it was like walking into a virgin Yosemite Valley. Yet there was one big difference. In this Shangri La, peaks rising to 24,000 feet formed the backdrop. It is simply the jewel of Nepal. The beauty intensified until on the eleventh day we skirted a rocky hillside, turned north onto a lateral moraine, and there it was. Towering more than two vertical miles into the atmosphere and rising in one massive sweep to a perfect summit pinnacle stood the Great Black One.

On April 1, we reached a clearing in the moraine beneath the south face of Makalu at 16,000 feet. It was the site of the Base Camp used by Sir Edmund Hillary during his unsuccessful attempts on Makalu in 1954 and again in 1961. Here most of the porters turned back, but a stalwart group remained over the next few days to help shuttle loads up to Advance Base at 17,500 feet. Located on a small plateau above the rocky moraine of the Barun Glacier, the views of Everest, Lhotse and countless other peaks were simply awesome. However, nothing was more impressive than Makalu's west face which loomed directly overhead.

After settling into our permanent Base Camp and organizing the loads destined for the upper part of the mountain, on April 5 the weather was good and we were ready to begin the climb. The route up to Camp I was a classic grind. The first couple of hours involved a tedious ascent through miles of loose boulders on the glacial moraine. Above the boulderfield was what looked to be a solid band of ice, hundreds of feet high, which appeared to block all access to the mountain's lower snow slopes. However, after crossing a frozen lake and scrambling up steep glacial debris, a corridor the size of a four-lane highway appeared on the right side of the icefall. It was like the parting of the Red Sea.

For nearly an hour the route ascended this alleyway flanked by huge cliffs of overhanging ice. At roughly 19,000 feet the corridor was history and a short steep headwall of glacier ice led to a snow bench nearly a mile long. After

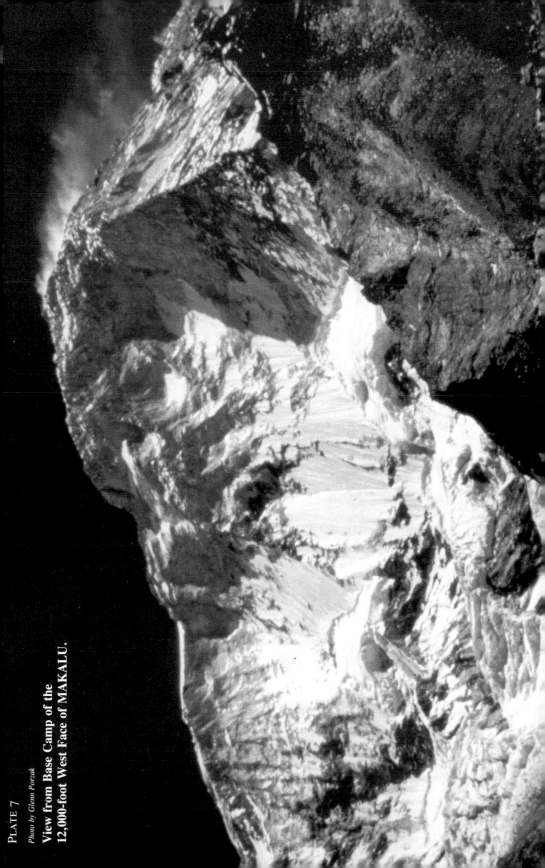

postholing across this wide expanse for what seemed an eternity, one last rock slope nearly 500 vertical feet in height had to be climbed before Makalu's lower tier of glaciers was reached.

Camp I was in a flat but wind-exposed area on the Barun Glacier at 20,000 feet. After days of hauling loads up to Camp I, we began the first foray towards the mountain's upper slopes. While heavily crevassed, the route to Camp II was straightforward and not too difficult. The sole exception was one prominent steep section midway, which we secured with a small amount of fixed rope. The plan was to try to locate the next camp beneath the towering couloir which provided the most direct access to the Makalu Col, the 24,300-foot saddle which was the gateway to the summit plateau.

As a result, we sited Camp II at approximately 21,700 feet in the last flat area before the slopes began to steepen dramatically towards the base of the massive snow gully. While lower than we would have liked, the camp was well protected from any avalanche danger by the surrounding séracs, and the views were spectacular. From this camp we were high enough to look north over a neighboring saddle into Tibet. Directly to the west, Lhotse and the southeastern flank of Everest appeared so close that you could study every detail of the summit slopes of these two giants.

Perhaps the greatest difficulty of the climb was establishing and stocking Camp III on the Makalu Col. That, in turn, required climbing and fixing the so-called Messner couloir, a snow-rock-and-ice gully which extended over 2000 vertical feet at an average angle of nearly 45°. The climb was unbelievably strenuous. Consisting of thirteen sections of fixed rope, each approximately 300 feet long, it took a minimum of 6½ hours to make the ascent. With the wind constantly funneling spindrift right into one's face, this section was downright torturous. Mentally and physically it was a challenge that stretched everyone to his absolute limits. Moreover, as if to provide a gruesome reminder of what can happen if you press beyond your limits, there on the col, encased in ice, was the body of a climber from a past expedition. All things considered, without the assistance of the Sherpas, I seriously doubt that we could have fully stocked the higher camps. They were a major force in keeping the mountain within our limits.

After four solid weeks of hard work and countless carries by every member of the team, we were ready to mount our first serious effort on the summit. Camp III was now stocked and Chris Pizzo, Gary Neptune and I moved up with the four Sherpas to occupy that camp for the first time. If all went well the following day, three of the Sherpas would carry the food, tents and other supplies required to establish the final assault camp. At the same time, Chris, Gary, Lhakpa Nuru and I would move up to Camp IV and make a summit attempt the ensuing day.

However, no sooner had we occupied Camp III than a severe storm struck. On May 1, with visibility only a few yards and winds well over 50 mph, we made an attempt at establishing Camp IV. But in such conditions it was ridiculous to think that we could actually pitch the tents and ready ourselves for a summit try. Instead, we gratefully settled for the efforts of the three Sherpas who cached their loads at 25,700 feet, the future site of Camp IV, and then descended to Camp II. The first summit party returned to Camp III and dug in to try and wait out the storm.

The wait would be a long one. Two days into the storm there was no end in sight. With gale force winds and zero visibility, the last place that we wanted to be was at 24,300 feet on a saddle that was fully exposed to the elements. On Day 3 of the storm the first signs of trouble appeared. Gary's face began to swell and his throat was so sore that he was barely able to talk. He had developed the powerful virus which had already incapacitated four other members of the team and relegated them to the lower part of the mountain. The pro that he is, Gary immediately knew that he had to get down to lower altitude before his illness became more serious. Thus, that same day he descended the fixed ropes with Lhakpa Nuru and went all the way to Base Camp in an effort to recover.

Meanwhile, Chris and I held on, hoping against hope that the weather would break. However, the longer we remained pinned down at Camp III, the less likely we would have the strength to make a serious summit try. Nonetheless, the thought of descending and then reclimbing the giant couloir on another day deluded us into thinking that we could hang on a bit longer. Finally after five days both Chris and I were totally whipped. While the clouds had lifted, the winds were still blowing well over 60 mph. We barely had the strength to crawl down the fixed lines and descend to the world of the living.

The next morning, May 4, we were a sorry lot. Gary Neptune, Sandy Read, and Ed Ramey were at Base Camp trying to recover from the dreaded virus. Having spent nearly two weeks at Camp II providing much-needed logistical support, John Cooley was on his way to Base Camp for a well-deserved rest. Stefan Goldberg and Mike Browning were at Camp I, and while better, they were still plagued by the awful virus. It seemed almost impossible to shake. Meanwhile, Chris Pizzo, Dave Herrick, the Sherpas and I were all at Camp II and thoroughly wasted. Dave had made ten carries between Camps I and II, and the Sherpas had been working hard at all levels and needed a rest as well. It was clear that now was not the time to go charging back up the mountain. The camps were in place and still stocked and the summit would wait. Everyone pulled back to Base for rest and relaxation.

Back at Base Camp we heard the Nepalese Government radio reporting that virtually all of the 28 expeditions had withdrawn without summiting. Yet, we resolved to give it one more try despite the fact that our numbers had been substantially reduced by the virus and normal attrition. On May 7, Chris Pizzo, Lhakpa Nuru and I began the long journey back up the mountain, with Mike Browning, Dawa Nuru and Lhakpa Dorje in support. Stefan Goldberg also moved up with us to Camp II to provide any medical assistance.

Retracing our steps back up to Camp I and then Camp II was awful. The weather remained cold, stormy and very windy. On May 9, the weather was so bad that we had to spend an extra day at Camp II, all the time dreading the thought of going back up all those fixed ropes. The next day dawned clear, though windy and cold. We had to make our move now as food and fuel were becoming dangerously scarce.

May 10 was the most difficult day of the expedition. Without Mike Browning's mental and physical support I doubt that we would have made the climb back up to Camp III. Breaking trail every step of the way, Mike sacrificed himself to conserve the energy of those on the summit team. Halfway up the fixed ropes, the weather turned absolutely horrendous. Visibility was less than a hundred feet, and the cold and wind were torturous. It looked as if another major storm was setting in and we were moving back up with neither the food nor the physical ability to weather another prolonged stay at Camp III. But we were already committed. If we descended now, the expedition was over. Flooded with doubts, yet still somehow determined, we continued on.

At four P.M. we finally reached the col in a white-out and the wind approaching 100 mph. After a tearful goodbye and thanks to Mike, he quickly descended with Dawa Nuru. Chris Pizzo, Lhakpa Nuru and I remained to ride out one of the wildest storms imaginable. Throughout the evening the winds were simply unbelievable. Despite being fully anchored into the hard surface ice with 8-inch screws, the tents were being picked up and tossed around at will. It felt as if we were riding a bucking bronco.

That night a number of tents in Camp II, nearly 3000 feet below, were totally shredded and destroyed by the gale force winds. Yet somehow we managed to hold on. When dawn finally appeared, to my amazement the sky was clear. Despite a wind of 40 mph, by eight A.M. we were on our way. In less than three hours we made it to the site of Camp IV at 25,700 feet. With a renewed sense of strength and energy, we set about erecting the two tents which had been cached nearly two weeks before. As we worked on the tents, for the first time in weeks the wind began to die down. It was almost downright comfortable.

After pitching the tents and chopping enough ice to melt water, Lhakpa and I climbed a couple of hundred feet above Camp IV to get a good look at the route. It was impressive. While the distance was not great, we should have to ascend nearly 2000 vertical feet of mixed snow, rock and ice before gaining the final summit ridge. Then came the crux of the climb, the twin towers. The first, the false summit, was a 250-foot nearly vertical gendarme which provided access to the final summit pyramid. Separating the two was a 300-foot knife-edged ridge. It would be an interesting day. If only the weather would hold.

In the planning stages of the expedition there had been much discussion regarding the use of oxygen. In 1983, we had neither taken nor felt the need to use any oxygen on Shishapangma. Yet that mountain was nearly 1500 feet lower than Makalu and the oxygen saturation exponentially decreases above 27,000 feet. As a compromise, we took 12 bottles of oxygen—one bottle for virtually every member of the team, or more realistically one bottle for climbing and one for sleeping for six potential summit climbers. While a number of the team members harbored ambitions to climb Makalu without the aid of oxygen, in the end everyone that attempted the summit opted for its use. In fact, given the physical toll the mountain had taken, no one even gave it a second thought. Sherpas and members alike, each of us knew that it was the only realistic chance we had to climb the mountain. It's amazing how quickly aesthetics go out the window when your back is to the wall.

On May 12, at three A.M., we awoke and began the laborious process of melting water and fixing something to eat. The cold was beyond belief. By 5:30 A.M., we were ready to go with not a cloud in the sky and not a breath of wind. To the west Everest and Lhotse dominated the horizon. To the north there were the 25,000-foot peaks of Makalu II and Chomo Lonzo, with the contrasting brown foothills and plains of Tibet beyond. Eastward, the endless expanse of peaks culminated in Kangchenjunga. And to the south lay the route up Makalu. In one sweeping panorama, four of the world's five highest mountains unfolded before our eyes.

For the first two hours we climbed and traversed alternating broken rock and water ice. While primarily third and fourth class, as we moved higher the exposure increased and a fall would have been serious. Nonetheless, we climbed unroped as it was unfeasible to belay given the distance which had to be covered. At 7:30 A.M. we intersected the broad icefield which runs directly up the center of the north face. A short but steep traverse brought us to its top where we took our first rest. We were at 26,700 feet and climbing far more rapidly than we had estimated during the previous day's reconnaissance. Our confidence grew.

Pressing onward, we gained the base of the couloir which provides access to the mountain's northwest summit ridge. Since a rock constriction forms a barrier midway up the couloir, at just over 27,000 feet we decided to climb the rock buttress on the left flank of the couloir. It was fourth-class rock powdered with snow and an occasional section of ice. The climbing was magnificent and if not so exhausting, it might have been downright enjoyable. After an eternity, we gained the final summit ridge at 27,500 feet. It was still only 9:30 A.M. But any triumphant notions were quickly erased when we took our first good look at the twin towers. They were awesome.

After a brief rest we lost no time in reaching the base of the first tower, where we roped up for the first time during the summit day. We initially tried to climb directly up the tower's nearly vertical northern face, but the snow and ice were so rotten that we backed off. As the left or east side of the tower overhung 9000 feet down Makalu's southeastern face, there was little doubt that the right side was the only feasible route. Gradually we arched our way up and around this western flank on climbing that was extremely steep and at these altitudes, very strenuous. I turned my oxygen regulator up to 3 liters per minute. While that helped my breathing, it did nothing to alter the fact that we were climbing 70° rotten ice without good belays.

After nearly an hour and a half we gained the false summit, only to come to the most pronounced knife-edged ridge imaginable. While generally uncorniced, the wind-scoured snow which plunged radically off each side was hollow to the core. After two rope-lengths of delicately traversing on this knife blade, it was a scant fifty feet up the second tower to a pinnacle of snow just big enough for one person to straddle. Formed by four spectacular ridges which all culminate at a single point, at 11:15 A.M. I unfurled the U.S. and Colorado flags atop the most perfect summit, of the most perfect mountain, on the most perfect of days.

For Lhakpa Nuru, it was his first 8000-meter peak. At age 24, I have no doubts that he will go on to reach the summit of many more Himalayan giants. He is one of the strongest and most engaging individuals you can imagine. For Chris Pizzo, it was the summit of his third 8000er, which equals the most by an American. And for me it was my second one; thus I became the fourth American to have climbed two or more. While intensely proud of this accomplishment, I was far more proud of the other members of the team whose efforts made possible the most incredible moment of my life.

Four days later, Gary Neptune, Dawa Nuru and Motilal repeated the ascent by climbing directly to the summit from Camp III, thereby capping off a true team effort. This made Gary the fifth American with two or more 8000ers.

By the 24th of May we had force-marched our way back to Tumlingtar and were listening to the government radio station reporting that we were one of the few expeditions to succeed in climbing a major Himalayan peak that season. It was time for celebration. Plans for the next adventure could wait for another day.

Summary of Statistics:

AREA: Nepalese Himalaya, east of Mount Everest.

ASCENT: Makalu, 8481 meters, 27,825 feet, via the northwest ridge, on May 12, 1987 (Porzak, Pizzo, Lhakpa Nuru) and on May 16, 1987 (Neptune, Dawa Nuru, Motilal).

PERSONNEL: Glenn Porzak (leader), Mike Browning, John Cooley, Dr. Stefan Goldberg, Dave Herrick, Gary Neptune, Chris Pizzo, Ed Ramey, Sandy Read, Lhakpa Dorje (Sardar), Lhakpa Nuru, Dawa Nuru and Motilal.

Trisul's Aleš Kunaver Memorial Route

VLASTA KUNAVER, *Planinska Zveza Slovenije, Yugoslavia*

TRISUL, THE FAMOUS MOUNTAIN with its three summits, had long fascinated us. Trisul stands for the three-pointed trident of the goddess Nanda, Shiva's consort. It is one of the highest peaks of Garhwal, which is said to be one of the most beautiful parts of the Himalaya. Garhwal is also one of its holiest regions; so many of the gods have their home there. That is the reason why you always see so many people, poorly dressed, with walking sticks and begging bowls, heading for the holy sanctuaries. But the gods and the Ganges was not why we chose Trisul. We had been drawn by the enormous virgin west face with great possibilities for climbing, skiing and paragliding.

We left for India on April 28, hoping to make the first ascent of the west face of Trisul I, to traverse the three summits and to descend from the top both by paraglider and by skis. We started from New Delhi on May 7 with a rented bus and at the end of two days got to Ghat at the end of the paved road. Sandi Marančič flew with a paraglider for the first time at the village of Ghat. News spread through the Nandakini valley like fire, "Flying people have come!" On the day of the harvest festival at Sutol, the biggest attraction again was paragliding. The view of the colorful paraglider soaring above the rice fields in the last rays of the sun made it a memorable holiday.

A five-days' walk up the Nandakini valley brought us to Base Camp at 3900 meters. It was about 600 meters lower than we wished, but the porters refused to carry any higher because of snow and bad weather. From there we made two acclimatization climbs.

On May 17, we made a new route on the lower 1500 meters of the west face. The rock was of UIAA IV difficulty and the ice from 45° to 60°. In 14 hours we reached the big snow plateau below the main west face, left gear and descended to Base Camp. Marinčič tested high-altitude flying and landed in Base Camp. On the 22nd, we made a second acclimatization ascent to the slopes of Nanda Ghunti and the Trisul snow plateau.

On May 27, we started on our main ascent. We climbed back to the snow plateau and rested there until midnight before setting on up the main west face of Trisul I. The first 1400 meters had ice up to 65° and rock of IV difficulty. The conditions in the lower part were good, but from the middle of the face on,

PLATES 8 AND 9

Photos by Lado Vidmar

On the West Face of TRISUL.

we had green ice with rock bands. It was not until eight P.M. that we climbed the last rocks and emerged onto a small snow patch, where we bivouacked.

The next day we progressed slowly because of the tremendous efforts we had already put in. We climbed a sérac barrier to reach the snow slopes that would lead to the top. There we were caught by a severe snowstorm and thick fog. Although we had gained only a few hundred meters, we were forced to bivouac in the early afternoon. Luckily we found shelter in an enormous crevasse. Fantastic ice sculptures on the ceiling and walls kept our tired minds working overtime.

A splendid sunny day greeted us the next morning. We knew that we'd reach the top and fly from the summit. We took only two hours to get there. Breathing deeply and sinking into the snow, one by one we arrived on top. What do you feel when you get there? I must admit, the strongest feeling was one of relief.

Kisses, congratulations, the view of Nandakini, Changabang and all around made us jubilant. Our oldest, Vanja Matejevec, lit a pipe on top, like Tom Longstaff, the first to climb Trisul. In 1907 he had ascended the northern slopes, the easiest and most frequented route up the mountain. We named our route after my father, Aleš Kunaver, who in 1984 died in a helicopter accident with his German friend, Toni Hiebeler. He had been on Trisul in 1960. During that first Yugoslavian Himalayan expedition, he and his friends made the first ascents of Trisul II and III, but bad weather prevented their getting to the top of Trisul I. This was the first of his many notable Himalayan expeditions. And so, after 27 years we climbed a new route in his memory.

Cumulus clouds floating up the south face forced Sandi and me to hurry preparing our paragliders. There was almost no wind, but there was no time to waste. Sandi pulled out the lines, ran eight or ten steps and was gliding down into the valley. I followed shortly after him. In fifteen or twenty minutes we were together again, in Base Camp. We remembered just split images: high icy peaks all around us, the west face below our feet, rising cumulus clouds, grass coming up at us, the broad smiles of our cook and liaison officer while we were landing. (Vlasta Kunaver thus established a record. No other woman has taken off from such a high altitude.—*Editor.*)

The other four members of the expedition continued along the ridge, making a difficult traverse of Trisul II and III. They descended the slopes of Trisul III and returned to Base Camp a day later.

Summary of Statistics:

AREA: Garhwal Himalaya, India.

NEW ROUTE: Trisul, 7128 meters, 23,386 feet, just left of the center of the West Face. Summit reached on May 30, 1987. Kunaver and Marinčič descended by Paraglider; the other four descended over the summits of Trisul II, 6690 meters, 21,949 feet and Trisul III, 6170 meters, 20,243.

PERSONNEL: Lado Vidmar, leader, Vanja Matijevec, Slavko Frantar, Janez Kastelec, Vlasta Kunaver, Sandi Marinčič.

Pumasillo and Mellizos, Cordillera Vilcabamba

CARLOS BUHLER

THE STEAMING JUNGLES of southeastern Peru seem a strange place to begin an exploration of the northeastern side of the Pumasillo massif. Hidden from all but the most remote mountain trails, the Pumasillo group is comprised of a jagged spine of peaks in the eastern Cordillera Vilcabamba. This seldom visited chain is chock full of Incan history. Incredible Incan highways of stone and stairways wind through the heavily vegetated valleys and passes. Pumasillo lies not more than 25 air miles from the ruins of Machu Picchu.

Paul Harris, an English climber I had met in Washington State, joined me in Cuzco a week earlier. From a few sparse maps and a satellite photo, we concluded that a two- or three-day walk would put us in a position to climb from the northeast side. Hoping to meet our *arriero* Washington Delgado early in the morning, we caught the last train from Cuzco to Santa Teresa.

Unfortunately, there is not space here to tell of our arrival in the ramshackle tiny jungle town at two A.M. and our finding the unmarked "hotel." The next day went smoothly. We met Washington Delgado and his assistant Ricardo as planned. Our food and gear arrived by freight car at eleven A.M. We loaded our supplies onto six burros and began the hike into the mountains.

Over the next three days, we walked and rode through a remarkable variety of ecological zones. Beginning with the *montaña* jungle, we traveled up into alpine grasslands. On the first day we were delighted to see tree branches in the dense vegetation bending under the weight of swinging monkeys. Occasionally, the children of the tiny settlements along the way followed us for kilometers, offering us fruit and laughter to bolster us along. Even Washington had not been far enough up the valley to see the snowy peaks above the grazing grounds.

Bamboo and broadleaf plants gave way to thick forest. We repeatedly crossed the Sacsara River as it plunged from its glacial origins at 5000 meters down to 1500 meters, where we had begun at its junction with the Urubamba. So steep was the trail that we were hard pressed to find a flat piece of ground for our tent on the first night. Our second day took us out of the jungle. We

PLATE 11

Photo by Carlos Buhler

PUMASILLO from North, seen from Mellizos' Southeast Face. Ascent was up East Face at left and descent down North Ridge facing photographer.

glanced skyward to check the enormous ridges that flanked our gorge, their slopes deep in vegetation. Yet, by five P.M. on our second day, we were camped at the upper end of the beautiful Sacsara valley. Heavy clouds obscured any view we might have had of the nearly 6000-meter peaks we knew were above us. The valley split and both forks abruptly climbed to glaciers we could just see beneath the rolling mists. The next morning we ascended the more northerly of the two *quebradas*. Paul and I walked ahead to search for a Base Camp site while Washington and Ricardo followed with the pack animals.

A couple of hours higher, we came to a flat terrace of dry glacial silt in the center of an enormous amphitheater of soaring peaks. On top of 500-foot rock walls were perched the huge séracs of Pumasillo's east glacier. That afternoon we climbed the moraine to get an idea of the layout of the peaks. One peak had stood out in the early morning clearing. Its upper eastern walls resembled the petals of a blossoming flower. The deep flutings of ice opened like a Japanese paper fan above an inaccessible hanging glacier high on the face. We assumed it had to be the famous Pumasillo itself—the Claw of the Puma. There were other impressive peaks around, but this one caught our imagination. With only nine days to climb, we agreed that if the weather improved, it should be our first objective.

Luck was on our side. The following nine days gave us steadily improving weather. The next day we set off on a conditioning ascent up the lower portion of a long rock-and-snow ridge. Our first day's climb in the fog took us up an impressive knife-edged ridge. During the occasional breaks in the mist we gained a better understanding of the cirque we were in.

With Pumasillo still first on our list, the next day Washington helped us carry our gear to an easy breakover point on the ridge we had climbed the day before. We chose a line up the southeast face which led to the 20-meter sérac barrier of the hanging glacier in the face's center. If we could climb this and get into the bowl, we could climb the fluted face above.

We began the next day at 3:30 A.M. At the outset, the snow was calf-deep. Our concern with avalanches became eclipsed by the uncertainty of immense snow bridges we had to cross in the dark. We reached the sérac wall with the sun. Something obviously did not jibe. The peak behind us, which had appeared smaller from Base Camp, now loomed far larger than the one we were on. We were not climbing Pumasillo; that was the great mountain over our shoulder. We were on Mellizos, a 5700-meter peak to the north.

We surmounted the sérac in two short, exciting pitches. Unfortunately, this put us on the edge of a heart-breaking crevasse, which cut a clean slice of the hanging glacier away from the icefield behind it. We nearly had to admit defeat. With a surge of determination, I led out on a paper-thin leaf of ice that partially bridged the five-meter gap. With some scary moves, I managed to climb part way down the crevasse and back out the far side. Now our way was clear to the ice flutings above.

Photo by Carlos Buhler

PLATE 12

On the East Face of PUMASILLO.

The upper face consisted of 300 meters of enjoyable ice runnels and snow mushrooms, varying in steepness from 50° to 75°. Fifteen meters from the ridge crest, Paul spotted a natural tunnel. As I ducked through, I felt a moment of terror at the thought of the many tons of ice that would squash me if it should come collapsing down. We had less than 100 meters to go up the east ridge to the summit. The last forty meters were a summit block of rotten ice guarded by a ten-meter overhang of collapsible crud. Paul graciously belayed me up the final pitch, noting that the ridge was so narrow and unstable that he could see clear through it in places. Paul logically declined to do the final pitch. Finding a rock wall that barred access to the south ridge for the descent, we decided on the low-angled but crevassed northeast snow slopes in order to drop back to our glacial basin from the southeast ridge. Having made only one rappel, we were back at our tent by five P.M. A quick look at our lack of food convinced us to trudge back over the break in the ridge. We reached Base Camp at 7:30 exhausted. Washington and Ricardo had read our minds. Fresh lamb stew was waiting. We wolfed it down like children eating birthday cake.

After a rest day, we had to come to grips with the nagging reality that we had not climbed Pumasillo. With four days left, we admitted that the next project had to be the Claw itself. We chose a route on the ice face which lies just to the right (north) of the highest point. We packed four days of food and fuel plus a light bivouac tent. It took us a long day and a half to climb the complex glacier which protects the east face. We made better time by ascending the south side of Pumasillo's east glacier. We could see that once we were up closer, we could traverse back north. That first afternoon we gained about 650 meters. We slept at 5200 meters on a safe spot on the glacier. The next day we moved up and right across slopes covered with deep snow. There was some debris that had come down, but in general the slopes offered the line of least resistance.

We pitched our tent beneath a sérac tucked up under the 55° final ice slopes of the east face at 5500 meters. Since the upper grooves in the face were clearly scoured by falling rock and ice during the heat of the day, the only safe time to climb them would be at night. Our second day had been short and so we could rehydrate fully and begin climbing long before the sun rose on the third day. Hoping to descend the normal west flank and walk back around, we carried all our gear with us. By the time the sun rose we were well past the frightening pock marks and nearing the top of the face. The climbing was entirely on ice and snow and we made excellent time by climbing together on all but the last 500 feet to the ridge. The weather could not have been better.

At 7:30 we reached the ridge crest. It was then only another twenty minutes of easy cramponing up the north ridge to the summit. Our descent was more difficult. Immediately upon attempting to drop down the west ridge, Paul took a scary eight-meter fall when a snow ledge gave way under him. I had ten tense minutes of doubt holding a taut rope until I could feel his movements as he struggled to climb back onto the ridge. He emerged unhurt but shaken.

PLATE 13

Photo by Carlos Buhler

Paul Harris on PUMASILLO.

PLATE 14

Photo by Carlos Buhler

On PUMASILLO's East Face.

Considering our lack of equipment for rappelling, we decided to descend the unclimbed north ridge.

All day we climbed down the north ridge. Rotten ice and gaping crevasses prevented quick progress. Chiseling bollards for anchors, we made two fifty-foot abseils down overhanging ice walls. By the day's end we had reached a col on the ridge at 5600 meters. A heavily corniced horizontal section would stop us on the ridge. In the last light we climbed out to a prominent bump on the ridge. Looking back from there, we spotted a possible descent down the eastern slopes which would take us back to the upper east glacier. We had used up our food and were afraid of getting caught in the complex glacier and being forced to backtrack.

After a restless night, we were up and moving on the fourth day. Fortunately, the pieces fitted together. Our descent over some risky sérac avalanche debris connected with the glacier after only one short rappel off a snow stake. We traversed south underneath the ice face we had climbed and eventually found our tracks coming up from the first night's camp. At three P.M. we stepped off the glacier thirty minutes above Base Camp. As we removed our crampons, we were elated to see Ricardo bounding up toward us. He greeted us with a heart-warming hug and explained how they had watched our every move with binoculars. On the last slopes, Paul and I shared the luxury of letting Ricardo take turns carrying our packs. With Pumasillo climbed, one of my long-standing dreams had come true.

Summary of Statistics:

AREA: Cordillera Vilcabamba, Peru.

NEW ROUTES: Mellizos, 5700 meters, 18,701 feet, via Southeast Face, August 23 and 24, 1987 (Carlos Buhler, Paul Harris).

Pumasillo, 5996 meters, 19,673 feet, via East Face, August 26 to 29, 1987 (Buhler, Harris).

Torre Egger's Southeast Face

SILVO KARO, *Domžale Alpine Club, Yugoslavia*

ALL THREE OF US, Janez Jeglič, Franc Knez and I, had been to Patagonia twice before. In 1983 we had made the first ascent of the great dihedral on Fitz Roy's east face and a new route on the Aguja Mermoz too. (*A.A.J., 1984,* pages 218-219). On January 16, 1986, together with three other members of a Yugoslavian expedition, we had reached Cerro Torre's summit, having climbed a difficult new route on the east face (*A.A.J., 1987,* pages 114-122).

Our third sojourn in Patagonia in November and December of 1986 was the most successful of all. We scaled the southeast face of Torre Egger, the impressive tower which lies in the shadow of the higher Cerro Torre. Our route was the most direct one and abounds in extreme difficulties. We stood on the top on December 7, 1986. Later in December we climbed a new route on the north face of El Mocho.

On November 9, we pitched Base Camp beside the Laguna Torre. During the following days we carried food and equipment to a bivouac site at the foot of the southeast face. We had to make use of every *hour* of decent weather; changes are sudden and dramatic. We outwitted the weather, often walking from Base Camp to the bivouac in order to climb that same day.

November 18. This was the first real day of climbing. In cascades of water and with falling snow, we climbed the first 180 meters of ice. It soon became apparent that we should have to ascend the first section expedition-style. The upper part would be scaled alpine-style.

November 19. Although the weather was bad, we succeeded in climbing 40 meters of great technical difficulties on ice. This part was extremely dangerous because of ice falling from both Cerro Torre and Torre Egger.

November 20. We managed 95 meters of extremely difficult free climbing in the "Chocolate Dihedral," despite great cold and ice-filled cracks. From our high point, the mountain towered up, completely vertical.

November 21. The long system of cracks was running out. We were at the crux of the route. The aid climbing was of utmost technical difficulty (A3), but we did manage to find our way into a new crack system. From there to the top, the wall was a great overhang.

November 29. We could scale only 40 meters of the overhanging wall. The weather was foul with gale-force winds and snow falling horizontally and building up on any slight irregularity.

PLATE 15

Photo by Silvo Karo

TORRE EGGER's Southeast Face.

December 1. We surmounted 90 meters of cracks and a dihedral. Despite the overhang, all was covered with thick snow.

December 6. Finally, we succeeded in climbing the "Bloody Crack," which was wide enough for N° 4 Friends. Filled with ice, it was very dangerous aid climbing. We were now 550 meters up on the route. We had no more rope to fix. There was only one possibility: to climb from there to the top as fast as possible, alpine-style.

On December 7 at three A.M., we set out. Before dawn we were already at the top of the fixed ropes. Lightly equipped, we had no bivouac gear and so could not look forward to spending the night on the face. It would have to be ascent and descent on the same day. The snowy summit seemed far above the vertical wall. The climbing was difficult and slow. It was not until seven o'clock in the evening that we reached the summit snow-cap. Powder snow was a terrible obstacle, but we found an icy channel which led us to the summit. At eight P.M. we finally stood atop Torre Egger in a clear evening but in a gusty gale. As we happily and proudly shook hands, we admired Cerro Torre, where we had stood only ten months before.

A quarter of an hour later, we started the descent. Near the top, one of us had to stand on the long ice pitons in the powdery snow while the other two rappelled one after the other. It was certainly risky. We speeded up, and yet when night fell, we still had 700 meters to descend. We lit our headlamps and reached the bivouac at one in the morning. We had had 22 hours of climbing and extreme effort without rest or food. Only ten years of mountain experience gave us the proper psychical and physical conditioning.

On December 8, we removed the fixed rope from the route on Torre Egger. On the 9th and 19th we were joined by Roberto Pe from an Italian expedition and together we made a new route on the north face of El Mocho. On the first day we climbed 250 meters. We slept at the bottom and the next day climbed the upper part of the face, following prominent cracks.

We must admit that our triumph was only possible because of the network of fixed ropes. Taking into consideration the height of the faces and the rapid and unpredictable weather changes, it was almost impossible to climb in pure alpine style. The proof is that almost all routes in Patagonia have been first done with fixed ropes. Some day the routes may be climbed free, solo and in one day. This is a natural development, a kind of staircase where every new step follows the older ones.

Summary of Statistics:

AREA: Patagonia, Argentina.

NEW ROUTES: Torre Egger, 2987 meters, 9800 feet, Southeast Face, Summit reached December 7, 1986 (Janez Jeglič, Silvo Karo, Franc Knez).

El Mocho, c. 2000 meters, 6562 feet, North Face, December 9 and 10, 1986 (Jeglič, Karo, Knez, Roberto Pe).

PLATE 16

Photo by Elio Orlandi

Near the Summit of TORRE EGGER.

The Eastern Pillar of Torre Egger

ELIO ORLANDI, *Club Alpino Italiano*

HAVING REACHED Fitz Roy National Park on October 15, Maurizio Giarolli and I immediately headed for the triad of the Cerro Torre group: Cerro Torre, Torre Egger and Torre Standhardt. In climbing circles, these three peaks represent some of the most difficult objectives in the world. We had come with the idea of attempting the traverse of all three spires without descending for any reason, without outside help and without any previous route preparation.

This was, frankly, an insane idea of the kind we climbers dream up, but doubtless nearly impossible to carry out, all the more so because the climate of the region with its sudden and frequent storms affect negatively about all expeditions. One must consider the objective dangers of the route as well as whether the weather would hold long enough to do the traverse.

Our preparations and enthusiasm encouraged us, however, to give our adventure a try by setting out to climb Torre Stanhardt, the first of the Triad.

The tremendous weight of our gear and of ten days of food needed for such an exploit and the enormous expenditure of energy that a team of two has to summon made us give up when in the teeth of a buffeting snowstorm we were only 100 meters from the summit of Torre Stanhardt. The foul weather then stuck in its little paw, notably complicating the descent.

After several rest days in Base Camp, our desire to pick up that painful project never returned. We persuaded ourselves to choose another objective to which our attention had been attracted, namely the sharp, elegant eastern pillar of Torre Egger. The colossal queen of ice and rock stands proudly between the king and the maid of honor of this fabulous triad.

For the past month, its vertical dihedrals had been attacked by another Italian team, composed of Guido Cominelli, Lorenzo Nadali and Andrea Sarchi, who during repeated attempts had climbed 500 meters, fixing much rope. They finally gave up because of the difficulty and the weather.

On November 1, we returned to the glacier at the foot of the giant east face of Torre Egger to dig a snow cave that was to serve as a logistic base and refuge in case of bad weather. The next day, in unbelievably stable weather, we attacked the smooth granite slabs and icy couloirs. The line rose up the great

PLATE 17

Photo by Michael Horan

Cerro Torre, Torre Egger and Torre Stanhardt.

east pillar to the left of the amphitheater of the hanging glacier. It began left of the Giongio-De Bonà route in the middle of the buttress up the vertical slabs and headed towards an ice couloir which soared upwards at 75° to 85° for six 50-meter pitches. Difficult, smooth granite slabs then took us to the first bivouac 500 meters above the start of the route. Immediately higher, in the middle of the wall, rose the extraordinarily steep snow arête at the top of which we again bivouacked, having gained 250 meters. The upper part of the wall had a series of cracks almost on the edge of the great buttress, which here had the form of a huge overhanging prow. We then deviated slightly to the right to a couloir below the summit mushroom, which on the eastern side has a vertical height of 90 meters. We bivouacked there a third time after a gain of 420 meters.

Up to there, our elegant route proved to be very free of objective dangers and of falling ice and rock because it rises vertically on the pillar. It is probably the safest of the four routes by which Torre Egger has been climbed. The rock on the whole route is optimal and offers largely free climbing with good cracks especially on the upper part. We rate the climb at VI + , A2 UIAA difficulty.

The summit mushroom was curious and almost unbelievable. There was a combination of very narrow, vertical trenches and tunnels etched by the wind in the interior of the overhanging, unconsolidated snowcap which let us emerge on the morning of November 5 directly onto the summit under a brilliant azure sky to scan this fantastic region.

We suggest the name of Titanic for our route. The smooth granite of the upper part of the pillar has the form of a great overhanging prow of a mysterious ship.

Summary of Statistics:

AREA: Patagonia, Argentina

NEW ROUTE: Torre Egger, 2987 meters, 9800 feet, Eastern Pillar, November 2 to 5, 1987 (Maurizio Giarolli, Elio Orlandi).

To the Very Summit

SILVIA METZELTIN BUSCAINI, *Club Alpino Italiano*

S MOUNTAIN CLIMBING develops, more and more ethical questions arise nowadays in the mountaineering world. Having become a mass sport, climbing has shoved aside or changed earlier standards. Some were perhaps false, such as nationalistic pride. Others have a definite ethical basis, such as mutual assistance among climbers. Adams Carter and Charles Houston have discussed some of these points courageously and emphatically in the *American Alpine Journal* of 1987.

From a purely sports point of view, there is a trend today which we must contemplate. Although climbing represents first of all free spirit, it is essential to heed self-discipline and certain unwritten rules if such freedom does not lose all its meaning and attractiveness. Despite accommodation to the present-day developments of technique and to modern society, climbing can keep its basic values only if . . . if . . .

A climber must remain true and honest to himself and to others, including non-climbers and sponsors. In this sense one should think through whether the present tendency to consider the summit as incidental is correct or not.

Naturally each region has its own particularities. The problems of the Yosemite are very different from those of the Himalaya. We must consider each in perspective.

Recently I have been compiling a history of climbing in Patagonia. The following cases arose more and more often: 1. the climb ends before the summit is reached on an established route; 2. a new route is not completed to the summit; 3. the climb stops where a new route joins an already established route. There is a tendency to consider the climb successful and completed if the greatest technical difficulties have been overcome, even though one has not got to the summit.

It is necessary to point out that in Patagonia the greatest difficulties do not always lie in the technical problems but more often in the hostile climate that surrounds the peaks. Until now, very few climbers have decided to bridge over the technical difficulty without placing bolts. (Alan Kearney and Bobby Knight are praiseworthy exceptions.) Therefore, in my opinion, the last meters in Patagonia, even if they are the easiest, are part of the whole. There, luck with the weather is part of the game and whoever doesn't like it should go somewhere else.

Certainly one's inner experience even without the summit can be very deep. I have in several attempts had to rappel a total of 6000 meters off Fitz Roy without having reached the summit. But three *Supercanaletas* are still not a single ascent of Fitz Roy.

On certain mountains there is a peculiar problem. On some summits the ice mushroom sometimes is absent, sometimes is easy and sometimes simply cannot be stood upon. But that is a special case. You can at least *reach* the summit mushroom in order to claim a successful ascent. And then you must state it clearly as, for example, Shipton did on Murallón and Rouse on Volonquí.

I really have to read some reports with great care to find out whether the summit was actually reached or not. In some cases the accounts in different mountaineering journals do not agree. I must state that the most reliable descriptions of all are given in the *American Alpine Journal*. But not even there! Who can check on everything when you can no longer count on the sporting fairness and honesty of the climber? Granted that one cannot always rely on assertions of how long the climb took or how much gear was used. But at least the mountain historian should be able to rely on the most essential fact: whether the summit was reached or not.

It concerns not only the individual—he can do in the mountains what he wants—but rather the whole climbing community. I wish to state here that most of the doubtful cases occur when the climber has been sponsored. On these occasions I find the lie, or the fib if you limit yourself to call it that, particularly serious. It points out the weak position of the climber in his relation to the sponsor. The same weakness can lead to an ethical collapse in which the climber puts his sponsor's interests ahead of his mutual interdependence with his fellow climbers.

I wish to recommend that one should think searchingly about such simple but also basic, though unwritten rules. In climbing one must be honest to one's self and to others. What sense is there to avoid touching pitons on practice cliffs when in the great mountains you give up honesty about summits?

To simplify the difficult task of mountain historians, I make a drastic suggestion: all climbs in which the actual summit is not reached are simply *attempts*, regardless of how difficult it may have been technically.

Every Man for Himself?

DAVID BREASHEARS

O VER THE PAST SEVERAL YEARS
we have witnessed an unprecedented number of climbers and expeditions
active on the highest peaks of the world. Through no fault of their own or
because of errors of judgement, these climbers are increasingly being confronted with extreme situations in which they must make difficult decisions.
These decisions can determine whether they and their companions will survive.

Often these decisions are admirable and selfless. Sometimes they are
self-serving and regrettable. Commonly they lie somewhere in between.
Recent events have focused attention on extreme or difficult situations that
highlight the moral geography of mountaineering. For example, when a
climber's companion becomes weak and unable to continue, with the summit
within reach after weeks of hard work and sacrifice, should the climber
continue alone to the top, or descend with his faltering companion? Or, as the
leader of a large expedition, does one divert the resources and energy of the
team in an effort to rescue an injured member of a different expedition on a
nearby peak, thereby sacrificing a team's chance for success? At what point
does one decide to abandon a stricken companion in an effort to save his or her
life?

Each situation in mountaineering presents a different and entirely subjective experience with a unique dynamic (weather, terrain, snow conditions,
altitude, and so on) that influences the decision-making of each individual.
Many times, when faced with a crucial decision, the climber is exhausted,
dehydrated and suffering from the debilitating effects of high altitude. One can
become concerned exclusively with one's own survival while neglecting or
forgetting the welfare of one's partner. More darkly, driven by an overwhelming desire to reach the summit, one might simply ignore or trivialize the
condition of a fatigued companion in order to justify continuing onwards.

This raises important moral questions for climbers seeking the great
summits. Does our passion for achievement, adventure and success sometimes
overshadow our commitment to the welfare of our fellow climbers? And what
are the moral obligations and responsibilities of climbers to one another in
uncommon and extreme circumstances?

Certainly, the final answer to these questions is that the welfare of our
companions must always be paramount. But in a society that readily rewards
success, yet casts a shadow on perceived failure, there will rarely be any

glamour or glory for those who return unsuccessful because they chose to assist stricken companions. Therein lies the problem.

If climbers are to make conscionable decisions in difficult situations, whether at Base Camp or in the chaos of a Himalayan storm, they must be imbued with basic moral values that enable them to make decisions with good judgement. We rarely climb alone. Therefore, we must accept the risk of having to forsake a summit for the sake of another person; it is simply too self-serving to do otherwise. That declaration may seem contradictory regarding an activity in which the element of risk is one of its most compelling aspects. But even the intentionally violent and deadly activity of war has produced profoundly compassionate and selfless acts. A life is a vibrant and vital thing. A summit is only a summit. It cannot give life or replace fingers or toes lost in its pursuit.

Mountaineering is, of course, fraught with risk, particularly in the high mountains. Rockfall, icefall, avalanche and storm take lives suddenly. But those are the objective dangers we accept when climbing. The risk of jeopardizing one's life because of the poor decisions of an over-zealous or incompetent companion is a subjective one, one we should never accept.

One of the hallmarks of mountaineering is that it is both character-building and character-revealing. Under conditions of prolonged physical and, more importantly, psychological one's moral fiber and true character emerge. It is exactly this element of mountaineering—the opportunity to test one's physical and psychological limits and resources—that makes an ascent so satisfying. It also gives point to our introspection as we examine the substrata (for example, fear, self-doubt, fatigue and the desire to succeed) of the decisions we make. We don't always make the best decisions. Who hasn't felt dismay, on occasion, at his companions' or his own actions? Yet the fact that we do make errors in judgement emphasizes the need for mountaineers to examine not only the romantic nature of their sport, but also its grimmer realities.

Despite different tactics, languages, nationalities, objectives and abilities, mountaineers share a common bond. Chief among them are a deep love and respect for the mountains, the excitement of a new challenge, and the freedom of spirit and comraderie. Because we share these bonds in common, we are all companions and tacitly agree to certain basic rules of behavior. One of those rules is that we are bound to offer every reasonable assistance, regardless of circumstances, to a beleaguered companion. In the mountains, companionship and humanity come before self-gratification.

Moral issues are always complex. Just the same, their consideration is vital if we wish to maintain mountaineering's respected traditions. It is crucial to the spirit of mountaineering that we always act with concern for those who climb with us.

Arapiles, Australia

ALISON OSIUS

T HAD BEEN a slow morning, rainy. Wolfgang was lecturing on training, Kurt singing, Didier smoking, me eating borrowed prescription anti-inflammatories.

But now we were at the base of India, 29, which several years ago was Australia's hardest route, a bulgy, gold-colored wall with white-and-gray streaks. Kurt had just re-named it "Kurt's Execution." He had also just given it the finger. He and Wolfie were taking turns. It was like watching rockets take off: launch *right* German, launch *left* German.

Wolfie had done the route before, and waxed pedantic. Kurt, his clowning sidekick, had been working on it for days and could do the crux beautifully, but his feet kept popping from the steep smears above. He was falling off all over the place. "Can't keep your silly mind on it," a friend scolded him.

Wolfie wandered off while Kurt had a rest and a smoke. "I know I can do it," he said. "Just concentration."

He lifted his shoes again. The ABC camera began rolling. Six hand cameras raised. Twenty-two spectators sat up straight.

Kurt started up, palming and pinching on the overhanging wall. He passed the crux strongly. Abruptly, his foot skidded. He dropped.

"Please . . . beat me," he asked. He lowered off, panting, to sit. Flies crawled on our faces.

He looked up again, alert as a beagle. "Oh, Gott, here comes Wolfgang." They spoke in German.

Wolfgang rolled his eyes. "How can you fall off that move? It's impossible."

Kurt's head dropped on his arms. "I have to do this climb, I have to do this climb," he chanted. "Everybody in Germany will hate me if I don't."

* * *

In recent months, it had seemed safe to assume that professional climbing contests were *the* scene. In the past, however, the only "climbing contest" you really heard about, the California Bouldering Championship, was like a charming county fair. The atmosphere was mostly low key: people wandered about sharing news of which climbs were easy scores, or even which move sequences worked on certain routes. But in 1985, things changed for good

60

when Italy introduced the First International Professional Rock Climbing contest, a three-day circus heavily advertised on billboard and airwaves, viewed by thousands—and, in what was truly unheard-of, with prize money as reward. *Prize money*—when the top rock athletes in this country sadly decide against buying a David's Cookie because (said in injured tones), "It's 70 cents?!" Then, in 1986, the second Italian contest featured a prize car, more money, more rivalry; less talk and sharing.

Overall, more was the word. Climbing competitions suddenly proliferated in Europe. France added indoor contests. Meanwhile, in the States, extra bouldering competitions sprang up East, West, and in between.

Many climbers, however, find the trend faintly horrifying. Some folks, for example, were first attracted to climbing because they wanted to get away from competitive sports. "Climbing is something I do for myself, not against someone," they'll say. Others are, and may even admit to being, very competitive, but they'd like to keep climbing a game, not take that long step into the realm of the professional.

So, OK. The colorful, thronged, commercial contests seem to have left far behind the idea of climbing's spiritual side. Ah, yes . . . well, it's no use railing against progress, particularly against steps already made.

Actually, climbing competitions don't offend this writer. I just generally like sports performances—and whoever thought of the ski runs of say, Jean-Claude Killy, as less than noble?

Granted, it would be bad if climbing contests drew thousands more to further crowd our cliffs, but I don't think climbing will ever become that popular.

But I would truly be sad to see meets, whose existence is a longstanding, grand tradition in climbing, take a back seat to the competitions; to see meets, which are often exchanges and often sponsored by national mountaineering clubs, fade or even die out. International meets in different countries have for many, many years been hospitality, culture, international gestures of friendship in which locals showed foreign guests around their turfs. Meets also seemed, for many young and not-so-young climbers, the big time—hosted and attended by greats; noticed; written up, often. They were non-competitive. Ostensibly.

When I decided to go to the meet my friend Louise Shepherd had organized at Arapiles, the center of Australian rock climbing, for autumn 1986, I wondered if the event might represent some sort of showdown. I asked my 18-year-old hotshot friend Jim Surette if, given the choice, he'd attend a competition or a meet. "Oh, the competition," he said easily.

Louise, an exceptional climber who runs with the international hard-core, surely had great drawing power, especially when you throw her humor and spark into the equation. But, with competitions all the rage, would many, or would high-caliber, climbers appear? Then, protectively perhaps, I decided this example didn't count. Because Australia is so far away from everywhere else, it wasn't fair to compare its magnet factor to that of a European country.

Plus you had to consider the scare factor. Arapiles has a reputation for cliffs so steep climbers trash their egos and elbows. One-third of the Araps regulars supposedly have tendinitis, and innocent tourists came in for nasty surprises.

Not to mention that many climbers have heard or read of Australian anti-Americanism. Of a route listed as "Dead Americans," the guidebook author Kim Carrigan, for years Australia's leading rock climber, editorializes, "There should be more of those."

But when I walked into Louise's home at Natimuk, the town nearest Araps, the first thing I saw was Wolfgang Güllich of Germany. Wolfie, the guy getting attacked by lightning bolts—in those silly ads for Edelweiss ropes. Wolfie, one of the best climbers in the world, and one of the sweetest-tempered. With him was the mobile-faced Kurt, affectionately known as Kurtel, who was wont to pick up a guitar and start banging out chords amidst a conversation. The two had just come from making a film in Yosemite, for which Wolfie had soloed the gigantic overhang called Separate Reality, and were on their way to climb in China.

Kim Carrigan was here, too, though he'd recently moved to Switzerland and become a triathlete. In fact, only the week before he had also married one—and here was Herself, Meg, with him now. Geoff Weigand, Kim's peer and frequent partner on rock, had just pulled in from Sydney. A year-and-a-half ago, he and Kim had done the first ascent of a 5.12 in Yosemite they dubbed America's Cup. "When you get good enough, you can take it back!" they had crowed at locals.

Then into the kitchen walked Didier Raboutou and Jean-Claude Droyer. Didier, five feet, five inches or so and very slender, is one of France's premier rock climbers, a consistent star on the competition circuit. Jean-Claude is perhaps France's best-travelled climber.

The previous season Didier had been part of a team of four sponsored by a French mountaineering magazine to travel to different crags and competitions. The other climbers who, like me, were staying at Louise's might have been expected to think this was a great idea. But, "That would suck," said one. "Being told where to go and what to climb."

Didier, I had heard, barely cracks a smile at the competitions, though he told me he likes their excitement and pressure. At this meet, however, he showed a calm, contained enjoyment of the easy counterbalance, managing much humor on little English. Turning over my hand to look at a rope burn, he said, straight-faced, "Too much washing?"

Six years before, I had been to a meet in France at which I'd had a very good time. I'd been uncomfortable in the mornings, however, when everyone lined up and, in an embarrassing process, paired off to climb. Louise's philosophy for this meet, however, was Fend For Yourself. And in this country, it seemed, anything else wouldn't have been fitting. As John "Crunch" Smoothey informed me, "The only organization Australians are interested in is the DSS."

"What's that?" I asked.

"Department of Social Services, dear. The dole."

A contest, of course, must by its nature be organized. You're sent to one climb or boulder problem after another, in sequence, sometimes waiting in tents before your turn so you won't have the benefit of seeing a competitor solve a route. You are indeed told where to go and what to do.

* * *

I stayed at Louise's, but up to 100 people—English, American, Japanese,—made up a changing campground kaleidoscope by the cliffs. This campground, only a decade ago, was practically deserted.

In fact, the local scene has always been small; everybody knew everybody. Isolated from the rest of the climbing world, Australia's pace was in fits and starts, spurred by visits from foreigners. Australian rock climbing really began in the late 50s through two Englishmen, Bryden Allen and John Ewbank, and thus its styles and ethics originally reflected those of the British.

But the big push came in 1975 when Henry Barber of North Conway, New Hampshire, came to Australia: it was never the same again. Barber picked plums at a dizzying pace. He climbed many, many routes up to grade 23, and of equal significance, he made futuristic attempts to climb routes such as Manic Depressive, later done at 25, two grades harder. Australians had looked at such routes, even thought they might "go," but not tried them. Henry made Australia take an intuitive leap.

Still, in the late 70s, Chris Peisker seemed a loner most of the time at Araps, except on weekends. But from about 1980–85, the place went wild with an explosion of hard new routes. But it was a contained explosion—Araps was the fiery center in a small world. Among the most visible climbers were Kim Carrigan, Louise Shepherd, and her two brothers. The first two travelled widely overseas, scoring high on the turfs and in the appraising eyes of foreign climbers. 1984–85 brought European traffic, and techniques honed on Europe's steep limestone, to Australia. One of the most significant visitors was Wolfgang Güllich, who, after a gargantuan six-day effort, created the showpiece Punks In the Gym (grade 32), a route as hard as any in existence today.

Lincoln Shepherd said the local scene during those unruly glory days "used to be more punked out, more anti-social, more 'I'm bored.' It was very elitist."

The scene was nuts, too. During "mice plagues," climbers trapped mice all night and threw them in the fires, or did worse. They threw aerosol cans in the fires, too.

The guys wore huge earrings, punk and Mohawk haircuts, women's clothes in flaming colors. All of which they flaunted abroad. Other climbers thought they were hyper-weirdos—or emulated them.

Until about three years ago, if a climber from overseas came to visit Arapiles, everyone knew it, and he might be sandbagged (sent up on a hard route described nonchalantly) into extinction. But more and more climbers have been drawn to Araps as the area has become a winter hot spot. Today

PLATE 19

Photo by Alison Osius

Geoff Weigand on "Orestes" (24), Arapiles.

internationalism reigns. With so many good foreign climbers around, it's harder for a local to be at the top. "In a lot of ways it's healthier here now," said Lincoln Shepherd, "less elitist." Less anti-American, probably; certainly the locals were warmly hospitable with their many visitors. Today, too, the sartorial self-proclamation has faded at Araps, because the rest of the climbing world's getting into drop-dead colors. Australia is a step ahead.

But the frontier spirit has hardly vanished. One day Geoff Weigand and I arrived at a route to find two climbers starting up. We settled down to wait. When the pair's leader beat a (mostly airborn) retreat, a newly arrived New Zealander named Alan jumped up to tie in.

"Come on, mate," said Geoff pleasantly, "we bagged it. We've been waiting for ages. Bloody New Zealanders," he, an animated character, joked. "You come over here, take our dole, steal our routes, steal our women."

Said Alan, scornful, "I'd take your dole and I'd take your routes—but I wouldn't touch your women."

Today Araps is populated by no fewer locals, but less ferocious ones. For various reasons, top climbers strayed from the scene or sport. Mike Law, the flamboyant "Claw," a leader of the scene since he was 15, is a confirmed urbanite. He avoids campgrounds and "their autistic young males," races motorcycles, plays bridge, and concentrates on doing new routes on the sea cliffs of Sydney. The said cliffs sport slimy, crumbly, peeling rock; winos; barbed wire; broken glass and gravestones. Kim Carrigan is in Switzerland. Geoff Weigand took a year-plus off for elbow rehab and bicycle racing, and is only beginning to climb again. Mike Moorhead died on Makalu in the Himalaya.

The Australian climbing scene is infused and dispersed, but a death reverberates through it. Everybody knew the person.

Everyone knows a lot, in fact. And what he doesn't know he reads in the trade's magazines, whether it's regarding local slander (a favorite pastime), or Louise's love life.

The climbing meet both symbolized Australia's new diversity, and the fact that, like the Australian community, the idea of the meet goes on. For one thing, this meet hardly lacked the excitement of competition.

Scraps of conversation reflect the intensity of the rock warring:

"Did you flash it?"

"No, third try."

"Steve flashed it?"

"One fall."

"I flashed the direct start, then fell off the rest."

"You idiot."

"Kim had some crazy sequence. People are doing it easier these days."

What struck me about the competition here, however, was that it was up-front, playful. In the past, I've gotten some put-downs that were wounding because of the pretense of off-handedness.

At a professional contest, competition is also honest and up-front, but it's serious business. People's reputations, endorsements, contracts, commercials, films, expeditions, et al are at risk.

In Australia, however, failure was pretty funny. One day after I had done poorly—pumping out, I fell off every move on a climb after I had supposedly done the crux—Geoff instantly said, "Serves you right. Think you can come over here and cruise our routes!"

All the locals were more than generous when I or any visitor got up something hard.

Evenings at Louise's tended to be hilarious flack (usually aimed at Wolfgang, who would look an innocent appeal) sessions, or people talked of elbows. Midway through the meet, I had such sharp pains I had to take two straight days off. And diets. People talked about diets a lot. "I am so totally fat," said Wolfgang. "Sometimes it is difficult to breathe."

Wolfgang gave his views on competitions. "I hate them. I want to do routes I have dreamed of. I do not want to climb to try to beat other people off the rock." But he will be in a competition soon "because I hate work even more."

Actually, the only slated competition was an eating contest; Australian climbers are as well known for these as anything. This one featured three weight categories—light, medium, and mega—and 17 rounds of pastries, breads and milkshakes. Townspeople walked by, wearing expressions that said, "The horror." One year someone drank seven thick shakes at a competition. He got the record, but he also got hypothermia.

My last day at the meet I climbed with Louise at a quiet cliff in an area called the Grampions, after passing through groves of twisting trees to reach these hills that rose right out of the plain. We heard koalas rat-tat-tat and were startled by the sight of a dead snake on the path (most Australian snakes, I'd found out late in my stay, are terminally poisonous). As I had on the other days I'd climbed with her, I found myself telling Louise my life story. Louise is a combination of inscrutable—because she often makes no editorial comments on what has just been said, or skips the little reassurances that frantically would-be tactfuls like me are always sticking in—and terrifically open. She doesn't care who thinks or knows what about her, or who she's arguing with and whether it might be impolitic.

The meet was memorable in its internationalism, but ultimately, in the context of *its* context, the overhangs and the cracks and Louise and the gang. Like her, the local climbers seemed remarkably unfazed and outspoken. They laughed at the American pastime of bolt-chopping. "That's the stupidest thing I've ever heard of," they said. They were sometimes arrogant, but were good-hearted and consummately tolerant. They seemed to forget grudges and fights easily, seemed pretty unflappable when old boyfriends, old girlfriends, and new spouses showed up. You can call it callous, or you can call it a pretty cool way to go through life.

* * *

Today I'm doing reps on a Cybex machine, a creature I'd never heard of until now; getting blue slime and ultrasound rubbed into my elbows; being juiced with electric shocks that make my arms jump around the table.

Recently, a climber asked me dubiously if my trip for the meet had been worthwhile. I thought he had my injured elbows in mind. But he was referring to the fact that I hadn't climbed much at my outer limit—I'd done a handful of 24s and 25s and tried nothing above. Actually, he put it pointedly. "You went all that way and didn't even do anything hard."

Surprised, I said, *"Of course* it was worth it. It was great." Later, I wondered whether, if it had been a competition I'd travelled to in Australia, I might be less indifferent. Rankings at a contest matter more. People go to one to have some fun—but mostly they go to compete.

Just as climbing is as safe or as dangerous as you want to make it, it is as competitive as you want it to be. The difference between the competition at a contest or a meet, I think, is that a meet, like climbing in general, retains a sense of teamwork. Though one often feels very alone on a difficult section, overall you are a duo: talking, coaching, exhorting. In a competition, of course, people are glad to see each other fall.

The magic thing about climbing is the bond that forms, symbolized by the rope that links. Competitions, where an official, not a partner, stands by checking your progress, have foregone that aspect. This is not wrong, just different, and competitions have other rewards.

But that difference, I hope, will guarantee that meets retain their place, and not as removed cousins to their glamorous relatives. Meets, if you want them to, can add pressure and inspiration to performances, can offer some—maybe many—of the thrills of competitions. But they kindly pad things out.

* * *

Kurt worked on India every day. At various times his friends came, watched, straggled away. The day I came along was his last chance; he and Wolfgang had to leave the next day for China. With the cameras rolling, with all of us roaring with joy, Kurt finally crossed India, too.

Gumbies on Gurney

CONRAD D. ANKER*

T HE KICHATNAS are located approximately 45 miles southwest of the Denali massif in the Alaska Range. Although the peaks are all under 9000 feet in elevation, what they lack in altitude, they make up for in steepness and intensity. The Kichatnas have been described as an Alaskan Yosemite or a big version of the Bugaboos. In addition to vast granite walls, the range is blessed with all the nastiness of Alaskan weather. Unlike the Yosemite or other wall areas in the Lower Forty-Eight, help is not a shout away. Our goal was to climb the southeast face of Gurney Peak, which had been climbed twice before, but from the north.

Our team consisted of four Salt Lake climbers: Bob Ingle, Seth "ST" Shaw, James Garrett and me. We hoped our training on Utah crags and frozen waterfalls would prepare us for the wretched chimneys, cataclysmic storms and loose rock we expected to encounter. Were we ready for this? Being Alaska Range Gumbies, we hoped so.

After a long drive in the Blue Salmon (aka '72 Ford Van), we arrived in Talkeetna. The weather was fine and our ace pilot Doug Geeting blasted us in after only one day. The Cessna 185 was full of gear and food. Forty-five minutes later, we were circling the main summits of the Kichatnas. After our landing, the mountains took on a different perspective. From Base Camp on the Trident Glacier, the mountains rose abruptly out of the smooth silk of the glacier, touching the sun as it worked its way across the sky.

The southeast face of Gurney Peak lay four miles to the south over two passes. The first pass appeared to be a casual walk-up with a few patches of rock. The rocks were overhanging, the snow waist-deep and the crevasses moving. We made it over the pass, but not at the low point. We fixed three ropes and christened the pass "Bust Ass." We ascended and descended the pass eight times to ferry our gear to the base of the route. Each time it was a new adventure: big spindrift avalanches, frayed ropes or, our favorite, iced ropes. The second pass was a tedious hike up a steep slope.

The spectacular scenery made up for what the hard work took out of us. The days developed into a routine, interrupted only by a short storm now and then. Papier mâché (oatmeal) for breakfast, Snickers for lunch, noodles for dinner and lots of grunting in between.

*Recipient of an American Alpine Club Climbing Fellowship Grant.

PLATE 20

Photo by S.T. Shaw

Southeast Face of GURNEY PEAK.

Finally we touched the wall, ready to climb the orange granite. From the platform we hacked out at the base of our route, the rock looked good, except for a few bands of lighter rock. Drill fests in bad rock? The unknown awaited. The first pitch started with a few wide moves and then petered out to a thin crack. This took blades well until one decided to pivot and sent me on a short flight. I got back up, taped the gobi and hammered a bashi into submission. At the first belay, clouds were appearing. ST headed up the second pitch, a steep chimney which exited to some hooking on portable flakes. The weather turned nasty. Snow flowed off the summit in waves, while the wind drove it like a hawk. With two ropes fixed, we retreated to a snow cave like beat puppies. Cooking in a drenched tent that was continually flattening out had been as much fun as playing Twister with a blowtorch in the center. The challenges never ceased.

Thin cracks and loose flakes created the vertical topography of the next 100 meters. I could either spend two hours nailing or 45 minutes running out some 5.10. Which to choose? I took off my plastic boots and slipped into my On-Sights for some truly *à-vue* climbing. About every four meters a pocket appeared into which I gratefully stuffed camming devices of various sizes. Stemming out to a small nubbin, I cleaned a slot for a #1 TCU with my nut pick. Clipping into the little wonderpuppy, I glanced down at Bob, secure at the belay. It looks good, I thought. I moved up another three meters, but still no good gear. I'd better get moving—nothing happening here. A good flake with a notch for my fingers. Great! I grasped the flake only to have it pop out as quick as a wink. A hurtling "typewriter" headed for Bob, exploding above him and showering him with shrapnel. Luckily, his helmet prevented any mishap.

With four ropes fixed, James and ST led up to the first bivouac while Bob and I wrestled with two bloated pigs (aka haul bags) and a pack. Hauling took on a new dimension of brutality as small roofs and coarse rock hindered progress. Bob and I met James and ST at a blank spot with snow clinging below it. This was our home for two days; we set up portaledges and began cooking noodles and tuna fish, the official expedition dinner. The harshness of the wall disappeared in the horizontal security of the portaledges.

On May 4, we were at the base of the light-colored bands. Lucky us! The intrusions were created for climbers: tight cracks and no loose rocks. Bob led out over a roof, carefully avoiding threatening sword-shaped rocks which would not be welcome on our ledges. On with the sticky shoes, a few wraps of tape and I was off up 5.10 hand jams in a vertical crack. Yee ha! A little more work and we set up the next evening's camp. The Monkey Terraces sit with three dots of snow below the Flying Monkey Roof, a feature visible from the ground. The next pitch looked like awkward nutting in an overhanging dihedral. Always one to avoid strenuous aid, I liberally back-cleaned, adding to the excitement of A2 climbing in the middle of nowhere. ST and James led the next three pitches and fixed the ropes. The climbing was exhilarating, weaving in and out of gullies and chasms. Which one was the correct one?

PLATE 21

Photo by Bob Ingle

Hanging bivouac on Gurney Peak.

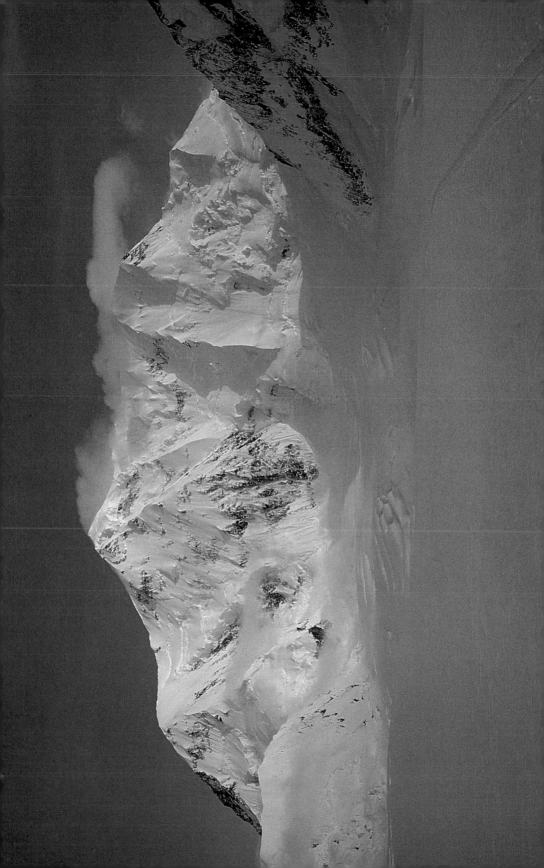

The sun set on the spectacular west face of Lewis Peak as we rappelled down the ropes to our Flying Monkeys bivouac. (I knew that Dorothy and the Tin Man were around somewhere. The flying monkeys kept singing with the wind.) Hanging high on the southeast face of Gurney, we looked out over the vast expanses of glaciers and minor peaks to the east. One of the benefits of being on the wall, aside from the fact that it was warmer than on the glacier, was the reception of the Anchorage rock station. Our contact with civilization was shocking. Ads for discount flights to Hawaii, all-you-can-eat restaurants (later to be our nemesis), and perm specials interspersed with generic rock music reminded us we were tied to a wall in Alaska and not on some other planet. The weather reports usually were the opposite of what was happening around us. All unsavory reports of big storms and low-pressure systems meant nice weather. Anticipation was running high. What would the weather do?

The weather dawned thick with fog. It wasn't snowing and the calm wind frosted our exposed ears. We stuffed packs with a supply of candy bars and clipped our Jümars into 11mm of security. The first rope passed over the Flying Monkey Roof, spinning us around on a thread half-a-mile above the glacier. A quick snap of adrenaline heightened the mystical morning. After four ropes we joined the ridge. Through cornices with interspersed boulder problems, we laced our way to the summit crest. The clouds surrounded us, but we knew the sun was near. The climbing was relaxing, hiking through boulders at an angle that felt flat after five days in vertical living. A final chimney set us on the summit. This is the summit! I'm in an airplane flying through clouds. Or am I stationary as the clouds race by?

We were sheltered from the wind which was chasing the clouds off the summits of the Kichatnas. We couldn't view the panorama in its entirety, each peak allowing a glimpse of itself one at a time. The east face of Kichatna Spire winked at us while the Triple Peaks carved holes in the clouds. Belayed downclimbing led to the edge of the wall. Rappelling was not tedious as the scenery presented itself anew. The surrounding peaks closed in on us, cathedral-like. The wind created a calling sound as our hushed talk echoed into the chanting of monks. The strips of webbing at the belays looked like smiles above us. Who would visit these slings next? We soon bedded down in our cocoons for a satisfying rest.

The southeast face of Gurney is a steep line, following cracks for its entirety. We placed 27 bolts for belays, none for upward progress.

The next morning was blustery. Snow obscured our view beyond 100 meters. After a bit of oatmeal, Bob and I descended to our camp which was complete with rum and pancakes. ST and James spent another day on the wall, enjoying the view from the comfort of their portaledge.

We arrived back at Base Camp with a week to spare. ST skied over to P 7360 for a solo ascent. One day we skied to the tongue of the Trident Glacier. The alders were budding, the birds were chirping, and we soaked our feet. The smell of vegetation overpowered our senses, a delightful break from the stench of unwashed poly-pro and smelly climbers.

PLATE 22

Photo by Bob Ingle

**Conrad Anker on Southeast Face of
GURNEY PEAK.**

The sky shone blood-red at three in the morning. Not to worry! Doug would airlift us from this surreal playground today, May 17. Ten o'clock rolled in with a thick wall of snow. As most storms in the past 31 days had lasted 36 hours, we were not overly concerned. By the fourth day, it had become a sad joke. On the ninth day we had run out of all food but for 30 cans of sardines. By the tenth day we had read all our books. During this huge snowstorm, Doug Geeting had made nine attempts to pick us up. He was as stressful as we about the situation (although probably not so hungry). On the eleventh night the clouds lifted and Doug flew up the glacier. The whine of the engine was like music. Emaciated, we flew to Talkeetna for a night of merry making and a day of gluttony.

Summary of Statistics:

AREA: Kichatna Mountains, Alaska Range.

NEW ROUTE: Gurney Peak, 2560 meters, 8400 feet via Southeast Face; May 3 to 8, 1987 (whole party).

PERSONNEL: Conrad D. Anker, Robert Ingle, Seth (ST) Shaw, James Garrett.

Augusta and Logan Twin Pack

DON SERL, *Alpine Club of Canada*

$\mathbb{W}$HERE I COME FROM, you've climbed a mountain when you can spit off the far side. Also, where I come from, Mount Logan is the biggest mountain there is, with a south face that is absolutely Himalayan in size and seriousness. It was thus that, while never having had personal acquaintance with the great peaks of the Saint Elias Mountains, I reacted with considerable pique to a report in the 1986 *Canadian Alpine Journal* in which four Yanks claimed to have "established a new route on the south face of Mount Logan." The report went on to reveal that they had, in fact, been soundly trounced by the mountain, turning back, frostbitten, "a few hundred yards" short of even gaining the existing Hummingbird Ridge route. At least 4000 feet of mountain still stood above them. These guys, I decided from the comfort of my living room, were plainly wankers. Somebody ought to do something about it!

And so it came to be that four of us found ourselves on the Seward Glacier early last May, intent on *climbing* the Early Bird Buttress. Because the putative plan called for an alpine-style ascent as that would entail 11,000 feet of difficult climbing leading to a 19,500-foot summit followed by stumbling six to eight kilometers across the summit plateau at 17,000 feet to find a descent route none of us had ever seen, it seemed prudent to climb something a little lower and less serious first. The north rib of Mount Augusta, the most aesthetic route on the prettiest peak on the Seward, beckoned.

After 15 kilometers and seven hours of sledding from Base Camp, we tucked into our bags in the basin below the rib. A typical "Saint Elias alpine start" at eleven A.M. the next morning saw us over the schrund at noon and the adventure began. Easy snow slopes led right to a short sérac wall at the base of the arête that forms most of the route. The arête, once gained, proved steep and exhilaratingly exposed, although belays were necessary only a handful of times. Four thousand feet and eight hours up, in high winds and spindrift, we dug in where the ridge begins to fade into the face. A miserable night, buffeted in our little "frost-boxes," followed. There seems to be no alternative to these little Gore-Tex wedge tents for hard routes where weight counts, but to pretend that they are anything more than cramped and icy is a cruel joke. Luckily, the storm let up by mid-morning and by one P.M. we made another "alpine start" and moved into the mists that supplanted the sun. By early evening we had climbed the upper 2000 feet of the face and topped out onto the crest of the west ridge. Cold, wet Pacific breezes surged up the south face from the

76

PLATE 23

MOUNT AUGUSTA from the Northeast. Ascent is marked. Descent was via North Ridge outlined by sun.

Malaspina Glacier. Fortress-height snow walls to protect the tents seemed advisable. We were a long way out on a limb if the weather worsened.

Morning dawned crisp, calm and reasonably clear. It was tremendously exciting to gaze out across the vast swirls of the Malaspina and stare into the sea. The ridge crest, while heavily corniced on the north side, offered reasonably straightforward travel along the top of the south-facing slopes. Once again, only a few belays were necessary and by 6:30 we had plugged up the final soft slopes, dumped our packs and plowed the final couple of hundred meters to the top. A third of a century after this fine peak was first climbed, the second ascent was ours!

The descent of the original route*, the north ridge, went smoothly enough, although the lee-side mists obscured the initial 1000 or 1500 feet down steep, icy slopes and confused us greatly. The long gentle section at mid-height was a delight, with fabulous golden views from the Bering Glacier to Kennedy and Hubbard, but the slopes below had us very much on edge. Fortunately the snow conditions were good and we regained the basin without incident. Just after one A.M., tired but elated, we slogged back to our campsite and plunged into a midnight snack of Dagwood proportions. An amazingly quick return ski trip, just 2½ hours, on a fast, frozen track got us back to Base Camp the evening of the following day. The "acclimatization" part of the trip was over. It was time to turn our thoughts to Logan!

It turns out maybe that the South Tahoe guys, whoever they were, might not be such wankers after all. It turns out that they may just have climbed a lot of hard, hard terrain on their attempt. All right, they certainly overstated the case by claiming to have done the route, but I've got to say my hat is off to them. We thought and talked, talked and thought, and we came to the considered opinion that that route was simply too big and too serious for us. To be humbled by a mountain is no shame. In fact, to be able to put aside one's ego and analyze each situation as one comes upon it is a key to staying alive in the hills. It is surely one of the great lessons that one can bring back to sea-level life from these adventures. If you are not ready, know so and go away. The mountain can't go away, and you can always come back! And so, without so much as setting foot on it, we turned our backs on it and sought an alternative.

The second half of the trip, while still a challenge, was, it must be admitted, somewhat anticlimactic. We knew there were parties on Logan's east ridge and reckoned they'd have tracks in and all the hard sections fixed. We also felt that we'd spent enough time at altitude and were fit enough to have a go at "flashing" the route. We'd pack for six days, take a single screw and a

---

*It should be noted that the account of the first ascent of Augusta in the 1953 *Canadian Alpine Journal* is terribly confusing as to points of the compass. The climbers refer to a northwest orientation of approach and to a col on the northwest side of the mountain, whereas they were approaching from the northeast to a col directly north of the summit. They climbed a ridge that might best be called the north ridge but which actually lies east of north relative to the summit. Similarly, the "west" face is the north face and their "north" face is the northeast face.

solitary picket per pair plus a 7 mm rope for the bunch and see if we could make it to the top. If anything went wrong, we'd fail, but that was simply the game.

Everything clicked. We got away from the landing site at noon, skied to the base of the route in 2½ hours and set up tents for a siesta till the sun went around the corner and the temperatures plunged. By ten o'clock, we were sipping soup and renewing friendships in the 11,000-foot campsite at the base of the first knife-edged section. Just after midnight, we dropped our packs 1000 feet higher and set about waking everyone in the camp by scrunching out platforms for the tents. Blustery snow the next day ended progress above the second knife-edge, only 1000 feet higher, but clear, calm weather reappeared in the evening. Superb views broadened and lengthened as we continued up slowly easing slopes to the plateau rim at nearly 16,000 feet on our third afternoon. Another hour-and-a-half saw us into the basin below the east peak for the night. Excitement and anticipation contended with headaches and lack of appetite. We were clearly too high too fast. We bedded down just as prepared to dash down for lower elevations at the first sign of edema or of bad weather as to head for the top.

Summit day! Getting under way was hard, but once we were moving, progress was smooth and steady. Firm snow underfoot and a cold but windless day helped. Still, the higher we got, the longer the stops. Finally, high on the traverse of the south face of the east peak, we were forced to the conclusion that the main summit was unattainable. Even after we had dropped the packs on a rock outcrop, the last thousand feet to the east peak seemed a desperate blur of frantic panting and dragging footsteps. Somehow the urge to spit off the far side never came to mind, and not long after we'd reached it, the east summit was once again stark and empty against the sky.

A stormy night had me worried—none of us was feeling very well—but our luck again held. While the morning was misty with intermittent snow, it was fair enough for travel. Our strength came back fast as we dropped and we kept on blasting down the ridge all through the afternoon. Twelve hours after leaving the Plateau Camp at 16,500 feet, we doffed our packs for the final time at the landing site, 10,000 feet lower. The mountain stood serene. Early Bird remained unclimbed, but we had stretched ourselves on a great route and had succeeded. To fail on a greater route may be viewed as nobler, and to succeed on the greatest of routes is obviously the finest of all, but I admitted to no misgivings, no second thoughts as I dropped off to sleep, glowing with contentment. The mountain had been kind to us, we had been true to ourselves and now we were going home.

Summary of Statistics:

AREA: Saint Elias Mountains, Yukon Territory, Canada.

ASCENTS: Mount Augusta, 4288 meters, 14,070 feet; Second Ascent via a new route, the North Rib, May 13 to 15, 1987.
Mount Logan, East Peak, 5892 meters, 19,330 feet; via East Ridge.

PERSONNEL: Mike Carlson, Greg Foweraker, Jeff Marshall, Don Serl.

Barrill and Dr. Cook

D R. FREDERICK A. COOK in 1906 claimed that he and Edward Barrill, a horse packer from Darby, Montana, had made the first ascent of Mount McKinley. This claim has been hotly disputed over the years. A great many books and articles have been written, supporting or disclaiming Dr. Cook. Backed up by substantial evidence, Bradford Washburn and Ann and Adams Carter published a detailed article with many telling photographs in the *American Alpine Journal* of 1958 on pages 1 to 30; after a careful reading of the article, most readers will doubtless find it difficult to credit Dr. Cook with the ascent.

There is a second point about which there has also been disagreement: namely the spelling of Edward Barrill's name. To clear up this point, Washburn wrote in January 1988 to the Town Clerk of Darby, Montana to see what the town records had to say. To his amazement, an answer came back, not from the Town Clerk, but from Barrill's daughter. He then sent her a copy of the 1958 *A.A.J.* We quote her reply in full. The letter is on file at the American Alpine Club. This letter not only clears up the question of the spelling of the name but also gives new evidence about the validity of the ascent.

* * *

January 29, 1988

Dear Mr. Washburn,

I have begun to read the book you sent me but it will take a long time as I want to get every word of it. I do wish there was a map showing the position of the different peaks in relation to Mt. McKinley. Otherwise it is a very interesting story and I will treasure it.

I am sorry that I have no first-hand knowledge of the climb as I was not born until 1910. I have only Dad's stories to go by and he told and retold them so often and they were always the same so I believe he was telling the truth. So many people have worked so many hours trying to prove or disprove the climb. My Dad was not a man who would exaggerate or lie about anything he did to make himself look good. He always said they did <u>not</u> climb Mt. McKinley and so I believe him.

It was a very harrowing trip from the beginning. They had a pack train of horses to carry the equipment but it was a mistake to bring horses. The trail was too rough for them and the poor animals fell & injured themselves over and over, and some broke their legs and had to be destroyed. One remarkable old mare was swept over a waterfall, pack and all, and was still alive and sound when she was rescued. Even her pack was not too badly damaged. Anyway, the men finally wound up carrying all the supplies themselves.

Foraker and McKinley from Southeast. Upper line shows Cook's line up the Ruth Glacier and possibly his highest point. Lower line is up the side glacier. His false "summit" photos were taken on the 5300-foot peak marked by an arrow. The point to the right was where he took his "15,400-foot" photo.

RUTH GLACIER

When they reached their destination they began setting up base camps and on the day that the climbers started up on the real climb, the others had all dropped out except Dad and Dr. Cook. It must have been a grueling climb with no oxygen, no special clothing, nothing a climber can get now. Dad said that if you stooped over and put your head at knee level, you could see the blue shadows of deep crevases (sic). Finally Dr. Cook said, "Ed, let's just *say* we climbed Mt. McKinley." He and Dad started back down after taking the picture of Dad with the flag on a side peak. I always felt that if that had been the real top of McKinley, it would have been Cook getting his picture taken.

Just before they got back to the base camp, Cook said, "Now Ed, I don't want you to say anything about this to the men. Just tell them they will have to talk to me." When they arrived the men crowded around and said, "Well, did you make it?" Cook went to his tent and shut the flap and Dad repeated what Cook had told him to say. "You'll just have to talk to Cook."

Cook stayed in his tent for three days then suddenly came out, rubbing his hands and stamping his feet. "Well boys," he said. "We made it." Dad said he nearly fell over into a snowbank. He said, "I didn't think he would really lie about it. But he did."

In 1909 the Alpine Club or the Explorers' Club contacted Dad and offered to pay his way to New York City to testify at Cook's trial. While Cook was planning the North Pole trip, he wrote Dad & said, "If you will keep quit (sic) about the McKinley trip, I will bring you back a chunk of the pole." He never paid the wages Dad earned as a guide for the expedition and I guess this is what he meant. Dad got mad and threw the letter away but my mother rescued it & kept it and took it along when they went to New York. That letter is probably still in the files of one of those clubs or the National Geographic, which I believe had been in on some part of it. One of those clubs later paid Dad's wages. Cook never did.

As to any documents the family might have had, I don't know anything. My sister Delia Costello of Sunnyside, WN was very interested in this bit of family history, but she is gone now.

My sister Alaska is the one who put the E on the end of our name and Dad began using it to please her. However, the real spelling is Barrill. My own middle name is Mt. McKinley and altho I was proud to be named after such a grand mountain, it was a bit top heavy for general use so I shortened it to McKinley. May any Gods on Mt. Denali forgive me.

Cook came to Montana after the trial to "Face Ed Barrill" as he said, but everyone here knew Dad & believed in him. Cook didn't seem to want to face Dad after he got here, he only wanted to talk about the trip. He was booed and hissed so many times that he finally stalked off the stage in a rage.

His daughter defended him fiercely in a Life Magazine article I read, and I can understand that, but in later years Cook was arrested for selling phony oil leases. This climb is now part of our history and as such we must forgive them for their past mistakes.

This letter got too long but I hope it is what you wanted. Thanks again.

Sincerely, Marj. Barrill

Physiological and Neuropsychological Characteristics of World-Class Extreme-Altitude Climbers

OSWALD OELZ AND MARIANNE REGARD, *Universitätsspital, Zürich*

O N MAY 8, 1978, Reinhold Messner and Peter Habeler demonstrated that altitudes higher than 8500 meters could be climbed without bottled oxygen. Until then it had been widely assumed that such a feat was physically impossible due to the low oxygen tensions on the summit slopes of Mount Everest, K2, Kangchenjunga and Lhotse. This opinion was in part based on the experiences on the British pre-war Everest Expeditions when the altitude of 8560 meters could never be passed without supplementary oxygen. It is noteworthy, however, that members of these expeditions ascended to that altitude without oxygen and suffered no permanent ill effects. After Hillary's and Tensing's successful ascent of Mount Everest with massive use of oxygen, it seemed clear that future expeditions would use the same tactics. Some scientists also claimed that the eventual summiters of an ascent without oxygen would suffer from severe brain damage.

After Messner's and Habeler's summit success, "oxygenless" ascents of the four mountains were repeated by a number of climbers. However, it became obvious that the true limits of human tolerance to hypoxia are touched during those adventures and that there is no margin for errors. This point had already been stressed by Hillary, who expressed the opinion that the summit of Everest could eventually be reached without oxygen, but that the risks involved were enormous. In the last eight years this prediction has been sadly confirmed by the death of several world-class climbers above 8000 meters due to avoidable accidents and/or exhaustion.

The recent interest in the physiological problems connected with the climbing to altitudes higher than 8500 meters is illustrated by the exciting work performed during Dr. West's American Medical Research Expedition to Mount Everest in 1981 (1), and Dr. Houston's Operation Everest II in 1985 (2). This prompted us to study some characteristics of world-class climbers who all had reached the summit of one of the four highest peaks in the world without supplementary oxygen (3). Among them were the two climbers who have summited all fourteen 8000-meter peaks and climbers who have climbed 8000-meter peaks including Everest in 24 to 48 hours from Base Camp to the top and back. (See Table 1.) The studies were done two to 12 months after the last extreme altitude exposure, that is at a time when most physiological changes induced by hypoxia have presumably disappeared. We focused our investigations on the mechanisms responsible for oxygen uptake and delivery to tissues and on the permanent effects of hypoxia on the brain. In a number of tests the static and dynamic long-volumes were measured and found to be within normal limits for an age-matched control population. Interestingly enough the most successful climber has lung volumes at the lowest limits of normal. The dimensions of the right and left heart were measured by echocardiography, using ultrasound for imaging and were found to be normal. This was somewhat a surprise since we had expected that the right heart would be enlarged as a consequence of increased pressure in the pulmonary circulation induced by hypoxia. However, apparently these changes are rapidly reversible upon return to sea level. The morphology and metabolic activity of the muscle was studied in biopsies taken from the thigh. There was an increased content of certain slow-twitch, fatigue-resistant fibers in the muscles of these climbers. There were also changes in fiber size leading to a favorable condition for tissue oxygenation. This was further illustrated by the fact that the number of blood capillaries per area was significantly greater in these climbers than in controls. There were signs for an increased capacity of the muscle to oxidize fat, which may be of advantage during prolonged exercise.

Table 1
Subjects' Climbing History

Subject	Country of Origin	Age	Peaks over 8500 meters Without O_2	With O_2	Peaks Between 8000 & 8500 meters Without O_2
RM	Italy	42	5		13
JK	Poland	39	4		10
EL	Switzerland	28	2		7
MD	Germany	50	2	1	3
KW	Poland	37	1	1	3
WR	Poland	44	1	1	1
DS	UK	42	1	1	2
HK	Italy	31	1		6
NJ	Switzerland	27	1		4
FM	Italy	38	1		2
PH	Austria	38	1		1
HE	Germany	38	1		1

It has been suggested that climbers like Messner and Habeler might be extraordinary in their capacity to take up and/or to utilize oxygen. It was postulated that climbing without bottled oxygen to the top of Mount Everest might only be possible for individuals, characterized by an extremely high maximal aerobic power. We, therefore, performed studies on the maximal oxygen uptake in these climbers in two different laboratories under different experimental conditions. The maximal oxygen uptake represents the functional capacity of the cardiovascular system to transport oxygen to the tissues of the body and is defined as the maximal amount of oxygen a person can take in and use during physical work. Much to our surprise the maximum oxygen uptake of elite climbers, even though it was higher than observed in untrained subjects fell within the range of amateur marathoners but was well below the values of elite long-distance runners. The mean value for the whole group was 60 ml oxygen per kg per min, whereas world-class marathon runners reach values higher than 80 ml.

The main mechanism by which the body compensates for low environmental oxygen tensions is hyperventilation that is an increase in ventilation both in frequency and volume. Ventilation at rest was higher in the world-class climbers than in control subjects, both at sea level and at 5300 meters in a decompression chamber. This observation is in agreement with previous reports by Schoene and co-workers (4) who observed that among the climbers of the American Medical Research Expedition to Mount Everest the summiters were characterized by resting hyperventilation and by a greater ventilatory response to hypoxia. This is probably either the consequence of a persisting ventilatory acclimatization or an inborn advantage of these climbers enabling them to climb so high without too much punishment. The ventilatory response to exercise at sea level was virtually the same in climbers as in control subjects. During exercise at 5300 meters, however, the ventilatory response of the climbers was higher than in controls.

On the whole it appears that the main feature of a successful extreme altitude climber are a high capacity to oxydize fat in the muscles, a favorable geometry for blood-tissue gas exchange and respiratory control centers with immediate and sensitive reaction to hypoxia. The maximal capacity to take up and to use oxygen is not extraordinary in the group of climbers studied and far below that of world-class marathoners. However, it is reasonable to suggest that a skilled climber with a very high oxygen uptake capacity would perform better than the best of the present day's climbers. The most important feature, however, for climbing the highest peaks of the world without supplementary oxygen is a strong motivation and an exceptional drive. Reinhold Messner and Jerzy Kukuczka, the first mountaineers who climbed all the 8000-meter summits typify these climbers. They are characterized by rather normal physiological features, but by the obsessive need to be the first and best and to climb "by fair means," that is without the aid of oxygen in any phase of the ascent.

Hypoxia acutely impairs the function of the brain. Climbers to extreme altitude repeatedly have reported hallucination of the visual, auditive and somatosensory type. Impaired sensory, perceptual and motor performance has been observed in the laboratory under simulated high-altitude conditions and in climbers in the Himalaya. These impairments of vital cerebral functions may lead to faulty behavior and deadly mistakes. Most of these changes seem to be rapidly reversible upon return to low altitude although climbers have reported defective short-term memory for months after an expedition. The question whether there is any permanent residual brain damage particularly after repetitive extreme altitude exposure has been hotly debated, and it has been suggested that climbing to extreme altitude without bottled oxygen should be discouraged similarly to professional boxing since it might cause permanent brain injury.

We have therefore studied eight of our most successful extreme altitude climbers with a comprehensive battery of neuropsychological tests (5). These individuals had collectively climbed more than sixty 8000-meter peaks without supplementary oxygen. The clinical and neurological examination of all of them was entirely normal and most of them had a higher IQ than a control population. In a test of concentration, however, the majority performed irregularly and with a high error score. Memory assessment revealed a defective short-term memory in half of the subjects with normal long-term memory. The cognitive flexibility which was assessed with measurements for spontaneous word and figure idea production and adaptive flexibility was also impaired in half of the subjects. There was no significant impairment of motor performance. Altogether the dysfunctions found in concentration, short-term memory and cognitive flexibility as well as a lack of perceptual or other higher cortical defects suggested a dysfunction of the fronto-temporal basal brain areas. There was also some correlation of these changes with pathological findings in the electroencephalogram.

These climbers function entirely normally in daily life and in the challenging environment of extreme altitude. The subtle changes which are most likely a consequence of repetitive hypoxic stress to the brain can only be detected in certain tests. It should also be remembered that the British climbers who first ascended to extreme altitude without bottled oxygen in the years of 1921 to 1938 had subsequently very successful professional careers and remained astute and sharp into their old days.

REFERENCES

1. West J.B., Human physiology at extreme altitudes on Mount Everest. *Science* 1984; 223:784-8.
2. Houston C.S., Sutton J.R., Cymerman A., Reeves J.T. Operation Everest II: man at extreme altitude. *J Appl Physiol* 1987; 63:877-82.
3. Oelz O., Howald H., di Prampero P.E., Hoppeler H., Claassen H., Jenni R., Bühlmann A., Ferretti G., Brückner J.C., Veicsteinas A., Gussoni M., Cerretelli P. Physiological profile of world class high altitude climbers. *J Appl Physiol* 1986; 60:1734-42.
4. Schoene R.B., Lahiri S., Hackett P.H., Peters R.M. Jr., Milledge J.S., Pizzo C.J., Sarnquist F.H., Boyer S.J., Graber D.J., Maret K.H., West J.B. Relationship of hypoxic ventilatory response to exercise performance on Mount Everest. *J Appl Physiol* 1984; 56:1478-83.
5. Regard M., Oelz O., Brugger P., Landis T. Persistent cognitive dysfunction after repetitive exposure to extreme altitude. In press.

Beware the Future

ROBERT HORAN

IN THE EARLY 1980s, Boulder, Colorado area standards for free climbing began to rise. Now, well into the 80s, the standards have sky-rocketed. Once again, Boulder's free climbers are among the country's leaders of difficult free routes, with several 5.12 + s and over twenty 5.13s to date.

The incursion is primarily due to the transformation of the area's ethics. Preeminent locals have ventured onto an unconventional vision among the rock crags, now scrutinizing blank, unclimbable-appearing portions of rock as opposed to naturally protectable cracks or flake systems.

These new-age rhythmical performances are usually top-roped free, if possible, and then bolts are placed in the most accessible places for the lead. The modus operandi for bolting varies, although 90% of the bolt routes have been established on rappel. Ultimately the first ascentionist will red-point the route (climb from bottom to top without ever weighting the rope). Often this ends up as a race against boredom.

Boulder's climbing mecca is gifted with many talented, well conditioned climbers, many of whom have never established a 5.13 route. It is the climbing community as a whole that is behind the push to the extremely high standards on the scale. From the first route in the area to the new desperate ones, each route acts as a stepping stone to something greater, ultimately making climbing safer and more enjoyable for all.

The Boulder area's competitive nature has driven local rock jocks to incredible new horizons and the overabundance of steep, overhanging, high quality rock shows no limits.

In the summer of 1984 the area received its first 5.13 route when I free-climbed the *Rainbow Wall* (5.13a) on the south face of Wind Tower in Eldorado Canyon. This diagonaled up and left on small holds and was protected by five bolts placed on lead. In the following spring of 1985, Christian Griffith led up *Paris Girl* (5.13a), between Disappearing Act and Grande Course on the Redgarden Wall. The thin-edged route with its long reaches was protected by eight bolts placed on rappel. In the summer of 1986, on the north side of Tower Two's summit block, Griffith and Neil Kaptain freed the bulging 30-foot wall *Venus de Milo* (5.13a). Here, as below when not specifically mentioned, bolts placed on rappel protected the strenuous route. Then down on the outcropping at the beginning of the Redgarden Wall Gully

PLATE 25

Photo by Bob Horan

**"Five-Year Plan" (5.13b), Skunk
Canyon, Flatirons, Colorado.**

Trail, just right of Breakfast of Champions, Charlie Fowler and Joe Huggins established *Kaptain Krunch* (5.12d/5.13a). Small layaways led to a slap for the sloping lip; two bolts and a pin placed on rappel protected the overhang. Meanwhile Griffith added an even wilder roof climb by traversing out left from the C'est la Vie dihedral on small but good edges. The awesome *Desdichado* (5.13b/c) is very exposed. Following this monumental ascent, Griffith teamed up with Mark Sonnefield to establish yet another 5.13 route with the free ascent of *Wingless Victory* (5.13b). The leaning arête climb is another very exposed route just right of the fourth pitch of the Naked Edge.

The following year of 1987 brought on even more 5.13 action as young Chris Hill freed the severely overhanging wall left of Supremacy Crack. The *Web* (5.13a) follows good holds with long reaches between them. Up the road a bit on Peanuts Wall, Dale Goddard joined the action by establishing the *Sacred and Profane* (5.12d/5.13a). The vertical face follows a prominent rib with small edges. Across from Peanuts on the upper part of the West Ridge (also known as the Rincon Wall), Fowler freed *Surf's Up* (5.13). This overhanging dihedral right of Wendego is hardest at the start and slowly becomes manageable. Bolts and pins protect the climb. Down the West Ridge, on the south face of Long John Tower, I led *Incarnation* (5.13a). The overhanging thin face is capped off with a beautiful vertical slab. Six bolts and two pins protect this exposed face. Topping off Eldorado's 5.13s was the *Kloberdeath Roof* (5.13b). Bob Candelaria's overhanging route climbs up and out left from the Kloberdanz roof and then up onto a vertical face.

In the Flatirons the standards have also changed. In the summer of 1986, Goddard free-climbed the severely overhanging thin crack on the south face of the Back Porch in Skunk Canyon. The *Five Year Plan* (5.13a/b) is all naturally protected except for a bolt placed at the lip, a must for any crack monger. That same summer, Goddard also established a very thin vertical face climb just right of Stone Love across from the Finger Flatiron. *Cornucopia* (5.13a) ascends a beautiful smooth wall.

The following spring of 1987, I free-climbed an incredibly overhanging pocketed wall at the mouth of Skunk Canyon to establish the spectacular *Guardian* (5.13a). That summer in Bear Canyon, Dan Michaels created another desperate 5.13 route by free-climbing the *Fiend* (5.11a). The overhanging, leaning dihedral is protected by a pin and four bolts. That fall Michaels created another desperate climb on the west face of the first Ironing Board. *Slave to Rhythm* (5.13b/c) climbs out of a very overhanging pebbled wall. In early December I established another 5.13 free route on the west face of Satan's Slab, just right of the Doric Dihedral. *Watchmaker Steady* (5.13a) climbs up very thin edges on a slightly overhanging wall. Five bolts were placed on lead.

COLOR PLATE 8 (on following page)

Photo by Melanie Dieckman

Bob Horan on First Ascent of Solstice (5.13), Old Stage Crag, Colorado.

Down the range a bit, in Boulder Canyon, in the fall of 1984, Griffith freed *Tourist Extravaganz* (5.13a). The minute vertical granite slab is located on Castle Rock, right of Country Club Crack. Several years later, in the spring of 1987, Mark Rolofson and I led *Damaged Goods* (5.12d/5.13a). The intricate bulge and crack is just left of Rude Boys on Milkdud Rock and is protected by four pins placed on rappel. Soon after, Rolofson free-climbed the thin water groove to the right of the latter routes, *Blues for Allah* (5.13a). That same summer, Griffin put up another arête route by freeing *Verve* (5.13b/c). The overhanging, thin-edged arête is located just left of the Cosmosis dihedral on Bell Buttress. In the fall of 1987 I reestablished another 5.13 free route in the canyon by free-climbing *Hands of Destiny* (5.13b). On the steep-to-overhanging crack-and-flake system, it consists of face climbing and laybacking on small holds. Four pins were placed on lead.

Another Boulder area crag worth mentioning is the Left Hand Canyon's Olde Stage Crag. Several very steep face routes all with bolt protection are here. Most noteworthy is the *Soltice* (5.12d/5.13a), which I climbed in early 1987. The steep face begins at a very technical roof and then goes up an overhanging wall.

Even further down the range, a favorite area for Boulder's climbers, Buttonrock Resevoir, has seen much activity, notably on the *New Horizons* arête, a thin overhanging prow, which I led in 1987. All the routes described are of good or excellent quality.

Editor's Note. All American rock-climbers will not agree with these tactics. By publishing this article, the American Alpine Club neither recommends nor condemns the climbing methods described above.

Color Plate 9 (on previous page)

Photo by Michiko Takahashi

Kazuyuki Takahashi taking off by Paraglider from Cho Oyu for the World's Altitude Record.

Paragliders and Modern Alpinism

JOHN BOUCHARD

PARAGLIDERS OR *PARAPENTES*, as they are known in France, are the most radical development in alpine climbing since the ice-tool revolution in the seventies. Just as the new ice tools opened countless possibilities for more new exploits, paragliding is redefining the limits of what is possible in the mountains.

Weighing as little as four pounds, they take up as much room as a small sleeping bag. They resemble the conventional RAM AIR sky-diving canopies, but they use a different material, airfoil and plan-form. Their rate of descent is around 600 to 900 feet per minute and so a 5000-foot descent can be made effortlessly in under ten minutes. For take-off you need a 30-foot-wide area which is at least 20 feet long and 18° steep. You lay the canopy on its back, arrange the lines, tie in, snap it over your head, run a few steps and you are airborne. A paraglider can also be used for bivouacs.

During the last few years they have been the key element in arousing excitement for the *enchainement* or linking of more than one alpine wall. In the past helicopters were used to accomplish this and because of it few were interested. Christophe Profit used a *parapente* to descend the Walker Spur in his winter solo *enchainement* of the north faces of the Matterhorn, Eiger and Grandes Jorasses. Jean Marc Boivin used one to link in one day the Triolet, Courtes and Droites north faces. And even more extraordinary was the exploit of Jean Troillet and Erhard Loretan. A few months after climbing Everest in 36 hours from their Tibetan Base Camp, they used *parapentes* to attempt ten north faces in a row, starting with the Eiger and finishing with the Matterhorn.

They have also been used to eliminate tedious and painful descents like those from Mont Blanc or Mont Blanc de Talcul. With paragliders, climbers have left Chamonix in the morning, climbed a Brenva-Face route and flown to Chamonix that same afternoon. In the Himalaya, climbers have flown from the summits of Gasherbrum II, the Nameless Tower and Cho Oyu, among others. In South America, climbers have used them to descend from Chimborazo and Aconcagua. In the United States, they have been used to fly off Half Dome, El Capitan, the Grand Teton, Mount St. Helens and Denali.

91

Here in the United States, the liability issue and government safety regulations are a definite hindrance. To learn safely, you need a clear steep area like a ski slope and no ski area is willing to risk a lawsuit. National Parks prohibit this type of flying and enforce the rules with severe penalties. This is unfortunate, since paragliders are well suited to places like the Tetons and Yosemite. In contrast, European climbers have year-round lifts to use and unrestricted access to suitable terrain. In a few months, they can get several hundred thousand vertical feet and more than a hundred hours of flying, while here in the United States we would need many years to do this. One direct consequence, in my opinion, is our almost absurd casualty rate. With no places to practice, beginners (though usually very experienced climbers) attempt flights in dangerous areas under uncertain conditions with predictable results. Regardless of the rules, laws and risks, you can be guaranteed that if European climbers are flying off climbs to make these spectacular *enchainements*, top American alpinists are going to try as well.

The big drawbacks are the amount of time needed to learn and the obvious danger of flying. You can't use paragliders on all climbs, just as you can't use crampons on the Nose of El Capitan. Learning to manipulate the canopy is fairly simple and can be learned in a few hours. But hundreds of hours of air time are needed to read the wind conditions and air currents and to fly safely in the mountains. It is also essential to fly in many different areas. It isn't like learning to rappel. It is more like learning to ski. You cannot take it lightly; you must devote very many hours to learning it.

Paragliders will affect American climbing in a few ways. First, they bring home the idea of *enchainement*. Big walls are not getting any bigger, the mountains are not getting any higher, but climbers are getting better. Obviously, we can't change the routes to make them harder, nor can we make them longer. But we can link several routes to open a whole new world of adventure. Second, they make some descents easier. Curry Village is now five easy minutes from the summit of Half Dome. Lupine Meadows are now six minutes from the top of the Grand Teton. The road is now three minutes from the base of Castleton Tower. Third, they will renew interest in alpine climbing and heighten a sensitivity to the mountain environment. The best flights are the big flights and, as the younger climbers learn to use paragliders, they will want to make flights in the Sierra, the Cascades, the Tetons and other ranges. They will have to climb the classic routes and in the process they will gain a tremendous amount of alpine experience. More important, they cannot help but learn to respect the fragility of the terrain.

This will all happen, but it will take time. Who would have guessed in 1970 what type of icicles and frozen waterfalls would be routinely ascended a few years later? Just learning to fly will take several years. At the same time the technology will improve, as ice tools did. The canopies will get a bit lighter and fly a bit further. Once again, climbers have shown that when everything seems to have been done, just when all the new climbs seem to be mechanically alike, a wild flair has returned.

Mountaineering in Greenland 1977–1986

Dolfi Rotovnik and Peter Søndergaard, *Dansk Bjergklub*

T HE WORLD'S LARGEST ISLAND, Greenland, fascinates mountaineers throughout the continents. It is a vast country covered by ice and snow and with mountains as numerous as the stars in the sky. This region of mountains, fjords and arctic glaciers has been the goal of over 80 mountaineering expeditions during the decade of 1977 to 1986. Probably expeditions have taken place which were not registered. Some expeditions have also not responded to our request for a report. Adding to these all the scientific (geological, zoological, botanical) expeditions, probably more than 200 expeditions have been carried out.

Previously new areas and virgin summits were the principal destinations of expeditions. Today, as in the Himalaya, many climbers go for new routes on already ascended mountains. This is easily explained by the fact that the lack of transportation in Greenland makes it very difficult to get to other areas than the well known. The following areas are shown on the map. *West Greenland:* Umanak (11 expeditions); *South Greenland:* Kap Farvel (17 expeditions); *East Greenland:* Angmagssalik (22 expeditions) and Scoresbysund, including the beautiful Stauning Alper (18 expeditions). The best thing about Greenland is that there is room for all kinds of mountaineering from grassy slopes to extreme ice and rock.

Permissions. Greenland is a part of Denmark, but in 1979 the Greenlanders obtained a special status, called *Hjemmestyre*, a sort of autonomous government. Since then, the most important governmental functions have gradually been transferred to the Greenlanders and, as a consequence, been moved from Copenhagen in Denmark to Nuuk (Godthåb) in Greenland. For the time being, permission for mountaineering in Greenland must still be obtained from the Danish Ministry for Greenland in Copenhagen. It is, however, expected that in a few years this administration will also be transferred to Greenland. Today, already, permission for the East Greenland National Park, where for instance the Stauning Alper are located, must be accepted by the *Hjemmestyre* before being granted by the Danish Ministry for Greenland. Application forms are requested from *The Ministry for Greenland, Hausergade 3, DK-1128 Copenhagen K, Denmark.*

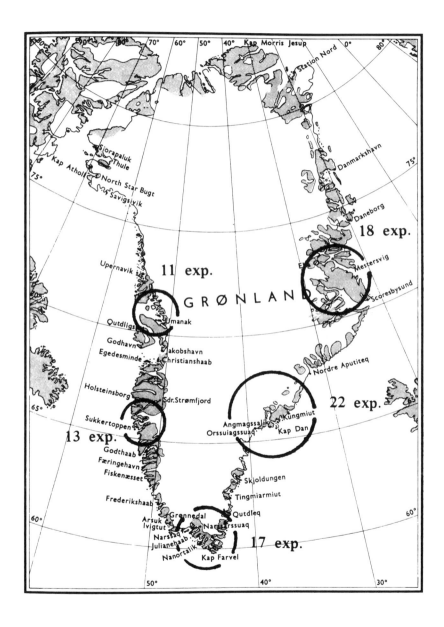

One should apply for permission at least six months before the expedition is scheduled to begin. Applications for the Stauning Alper must be filed at least twelve months ahead of the expedition. The permission will cover general mountaineering activities in the region applied for. Specific license for certain routes or summits is not required.

One of the conditions is likely to be a request for a guarantee of a rather large amount of money to cover possible rescue expenses. The Ministry for Greenland usually accepts a bank guarantee or an insurance policy for the amount. The size of the guarantee requested varies according to the character of the project and the remoteness of the destination. Another condition concerns radio equipment.

How to get to Greenland. Most travelers to Greenland by airplane from Copenhagen go to Søndre Strømfjord or Narssarssuaq. Another possibility is to fly to Godthåb from Frobisher Bay in Canada. Many expeditions set out from Akureyri in Iceland if their destination is the east coast. Information and travel arrangements can be obtained through *Grønlands Rejsebureau* (Greenland Travel Bureau), *Gammel Mønt 12, PO Box 130, DK-1004, Copenhagen K*.

Local Transportation. From the airports in the towns mentioned above, local transportation must be by airplane, helicopter or boat as there are no roads between towns. This transportation is generally very expensive. Adding a small boat to the expedition equipment might prove useful, especially an inflatable boat. The last part of the way to the desired range is now often done by helicopter. The price for renting a helicopter amounts to D.kr. 20,000 per hour. Local airplane and helicopter transportation can be arranged with *Grønlandsfly A/S* (Greenlandair), *PO Box 192, Gammel Mønt 12, DK-1004, Copenhagen K*. On the east coast it might be a good idea to rent a Twin-Otter, a small plane carrying 1500 kilograms, including persons, (an expedition of 8 to 10 members with equipment) from Akureyri in Iceland at the price of D.kr. 55,000. The Icelandic Pilots are rather fearless and might be persuaded to land in areas without landing strips in Greenland. Using that means of transportation also offers the possibility of surveying the area by air and perhaps of airdrops. Boat transportation must be arranged with local fishermen, which means that it is difficult to fix until the expedition arrives in Greenland.

Maps. Maps in the scale of 1:250.000 and aerial photographs can be bought from *The Royal Geodetic Institute, Rigsdagsgården 7, DK-1218 Copenhagen K, Denmark*. Nautical charts, which may be of interest as they contain other details than the surface maps, can be bought from *Søkortarkivet Farvnadsdirektoratet, Esplanaden 19, DK-1263 Copenhagen K*.

For naming mountains and other features in Greenland, as a rule only Greenlandic names may be used. (It is possible to obtain an exception to this rule.) Proposals for naming mountains may be sent to *Stednavneudvalget, Royal Geodetic Institute, Rigsdagsgården 7, DK-1218, Copenhagen K*.

References to climbs and expeditions. The following works are the most important summaries of expeditions and ascents up to now: expeditions before 1944 (*Berge der Welt*, Volume III, 1948); expeditions before 1966 (*Berge der*

Welt, Volume XVI, 1966/7) by Erik Hoff; "Mountaineering in Greenland, 1967-1976" by Erik Hoff in *American Alpine Journal, 1979,* pages 125-152; expeditions from 1977-1981 (Österreichische Alpenzeitung, 1984) by Adi Mokrejs. Further attention is called to *Montagne di Groenlandia* by Mario Fantin, which was an attempt to give a complete exposition of mountaineering in Greenland before 1969. Another book is the 1971 *Staunings Alps* by Donald Bennet.

Expeditions and Climbs in Greenland from 1977 to 1986. This is a continuation of the work of Erik Hoff, published in the *American Alpine Journal* of 1979. It summarizes, to the extent that has been possible, the ascents which have taken place between 1977 and 1986. As was the case with Hoff's list, the present one does not pretend to be complete. We have asked all expeditions that applied for mountaineering permissions to forward reports. Unfortunately a number have not replied. Also, ordinary tourism in Greenland does not require a visa. Expeditions unaware that permission is required for mountaineering may have escaped police control and made ascents we have not heard of.

We have recently taken over the large archive which Erik Hoff industriously built up over several decades, containing reports, photos, sketches, maps, etc. From that archive and from our own knowledge, we shall be glad to supply potential expeditions with mountaineering information on Greenland. We trust that future expeditions will be aware of the importance of keeping accurate records and will report back to us and thus continue the great work of Erik Hoff. Inquiries for information and reports should be sent to Dansk Bjergklub Expedition Committee, Dolfi Rotovnik, Snemandsvej 1a, DK-2730 Herlev, Denmark.

Abbreviations. In the following section, certain reference works appear repeatedly. We have used the following abbreviations. *AAJ (American Alpine Journal); AJ (Alpine Journal); Jahr (Alpenvereins Jahrbuch); M&A (Montagne et Alpinisme); CISDAE (Centro Italiano Studio Documentazione Alpinismo Extraeuropeo); FEM (Federación Española de Montaña); RCAI (Rivista del Club Alpino Italiano).*

1977

1. Scottish expedition to Northeast Greenland (University of Dundee). Members: C. Roger Allen (leader) et al. 3rd ascent of Petermann Bjerg (2940 meters) from Franz Joseph Fjord, northwest of Mestersvig. Private information.

2. German expedition to East Greenland, Stauning Alper (Schwäbische Grönland Kundfahrt). Members: Winfried Baumgärtner (leader), Ulrich Bayer, Dieter Brodmann, Rudi Laich, Dietrich Schlotz, Wilhelm Schlotz, Wolfgang Vögele. 17 ascents (16 first ascents) in the area of Borgbjerg Glacier of the southern Stauning Alper. *AAJ, 1979,* p. 222; *Jahr 1978,* p. 168; general report.

3. German expedition to East Greenland, Stauning Alper. Members: Karl Maria Herrligkoffer (leader), Helmut Böhme, Leo Glasl, Schorsch Kirner, Uli Bayer, Fritz Aumann, Doris Kustermann. 9 first ascents in Klosterbjerge, Alpefjord. *Bergsteiger, 1978*, n° 2, p. 92.

4. French expedition to East Greenland, Stauning Alper (Fédération Française de la Montagne). Members: André Zagdoun (leader) et al. 5 ascents (4 first ascents) in the central Stauning Alper. *AAJ, 1978*, p. 554; general report.

5. British expedition to West Greenland, Upernivik Island and Akuliaruseq Peninsula. (University of St. Andrews). Members: Philip Gribbon (leader), David Meldrum, Sandy Briggs, Adam Arnott, John Thurman, Colin Matheson, Peter Gribbon. 12 ascents, (3 first ascents). *AAJ, 1978*, p. 554; general report.

6. French expedition to South Greenland, Tasermiut Fjord (Club Alpin Français). Members: Marceau Agier (leader), Yves Payrau, Claude Vigier et al. Ascent of Suikarsuak Tower's northwest face. *AAJ, 1979*, p. 220.

7. Austrian expedition to East Greenland, Angmagssalik area. Members: Rupert Schitter, Hermann Höpflinger, Heinz Gotschy, Johann Trexl, Peter Wintersteller, Franz Zehetner. Several ascents (1 first ascent) in the Karale Glacier area. Private information.

1978

1. German expedition to South Greenland, Tasermiut Fjord (Nürnberger Grönland Expedition). Members: Herbert Voll (leader), Peter Bauernfeind, Thomas Handwerger, Gerald and Rainer Pichl, Klaus Stüllein, Helmut Unkold, Werner Zürsmeister, Margrit Stünzendörfer. First ascent of Ulamertorssuaq west face (850 meters, IV+ to VI−); attempted route on Ketil. *Jahr, 1979*, p. 232; *Mitteilingen der DAV Sektion Nürnberg*, n° 3, September 1978.

2. Italian expedition to West Greenland, Evigheds Fjord, Sukkertoppen area (Scoiattoli Cortina). Members: Franco Dallago (leader), Giusto Zardini, Giuseppe Gomirato. 4 ascents between 800 and 1650 meters. *CISDAE*.

3. Italian expedition to East Greenland, Sermiligaq Fjord, Angmagssalik area (Club Alpino Italiano). Members: Desiderio Dottori (leader), Jesi and Claudio Giudici. Ascents between Sermiligaq and Sangmilik Fjords. Private information.

4. Spanish expedition to East Greenland, Tasissarssik Fjord, Angmagssalik area (Club Montañeros Celtas de Vigo). Members: Constancio Veiga González (leader), Santiago Suárez Alonso, Antonio Dourado Iglesias, José Ramón Melón Iglesias, Albino Quinteiro Mora. 6 ascents (3 first ascents) in the Trillingerne area and second ascent of Storebror. *AAJ, 1979*, p. 222; *Peñalara, 1978*, p. 174.

5. British expedition to East Greenland, Stauning Alper (Army Mountaineering Association). Members: P.D. Breadmore (leader), R. Churcher, M.A.

Rough, L. Townsend, W. Parker, A. Leggat. 16 ascents (14 first ascents) between 320 meters and 2285 meters in southernmost Stauning Alper, Eastern Renland, Bjørneøer and the head of Vestfjord. General report.

6. Spanish expedition to East Greenland, Stauning Alper (Centro Excursionista de Catalunya). Members: Enric Font, J.G. Hernández, F.X. Gregori, J.M. Iglesias. 11 ascents in the area between Fangst Hytte Glacier and Sedgewick Glacier. *FEM, 1978,* p. 180.

7. Spanish expedition to East Greenland, Angmagssalik area (Club Alpino de Gijón). Members: Gonzalo Suárez Pomeda (leader), Pedro García Torano, Aurelio Alvarez Riera, Julio Bousono Paneda, Luis Antonio Ruiz Alonso, Félix Mejica Pérez. 35 ascents between Qiugorssuaq and Ikasaulaq Fjords. *FEM, 1978,* p. 195; general report.

8. Spanish expedition to West Greenland, Sukkertoppen area, Evigheds Fjord (Sociedad Excursionista, Club Alpino Maliciosa). Members: José Luis García (leader), Luis López Fernández, Pedro Nicolás Martínez, Arturo Romero Palacios, José Luis García Sánchez, Margarita Mayo Arlanzón, Juan Palacios Antón, Ramón Jaudenes-Atauri, Eduardo Martínez. 8 ascents from Base Camp in Kangiussaq. *FEM, 1978,* p. 178; Private information with map.

9. Spanish expedition to West Greenland, Sukkertoppen area, Evigheds Fjord (Agrupació Excursionista de Granollers). 11 members. 12 ascents. Information from Club Alpino de España.

10. Spanish expedition to West Greenland, Holsteinsborg area (Club Camprodón). Members: Manuel Bunsola, J. Busquets, P. Masferrer, J. Mercer, V. Aris. 14 ascents. Private information.

11. French expedition to South Greenland, Narssarssuaq area. Members: Jacques Rouillard (leader), Jean-Bernard Givet, Bernard Brigai, Robert Fargeas, Jean Macian, Gilbert Selz, Christian Meynier, Monique Larmoyer. First ascent of P 1881 northwest of Narssarssuaq. *AAJ, 1979,* p. 222; Private information with map.

12. Yugoslavian expedition to East Greenland, Angmagssalik area (Planinska Zveza Slovenije). Members: Janez Bizjak (leader), Renato Vrečer, Damian Meško, Marco Lenarčič, Matevž Lenarčič, Bojan Pajk, Vili Pistotnik. Rudi Pušnik. Andrej Pušnik, Bojan Šprogar. 26 ascents (7 first ascents) between 16 September Glacier and Glacier de France of 1540 to 2220 meters. *AAJ, 1979,* p. 221.

13. German expedition to West Greenland, Sukkertoppen area, Evigheds Fjord (Göppinger Grönland Expedition). Members: Alexander Schlee (leader), M. Albanus, F. Bässler, G. Vlach, I. Dölker, O. Dorka. R. Frick, M. Haase, R. Hauff, R. Niebling, U. Strom, P. Meier, H. Schlee. 38 ascents (16 first ascents) between 1600 and 2140 meters. *AAJ, 1979,* p. 223; *Jahr, 1979,* p. 231.

14. Austrian expedition to South Greenland, Tasermiut Fjord (Tiroler Grönland Expedition). Members: Gernot Pollhammer (leader) et al. 6 first ascents. Ulamertorssuaq northwest face (1100 meters, V/VI, A2). *Jahr, 1979,* p. 229.

15. Japanese solo traverse of Greenland from north to south. Member: Naomi Uemura. *AAJ, 1979*, p. 224.

16. French expedition to Southeast Greenland, Lindenow Fjord. Members: Jean Claude Marmier (leader) and 10 members. Several first ascents and new routes, among others Apostelens Tommelfinger's southeast wall (1300 meters, VI). *AAJ, 1979*, p. 219; *M&A, 1978*, n° 4, p. 446.

1979

1. French expedition to South Greenland, Narssarssuaq area. Members: Jacques Rouillard (leader) with 17 persons. Second ascent of P 1881, first ascent of P 1713 in Johan Dahl Land. *AAJ, 1980*, p. 569; private information with map.

2. British expedition to East Greenland, Stauning Alper and Lyell Land (Army Ordnance Corps). Members: John Muston (leader) with 8 persons. Ascents of Argandhorn, Snehaetten and Jeannet Bjerg in Lyell Land and Harlech in Stauning Alper. General report.

3. Swedish expedition to East Greenland, Angmagssalik area (Svensk Klatre Forbund). Members: Lars Gören Johanson (leader) et al. Fourth ascent of Mont Forel, ski from Kungmiut (20 kms). Private information.

4. German expedition to East Greenland, Angmagssalik area (Deutscher Alpenverein Sektion Goslar). Members: Ulrich Schum (leader), Theo Hilz, Wilhem Huber, Klaus Suess. Fifth ascent of Mont Forel (first of the south face), 9 first ascents up to 3100 meters. Helicopter to Base Camp and then with skis. *Jahr, 1980*, p. 104; *AAJ, 1980*, p. 569.

5. Czechoslovakian expedition to East Greenland, Angmagssalik area. Members: Sylva Talla (leader), Peter Pavlak, Jaroslava Tallova. Sixth ascent of Mont Forel by Swiss route and first female ascent. Ski from Tasilaq Fjord. Private information.

6. Italian expedition to West Greenland, Sukkertoppen area, Evigheds Fjord (Scoiattoli Cortina). Members: Modesto Alvera, Orazio Mollonto, Armando Dallago, Diego Ghedina, Bruno Pompanin Dimat. 5 first ascents up to 1400 meters. *RCAI, 1980*, n° 5/6, p. 216; *CISDAE*.

7. Italian expedition to East Greenland, Angmagssalik area. Members: Sergio Maccio (leader), Antonio Falconara, Enzo and Fabio Bianchini, Giovanni Rupi, Enrico Valentini. Ascents north of Sangmilik Fjord and northeast of Sermiligaq village. *CISDAE*.

1980

1. Yugoslavian expedition to East Greenland, Angmagssalik area (Mountain Club Kozjak, Maribor, Slovenia). Members: Inko Bajde (leader), Franci Gselman, Boro Jerebebek, Zvone Koklič, Adi Lep, Štefan Senekovič, Ivan

Šturm, Ivo Veberič, Janez Bizjak, Bojan Pajk. 55 ascents (13 first ascents) in the area east of the Midgaard Glacier. *AAJ, 1981,* p. 205; *Jahr, 1980,* p. 157.

2. British expedition to East Greenland, Stauning Alper and Nathorst Land. Members: H.W. Beaves (leader) and 7 persons. Several ascents, including first ascents. Private information.

3. North Irish expedition to South Greenland, Prins Christian IV Island (Queens University, Belfast). Members: Alistair Acheson (leader) and 6 persons. 20 first ascents. *AJ, 1982,* P 244.

4. British expedition to East Greenland, Hochstetter Forland. Members; Geoffrey Halliday (leader), A.J. Muston, Tim King, Dave O'Neil, Mandy Wilson. Ascents of Wildspitze and Matterhorn in Barth Bjerge. *AJ, 1982,* p. 244.

5. British expedition to East Greenland, Knud Rasmussen Glacier, Angmagssalik area. Members: Douglas Anderson (leader), William Jeffrey, Andrea Mountain, Dick Pert, Bob Dunken, Ian Carr, Rebecca Upham, Noel Williams. 4 ascents. *AAJ, 1981,* p. 204.

6. Italian expedition to East Greenland, Angmagssalik area. Members: Agostini Gentilini (leader), Rina Gentilini, Piero Favalli, Gianni Paisnetti, Tullio Rocco, Massimo Sanavio. 9 ascents (3 first ascents) in the Gobi Glacier area. *Jahr, 1981,* p. 157; *CISDAE.*

7. Swiss expedition to South Greenland, Kap Farvel area. Members: Irene and Wolfgang Freudenreich. 1 ascent (P 1511.) Private information.

1981

1. Italian expedition to West Greenland, Upernivik Island (Club Alpino Italiano, Bardonecchia). Members: Giuseppe Agnolotti (leader), Giorgio Pettigiani. New route on Palup Peak (2101 meters). *AAJ, 1982,* p. 167; *CISDAE.*

2. French expedition to Narssarssuaq area. Members: Jacques Rouillard (leader) and 15 persons. 7 ascents some 25 kms southeast of Narssarssuaq. Private information with map.

3. Swiss expedition to Tasermiut Fjord. Members: Beat Streich (leader), Beni Tscherrig, Egon Feller, Bruno Pfaffen, Bruno Leiggener. Difficult climbs in Tasermiut area. 5 new routes. Private information.

4. Spanish expedition to West Greenland, Sukkertoppen area (expedition from Catalonia). Members: Monso i Molas (leader) et al. 5 ascents in the area north of Manitsup Sermilia Fjord. Private information.

5. Italian expedition to West Greenland, Akuliaruseq Peninsula, north of Upernivik Island (Club Alpino Italiano). Members: Lodovico Gaetani, (leader), Franco Alletto, Giuseppe Cazzaniga, Giancarlo Delzotto, Bruno Gabaglio, Fabio and Mariola Masciadri. 2 ascents, first ascent of Nanupniaqua (2200 meters). *Lo Scarpone,* October 1, 1981; *AAJ, 1982,* p. 167; *CISDAE; RCAI, 1982,* 5/6; private information.

Magnus Nilsson on Pyramiden. On the left, Ulamerssuaq. On the right, Tasermiut Fjord.

6. Yugoslavian expedition to East Greenland, Angmagssalik area (Slovenian Alpine Clubs Domžale and Mengeš). Members: Stane Klemenc (leader), Janko Kos, Matjaž and Borut Veselko, Franci Vrankar, Miro Štebe, Marko Grad. 25 ascents with many difficult climbs 180 kms northeast of Angmagssalik in Kronprins Frederiks Bjerge. Third and fourth highest ascents (3355 and 3250 meters) in Greenland. *AAJ, 1982,* p. 168; *Jahr, 1982-3,* p. 154.

7. Italian expedition to West Greenland, Sukkertoppen area, Evigheds Fjord (Club Alpino Italiano, Albino). Members: Claudio Allegrini, Aurelio Bortolotti, Benito Cabrini, Renato Saffi, Lorenzo Carrara, Ubaldo Cortinovis, Antonio Gamba, Antonio Pondi, Dinuccia Zanetti, Ricardo Zanetti. *Lo Scarpone,* March 16, 1982, *CISDAE.*

8. Swiss expedition to West Greenland, Umanak and Upernivik (Akademischer Alpen Club, Bern). Members: Jürg Müller (leader), Thomas Kopp, Werner Munter, Hans Stämpeli, Beat Geissbühler, Margrit Munter, Johannes Walther, Fritz Willen. Second ascent of southeast ridge of Umanaktinde (1200 meters); ascents on Upernivik Island. *Die Alpen,* 1st Quarterly, 1982, p. 43.

9. Swiss expedition to West Greenland, Qioqe Peninsula, north of Umanak. Members: 15 persons. 4 first ascents up to 2120 meters. *Die Alpen,* 1st Quarterly, 1982, p. 43.

10. North Irish expedition to South Greenland, Kap Farvel area. Members: R.J. Finlay (leader) with three persons. 16 ascents (11 first ascents) on Pamiagduluk Island, south of Aupilagtoq village. Private information.

11. Italian expedition to East Greenland, Stauning Alper, Vikingebrae area. Members: Giuseppe Dionisi (leader) and eight persons. Ascents of Hjornespits, Nosketinde and Dansketinde. *AAJ, 1982,* p. 167.

1982

1. Austrian expedition to East Greenland, Angmagssalik area (Österreichischer Himalaya Gesellschaft). Members: Bruno Klausbruckner (leader), Eduard Frosch, Ernst Gritzner, Werner Hölzl, Hans Höran, Leopold Krenn, Oswald Pletschko, Franz Pucher, Peter Schier, Helmut Wimmer. Seventh ascent of Mont Forel (new route on southwest ridge), 6 first ascents in the Femstjernen area, third ascent of Laupersbjerg. *AAJ, 1983,* p. 180; *Österreichische Alpenzeitung, 1984,* 7/8, p. 22.

2. French expedition to South Greenland, Narssarssuaq area (Club Alpin Français, Section de Belfort). Members: André Mairot, Marie-Dominique Beluche, Claudine Colin, Michel Deloye, Bernard Dieterich, Robert Hottinger, Christian Machet, Janine Mairot, Michel Paviet, Jean-Luc Riblet. 2 ascents between Narssarssuaq and Johan Dahl Land, Valhaltinde (1650 meters) and P 1960 in Kornerup Land. General report.

3. Austrian expedition to West Greenland, Wegener Peninsula north of Umanak (Voralberger Grönland Expedition). Members: Karl Malin (leader), Emil Galehr, Heinz Grasbon, Bernhard Grimm, Gerhard and Waltraud Huber,

Helmut Koch. 11 ascents (10 first ascents), many of UIAA V difficulty. *AAJ, 1983*, p. 183; general report.

4. Italian expedition to East Greenland, Stauning Alper (Club Alpino Accademico Italiano, Torino). Giuseppe Dionisi (leader), Giuseppe Alasonatti, Eugenio Ferrero, Luciano Luria, Sergio Martini, Franco Ribetti, Mario Solero, Gian Luigi Vaccari. First ascent by north ridge of Norsketinde (2789 meters), first traverse of Dansketinde (2930 meters), highest peak in the Stauning Alper, and several other ascents. *AAJ, 1983*, p. 180; *Jahr, 1982-3*, p. 154; *RCAI, 1983*, February; general report.

5. Italian expedition to East Greenland, Angmagssalik area (Club Alpino Italiano, Veneto-Friulana). Members: Gianni Pais Becher (leader), Daniele Zandegiacomo, Ferruccio Svaluto Moreolo, Maurizio Dall'Olmo, Oliviero Di Zoldo, Gigi Dal Pozzo. 10 first ascents of from 1900 to 3270 meters between Kristians Glacier, Femstjerne and Glacier de France. *AAJ, 1983*, p. 180; *RCAI, 1983*, 3/4; *CISDAE*.

6. Italian expedition to West Greenland, Akuliarueseq north of Upernivik Island (Club Alpino Italiano, Lanzo-Asso). Members: Graziano Bianchi (leader), Ginetto Mora, Giuseppe Colombo, Vittorio Duroni, Maco Cipriano, Lorenzo Spallino, Ambrogio Fogar. 5 first ascents between 1700 and 2100 meters. *CISDAE*.

7. French expedition to South Greenland, Søndre Igaliko. Members: Jacques Rouillard (leader) et al. 3 ascents (P 1410, P 1370, P 1530). Private information with map.

8. German expedition to West Greenland, Umanak area (Deutscher Alpenverein, Sektion Lindau). Members: Walter Föger (leader) with 7 persons. 9 ascents (3 first ascents) on Qioqe Peninsula. *Jahr, 1984*, p. 164.

9. British expedition to East Greenland, Angmagssalik area. Members: Cormac Higgs, Colin Wootton, Geoffrey Monaghan. Difficult climbs in Sermiligaq Fjord area 80 kms northeast of Angmagssalik. *AAJ, 1983*, p. 183.

1983

1. Italian expedition to East Greenland, Angmagssalik area (Club Alpino Italiano, Ligure). Members: Gianni Fasciolo (leader), Anthony House, Marco and Enrico Chierici, Emma and Gianni Bisio, Paolo Gardino, Bruno Vian, Magda DeFerrari, Carlo Malerba, Mino Girelli, Rosana Pisoni, Camillo Cortemiglia, Bruno Messiga, Battista Piccardo. 10 ascents between 16 September, Karale and Knud Rasmussen Glaciers, the highest of which was 1780 meters. *AAJ, 1984*, p. 194; *Jahr, 1985*, p. 193.

2. French expedition to South Greenland, Søndre Igaliko. Members: Jacques Rouillard (leader) et al. 6 ascents up to 1650 meters; only Nutluartoq previously climbed. Private information with map.

3. British expedition to West Greenland, Søndre Strømfjord area (British Army expedition). Members: S. King (leader) with 10 persons. 16 ascents, several first ascents in Sukkertoppen Icecap area. General report with map.

4. British expedition to East Greenland, Stauning Alper (Salford University Mountaineering Club). Members: Gerry McCullough (leader) with 8 persons. 11 ascents (6 first ascents) in Berserkerbrae-Dunnottar Glacier area. First ascent of south face of Dunnottar. *AJ, 1984,* p. 188: private information.

5. French expedition to West Greenland, Umanak (Club Alpin Français, Grenoble). Members: Jean-Marie Delacroix (leader) et al. Ascent of West Pillar of Umanakfjeld. *M&A, 1987,* n° 1, p. 22.

6. Danish expedition to East Greenland, Stauning Alper. Members: Søren Eisenhard (leader), Gertrud Andersen, Ole Haug. Two attempts on Glamis and ascent of one minor summit east of Bersaerkerbrae. Bad weather. *Dansk Bjergklub, 1983,* p. 4.

1984

1. Italian expedition to East Greenland, Stauning Alper (Club Alpino Italiano, Rome). Members: Sandro Pucci (leader), Franco Alletto, Paolo Caruso, Paolo D'Ugo, Mauro Dainese, Marcello Paterno, Giampaolo Picone, Marco Re. 10 first ascents at 72°N between 2000 and 2600 meters. *AAJ, 1985,* p. 220; *RCAI, 1985,* p. 310.

2. French expedition to East Greenland, Stauning Alper (Club Alpin Français, Section de Paris). Members: Marc Breuil (leader), Pascal Elleaume, Jacques Girand, Lubomir Krizenecky, Philippe Nonin, Bernard Odier. Traverse on skis west-to-east from Alpefjord to Mestersvig. 8 ascents, all over 2000 meters. General report.

3. International expedition to East Greenland, Angmagssalik area. Members: Italians Gianni Pais Becher (leader), Antonio Colli, Mauro Corona, Maurizio Dall'Omo, Luciano de Grignis, Fabio Delisi, Lino Di Lenardo, Roberto Mazzilis, Cristina Smiderle, Luciano Zardini; Slovenes (Yugoslavia) Peter Podgornik, Janko Humar; Greenlanders Ane Kuitze, Ferdinan Maqe. 28 new routes, 20 first ascents in Kristian Glacier area of peaks between 2000 and 3240 meters; several ascents of UIAA V to VI difficulty. *AAJ, 1985,* p. 221; *RCAI, 1985,* p. 73.

4. Yugoslavian expedition to East Greenland, Angmagssalik area (Slovenian Zgornje Savinjska Mountaineering Section). Members: Ludvig Petek, Ana Laznik, Marjana Skornšek. 25 ascents (18 first ascents) north of Karale Glacier. General report.

5. British expedition to East Greenland, Angmagssalik area (Eagle Ski Club). Members: Derek Fordham (leader), Graham Elson, Michael Esten, Rupert Hoare, David Waldron. Two attempts on Mont Forel abandoned 200 and 300 meters below summit due to high winds and bad snow conditions. *AAJ, 1985,* p. 220; general report.

6. British expedition to West Greenland, Søndre Strømfjord area (Military expedition). Members: A.J. Muston (leader) with 10 persons. Several ascents between Søndre Strømfjord and Itivdleq Fjord. General report.

7. French expedition to West Greenland, Søndre Strømfjord area. Members: Jacques Rouillard (leader) et al. 3 ascents south of Itivdleq Fjord. Private information with map.

8. Italian expedition to West Greenland, Umanak area (Club Alpino Italiano, Rieti). Members; Alberto Bianchetti (leader), Enrico Ferri, Eliano Pessa, Millesimi Arnaldo, Angelo Sebastiani, Roberto Antonucci, Franco Basso, Pietro Ratti, Rocco Venditti, Mario Sciarra. Ascent of Qilertinguit Tunuliet (2070 meters) and other peaks on Nugssuak Peninsula. Ascent of Umanak Tinde by new route. *CISDAE*.

9. Spanish expedition to South Greenland, Tasermiut Fjord (Catalan Expedition, Barcelona). Members: Martin Xavier, Nicolau Xavier, Emili Ortega, Jordi Verdaguer. First ascent of 1450-meter-high west face of Ketil (VI, A3). *AAJ, 1986*, p. 185.

10. Swiss expedition to South Greenland, Tasermiut Fjord. Members: M. Piola (leader), C. Dalphin, N. Schenkel, B. Watson. New route on west face of Ketil. Details missing. *Vertical, 1984*, n° 3.

11. Czechoslovakian east-west traverse from Johan Petersen Fjord to Søndre Strømfjord. Members: Vladimír Weigner, Jaroslav Pavilíček, Miroslav Jakes. *AAJ, 1985*, p. 223.

1985

1. Belgian expedition to East Greenland, Stauning Alper (Club Alpin Belge). Members: Jacques Borlée (leader), Jean-Marc Piron, Daniel Caise, Gérard Miserique, Didier Dubosse, Philippe Soertaert, Jean-Pierre Deveaux. 3 ascents, first ascent of south face of Dunnottar (2450 meters). *AAJ, 1986*, p. 186.

2. British expedition to East Greenland, Stauning Alper (Liverpool Polytechnic I.M. Marsh College). Members: Michael Peckham (leader), David Huddart, Paul Potter, Adrian Pringle, Tom Saxlund, Steve Gebbels. 10 ascents (3 first ascents) in the region of Bersaerkerbrae and Dunnottar Glacier. *AJ, 1986*, p. 228.

3. Finnish expedition to East Greenland, Angmagssalik area. Members: Eino Putkonen (leader), Heikki Leinonen, Anne Kaitila. Attempt on Mont Forel frustrated by bad weather; only mountaineering on Angmagssalik Island. Private information.

4. Austrian expedition to West Greenland, Upernivik Island (Alpenverein Tirol and South Tirol-Italy). Members: Klaus Gogl (leader) with 16 persons. 25 ascents (5 first ascents) on Upernivik Island between 1020 and 2120 meters. Several climbs of UIAA V to VI difficulty. General report.

5. Spanish expedition to West Greenland, Sukkertoppen area, Evigheds Fjord (Unió Excursionista de Catalunya). Members: Jordi Colomar (leader), Josep Barrachina, Alex Alom, Jaume Real, Lluis López, Ramón Bramona, Francesc Sanahuja, Jordi Sans, Miquel Angel Martínez. 7 ascents; third ascent

of Mount Atter (2190 meters) by new route, east ridge, highest peak in West Greenland. *AAJ, 1986,* p. 186. General report.

6. British expedition to East Greenland, Kejser Franz Joseph Fjord (Scottish Mountaineering Club). Members: Malcolm Slesser (leader), Iaian Smart, P. Sellers, P. Todd, R. Zeyen. Fourth ascent of Petermanns Bjerg (2940 meters) and two other ascents in the area, one of them a first. *AAJ, 1987,* p. 186.

1986

1. German expedition to West Greenland, Sisermiut area (Deutscher Alpenverein, Sektion Siegburg). Members: Jochem Becker (leader), Erwin Diesler, Klaus Eiler, Michael Hagena, Beate Hasenjaeger, Axel Klier, Thomas Meier, Klaus Scherer. 6 first ascents in area 67°N, 63°W. *Mitteilungen der Sektion Siegburg,* March, 1986. *Mitteilingen des Deutschen Alpenvereins,* January, 1987.

2. British expedition to South Greenland, Kap Farvel area (Salford University). Members: Les Thurbull (leader), Andy Leslie, Rob Cooper, Martin Sluce, Stas Chobrzynski-Rawicz, Paul Hodkins, Brian Hull, Andy Greenwood. 16 first ascents and 4 second ascents on Kangerssuaq Qingordleq. General report.

3. British expedition to Northeast Greenland (Austrian Alpine Club, U.K. Section). Members: John Shrewsbury (leader), Mike Garrett, Margaret Graham, Malcolm Sales, Anne Wheatcroft, Chris Whitford. 4 first ascents of from 1120 to 1510 meters on Milne Island. *AAJ, 1987,* p. 187; general report.

4. French expedition to Northeast Greenland (Groupe de Montagne Chamalierois). Members: Bernard Thomas (leader), Christian Paour, Monique Thomas, Philippe Rousseau, Michel Thomas, Pierre Brajon, Brigitte Thomas, Christian Béal, Michel Quanty. First ascent of P 1831, the highest point in Strindberg Land at 73°42'N, 24°25'W. General Report.

5. Italian-Yugoslavian expedition to East Greenland, Ingolffjeld (2560 meters). Members: Italians Gianni Pais Becher (leader), Ferruccio Sveluto Moreolo, Pierantonio Zago, Sergio De Longhi, and Slovene Peter Podgornik. Attempt on 1500-meter-high north face of Ingolffjeld to 1030 meters. The peak lies 150 kms northeast of Angmagssalik. *AAJ, 1987,* p. 186.

Addition to Chronicle 1967-1976

Irish expedition to South Greenland, 1975. Members: David A. Welsh (leader), Joe Mulhall, David Mitchell, Alan Douglas, Paddy O'Brien, Roger Greene, Ray Finlay, Philip Holmes. 12 first ascents north of Augpilagtoq village. Private information.

Climbs and Expeditions, 1987

The Editorial Board is extremely grateful to the many people who have done so much to make this section possible. Among those who have been very helpful, we should like to thank in particular Michael J. Cheney, Kamal K. Guha, Harish Kapadia, Mohan C. Motwani, H.C. Sarin, Józef Nyka, Tsunemichi Ikeda, Muneeruddin, Trevor Braham, Renato Moro, César Morales Arnao, Vojslav Arko, Franci Savenc, Paul Nunn, Xavier Eguskitza, José Manuel Anglada, Josep Paytubi, Elmar Landes, Robert Renzler, Sadao Tambe, Annie Bertholet, Fridebert Widder, Silvia Metzeltin Buscaini, Luciano Ghigo, Zhou Zhen, Ying Dao Shui and Hanif Raza.

We are grieved to report that Mike Cheney died in his sleep on February 20, 1988. He was a most valuable correspondent to the A.A.J. and assisted innumerable expeditions.

METERS TO FEET

Unfortunately the American public seems to be resisting the changes from feet to meters. To assist readers from the more enlightened countries, where meters are universally used, we give the following conversion chart:

meters	feet	meters	feet	meters	feet	meters	feet
3300	10,827	4700	15,420	6100	20,013	7500	24,607
3400	11,155	4800	15,748	6200	20,342	7600	24,935
3500	11,483	4900	16,076	6300	20,670	7700	25,263
3600	11,811	5000	16,404	6400	20,998	7800	25,591
3700	12,139	5100	16,733	6500	21,326	7900	25,919
3800	12,467	5200	17,061	6600	21,654	8000	26,247
3900	12,795	5300	17,389	6700	21,982	8100	26,575
4000	13,124	5400	17,717	6800	22,310	8200	26,903
4100	13,452	5500	18,045	6900	22,638	8300	27,231
4200	13,780	5600	18,373	7000	22,966	8400	27,560
4300	14,108	5700	18,701	7100	23,294	8500	27,888
4400	14,436	5800	19,029	7200	23,622	8600	28,216
4500	14,764	5900	19,357	7300	23,951	8700	28,544
4600	15,092	6000	19,685	7400	24,279	8800	28,872

NOTE: All dates in this section refer to 1987 unless otherwise stated. Normally, accounts signed by a name alone (no club) indicate membership in the American Alpine Club.

UNITED STATES

Alaska

Denali National Park and Preserve Mountaineering Summary, 1987. For the second year in a row, a new record was set for the number of mountaineers attempting to climb Mount McKinley. Despite the increase in attempts, extended periods of poor weather throughout the Alaska Range resulted in the lowest success rate since 1971. The previous winter's snowfall was about average. However, extended periods of clear weather during the late winter and early spring created extensive avalanche conditions. At least five and possibly six persons died in avalanche-related accidents within the boundaries of Denali National Park and Preserve. An Alaskan team, Art Mannix and Chris Leibundgut, attempted a winter ascent of the South Buttress of McKinley from the west fork of the Ruth Glacier. They reached 15,000 feet before frostbite caused their retreat. The only other winter mountaineering in the park was a first winter ascent of Mount Silverthrone by Alaskans Brian and Diane Okonek and Rick Ernst. The High Latitude Research Project was not funded this season, but a short research was conducted by medical personnel. Dr. Peter Hackett coordinated the project in which they investigated a possible link between retinal hemorrhaging and cerebral edema of climbers at altitude. Following the completion of the project, the Mountaineering Rangers staffed the camp for the remainder of the season. Once again, the transportation of the camp to and from the mountain was provided by the U.S. Army, 242nd Aviation Company, Fort Wainwright, Alaska.The National Park Service conducted two 3-week expeditions on Mount McKinley, all on the West Buttress. We continue to emphasize environmentally sound expeditionary climbing and sanitation practices. In addition, mountaineers are encouraged to conduct their own evacuations whenever possible. During emergencies, the 14,200-foot medical-and-rescue camp serves as a base from which most Mount McKinley rescue operations are coordinated.

Interesting Statistics. In 1987, new all-time records were set for the number of people attempting Mount McKinley: 1978 = 539; 1979 = 533; 1980 = 659; 1981 = 612; 1982 = 696; 1983 = 709; 1984 = 695; 1985 = 645; 1986 = 755; 1987 = 817. *Success Rate:* 251 (31%) of these attempting Mount McKinley were successful. This was the lowest success rate since 1971 when 29% of the 163 climbers reached the summit. None attempting either Mount Foraker or Mount Hunter was successful. *Acute Mountain Sickness; 128* (16%) had symptoms. 91 (11%) were mild; 32 (4%) were moderate; 5 (1%) were severe. *Frostbite:* 55 (7%) reported some degree of frostbite, two of which required hospitalization. *West Buttress Route:* 687 (84%) of the climbers were on the popular West Buttress route. *Mountain Guiding:* 244 (30%) of the climbers traveled with one of the authorized guiding companies. The overall success of these groups was 23%. Most were on the West Buttress, but other guided parties were attempted on the Muldrow, West Rib and South Buttress. No guided party reached the summit of Mount McKinley by any route other than the West Buttress. *Foreign Climbers:* 232 (28%) of the climbers were from foreign countries. 16 nationalities were represented: Australia 23, Austria 18, Canada 27, France 21, Great Britain 40, Israel 2, Italy 4, Japan 33, Netherlands 6, New Zealand 2, Romania 1, Mexico 4, Poland 6, Switzerland 29, West Germany 14, Yugoslavia 2. *Number of Climbers on McKinley during a Given Week:* A new all-time high of 314 climbers were on the slopes of Mount McKinley for the week ending May 19.

New Routes and Interesting Ascents. *Mount McKinley:* No new routes were completed in 1987. The Northwest Buttress was climbed by a team of four, two of whom reached the North Peak. The South-Face Haston-Scott route received its third ascent by Americans Paul Cagner and Bill Crouse. *Broken Tooth:* Mugs Stump and Steve Quinlan climbed a new technical route on the south face. Tom Bauman and Jack Lewis did the first ascent of the west ridge. *Ruth Gorge Peaks:* Austrians Andreas Orgler and Sepp Jöchler did some fine climbs above the Ruth Gorge, reported below. *Kichatna Spires:* Seth Shaw, Robert Tingle, James Garrett and Conrad Anker ascended the southeast face of Gurney Peak. (See article.) *Mount Mather Area:* A new route on P 9810 was completed by Italians led by Cosimo Zappelli. *West Tripyramid:* Scott Gill, Randy Waitman and Cliff Beaver of the National Park Service completed the first ascent of the northwest ridge.

Accidents. On May 3, a large British group was descending the West Rib. At 14,800 feet, one member slipped and fell 800 feet, sustaining serious head injuries. The group's CB radios were set to broadcast on a frequency not monitored by Base Camp, the air taxi operators or the National Park Service. Thus, a climber had to ski to Base Camp to report the accident. Word was relayed to the Talkeetna Ranger Station at 10:30 P.M. Insufficient light remained to conduct a rescue that day, so plans were made to attempt a helicopter hoist evacuation early on May 4. No private helicopters with winch capabilities were available. Assistance was requested through the Rescue Coordination Center at Elmendorf Air Force Base. The following morning, an Air Force C130 arrived to orbit the mountain to provide radio communications and the Army Chinook helicopters lowered an Air Force "PJ". The injured climber was stabilized and then hoisted from the accident site. This was only the second hoist operation ever conducted on Mount McKinley.

Also in early May, an experienced Yugoslavian pair arrived to climb the West Buttress. They had been delayed by baggage lost by the airline and hoped to make up lost time by climbing rapidly. They moved to 14,200 feet in three days. When they began the ascent the next day, one felt ill and returned to 14,200 feet while his partner continued. The following day, the ill climber's condition deteriorated and he became severely ataxic. Fortunately, he was found by a NSP patrol, who sledded him down to Windy Corner where his condition improved enough for him to begin his own descent. Meanwhile, oxygen was flown via helicopter from Talkeetna, but clouds prevented direct delivery to the Yugoslav. It was dropped to another party that shuttled it to the Yugoslav, who skied back to Base Camp without further assistance.

At the beginning of May, two Alaskans registered for a climb of the southeast ridge of Foraker. The next day, two Canadians registered for the same climb. On May 15, the Alaskan team's due-out date, their air taxi operator could find no sign of anyone on the route. The National Park Service searched the route by helicopter and found tracks leading into an avalanche starting zone. Mountaineering equipment was discovered mixed with avalanche debris at the bottom of the avalanche nearly 3000 feet below where the tracks were seen. A ground search was determined to be too hazardous. Although no bodies were seen, the observations of the equipment from the hovering helicopter and the recovery of a stuff sack definitely linked the Alaskans to the accident. A yellow climbing suit was also seen which matches the description of a suit worn by one of the Canadians. All evidence points to the four men having been swept to their deaths in the avalanche. In 1978, two Japanese were killed in an avalanche just above where the Americans and Canadians were hit. During the intervening years, climbing parties have regularly reported close calls near the 10,500 to 12,000-foot level of the southeast ridge.

On May 15, a pair from Anchorage registered for an ascent of the west ridge of Mount Hunter. On May 22, the two men were approaching the summit when they triggered a soft slab avalanche which swept them both about 200 yards down the slope they had just ascended. One man was almost completely buried. After considerable effort and after between 30 and 45 minutes, he extricated himself. He then followed their rope to his partner who was completely buried. It took another 10 minutes to extricate him. There was no sign of life. The weather was severe and the pair had carried no bivouac gear. The survivor was forced to begin an immediate solo descent down the heavily crevassed and corniced west ridge. After several close calls, he was able to reach another climbing party at 10,600 feet. Poor weather prevented their descent until May 27.

Toward the end of May, a female member of a three-person Japanese expedition became ill at 17,200 feet on the West Buttress. The weather began to deteriorate and so they descended to the 14,200-foot basin. Once there, her condition did not improve but the other two did not seem concerned. A member of a nearby French expedition noticed she was unable to walk and sledded her to the medical camp, where she was diagnosed as having pulmonary edema. There she was treated with Diamox and continuous oxygen. The following day she was still unable to walk. The weather prevented an air evacuation and so a ground team was organized to sled her to 11,000 feet where a French and American team then continued on with her to Base Camp. Throughout the entire evacuation her party seemed unconcerned and unwilling to assist. She recovered once back near sea level in Talkeetna.

At the end of May, a West German team of two made a rapid ascent of the West Buttress. They climbed from 7200 feet at Base Camp to the 17,200-foot camp in five days. On the sixth day, they began their summit push, each traveling separately. Bad weather turned one man back at 19,200 feet. That night both men were tired but seemed all right. The next morning, one man was unresponsive and had a pulse of 90 and respiration rate of 56 per minute. He was placed on supplementary oxygen, lowered down the Rescue Gully and reached the 14,200-foot medical/rescue camp at two P.M. His condition remained serious but he was stabilized. He was air-evacuated the following day. The diagnosis was severe pulmonary and cerebral edema.

In early June, an American was descending the Messner Couloir, plunge-stepping into soft snow. During one of his steps, his cramponed boot snagged either on a pack strap or something dangling from his harness. He lost his balance, pitched forward and took a 1500-foot tumbling fall. A soft patch of snow stopped him but he was battered and sustained a broken hip. Fortunately, the fall had been seen by climbers in the 14,200-foot basin. A rescue team was quickly organized, and the injured climber was lowered to a landing site and air-evacuated by helicopter.

In early June, two Poles ascended the Messner Couloir. Their final camp was at 18,900 feet. From there they went to the summit and descended to their camp. They then began to glissade diagonally down the 30° to 40° slope toward the 17,200-foot camp on the West Buttress. During the glissade, the lead man hit an icy patch, lost control and fell 2600 feet. His partner cut over to the West Buttress and made a rapid descent to the 14,200-foot basin. From there, climbers ascended and located the lifeless victim. The team brought the body down to 14,200 feet, where it was flown off the mountain.

In early July, an 11-member guided expedition was camped below Windy Corner at 12,900 feet. It had been snowing but the guides said the large couloir and adjacent face of the buttress of the West Buttress had been sloughing off, thereby cleaning itself. At 5:30 A.M. the deposition zone created by the sloughing broke loose and the resulting slide tore through the camp and buried four of the five tents which held nine of the eleven expedition members. The two guides extricated themselves and with the help of the two team members who were not buried, located and freed all the rest. Miraculously, no one was seriously injured. Four tents were destroyed. By good luck, the weather was mild with little wind. All had been sleeping at the time of the avalanche and so protective clothing was at a minimum. This is the third avalanche incident at this location.

In mid-June, an American soloist registered to climb the southeast ridge of Foraker and the Cassin Ridge of McKinley. Other climbers persuaded him to change his plans to the West Buttress. Once at the 14,200-foot basin he switched to the upper West Rib and successfully reached the summit. He descended to the northeast fork of the Kahiltna Glacier and announced his plans to another party to travel up and "take a look" at the Cassin. He was never seen again. During the search for him, tracks were seen proceeding up

DENALI NATIONAL PARK AND PRESERVE
1987 MOUNTAINEERING SUMMARY

	Expeditions	Climbers	Successful Climbers
Mount McKinley			
West Buttress	154	483	165
West Buttress (Guided)	27	204	56
Muldrow	1	3	0
Muldrow (Guided)	1	14	0
West Rib	6	44	12
West Rib (Guided)	2	13	0
Cassin	8	17	9
Cassin (Guided)	1	4	0
South Buttress	4	11	2
South Buttress (Guided)	1	9	0
East Buttress	1	3	0
Messner Couloir	3	6	3
South Face	12	2	2
Northwest Buttress	1	4	2 (N.Peak)
East Buttress	1	3	0
	211	817	251 (31%)
Mount Foraker	4	8	0
Mount Foraker (Guided)	2	11	0
Mount Hunter	6	17	0
Mount Huntington	2	4	2
Mount Huntington (Guided)	1	4	0
Kahiltna Dome (Guided)	1	4	4
Mount Bradley	1	2	2
Mount Barrille	1	2	2
Mount Dan Beard	1	2	0
Mount Dickey	1	2	0
Peak 11,300	4	12	6
Peak 11,300 (Guided)	1	4	4
Mooses Tooth	11	34	14
Mooses Tooth (Guided)	1	3	3
Broken Tooth	3	6	4
Mount Silverthrone	1	3	3
West Tripyramid	1	3	3
Kitchatna Spires	2	6	4
Mount Russell	1	2	0
Little Switzerland	3	3	N/A
Miscellaneous Ski Trips	23	116	N/A

NOTE: Since registration is required only for Mount McKinley and Mount Foraker climbs, statistics for other climbs represent those climbers who voluntarily checked in with the Mountaineering Rangers. Other climbs, especially in the area of the Ruth Glacier, are likely to have occurred.

the northeast fork but then turning into a cirque and to the west of the start of the West Rib. The tracks ended in avalanche debris.

Items of Special Concern. Seven people lost their lives in climbing accidents in 1987. This is a significant increase over the past five years and the greatest number of fatalities since 1980, when eight people died. This was the first year since 1979 that a fatality has occurred on a mountain other than McKinley (four on Foraker and one on Hunter). In 1987, we expanded the slide-and-tape mountaineering orientation to include French and Spanish versions in addition to the German, Japanese and English versions which were available previously. We also constructed a storage box to house rescue equipment at 17,200 feet on the West Buttress. The cache is now in place. The information brochure *Mountaineering* was revised and we hope to expand it to Spanish and French in 1988. It is currently available in English, German and Japanese. For more information, or to request mountaineering information or registration forms, please contact Robert Seibert, South District Mountaineering Ranger, Talkeetna Ranger Station, P.O. Box 588, Talkeetna, Alaska 99676. Phone: 907-733-2231.

ROBERT SEIBERT, *National Park Service*

Peaks above Ruth Gorge. Sepp Jöchler and I spent two weeks climbing peaks that rise above the Ruth Gorge. We set up Base Camp below the east buttress of "Mount Bradley" on July 3. On July 4, we climbed the 5000-foot-high east buttress of "Bradley" in 14 hours. We used no pitons, just nuts. We roped for the first ten rope-lengths and climbed unroped from there to the top. The bottom of the route ascended a prominent buttress that plunges for 700 meters steeply to the Ruth Glacier from the east ridge. We got onto the buttress by means of a 60-meter couloir and then followed cracks to the top of the buttress. We did two rope-lengths to the right of the ridge crest on slabs and climbed the last 700 meters up the heavily corniced and mixed ridge. We descended the also unclimbed south ridge to the col between "Bradley" and "Wake" and in eight hours completed the descent to the Ruth Glacier down a crevassed tributary glacier. The most difficult rock was of UIAA VI difficulty, though mostly III to V. Though the ice was principally of 50°, there was one pitch of 70°. An attempt on the right east buttress of Dickey on July 9 failed. On July 10, we climbed the 6200-foot "Hut Tower," the farthest right tower of a chain opposite "Bradley" and "Wake" on the east side of the Ruth, by its 300-meter-high southwest face. We made our approach up the lowest rock rib and started the serious climbing in the leftmost notch on the southwest buttress (VI−). Our attempt on the "Grand Asses Wall" on July 12 failed after we had climbed 350 meters of this smooth 800-meter-high face. It is directly opposite "Bradley" and 600 meters north of the "Hut Tower." We made a new route on the east face of Barrille but stopped at the end of the difficulties, 500 meters up the 800-meter-high face. We crossed the schrund and attacked the giant

PLATE 28

Photo by Bradford Washburn

"Mount Bradley," Ruth Gorge.
Ascent was up right ridge. Descent
was by left skyline and then down
the glacier on the left.

gray-yellow buttress in the middle of the face. We climbed eight pitches on cracks on the right side of the buttress (VII, A3), rappelled diagonally left for 20 meters, climbed four more pitches (VII, A3) until we could traverse left to the top of the buttress. A severe storm with rain, snow and high winds hit us there and we rappelled off. We were flown out the next day, July 17.

ANDREAS ORGLER, *Österreichischer Alpenverein*

Rooster Comb, Northwest Ridge of P 9680 to P 9220. Andy Cunningham and I climbed the northwest ridge of P 9680 to an upper snow shelf on May 14 and 15, traversed left and climbed to the summit of P 9220 on May 16 and descended the same route on May 16 and 17. The initial rock wall was avoided on the left with a brief exposure to sérac fall. We returned to the crest by a fluted snowfield. We bypassed the next rock wall by a zigzag to the left before we followed the crest to the crux section of the route. A very difficult pitch of mixed climbing led to a big cornice which we passed on the left by a long unprotected pitch of steep insecure snow. The snow arête led to a bivouac site. We had climbed 19 pitches in 17 hours. May 15 started with three difficult pitches on the right of the crest. The final rock buttress was passed by an ice gully on the right directly under séracs and then through a sérac wall further right (13 pitches). We were now on a snow slope under P 9680, which had an enormous cornice. We went left to a bivouac below P 9220 (12 hours). A long pitch led to the summit of previously unclimbed P 9220. The mountain had the last laugh, however, because the summit was hollow and on my final step onto the highest point, I fell into a crevasse! In view of this, the cornices on the summit ridge, the lack of food and the dangerous appearance of the descent from the main summit of the Rooster Comb, we climbed down and abseiled the ascent route, reaching the glacier just as the weather broke.

ANDY NISBET, *Scottish Mountaineering Club*

Foraker Correction. On Plate 5 of *A.A.J.*, *1985* and Plate 27 of *A.A.J*, *1987* the line of the Pink Panther route on Mount Foraker should move ⅛ to ¼ of an inch to the right to the obvious S-shaped gully for the initial 2500 feet.

Broken Tooth South Face. Mugs Stump and Steve Quinlan completed a new route, the second, on the Broken Tooth in mid-May, when they spent four days on the south face. They found two good bivouac sites a third and two-thirds of the way up the 22 pitches. They rated the climb as VI, 5.10+, A3.

Broken Tooth, West Ridge. Jack Lewis and I climbed the west ridge of the Broken Tooth, gaining the ridge from the southwest and making the third ascent of the peak. Our route is probably the easiest of the three routes that

Photo by Bradford Washburn

BROKEN TOOTH from South. Solid line on left is Bauman-Lewis route. Dotted line on right is Stump-Quinlan route.

have been done. The major problem was the weather and it was good enough only on the third try. Two rock pitches and a lot of wallowing in depth hoar put us on the west ridge. Snow steps on the ridge took us to a rock tower, which we climbed on the right. Then hard ice brought us to the summit tower and three pitches of good rock climbing to the summit ridge. It was then a hike to the top. (IV, 5.9).

THOMAS BAUMAN

West Tripyramid, Northwest Ridge. On August 22, Scott Gill, Randy Waitman and I climbed a new route, the northwest ridge of West Tripyramid (3572 meters, 11,720 feet). We established our high camp at 6400 feet on the Traleika Glacier after a five-day approach via Wonder Lake, the Peters Glacier and Gunsight Pass. This included one storm day. The Peters Glacier has surged and is generally impassable below the Tluna Icefall. The Muldrow Glacier between Gunsight Pass and the Traleika was heavily crevassed, necessitating caution. Tripyramid is 11 miles east-northeast of Denali. The route rises 5300 feet and we rate it Grade III. All climbing was unroped except for two pitches of 40° to 50° ice directly below the summit, which we climbed simultaneously with protection. Descent was by the ascent route. The climb took 13 hours round-trip.

CLIFF BEAVER, *Unaffiliated*

Silverthrone, Winter Ascent. On March 5, my father Jim Okonek of K2 Aviation flew my wife Diane, Ricardo Ernst and me to Kantishna. We skied to the Muldrow Glacier via McGonagall Pass and ascended the Brooks Glacier to the Silverthrone Col at 10,650 feet. Ricardo pulled moose steaks and smoked salmon from his heavy sled for us to dine on. Despite wind-scoured slopes, we never experienced the slightest breeze for the entire trip. On March 12, we followed the north ridge to the 13,220-foot (4029-meter) summit of Silverthrone. A thin, and in some places corniced, summit ridge added excitement to an otherwise easy climb. My Dad, returning to Talkeetna from the Ididarod Dog Sled Race, flew by as we neared the summit. The temperature was comfortable 0° F and it was calm and clear. Denali loomed so close it seemed we could touch it. On March 14, Diane and I walked up McGonagall Mountain under the full moon and northern lights. On March 16, the three of us ascended P 9240 from Gunsight Pass. This is the true beginning of Denali's Pioneer Ridge and the point the Cairns expedition had reached in 1912. The next day we descended to the Peters Glacier, which we followed to its terminus and along the Muddy River. In August of 1986, the Peters Glacier began to surge and in a few months advanced several miles. The surface of the glacier is an imposing jumble of dirty séracs and crevasses. We returned to Kantishna on March 21.

BRIAN OKONEK

P 11,091, P 10,300 and P 9810, Eldridge Glacier. Our expedition was composed of mountain guides: Bruno Musi, Giorgio Passino, Giuseppe Cheney, Eliseo Cheney, Henry Truchet and me as leader. We set up Base Camp on May 29 on the north fork of the Eldridge Glacier at 4600 feet at the eastern edge of Denali National Park. During the first days, we explored the very beautiful area. On June 2 we established Camp I at 5500 feet. The next day Musi and Passino made an unsuccessful attempt on P 9218 where they climbed several pitches of rotten rock before being turned back by bad weather. On June 6 we moved to Camp II at 7500 feet. On June 7, we all climbed P 10,300 at the head of the glacier from the east, where we found difficult ice up to 50°. (This same route was first climbed on July 4, 1958 by Adams Carter, Barrett Morgan, Harold Janeway, Sandy Weld, Fred Churchill, Bill Loomis, Doug Bingham, Dave Helprin and George Erlanger.) On June 8, Musi and Passino attempted the north ridge of Mather but had to give up because of bad weather. On June 9, Musi, Passino and I headed for P 11,091, which lies just east of Mather. We started up into the cirque which lies between it and Mather. After having overcome notable ice and mixed difficulties (ice up to 65°), we reached the summit at 12:30 A.M. (This same route was climbed on July 17, 1960 by Adams Carter, Tom Bisbee, Nat Goodhue, Doug Bingham, Brian Wilson and David Atherton.) Late in the afternoon of June 10, Musi and Passino headed for P 9810. They ascended a 2000-foot-high face and got to the summit in bad weather, having climbed hard brittle ice up to 70°. (The first ascent of P 9810 was made from the north from the Muldrow Glacier side by Adams Carter and Roger Dane on July 4, 1957.) They descended an easier ridge to the north and then to the east. Both the ascent and the descent routes were new. Bad weather prevented further ascents and we returned to Talkeetna on June 16.

COSIMO ZAPPELLI, *Società delle Guide, Courmayeur, Italy*

Deborah, West Face. Andy Reynolds, Keith Eckelmeyer and I made the third ascent of the west face of Deborah. Although it was a great climb, nothing really noteworthy took place. We repeated the straightforward west-face route, the most direct and easiest way to climb Deborah. We flew to the upper Yanert Glacier in early April and spent two days getting through icefalls, fixed 500 feet of line on the face and waited a day for weather. We then climbed the face in an 18-hour round-trip push from our 9000-foot camp. We skied down the Yanert to the Parks Highway.

GEOFFREY RADFORD, *Mountaineering Club of Alaska*

Mount Kimball, P 10,310 and P 11,288. Mount Kimball was climbed for the third time but by a new route by Jim Bouchard and José Rueter. In February, Doug Buchanan and Mark Wumkes made the first ascent of P 10,310 in the central Alaska Range. Bouchard and Dan McCoy climbed P

11,288, near the Black Rapids Glacier. McCoy fell on the descent but was not seriously hurt. Details are lacking on all these climbs.

Four Horsemen, the Angel and Other Peaks, Revelation Mountains, 1985. In 1985 Dan Heilig, Mal Miller, Greg Collins and I spent from late April to late May in the Revelation Mountains. Our Base Camp was at the head of the southernmost fork of the Revelation Glacier, in the cwm where Dave Roberts and crew camped in 1967 (*A.A.J., 1968*, pages 27-35). The weather was windy and stormy and we were barely able to climb a third of the time. All four of us ascended to the highest point of the Four Horsemen via the 4000-foot northwest couloir and west ridge (AI4, moderate 5th class). Heilig and Miller climbed the two Horsemen west of the highest one, both one-day mixed climbs. Collins and I concentrated our energy on the Angel, a peak Roberts' group tried six times without success. We made four attempts on the massive 4500-foot buttress, finally succeeding in a 24-hour push with a few fixed ropes in place. The route followed snow ramps with an occasional rock move or two along the left flank of the buttress. Upon reaching the broad crest, we climbed a difficult and poorly protected slab (5.9+), a vertical dihedral (5.8), then seven or eight mixed pitches until snow-and-ice ramps could be connected to the top of the buttress. Some exposed ridge running took us to the main peak; two pitches of ice brought us to "Terror Tower," a two-pitch horror of vertical loose blocks. This required a few moves of aid in addition to nerve-wracking crampon-clad free climbing. From the top of the tower a few ice steps brought us to the summit snowfield, a few hundred feet before we got to the summit. Heilig, Collins and Miller climbed the satellite peak east of Golgotha via the east ridge in an afternoon; Heilig and Collins ascended the Sentry via the north ridge; Collins and I climbed Hydra Sylph via the northeast gully. All were one day climbs with moderate mixed climbing. Collins and I also climbed the "Vanishing Pinnacle," climbed by Roberts and Fetcher in 1967 (5.6, A3). Greg led the crux pitch free at 5.11. On the top we found rusty pins slung together with a nylon belt left two decades earlier. Our rock was granite, generally of good quality. The Revelations are not massive, monolithic granite walls like the Kichatnas, but they do offer challenging mountaineering with 4000- to 5000-foot climbs in a very beautiful and remote place.

THOMAS WALTER, *National Outdoor Leadership School*

Marcus Baker, Chugach Mountains; Wrangell, Wrangell Mountains; and McKinley, Northwest Buttress. Todd Frankiewicz, Leo Americus and I completed a winter ascent of Marcus Baker (13,176 feet) on March 1. Though technically not difficult, it has rarely been ascended in winter. We skied up the Matanuska Glacier and set up a high camp at 10,500 feet. A terrible storm moved in. We went for the summit in a break in the storm and consequently ended up in terrible weather. We reached the summit in frigid conditions and quickly descended to the snow cave. Unfortunately Americus froze one toe quite badly. The three of us skied over a 9000-foot pass, dropped onto the Marcus Baker Glacier and skied that to the Knik Glacier and on into Palmer, completing an 80-mile trip. My next adventure was a traverse of the Wrangell Mountains from the confluence of the Sanford and Copper Rivers at the Glenn Highway to McCarthy at the toe of the Kennicott Glacier, a distance of 150 miles. Howell Powder, Alex Swiderski and I skied up the Sanford River to the west side of Mount Zanetti (13,009 feet) and camped at 9000 feet. From there, on April 12, we climbed to the summit up 30° to 40° hard packed snow and ice. This was good acclimatization for Mount Wrangell (14,164 feet). We gained the 13,000-foot plateau, dropped our gear and proceeded to the base of the south face at 13,200 feet. On a wonderfully sunny day, April 17, we chose a direct route through the wind-sculptured gargoyles hanging off the face in all directions. The last 200 feet of the climb was up a 50° ice gully. The Nebesna Glacier is gigantic! It took three days to ski from the Wrangell plateau to the base of Blackburn. Our route was from 8000 feet on the western end of the north face. In one long day we got past many crevasses to 13,000 feet. The following day, Alex and I battled our way through blowing snow to 14,500 feet, where the north-face line meets the north ridge but had to retreat because of the weather. We still had 50 miles to ski to reach McCarthy. In May, Tom Kelly, Howie Baer and I climbed the northwest buttress of McKinley. This wonderful route is rarely attempted partly because once Kahiltna Pass is reached at 10,000 feet, you have to drop 3000 feet to the Peters Glacier. It took us 27 days from the Kahiltna Glacier Base Camp and back. Kelly and I reached the summit of the North Peak on May 26. The better weather never came for our climb to the South Peak. According to the Park Service, our climb of the northwest buttress was only the fifth ascent.

JOHN BAUMAN, *Mountaineering Club of Alaska*

Peaks Above the Matanuska Valley. Greg Higgins, Tom Choate and I made several climbs from the Matanuska Glacier from July 15 to 20. On July 16, we climbed Mount Wickersham (7415 feet) from the southeast, finding only two entries in the summit jar: Grace Hoeman solo on July 5, 1969 and an ascent from the west on August 8, 1978. We traversed the ridge over rotten rock to P 7000 + , where we found evidence of a previous ascent. On the 17th we climbed P 8400 + via the east ridge for a second ascent. (This was mistakenly called P 8380 in *A.A.J, 1976,* page 437.) On the 19th we made the first ascent of P 8555 via the western side. If one follows the long ribbons of rock-covered ice, most of the glacier can be traveled without using crampons.

WILLY HERSMAN

Valdez Ice Festival. The Fifth Annual Valdez Ice-Climbing Festival, sponsored jointly by the American Alpine Club and the Valdez Alpine Club, was a great success. More than 60 participants came from Fairbanks, Anchorage, Cordova, Talkeetna, Girdwood, California, Colorado, Washington and Oregon. Vast numbers of routes were climbed, both of moderate and extreme difficulty. Climbers heading for the Himalaya came to train on steep waterfall ice. Climbing conditions were good, with temperatures a little below freezing, light winds through Keystone Canyon and several days of sunshine. Luckily, the Lowe River was frozen, permitting hiking across the ice to climbs on the other side of the river from the Richardson Highway. Some of the difficult ice routes were these: the fourth ascent of *Wowie Zowie* (Grade VI) by Steve Garvey and Jim Sweeney; the first ascent of *Sans Amis*, an extremely difficult (Grade VI) route on the slabby, nearly vertical east wall of Keystone Canyon upstream from Bridal Veil Falls by Garney and Sweeney; the second ascent of *Love's Way* (Grade VI−) by Roman Dial, Kate Bull, Jon Krakauer and Brian Teale; and the first ascent of *Synapse* (Grade IV +) by Teale, Chuck Comstock and Joe Loffredo in Keystone Canyon to the right of Mud Slide.

ANDREW EMBICK, M.D.

Peaks Above Harding Icefield, Kenai Fjords National Park. Rick Dare, Dallas Virchow, Joe Sears and I spent 13 days on the Harding Icefield in June. We reached the icefield via the Exit Glacier and spent three days hauling loads to Base Camp at a group of peaks near the northwest corner of the icefield. We climbed four peaks there by mixed snow and rock routes: P 5178 (60°08′ N, 149°57′ W), P 4900 and P 5000 (just east of P 5178) and P 4800 (north of P 5000). We also climbed P 4815, which lies southwest of the Exit Glacier.

STEVE GARDINER, *Unaffiliated*

Needle Mountain Correction. On Page 159 of *A.A.J.,1987,* it states that Needle *Peak* was a *second* ascent. It should have been Needle *Mountain* and it was in fact a *first* ascent.

Blackburn and P 10,565. On May 3, Paul Claus flew a party from Anchorage Community College's Alaska Wilderness Program to 7300 feet on the Nabesna Glacier below P 9111, north of Mount Blackburn (4995 meters, 16,390 feet). Led by Todd Miner and me, the party consisted of Karen Cafmeyer, Larry Hartig, Jim Sayler and Blaine Smith. We established camps at 9800, 11,500 and 13,000 feet. Above 12,300 feet, where our route joined the north ridge, the tedious job of breaking trail in deep snow ended; in fact, we were forced to camp at 13,000 feet in a crevasse because there was not enough snow for a snow cave. The broad summit was reached on May 12 by all. On the way down, Miner, Cafmeyer and I climbed P 10,565 from a pass at 9800 feet on May 14.

WILLY HERSMAN

P 9110 and P 9105, Hole-in-the-Wall Glacier, Wrangell Mountains. The Hole-in-the-Wall Glacier and the mountains surrounding it are unique. The upper glacier is a large semi-circular basin which flows off a ten-mile-long ridge, the south side of which is a vertical wall that drops 2000 to 3000 feet. It contains numerous snow-and-ice gullies and waterfalls. Several high peaks lie along this ridge: P 8880, P 9008, P 9105, P 9110 and P 9124. The north side of the ridge first gently slopes into the upper glacier at 8500 to 8000 feet and then becomes a vertical wall over which the ice tumbles in spectacular 2500-foot icefalls; five tongue-like icefalls cut through the wall. On September 23, Bob Jacobs and I were dropped off by airplane at 5900 feet in a large basin a mile from the south wall. We climbed up a snow ramp to 7000 feet to camp. The next day we watched five inches of snow fall. On the 25th, we climbed further up the ramp and then through a couple of snow gullies in the rock bands in the wall. This brought us to the upper ridge above the glacier. We followed the ridge east over hoarfrost-covered rock to the summit of P 9110. We went along the ridge down to 8600 feet at the base of the west ridge of P 9105. I led 100 feet up the 45° ice before we were enveloped in a severe white-out. It was a race to get down before wind and snow covered our tracks. On the 26th, we traversed around P 9110 to reach the base of P 9105 again. Bob led the 500 feet up the west face to the top. The rime-covered summit was impressive. We moved camp down to the landing area later that evening and down to the Glacier Creek airstrip, some ten miles down the Chitistone River the next day. We believe that these were the first ascents of the two peaks.

DANNY W. KOST, *Unaffiliated*

P 9400, Chitina Glacier, Saint Elias Mountains. Dan Doak and I were dropped at Huberts Landing at 2000 feet on the Chitina River to complete a climb I had tried with another climber in July. On September 16, we hiked along the north side of the Chitina Glacier to the base of P 9400 at 2400 feet. We climbed scree and through spruces to establish camp at 5200 feet on the south face of the mountain at the same site we had used in July. On our trip in July, we had enjoyed great views of Logan, King Peak and Saint Elias, but on this later one, we were constantly threatened by snow clouds. On the 17th, we hiked through fresh snow to 6900 feet, the base of the actual climb, at the foot of the south face below P 9000. We climbed a 45° snow-and-ice gully which lies just east of P 8645, up over a couple of steep ice steps onto the west ridge at 8700 feet. (This was our high point in July, when we climbed a rock buttress up the south face to reach P 8645.) Dan and I then followed the heavily corniced ridge over P 9000 and P 9300 and on to the main summit of P 9400. We had no distant vistas, but the view 7000 feet down onto the Chitina Glacier was breathtaking. P 9400 lies three miles northwest of the junction of the Ram and Chitina Glaciers. I believe this was the first ascent of the peak.

DANNY W. KOST, *Unaffiliated*

Pyramid Peak, Saint Elias Mountains. On September 11, Dan Doak and I flew to 4200 feet 2½ miles south of Pyramid Peak, which lies 22 miles southeast of McCarthy, hoping to finish making the first ascent that Dan, Jesper Krogholt from Denmark and I had attempted two weeks earlier. Then, we had hiked in from the Dan Creek airstrip eight miles northwest of the peak, ascending the Dan Creek drainages to look at possible routes on its north and west sides. Seeing no feasible routes there, we attempted it by a glacier which flows off the mountain to the south from a basin between the east and west summits. We climbed the icefall to reach the basin and opted to try the higher eastern summit (8910 feet). We ascended a 45°, 400-foot ice couloir at the upper end of the basin to reach the north ridge. I led one pitch on the ridge to 8500 feet. Due to approaching bad weather and lack of time, we descended. So Dan and I had returned to finish the climb. Now we were looking at a different mountain with two feet of new snow. We camped at 6100 feet a few hundred yards from the south face. On September 12, we established a route through the icefall to 7700 feet. On the 13th, we hoped to return through the icefall, but it snowed and was foggy. On the 14th, after reaching the basin at 7900 feet, we decided to go straight up the west face to the east summit. It was a 50° snow-and-ice climb to within 300 feet of the top. Then we traversed to the right under the huge sérac which hung off the north side of the summit over shaky snow bridges and up the final steep ridge. Beautiful, surrealistic rime covered the rock and even the séracs. The 8875-foot west peak looked ominous with the top 150 feet resembling the summit mushroom of Cerro Torre. We didn't enjoy the view for long and our descent through the icefall in fog was interesting.

DANNY W. KOST, *Unaffiliated*

Mount Wade. In July Bruce Tickell and I climbed Mount Wade (Boundary Peak 173; 2426 meters, 7960 feet), which is 50 miles east of Yakutat, overlooking Nunatak Fjord. We ascended the East Nunatak Glacier from the beach and left the glacier five miles from the fjord to climb easy slopes to a camp at 4000 feet. From there we ascended snow and loose rock to a narrow ridge 1.5 miles south of the main summit. We then traversed the ridge on rock and snow, skirting obstacles whenever possible. After a mile we could descend onto the high cirque glacier which took us to the east ridge of the summit block. We waited two hours for better light and reached the summit with the sunrise of July 16 to enjoy unrivaled views of the St. Elias and Fairweather ranges. The ascent from the 4000-foot camp took 14 hours and the return only six hours.

GERALD BUCKLEY, *Unaffiliated*

Fairweather, Southeast Buttress, 1986. On June 27, 1986, Tad Pfeffer, Linda Sugiyama and I were flown by Mike Ivers to a camp on the upper Fairweather Glacier at 6000 feet. We benefited from the new rules under which

FAIRWEATHER's Southeast Buttress ascends from directly in front of the summit.

airplane landings appear to be permitted in most areas of Glacier Bay National Park. The east ridge of P 13,820, the south false summit of Fairweather, descends to 11,500 feet where it is abruptly truncated by cliffs to form a giant buttress. These cliffs drop 3000 feet to the glacier which tumbles from the massive high cirque between Fairweather and Quincy Adams. Our route went up a long couloir onto a hanging glacier on the right side of the south face of the buttress to the low point of the east ridge. It then followed the east ridge to P 13,820, where we joined the Carpé ridge route to the summit. The initial 1500 feet and to a lesser extent the rest of the route up the east ridge lay under hanging glaciers high on the face, but we observed little falling ice. The azure skies we had on our arrival soon disappeared and Linda and I waited a week before starting from camp at 1:30 A.M. on July 4, leaving behind Tad, who decided not to climb. An hour-and-a-half's walk brought us to the base of the face at 6000 feet. A short 60° ice slope and a labyrinth of schrunds and avalanche debris led to a right-trending snow slope, which we followed to the long snow-and-ice couloir. The 45° couloir was cut by a 200-foot rock band, much of which was streaming with water. The couloir, sometimes with only a foot or two of slush and thin ice over rock, continued up to a curving snow arête which formed the right edge of the south face. The danger of a wet snow avalanche was great. We waded through steep snow over ice up and left to the upper part of the prominent hanging glacier in the middle of the face, which gave us six pitches of 45° ice before a snow ramp led right to the sérac-guarded nose of the buttress. After a false start, we found a moderate ramp system which snaked onto the broad ridge crest at 11,500 feet, where we collapsed for the night at 10:30 P.M. Not until two P.M. the next day did we start up the steep part of the east ridge at 12,500 feet. This was an elegant uncorniced 40° knife-edge. We often had our left feet on slush on the south side and our right feet in powdery windslab on the north. At 13,300 feet the ridge broadened to moderate snow slopes which we followed to the top of P 13,820 to camp in the rays of a late Alaskan sunset. On the third day, July 6, 1986, we followed the Carpé ridge to the summit, skirting the ice nose on the right in crampon balling snow. Lenticular clouds on the peaks far below and high clouds signaled a weather change and we got back to camp as it began to snow. By nine A.M. a snowy whiteout roused us to an uneasy compass-and-altimeter descent of the Carpé ridge, spiced with plunges into unseen schrunds, near-plunges into giant unseen crevasses, ice and then man-eating slush. To punctuate the day, a large wet-snow avalanche wiped out our tracks ten minutes after we reached the rock ridge at 8000 feet, where we bivouacked on a cornice. After a humid but happy night in continuing sleet and fog, we woke to sunshine, descended the remaining 3000 feet of ridge and marched the four miles back to camp. Continued soft-snow conditions and another storm prevented us from serious climbing until Mike Ivers flew us out on July 15.

CHRIS BRETHERTON, *Unaffiliated*

P 5000, Chilkoot Inlet, Coast Range. John Brainard and I decided to attempt the first known ascent of this beautiful and oft-viewed peak above the eastern shore of Chilkoot Inlet, 2½ miles southwest of Sinclair Mountain. On July 1, we met at the landing strip near Haines with typical clouds and a 2500-foot ceiling. We went eight miles south to wait out the weather on the western shore of Chilkoot Inlet. We awoke early on July 3 to surprisingly clear skies. The canoe crossing required 55 minutes of dedicated, strong paddling. The killer whales and sea lions confused our landing on the opposite shore. We immediately set off through the most hideous devil's club and dense vegetation. After nine hours of exhausting effort, we bivouacked at 3000 feet. The next morning was also astonishingly clear. We forded a glacial lake and slugged up a 45° snow slope, having cached our technical equipment. At the top of the slope we found ourselves in a steep bowl with two possible summits. I favored the peak we could actually see, but Brainard had studied this mountain for two years and urged that we push up beyond the sheer mushy snow wall which blocked our view. A thousand vertical feet left us on a small shelf viewing another wall above us and avalanche cracks in the snow crust 300 yards to the left. Discretion lost out and we went up another 250 yards and happily topped out onto a 20° slope leading to a mixed rock-and-snow summit. We built a cairn and buried a canister at 3:10 P.M. on July 4. The descent was even more miserable than the ascent. We arrived at the shore of Chilkoot Inlet shortly after midnight, totally exhausted. The tide carried us, but the wind helped and we made the friendly western shore at three A.M.

JOHN C.D. BRUNO

Mount Ogden, 1986. In late June 1986 Bruce Tickell and I climbed Mount Ogden (Boundary Peak 86; 2281 meters, 7484 feet). It lies about ten miles south of the Taku River. We landed on the lake in front of the Wright Glacier, and hiked south on the glacier to under the peak. The climb was an easy snow slog until the last 1000 feet. From there we traversed under the west face and ascended a ridge from the northwest; it was mostly fourth class with a few harder sections. The climb took 16 hours from camp at 3000 feet. We also made two attempts on Mount Fremont Morse, but were turned back by technical difficulties both from the north and the south sides. Expecting little more than a few roped pitches, we had little other than a rope for assistance. A little more determination and hardware would suffice to make this ascent.

GERALD BUCKLEY, *Unaffiliated*

International Exchange

Czechoslovakian Exchange. In the summer of 1987, the American Alpine Club was host to a team of 12 climbers representing the Czechoslovakian Mountaineering Asssociation. American climbers had been admirably received and hosted in Czechoslovakia in 1986. After a warm welcome from Ad Carter

PLATE 31

Photo by Standa Vaněk

**Czech Petr Čermak on Chain
Reaction (5.12c), Smith Rocks,
Oregon.**

and Paul Kallmes, two masterminds of the affair, Henry Barber showed them climbs on Cathedral Ledge in New Hampshire. They got a chance to climb in the Shawangunks before heading west. Their path took them to the Devils Tower and then to difficult climbs in the Colorado Rockies, including Cinch Crack, Downpresser Man, Johnny Belinda, Naked Edge and several free ascents of the Diamond on Longs Peak. In the Boulder area, Mark Wilford renewed his friendships from his 1982 trip to Czechoslovakia and showed them Eldorado Canyon. These many difficult climbs got them in shape for Smith Rocks, where they redpointed a number of 5.13s, and other West Coast attractions. Alan Bartlett and I took on the task of hosting them in California. I began to sweat a little as I heard what they had done at Smith Rocks. But my longtime friendship with Vladimír Weigner, the leader of the group, made me comfortable in generously offering to allow them to go first on a few old classics where they might guard my own shaky progress with a tight belay from above. Meanwhile Bartlett and Kallmes directed some of the young tigers to the test places in Tuolumne and the Valley. There were one-day ascents of the northwest face of Half Dome and the Nose of El Cap. The North America Wall, an on-sight climb of Astroman and the south face of Watkins were also completed. Tomaš Čada renewed his acquaintance with John Bachar and went on to lead A Separate Reality.

MICHAEL WARBURTON

Washington—Cascade Mountains

Mount Stuart, Lost Planet Airmen. Between the northwest face and north ridge on Mount Stuart lie several pitches of superb crack and slab climbing. On June 27, Tobin Kelly and I climbed through small séracs just left of the northwest-face route and up a long thin finger crack on excellent rock. Another tricky pitch up a moss-infested corner brought us to the fourth-class ground on the northwest face. After three pitches of scrambling, we followed a flaring chimney and corner up and left to the base of a long left-facing corner. Stemming, laybacking and thin jams went on for 140 feet to where I stepped out onto a small ledge. Two more pitches on good rock ended on the third-class ledges of the north-ridge route just below the summit. (IV, 5.10b.)

ALAN KEARNEY

Castle Peak, Left Side of North Face. The north face of Castle Peak features six distinct granitic buttresses. Our climb ascended the last buttress on the left side of the face. On September 12, Sue Harrington and I climbed two pitches of slabs to gain a prominent small corner system in the center of the face. We followed the corner for one long lead which involved difficult stemming (5.10) until we could exit leftward and climb a thin crack through a small overhang to a belay stance. Directly above the belay are large roofs with less formidable roofs up and to the right. We jammed up a tiny left-facing corner for 20 feet (5.10b) to a small ledge. We pulled through a small overhang using a thin crack, moved right slightly to an alcove and then climbed up and left on face holds to surmount a second overhang (5.10c). From a semi-hanging belay stance, we jammed a beautiful long finger-and-hand crack which ended on a ledge. We traversed right for 50 feet and then climbed up and right into a large corner system on the west side of the buttress. We climbed 1½ pitches to the top of the steep portion of the buttress. We scrambled up and left four pitches to gain easier ledges that led to just below the summit of the buttress. We climbed a squeeze chimney on the right side of the summit block and then followed the east ridge to the true summit. (IV, 5.10c.)

ALAN KEARNEY

Big Kangaroo, South Face. On October 4, Chris Copeland and I climbed the first three pitches of the 1984 Thomas-Kearney route, but instead of exiting from the corner, we continued up it. From a small stance in the corner, we climbed a left-leaning flake for 75 feet which parallels the corner before rejoining it to climb up to a hanging belay just under a giant overhang. We climbed up and left using a thin crack beneath the overhang (5.10c and aid) and up to a belay above the left end of the overhang. We traversed left using tension and continued across to a large flaring crack. We ascended this a short way and traversed left again to gain the 1967 south-face route. Protection was up to 4 inches with emphasis on stoppers and small Friends. (III, 5.10c, A2.)

ALAN KEARNEY

Wallaby, North Face. On June 24, Andy Selters, Chuck Sink and I completed a four-pitch route up the north face of Wallaby on Kangaroo Ridge. We entered the face from the west on scree and began roped climbing at a ledge with whitebark pines. The route followed cracks, a small left-facing corner and ramp system to a recess three pitches up. A rising leftward traverse beneath an overhang ended at the top of the face. The rock was variable. (II, 5.9.)

ALAN KEARNEY

Dragontail Peak, Northwest Face, Stuart Range. On October 11, Alan Kearney and I climbed a new route on the northwest face of Dragontail via the prominent buttress between Serpentine Arête and the Boving route. We began in the huge corner system just to the right of the toe of the buttress. A pitch of third class led to a belay in the corner. From there, a 40-foot horizontal traverse brought us to a clean, discontinuous crack system. We ascended this for two pitches, occasionally diagonaling back to the corner. The second was hard with the crux moves protected by tied-off knife-blades (5.9). From a belay on ledges, we climbed a crack diagonally left through the steep wall of the corner to the crest of the buttress. We followed the crest for the rest of the route. It was fourth class for about three rope-lengths, but then the arête narrows and has four steep headwalls. The first two, 25-foot white walls facing right, were turned via hidden crack systems just to their left. The third wall is wider and slightly higher. It is split by a narrowing fist-to-finger crack which leads to a small stance (5.9). Then a short pitch ends on a flat ledge. Above, we climbed directly on the knife-edge for 75 feet to the fourth headwall, where a 15-foot traverse to the left took us to cracks (5.9) up through a notch. The final 200 feet up the arête to the summit ridge are pleasant scrambling on solid rock. (1200 vertical feet; 13 pitches; III, 5.9.)

PETER KELEMEN

Silverstar Mountain, 1986. A new route was made in September 1986 on the northeast buttress and finally the east ridge. Dave Beckstead and I found interesting, sometimes very challenging climbing on the slabs and towers of this ridge. The route begins from a small glacier and ends where it joins the Ulrichs route near the summit pinnacles. The rock is very solid, being part of the Golden Horn batholith. The route was long enough so that a bivouac was made in the trees on the descent. (III, 5.8.)

FRED BECKEY

Witches Tower, North Face Dihedral, 1986. On July 30, 1986 Dan Nordstrom and I hiked in over Asgard Pass to test this sunless dihedral. We started in a white dihedral to the left of the main open-book. The next two pitches followed the main corner and a hand crack thick with lichen to the base of an overhanging headwall. We could have escaped the cold by heading left in a gully, but by following discontinous cracks above, we arrived at a sunny belay. The final summit arête was memorable both for its exposure and its warmth. (III, 5.10.)

FRED YACKULIC

Prusik Peak, South Face of West Ridge. On August 16, Rich Romano and I ascended the leftmost crack system on the south face of Prusik. The large overhang on the second pitch was passed on the right. A short overhanging hand crack and airy face moves brought us to the west-ridge route. (The climb is left of the Boving-Christensen route.) (II, 5.10.)

FRED YACKULIC

Davis Peak, North Face, Southern Pickets. Andy Cairns and I made a difficult approach to the northern cirque of this outlier of the southern Pickets. The actual rock climbing, gaining 4000 feet, was delightful, as the numerous handholds buoyed us four pitches up the prominent central chimney (probably the melted-out version of the 1974 Kloke-Simon route). We then exited left for three pitches on an exposed rib for some delicate face climbing. Re-entering what was now a gully, we surmounted a succession of monstrous chockstones to top out near the full-moonlit summit. (IV, 5.10.)

BRYAN BURDO, *Affiliated Climbers of the Montlake Erratic (ACME)*

Mount Shuksan, Nooksack Cirque. Pete Doorish and I visited a summit immediately northeast of Nooksack Tower by climbing from a camp near the northeastern arm of the Price Glacier. The climbing was enjoyable at the outset, but the rock became increasingly friable. As the rock deteriorated, the views improved, with the summit providing a culmination of these extremes. (III, 5.6.)

BRYAN BURDO, *ACME*

Climbs in the "Skykomish Alps." The peaks south and east of the town of Index offer a variety of climbing opportunites on steep rock between 3000 and 6000 feet in elevation. All share the same kind of rock, a unique metamorphosed volcanic, which tends to be steep, hard and somewhat intimidating. Nonetheless, it has rewarding climbing and I have found several fine intermediate free climbs while Pete Doorish has put in some of the hardest wall climbs in the Cascades. In 1985 Bill Enger and I climbed Mount Persis' north face and Josh Medosch and I ascended a 400-foot dihedral system on the southwest face of Gunn's peak *(Gunnslinger)*. In 1987, I returned to Gunn to climb on its high quality *Rhinostone.* The two best routes were *Rhinostone Renegade* (II, 5.8 +) on the south face and *Belayed Runner* (II, 5.10 +) on the west face direct. Renegade, done with Andy Cairns, shares its start and finish with 1985 *Gunnslinger* and climbs a broken arête. Runner, done with Greg White, features some outstanding crack climbing on its final, crux pitch. Both climbs are three pitches long. To the south, Mount Baring presents a steep north face rising 4000 feet above Barclay Lake and has smaller crags on its southern exposure. I climbed one of them, a 400-footer, southwest of the summit which I call "Syko Rock." *Loconotion Arête* (II, 5.8) climbs this face on the southeast. The north face of Baring received a lot of attention until its ascent via the northeast corner in 1959 and then apparently went unclimbed for 20 years when Doorish and Dale Farnham repeated the Cooper-Gordon route in the rain. Doorish did this route free with John Siletto in 1983 (IV, 5.10). Doorish and Farnham climbed the route in winter conditions in February, 1984. This team was joined by Alex Cudowicz later in 1984 to forge a 26-pitch route directly up the north face (V, 5.10, A3). The Dolomite Tower, adjacent to the north face, dominates Baring's profile when seen from the west. It is an 1100-foot monolith of vertical and overhanging rock for which the approach itself is a climb. Doorish set upon it in the summer of 1985. His solo efforts over the summer established fixed lines less than halfway up its north prow.

Finally in September 1985, Doorish returned alone for an epic final push, which took 12 days and consumed 30 drill bits for 40 holes in rock with the consistency of marble. Despite foul weather and a broken hammock, which committed him to 11 sleepless nights, Doorish managed to top out in a hailstorm (V + , 5.9, A3). The Dolomite project does not stand alone as a testament to determination. A few miles south, and a year previously, Doorish, Farnham and Charlie Hampsen had laid siege to the seemingly impregnable North Norwegian Buttress of Mount Index. This 2200-foot tower, which looms over Lake Serene, had repulsed some of the area's leading climbers over the years, the high point being a mere five pitches up the northeast face. After an initial attempt during the snows of November 1984 to above this point, Doorish and company returned regularly on weekends the next season to jümar ropes and pound pins through the 30- to 40-foot roofs midway up the route. In July 1985, Doorish and Farnham finished the project in a six-day push, calling a 26-day, 24-pitch effort. The reward was a descent of the route, featuring a wild 300-foot free rappel through the roofs. (VI, 5.9, A3.)

BRYAN BURDO, *ACME*

Mount Baring, East Buttress of South Peak. On May 20, Ken Johnson and I climbed an interesting route on the south peak of Mount Baring. We approached via the straighforward south slopes of Baring from old logging roads. We followed up the remains of the road from a large washout and climbed through the timber clearcut to open forest. Then we traversed to the northeast for some way to reach the prominent snow gully which leads to the notch east of the south peak. We climbed the 40° snow-and-ice gully for several hundred feet. We got to an obvious notch, where I found an old steel carabiner. From there, four roped pitches of rock brought us to the summit. (III, 5.5.) We descended the northwest ridge. It took us eight hours from the road and eleven hours round-trip.

JOHN PETROSKE

Pyramid Peak, North Face. On March 29, James Ruch and I completed the first ascent of Pyramid Peak's north face. The climbing was almost entirely on good ice and snow with occasional mixed sections. In surmounting the difficult band via an ice ribbon, we encountered five rope-lengths of superb ice. The fourth surpassed the vertical for a three-meter section before easing back to a comfortable 80°. This concave pitch, as we called it, provided the only two placements in its entirety before a semi-hanging belay from a lone knife-blade piton. Though I would not dare to rob anyone of the exhilaration I sensed when leading this pitch, I might suggest that future parties carry more than two ice screws. (III-IV.)

ROBERT COTTER, *Unaffiliated*

Mount Rainier, Success Glacier Middle Finger. The Success Glacier sits in a cirque between Success and Kautz Cleavers. On the headwall are three snow fingers. The right finger was climbed in 1960 (Success Glacier Couloir). No information was available on the middle finger. Although it may have been climbed previously, we could find no record of it. Starting from Indian Henry's, we crossed the Pyramid Glacier to camp at 9200 feet on the Success Glacier. Our route then ascended to the schrund at 10,600 feet and into the middle snow finger. The angle being less than expected, we moved quickly, in part motivated after being bombarded by rockfall in the lower part of the couloir. The sudden rockfall came from everywhere as it bounced off the sides of the couloir. Fortunately no one was hurt. Keeping to the right, we ascended to near the couloir's head at 11,500 feet and crossed over, following the right side of the rib through rock bands to 13,000 feet on Success Cleaver. With evening closing in, we camped. The next morning we traversed under rock bands and up a short ice gully to Point Success.

JAMES COUCH, *Unicorn Adventures*

Storm King Mountain. On July 12, in a long push from Rainy Pass, I did a new route on Storm King Mountain. The north side of the peak has a small pocket glacier with two couloirs at its head. I followed the right one for several hundred feet on 50° snow and ice until being forced up class-5 rock on the left of the couloir. More moderate rock, followed by snow and ice, led to the final section and crux of the couloir, which was blocked by a large chockstone. The couloir ends in a notch between the west summit and a spectacular tower. I climbed the right side of the notch, not difficult but with a lot of loose rock. The north ridge of the west summit provided a fast descent to the pocket glacier (III, 5.7).

STEVEN C. RISSE

The Changing Cascades. In August, Mike Mooney and I packed into the Mount Challenger area. We hoped to carry over Whatcom Pass and then traverse by glacier to Perfect Pass, leaving Whatcom Peak to the west. Next we would cross the Challenger Glacier to Challenger Arm, skirt the Luna Cirque on snow to the hanging ice cliff under Mount Fury and, after two days of travel, gain the north buttress of Mount Fury. None of this is original, but what is remarkable is that our plan did not work. I had been in the area in 1974. In these 13 years the glaciers have receded and mountain travel is now substantially more difficult. The glacier traverse between Whatcom and Perfect Passes, a route clearly marked on a 1968 chart, no longer exists. The glacier that remains is several hundred feet higher, and the traverse would be foolish on a scree precipice and hanging ice. The way now is to climb over Whatcom Peak. Similarly, we were thwarted at the Challenger Arm. There is no snow below the west and south rims of the Luna Cirque. The glacier below the southern rim is an impossible remnant. The way to Mount Fury is to descend into the cirque, climb the opposite headwall and then work through broken ice at the toe of the glacier under the north buttress. This unappealing but necessary exercise took an extra day. Our planned approach was unfeasible in anything less than twice the time described by its pioneers in the sixties.

RICHARD LOREN DOEGE

Oregon

Elephant Rock, Sixes Mountains, Southern Oregon Coast Range. On July 4, Wayne Wallace, Tim Olson and I climbed five pitches up the Elephant's Trunk (as seen from the northwest) with a sixth pitch on the summit block, an incredible andesite plug. Long run-outs on the face climbing were protected by thin pins, which gave good belays.

ROBERT MCGOWN

California

Deadman Buttress, Sonora Pass Region, 1982 and 1984. In July 1982 Don Neer and I climbed the *Arête Route* up crack systems on the central of the three buttresses on the south side of Highway 108, ½ mile east of Chipmunk Flat. The route is on the arête on the left of the rock when viewed from the highway. (II, 5.9.) Dave Parks and I did the *Dike Route* in August 1984. This is a four-pitch route up a difficult dike system to the right of the previous route. The first pitch is the crux. At the top of it, one can climb straight up through a trough and a dihedral or one can traverse right on the third pitch and follow cracks through a roof (III, 5.11a.)

STU POLACK, *Unaffiliated*

New Routes in Pinnacles National Monument. Lifeline follows an indistinct water chute on the Hand, about 20 feet right of the Salathé route. There are many bolts. (I, 5.10b.) *Peregrine* ascends in four pitches the farthest west and most massive water chute on the southeast face of the balconies. A short bolt ladder on the second pitch is the only aid. (II, 5.10d, A1.) *Bullrun* ascends a water chute on the cliff opposite and to the north of the route on North Yak. A bulge is the crux. (I, 5.8.) All these were done by Dave Parks and me over the last few winters.

STU POLACK, *Unaffiliated*

Clyde Minaret, Southeast Edge. After much consulting, Joel Richnik and I were pleasantly surprised to find no recorded ascent of the beautiful line that runs just right of the southeast edge proper of Clyde Minaret. The route begins near the base of this edge, far to the left of the popular southeast face route. Begin climbing in a series of shallow corners and continue up an off-width crack which is visible from the ground. Move up a ledgy face, fade right and then cut back left to the base of a right-facing dihedral. From the top of the dihedral, contour along the ridge up and right. When the ridge ends, follow the last part of the southeast face route.

MIKE CARVILLE

Midway Mountain, East Ridge, South Face. This route starts 30 feet right of a prominent right-facing dihedral. The first pitch is the crux, with 5.7 stemming and jam cracks to a belay slab. The next two pitches wander up and slightly left to the east ridge at 13,000 feet. From there it is easy to the summit. It was climbed in July by Mark Hoffman, Mark Tuttle and me. (II, 5.7.)

ROBIN INGRAHAM, *Jr.*

Mount Humphreys Variation. In August, Mark Hoffman and I followed the regular route to a point just below the normal class-4 pitch, which climbs the left side of the ridge crest. We traversed to the right side of the ridge and climbed a thin crack in an overhanging corner. This leads to class 3 just below the summit. (I, 5.9.)

ROBIN INGRAHAM, JR.

Ericsson Crag 3, Vinland. Fred Beckey and Reed Cundiff climbed the first route on the north side of the Ericsson Crags in 1972. In July, I returned with Fred to do a direct line on the face he had climbed 15 years previously. Our route followed the most obvious cracks just right of a prow in the center of the face. The original line was in bowls and depressions left of the prow although the *High Sierra Guide* mistakenly lists that route as being right of the prow. While there was no evidence of a previous ascent, a climb in 1982 recorded in the summit register telling of repeating the original route may have ascended sections of our route. In any case, we climbed cracks and chimneys right of the prow until we were led left to a prominent ledge right on the prow itself. A 5.8 thin crack above was the classic pitch of the route, which gave way to much easier climbing. (11 pitches. IV, 5.9.)

ALAN BARTLETT

Glen Aulin Area, Yosemite National Park. A number of fine routes have been done in this area over the past few years. The best approach is from near Pothole Dome in Tuolumne Meadows. This cross-country approach is much quicker than the trail from Soda Springs. Local climbers have taken to calling the main formation above the High Sierra Camp "Pluto Dome." This is the formation with the route Hiatus listed in Roper's *High Sierra Guide*. Below and right of Hiatus is a slab containing a number of fine one- and two-pitch routes done in 1987. These were reported in the December 1987 issue of *Climbing* and will not be listed here. In addition, the following routes have been done. *Primate Crossing* is a right-diagonaling flake/crack to the right of Hiatus. This three-pitch route was done by Rick Hooven and David Chen. (II, 5.11c.) *Bad News Bears* was done by Don Reid and me in 1985. It is the farthest right chimney system on Pluto Dome, easily visible from the High Sierra Camp. (II, 5.10c.) *Cooking with Teflon* lies on a northwest-facing slab across the river (west) from the camp. It is a finger crack in low-angle, very polished rock. This three-pitch climb was done by Mike Forkash and me in 1987. It requires a large assortment of thin protective devices. (II, 5.10b.) *California Corner* was climbed by Walt Shipley and me in 1987. This route is a mile downstream from the previous route and ascends a large, left-facing corner. (Four pitches. II, 5.9+.)

ALAN ROBERTS

Mount Whitney. This long route, *The Hairline*, ascends between the Great Book and the Direct East Face. It starts with 5.10 face climbing (bolt protected) to attain cracks which don't quite reach the ground. It crosses the East Face route just below the Fresh Air Traverse and stays left of the upper pitches of the Great Book. The route is about 30% aid. 20 to 25 pitons should be carried, as well as several kinds of hooks, nuts and Friends up to five inches. Bernie Bindner and I climbed it in August. (V, 5.10, A3.)

ALEX SCHMAUSS

Mount Whitney Area. The cirque south of where Pinnacle Ridge hits the main crest contains many fine possibilities and has generally been overlooked by climbers. The following four routes were climbed by Scott Ayers and me over the last few years. *Aiguille du Paquoir* is a squat tower immediately south of Aiguille Extra. Our route ascends corners for 11 pitches to the summit. (IV, 5.9.) *Aiguille Jr.* is the next tower south, taller than Aiguille du Paquoir. We started up the right buttress and climbed eight pitches to the top of the buttress before traversing to the left edge of the tower. (10 pitches. IV, 5.10.) *S'brutal Tower* is the next tower south. Our route climbs the prow for eight pitches, staying left of the prow for the first three. (III, 5.9.) *So Many Aiguilles, So Little Time* is on the south face of Pinnacle Ridge and climbs cracks in the center of the whitish face for six pitches. (III, 5.10+.)

MIKE STRASSMAN

North Dome, Kings Canyon. During the weekend of July 4, 1986, Gary Hinton, Blaine Neely and I climbed a new route to the right of Dolphin Dreams. *Freak Show* is mostly free climbing with aid consisting of hooking, thin flakes and steep, flared cracks. (V, 5.10, A3 + .) Between October 1985 and August 1987, several high-quality routes have been climbed on the polished apron near the right side of the "Roman Arch." This apron has been dubbed "Chernobyl Wall" due to the effect of the sun on a hot day. From left to right they are *Enchanted Pork Fist* (II, 5.10a; 2 pitches, face and crack climbing) by Mike Meng, Hinton and me in 1986; *Rainbow Warrier* (II, 5.11; 4 pitches, face climbing) 1st pitch in 1986 by Mike Stewart, Tom Grannaman, Hinton and me, 2nd, 3rd, 4th pitches in 1987 by Stewart, Miguel Cormona and Malcolm Ball; *Jerks on a Joyride* (II, 5.10b: 2 pitches, face and knobs) by Stewart, Grannaman, Hinton, Glen Short and me in 1986; *You Had a Hand in This Too* (I, 5.11a; 1 pitch, face climbing) by Herb Lager, Stewart, Pete Bishop, Greg Vernon and Neely in October 1985; *Split Lips and Broken Bits* (II, 5.10a; 2 pitches, crack and face climbing) by John Anders and me in June 1986; *Kibbles and Bits* (II, 5.10a; 2 pitches, crack and face climbing) by Anders and me in June 1986. Topos are available at the Cedar Grove Ranger Station.

CRAIG PEER, *D.O.C.C.*

Summit Registers. The focus of our club is climbing difficult routes on remote high-country peaks, seeking out the few remaining registers in the Sierra, and, more importantly, preserving this history and these records. Through our endeavors, I have seen five registers that date back to 1940 and in 1982 my climbing partner Mark Hoffman came upon a 1910 register on East Vidette. The record was filled up and has been removed. It served its purpose as a record for 72 years. Other records have not been so lucky. In 1912, Francis Farquhar, William Colby and Robert Price made the first ascent of Midway Mountain in the Great Western Divide. We know of the 1912 record because the *Climbers' Guide to the High Sierra* by Steve Roper states that Midway unquestionably had the oldest register in the range. When we reached the summit of Midway after our first ascent of the east ridge's south face, we found that the 1912 register had been stolen. A group of climbers calling themselves the "Purple Mountain Gang" claimed responsibility for the theft. One climber had the audacity to write, "I'm sad all old registers aren't left on peaks, or there would be no need for the register exchange program!" The Purple Mountain Gang's "register exchange program" involves taking a register from one mountain and placing it on another summit, possibly even in a different state. This I know, for in 1982 two friends of mine ascended Mount Dade in the Sierra Nevada. On the summit was a register labeled "Mount Dailey," and so this isn't just a local problem. Other incidents include the removal of the register from the northwest summit of Deerhorn Mountain. Up to 1976, the record dated back to 1931, with fewer than ten ascents. There is no way that with so few ascents the register could have been filled. In addition, Mount Humphreys unfortunately fell into this same category. On August 16, 1987, we reached this summit and found the register inside dated 1986. On the very first page, a climber wrote, "Six years ago this register dated back to 1935 and was only half full. I'd like to know who the idiot was who removed it so that I could have a few words with him." Climbers will not tolerate stealing historic summit registers. Possibly by increasing climber awareness in the area, the few remaining registers will survive for our children to see. The bottom line is LEAVE THE REGISTERS ON THE SUMMITS UNTIL THEY ARE FULL! These registers are not meant to be removed until they are full and state so on the very first page.

ROBIN INGRAHAM, JR., *High Sierra Alpinists of Merced*

Utah

Utah Desert Climbing. River Road Area: This is a local name for the section of State Highway 128 that follows the Colorado River east from US 191 at the Colorado River Bridge in Moab. *Rick's Rotten Ramp.* Rick Norman, Mike Meyer, Brett Maurer and Christine Blackman ascended this left-sloping ramp two crack systems right of Split Pillar in the River Road Dihedrals area on July 26. (I, 5.7.) *Frankin-Tony* was climbed in May by Tony Valdes and Steve Frank. The 70-foot route is on the rimrock above the River Road just west of mile-marker 6. (I, 5.10d.) *Fried Flounder* is on the west face of Big Bend Butte 7.5 miles up the River Road. The route is 350 feet right of the left edge of the landform. Rappel slings are visible from below. (I, 5.10b.) *Vivaldi Pinnacle* was first climbed by West Germans Franz Nebbe and Renate Stockburger. The four-pitch route is 200 feet left of the notch between Dolomite Spire and the right edge of Big Bend Butte. (II, 5.9, A0.) *Grim Reaper* was climbed on March 24 by Benny Bach and Cameron Burns. The route is 500 feet right of Dolomite Spire on the northeast side of the butte. (III, 5.10a.) *The Scorpion* was climbed by Harvey Carter and me on April 23. The 200-foot-high landform is in Richardson Amphitheater, east of mile-marker 23 on River Road. (III, 5.9.) *Farewell to the Desert* was climbed by Nebbe and Stockburger. The four-pitch route makes the first ascent of the Rectory from the east side. All other routes follow fracture lines on the mesa's west walls. The Rectory is immediately north of Castleton Tower (II, 5.8, A2.). *Renate Goes to Africa* was climbed by Nebbe and Stockburger on August 19. It is 300 yards from the north end of the west face of the Convent (the mesa north of the Rectory). (III, 5.8, A2.)

Potash Mine Road, Long Canyon Area: King's Left Hand was climbed by Bego Gerhard and Barry Miller on September 8. It is on the Potash Mine Road (State 279 a mile north of the Colorado River bridge, north of Moab), ¾ mile upstream from "Indian Writings." (II, 5.9.) *King's Right Hand* was climbed the same day by Tony Valdes, Paul Frank and Bob Milton. (II, 5.10.) *Seam As It Ever Was*, 5.2 miles up the Potash Mine Road, was first climbed by Dan Mannix and Alison Sheets. Rappel anchors are visible. (I, 5.11.) *Last Tango in Potash* was climbed by Kyle Copeland and Sheets on November 30. The route is 4.5 miles from Highway 191. (I, 5.11+.) *A Fistfull of Potash* was made by Charlie Fowler, Geoff Tobin and Tom Dickey. The route is the first crack system right of the previous route. (I, 5.11.) *Necro Dancer* is on the north side of Long Canyon 1¾ miles from Jug Handle Arch. (I, 5.10+.) *Dawn of an Error* is left of Necro Dancer (I, 5.11.) Both were done on April 9 by Copeland and Sue Kemp. Rappel anchors are visible from below. *Carter Chimney* was soloed by Harvey Carter in April. It is on the left side of Maverick Buttress. (I, 5.9.) Five climbs on Maverick Buttress were done in January by Charlie Fowler and Jack Roberts: *Hot Toddy* (I, 5.10b), *Tequila Sunrise* (I, 5.10d), *Gunsmoke* (I, 5.11a), *Miss Kitty Likes It That Way* (I, 5.11d), *Rawhide* (I. 5.11d).

Fisher Towers: Road Kill is a new route on the north side of Cottontail Tower and was climbed by Earl Wiggins, Art Wiggins and Katy Cassidy on November 13. The 7-pitch, 750-foot route begins at the right of an obvious buttress right of the original West Side Story route. (IV, 5.9, A4.) *Phantom Spirit* was soloed by Jim Beyer on February 25 and 26. The route ascends the east face of Echo Tower. (IV, 5.9, A3.) *World's End* was also soloed by Beyer in March. The 8-pitch climb begins 40 feet right of the Sundevil Chimney on the southwest face of the Titan. (VI, 5.9, A5.)

Moab Area: Mill Levy was climbed on December 1 by Earl Wiggins, Katy Cassidy and Dan Mannix. It is in the Airport Towers north of Moab and ascends 230 feet in three pitches up an obvious line on the prow of rock across from Echo Pinnacle at the entrance of Mill Canyon. (II, 5.11.)

Valley of the Gods: Eagle Plume Tower. The first ascent of the north face of this 350-foot route was done in the spring by Chip Wilson and Steve Bartlett. This route is on the opposite side from the original ascent line. (II, 5.4, A3.)

Texas Canyon: Texas Tower was first climbed on April 26 by Tim Toula and Kathy Zaiser. It rises 650 feet and is a desert classic, rivaling Spider Rock and Moses in beauty. (IV, 5.10+, A1.) Driving south on US 191 to State Highway 95, you follow signs to Bridges National Monument and at the visitor center you may get directions to the tower.

Indian Creek: There continue to be hundreds of ascents done each spring and autumn in the popular Indian Creek area. The location of the following routes requires a detailed topo of the region and thus they are listed only to document their ascent. Detailed approach may be researched in the new *Desert Rock Guide*, published in 1987 by the Chockstone Press of Denver. *Wild Works of Fire*, on the Supercrack Buttress, by Austrian Martin Wilberger and Swiss Romain Vogler (I, 5.11-); *Digital Readout*, by Alan Lester and Chip Chace (I, 5.12); *Zigi*, by Chace and Monika Lou (III, 5.12); *Fuel Injected Hard Body*, by Steve Petro and Kelly Moore (I, 5.12); *Little Face Climb*, on the Supercrack Buttress, by Germans Michael Beuter, Carmen Moritz and Christian Strasser (I, 5.11c); *Christmas Tree*, by Antonine Savelli and Teri Kane (I, 5.12c); *Paragon Prow*, by Stuart and Bret Ruckman (II, 5.11); *North Face of Six Shooter Peak*, by Dave Dawson and Dave Insley (II, 5.9).

Glen Canyon Recreation Area, Bathtub Butte: North Tower by Tom Thomas and Dan Mathews. 360 feet, 4 pitches. (III, 5.11, A2.) *Gunsight Pinnacle* by Thomas and Mathews. 360 feet, 4 pitches. (III, 5.11a.) Both are on Bathtub Butte which appears on the USGS quad as P 6229, east of Fiddler Butte.

ERIC BJØRNSTAD

Arches National Park. The park experienced its busiest year both in tourist visitation and climbing activity. A number of new routes were established on its relatively dense Entrada Sandstone walls. The park continues to encourage climbing (although a free permit is requested) and keeps an up-to-date loose-leaf notebook of new climbs at the visitor center. *Three Penguins.* Although it was originally climbed by Michael Kennedy and Molly Higgins in 1976, eleven years transpired before the second ascent was made in June 1987 by Tony Valdes and Sonja Paspal. *Argon Tower* had its first free ascent on October 12 by Tim Coates and Bret Ruckman (5.11). *Weapons of Love.* This 140-foot route climbs the Sand Bag before traversing left 250 feet and ascending to rappel anchors. The first ascent was made by Valdes and Kirk Miller. (5.10d, A2.) *Hall of Flame* was put up by Kyle Copeland and Alison Sheets. It is on the left side of the Candalabrum and climbs to the summit in three pitches. The only aid is on the final moves. (I, 5.11c, A2.) *Fledgling* was climbed on the 100-Yard Wall in January by Terre Lashier and Steve Swanke. It is located two landforms left of the popular Doil route on the 100-Yard Wall. Chris Begue and Scott Carsson made three new routes on the Park Avenue West area of the park: *Sand of a Beach* (I, 5.10a), *Black Celebration* (I, 5.10c), and *Many Miles Away* (I, 5.11a). Copeland and Sheets climbed *Hamburger Hell* on Headquarters Hill on December 1 (I, 5.11). This aesthetic route is 100 yards left of the Libbus Maximus route. *The Pickle* is a 150-foot spire between mile-markers 130 and 131, north of Moab, on US 191. Benny Bach, Cameron Burns and Ethan Putterman made the first ascent from May 19 to 21 (I, 5.9, A1). *Owl Rock*, first climbed solo by Ron Olevsky solo in February 1978, remains the most popular tower climb in the Arches. In March 1987 Italians Marco Ferrari and Patrizia Spadon climbed *Ala Sinistra* (Italian for "Left Wing"; I, 5.11, A0). This difficult route is on the west face of the tower, 20 feet left of the original ascent line. The same Italian pair also made a new route on Off Balanced Rock. *Camino* is at the right side of the chimney formed by the stout pillar-like structure on the north face (I, 5.10+). The first-ascent line follows the crack system left of the pillar. Jim Beyer, solo, established a fourth route on March 12 and 13 up the imposing walls of *The Organ*. The northwest buttress ascends to the summit in seven pitches (IV, 5.10, A3+). *Beached Whale-Whale of a Time* was climbed by Chris Begue and Alf Randell in April (I, 5.11a, A0). The route is south of the Eye of the Whale formation in the Herdina Park region. In the remote Klondike Bluffs four new routes were made in 1987. *False Start* was done by West Germans Franz Nebbe and Renate Stockburger in the Marching Men area (I, 5.8, A2+).

They also climbed two new routes on *Bouquet Tower* (I, 5.7 and I, 5,9). *Sand Hearse* was put up by Charlie Fowler and Jack Roberts on the northeast face of the landform four towers south of North Marcher (I, A2).

ERIC BJØRNSTAD

Canyonlands National Park. A free climbing permit is now required in both Arches and Canyonlands National Parks. *Druid Arch*'s south leg, east side, was climbed solo on February 7 and 8 by Paul Midkiff. This arch is in the Needles district of the park. *North Butte of the Cross* was first climbed by Paul Horton and Lyn Watson on May 15. They used no pitons or bolts (III, 5.9). It is near the northeastern border of the Glen Canyon National Recreational Area in the Maze of Canyonlands National Park. Four new routes were established in Lockhart Canyon on the cliffs behind the sandbar which is the first stop on the Colorado River for those running Cataract Canyon. The site is 20 miles down river from the standard put-in at the Potash Mine. This is roughly five miles southwest of Monster and Washerwoman Towers, although the climbs can only be reached by river. These routes were climbed in July by Mike Mayer, Brett Maurer and Christine Blackman: *Fist Fight* (I, 5.10b), *Beach Layback* (I, 5.8), *Dawn Delight* (I, 5.10a) and *Finger Fun* (I, 5.11b). In the *Taylor Canyon* area of Canyonlands National Park a number of new climbs were made. *Saddle Tower Buttress* was climbed by Tom Thomas and Dan Mathews (IV, 5.11-, A2). The tower is at the head of Rough Canyon, an offshoot of Taylor Canyon in the northwestern part of the park. The same pair made the first ascent of *Ekker Butte* (II, 5.11-), in the Maze district of the park. *Antelope Tower* was climbed by Thomas and Tony Moats (II, 5.10, A2). This is near Horseshoe Canyon. Jake Tratiak and Robert Alledrege climbed *Monkey Pin* (I, 5.8) 2½ miles from the junction of Beef Basin Road #104 and Bobbys Hole Road in the Needles District of the park.

ERIC BJØRNSTAD

Central Utah Ice Climbs. Several new ice climbs of high quality were done in January and February of 1987. These were located in Straight Creek Canyon, near Orangeville. Easy access via a maintained road and steep ice in a sandstone setting are ingredients of these classic waterfall climbs. *Beehive:* This 100-meter climb with overhanging cauliflower ice is up the most independently freestanding ice pillar in Utah. The crux involves a 10-meter section of overhanging ice. First ascent by Dean Hannibal and me in February (WI 5). *Angelic Life Form (ALF):* A series of vertical steps through vertical sandstone. Bob Ingle and I dedicated it to the memory of John Alf Engwall when we made the first ascent in January (WI 3). *Easy Wind:* A three-pitch ice climb west of ALF on the same cliff band. The third pitch ascends a beautiful pillar to a stance which is followed by a 5.6 move to the mesa top. First ascent by Bob Ingel and me in January (WI 3 +). All three have rappels off the mesa.

PHILIP D. POWERS, *National Outdoor Leadership School*

Provo Canyon. In August, Mark Galbraith and I climbed the prominent pedestal between the ice climbs "Finger of Fate" and "Bridalveil Falls." A long fist crack in the big left-facing corner is what attracted us. The climb starts just right of the pedestal and follows steep cracks interspersed with leftward traverses for two pitches to the base of the corner. One long lead up this corner on good rock landed us on the top of the spectacular pedestal. (II, 5.9.)

BRIAN SMOOT

The Organ, Zion National Park. During a week with three spring snowstorms, members of the Memphis Mountaineers climbed a new route on the Organ which starts 50 feet left (west) of the major gully system on the southeast corner of the formation. Pitch 1 ascended a long 5.6 slot with several small traverses to a major ledge system. Pitch 2 climbed a 5.7 off-width crack. Two long, loose fourth-class sections completed the route to the top of the eastern shoulder of the Organ. I led Dan Mauney and Eric Painter up the 610-foot route on March 8.

JIM DETTERLINE

Arizona

Navajolands. The Navajo still discourage climbing on the reservation. Spider Rock and Shiprock are definitely sacred to the Navajo. The northeast face of *Jacob's Monument* was a new route made on April 11 by Kyle Copeland and Sue Kemp (III, 5.10, A2). This spire is a few miles northwest of the Monument Valley Navajo Tribal Park. The first ascent of *West Elephant's Foot* was made by Kyle Copeland and Alison Sheets on November 28 (I, 5.9, A2). The second ascent was made on the same day by John Middendorf and Allen Humphreys. The Elephant's Feet formations are located beside Arizona Highway 64 near Red Lake in north central Arizona.

ERIC BJØRNSTAD

Montana

Castle Mountains. On June 7, Keith Brunckhorst and I climbed the west hanging buttress on the Stone Pillar behind the Stone Pillar Ranch. The first pitch was up a 5.10a slab now protected by two bolts to gain a 70-foot finger to hand crack. The second pitch went up a short vertical corner, then left onto a ledge, around a hanging corner to gain a class-4 ramp. The final pitch is easy fifth class. (I or II, 5.10a.) On September 11, Tom Bozeman and I climbed the largest formation in the Castle Mountains, a six-pitch route on the southwest wall. We followed the line of least resistance up the blank-looking wall. To gain the summit block, we scrambled 150 feet northwest to an easy 5th-class chimney. (II, 5.9.)

RON BRUNCKHORST, *Unaffiliated*

Tweedy Mountain, East Pioneers Mountains. In August, Craig Zaspel and I made the first ascent of Tweedy Mountain's north ridge, including the prominent tower. There were seven pitches of enjoyable alpine climbing followed by 500 feet of 4th-class climbing. (III, 5.7.)

RON BRUNCKHORST, *Unaffiliated*

Flathead Spire, South Face, Blodgett Canyon, Bitterroot Range. Wayne Wallace and I began this route by climbing the first two pitches of the Ballard-Everingham route to a good ledge below the base of a large dihedral, just to the right of "Afterburner." We followed the righthand dihedral with some loose rock to a large expanding flake which ends with a hand traverse to a small sloping ledge. Above the ledge is an improbable-looking groove; protection became better higher up. From an exposed foot ledge, we moved up and then crossed right to the second of two dihedrals. From its top we stepped to the right from below a small roof and continued up over several loose blocks to a large ledge with an anchor tree. We finished the route via an obvious crack that splits a small roof. (IV +, 5.11−; 10 pitches.) We dedicate this route to the memory of Richard Pierce, who lost his life shortly after reaching the summit of Pumori.

MICHAEL CARVILLE

Wyoming

Green River Pyramid, Wind River Range, 1986. This pyramid is very apparent from the Green River valley opposite Squaretop. In June 1986, Carl Horton, Shawn Mitchell and I climbed it by its southwest face. (III, 5.10a.)

FRED BECKEY

Cloud Peak, East Face, Big Horn Mountains, 1986. During the first week of August of 1986, Steve Petro and I made the first ascent of the east face of Cloud Peak. The face is about 1000 feet high and consists of generally smooth solid granite with several ledge and dihedral systems. The route begins 80 feet left of a prominent left-angling black dike. The climbing went all free and had occasional run-outs on easier ground. The first three pitches went at 5.10 on steep slabs leading up to the first 5.11 pitch. This fourth pitch, the crux, was the steepest; it was the last on the slabs and connected the route to the dihedrals. It involved delicate face climbing and traversing on small edges. Two moderate pitches above led to grassy ledges and a bivouac after the second day. The last two pitches (5.9 and 5.11) were done on the third day during a building storm. An average free-climbing rack of RPs, Friends and stoppers is adequate for the route. Six bolts were drilled on the climb. We approached from above and needed ice axes to descend the northernmost couloir.

ARNO ILGNER

Colorado

Colorado National Monument. Details of routes in Colorado National Monument are available in the new *Desert Rock Climbing Guide* published in 1987 by the Chockstone Press of Denver. In February, a new route was established on the *Oliver Perry-Smith Buttress* by Kyle Copeland, Charlie Fowler and Alison Sheets. The 350-foot Windgate Sandstone climb is 50 feet left of the original route (III, 5.10). Protection was with medium to large nuts. From February 6 to 8, Jim Beyer climbed *Red Desert* on Independence Monument. The difficult, predominantly aid route ascends the fracture line a few yards right (east) of the South Face Direct route and overhangs the bottom of the rock by 25 feet.

ERIC BJØRNSTAD

Deer Ridge Buttress and Longs Peak, Rocky Mountain National Park. On August 10, Scott Hall and Skip Daniel ascended a new route on Deer Ridge Buttress (II, 5.8.). It begins 100 feet left of Rainbow Rock and follows a direct line up the slab from a large pine tree growing out of the base of the rock to a dead tree 165 feet above on a major ledge and thence directly to the top of the formation. The first pitch starts up unprotected 5.6 climbing to an area of good cracks for protection and eventually a 5.8 crux friction mantle move. A horizontal flake 150 feet up provides a good belay. Pitch 2 follows an enjoyable 5.6 handcrack, and the final pitch (5.4) continues into the Rainbow Rock route. Unreported from 1986 is a new route (III, 5.10) on the east face of Longs Peak done by Kurt Oliver and me on July 30, 1986. Oliver christened it "Detterlines's Folly" because of my inability to follow any easier established routes. The seven-pitch line, done as a finish to Alexander's Chimney and the lower Eighth route, ascends a chimney system on the right of the upper Teeter Totter Buttress on mainly moderate rock, passing through a 40-foot section of 5.10 fingercrack shortly before finishing on the regular Teeter Totter route. Also unreported from 1986 is a two-pitch 5.8 route on Alligator Rock done by Lisa Reilly and me on August 9, 1986. It ascends the center of the 305-foot slab between the rappel gully and the central crack. It is mostly unprotected face-and-friction climbing.

JAMES DETTERLINE

Revolution Rock and Montgomery Cliff, Durango Area. The approach is via a gully to the west of Sweeney's Restaurant parking lot, north of Durango. Revolution Rock is the lower-angled slab. *Sandinistas* is the 150-foot route that begins at the very lowest point and goes up past four bolts. There is a moderate runout near the crux and a long runout on a 5.8 section right off the ground. It was first climbed by Lynda Pritchett, Alex Duncan and me in July. (I, 5.10a.) *Path of Dissent* goes up 40 feet right of Sandinista. One point of aid was used to gct past the third bolt. (1, 5.10.) *Rebel Waltz* is 60 feet farther right. There were long runouts on easy rock. (I, 5.7.) The last two climbs were first done by Pritchett and me in August. On Montgomery Cliff, Duncan and I did *No Exit* in July. This route lies on the crag above the slab. On the north face is a right-leaning dihedral with several blocks in it. Go to the two-bolt belay and rappel off. (I, 5.8.)

DAVID KOZAK

CANADA

Yukon Territory

Mounts Logan, Steele, Wood, Augusta and Upton, Icefield Ranges. During the 1987 climbing season there were 14 groups that climbed in the Icefield Ranges, as well as five that skied. Most of the expeditions were on Mount Logan. Canadians Steve Langley, John Lajeunesse, Matthew Friesen, Stewart Buroker, Dave Chase and Matt Groll climbed Logan's east ridge, as did Americans Dick Ratliff and Paul Richins of a joint Canadian-American party led by David Loeks. Canadians Don Serl, Jeff Marshall, Greg Foweraker and Mike Carlson climbed Mount Augusta by its west rib and then ascended Logan's east peak by the east ridge. Canadians Pierre Bay, Don Daniel and Yves Gilot were successful on their climb of Logan via the King Trench. Five expeditions failed on Logan's east ridge: four American expeditions led by Wally Orr, Phil Boyer, Ron Beauchamps and Steve Young, and Scots led by Charlie MacLeod. David Cheesmond and Catherine Freer are missing after their attempt on the Hummingbird Ridge and are presumed dead. Canadians Martyn Williams, George Henry, Joseph Johnson, Liz Desmore, and Roger Mitchell climbed Mount Steele along the southeast ridge. Canadians Gerald Holdsworth, Rory McIntosh, Mary Clayton and Liz Hofer climbed Steele via the Washburn-Bates route which goes through the saddle between Steele and Lucania. Holdsworth later joined Donjek Upton, Garth Mowat and Paul Langevin in an unsuccessful attempt on Mount Upton. Canadians Pat Sheehan, Greg Horne and Jeff Weir climbed Mount Wood, although Ron Chambers, Bob Haney, Ray Breneman, Bruce Sundbo, Charlie Zinkhan and Clerence Summers did not make it to the summit.

LLOYD FREESE, *Kluane National Park, Canada*

P 10,500+, North of Queen Mary, Saint Elias Mountains, Icefield Ranges. After a week of poor flying weather, Bill Proudman, Deb Caughron, Bobby Bonnet, Peter Hampson and I abandoned our original goal of Mount Kennedy and flew to the large unnamed glacier five miles north of Mount Queen Mary at 8500 feet. The next day, May 13, in excellent weather, we climbed P 10,500 + three miles north of Queen Mary by its west ridge. We skied and hiked the 70 odd miles out of the range. Pulling sleds we swung north to the major glacier system seven miles south of Donjek Mountain and then down onto the Kaskawulsh Glacier. Sleds, radio and climbing gear were then flown out, allowing us a lightweight three-day and 45-mile ski and hike down the Kaskawulsh and out Slims River to the Alaska Highway.

MICHAEL FISCHESSER

British Columbia

Mount Waddington and Other Peaks. Andy Tuthill, Bruce Anderson, Mark Bebie and I and Canadian Joe Bajan climbed the south side of Mount Waddington on July 30. From Base Camp at 7000 feet on the Dais Glacier, in marginal weather we followed the original Wiessner-House line. We third-classed to the end of the ramp and roped up for 15 pitches over good rock and ice to a bare, rocky, cold summit. We saw several pitons left by the original party. In a gathering storm, we bivouacked in the schrund formed by the summit tower on the northeast side. The next morning we descended to the west via the Angel Glacier and down a 1200-foot couloir at the northernmost point of the Dais Glacier (IV, 5.7, 37 hours round-trip). On August 2, Bebie and I traversed Cavalier, Squire and Halbredier to an unnamed spire south of Halbredier. We ascended the north ridge from the notch between the spire and Halbredier (I, 5.9). On August 3, Bajan and Tuthill climbed a prominent buttress visible from Base Camp on the Dais-Regal divide (II, 5.7). Anderson and Bebie repeated this on August 5. That same day, Tuthill and I climbed a new route on the 3000-foot south face of the northwest peak of Waddington. Starting from a prominent couloir at the base, we ascended on some verglas to its head and cut back right across a prominent snowfield. Instead of following the main couloir, we exited right on a verglas-coated rock ramp and ascended left and up for several pitches to the top of a spectacular flying buttress. Following this to an obvious short couloir, we exited just below the northwest summit at the top of the Angel Glacier. We descended as on the previous main-summit climb (IV, 5.7, 17 pitches, 20 hours round-trip). Anderson and Bebie repeated this climb on August 6.

STEVEN C. RISSE

Mount Moore, British Columbia Coast Mountains. Located south of Tatlayoko Lake and west of Chilko Lake, Mount Moore is a prominent mountain that features a spectacular hanging glacier, ice sheets and couloirs on its 2500-foot-high, broad northern face. Irving Day, Jim Couch and I flew to a base near the mountain in September. The difficult climb of the north face was done in cold, windy weather. A snow crust had formed over ice in the morning, but this turned to slush during the day. I turned back because of crampon problems after five pitches in the couloir leading to the upper glacier, but Day and Couch completed the 25 pitches of the long, slow ascent. The upper section had much exposure and was difficult to protect. They made a chilly bivouac on the descent. We rate it as Grade IV. The angle is a constant 50° to 60°.

FRED BECKEY

Mount Winstone, North Face, British Columbia Coast Range, 1986. In August 1986 Gary Silver and I approached via Taseko Lakes. The climb began at the same place as the Pilling-Gerson climb of 1983 but bears directly up steep snow and ice toward the west summit ridge to the left of the previous route. The snow-covered ice proved too dangerous to complete to the ridge and so the final six pitches were done on class-5 rock.

FRED BECKEY

Thunder Mountain, Northeast Face and Glacier, Bella Coola Area, British Columbia Coast Range, 1986. In September 1986, Reed Dowdle, Han Timmer and I approached by float plane from Bella Coola to Compass Lake. We hiked through tundra to a tarn beneath the Thunder Glacier. The climb itself was via a long snow gully to the main upper glacier and then through a maze of séracs and short ice walls. Several major traverses to avoid ice cliffs brought us to the summit ridge between the two peaks, Thunder Mountain and Mount Tzeetsaytsul. There were three technical ice pitches that required ice tools and front-pointing with ice-screw protection. Three rappels on the descent were made from bollards.

FRED BECKEY

Gemse Peak, Anderson River Group, British Columbia Cascade Range, 1986. Maxim de Jong, Sybil Goman and I climbed a new route (5.7) on Gemse Peak, the southwest face, in May 1986. We made one pendulum. The rock is solid but quite mossy.

FRED BECKEY

Lindeman, North Couloir, British Columbia Cascade Range. On November 14, Rob Freeman, Tim Hudson, John Petroske and I climbed a four-pitch snow-and-ice couloir on the north face of the north peak of Mount Lindeman. The prominent couloir parallels the north-edge route and averaged 45°. We approached via Centre Creek; the last five miles of the road were passable with a four-wheel-drive vehicle. We followed the timber slope southeast up the valley, staying close to the stream. From a meadow, we could climb either of two gullies on the right (south) side of the basin; the west one was easier. We contoured east under the broad northwest face and climbed to the higher (southern) of the two saddles between MacDonald and Lindeman. The route begins on a low-angle ice slope and steepens to the base of the couloir. From the top of the couloir, we scrambled class-3 to the north summit and then worked along the ridge class-4 to the main summit. We rappelled down the south side of the west ridge of the north peak.

KEN JOHNSON

Interior Ranges

South Howser Tower, Minaret, Bugaboos, Purcell Range. Fabrizio Defrancesco and I arrived in the Bugaboos on July 18. We first repeated some of the routes on Bugaboo Spire and Snowpatch. We then climbed a new route on the Minaret, a prominent rock pillar on the south face of South Howser Tower. After three days of climbing with one bivouac on the wall, we reached the top, following a beautiful crack system. The climbing was of continuous 5.10, A4 difficulty. The route gained 650 meters.

FABIO STEDILE, *Club Alpino Italiano*

Trinity Spire, Purcell Range, 1986. Sybil Goman, Reed Tindall and I climbed the east buttress of Trinity Spire (5.9) in August 1986. It was mostly cracks and some mossy rock. It was hard to protect. It has a lovely setting in St. Mary Provincial Park near Totem Lake.

FRED BECKEY

Pigeon Spire, East Face, Bugaboos. Tom Thomas, Dave Knox and I made a new climb in 12 hours on August 26 which is sure to be climbed free in the near future. The route followed the southern (left) portion of the east face of Pigeon Spire (V, 5.10, A2: 11 pitches). A complete description exists at the Boulder Cabin.

GIL McCORMICK, *Unaffiliated*

Mount Niflheim, Monashee Range. Mount Niflheim is 1.3 miles west of Mount Thor on the Thor-Odin Creek divide. To our knowledge, the summit had been reached only once, by a traverse from Thor. Gary Speer, Keith Hertel and I flew to the basin west of the peak and then made an exposed new Grade III route on July 24. This was somewhat complex but can best be described as the west face and southwest ridge. The quartzite rock was generally sound, though friable at times, and we sometimes found it difficult to give good protection. Its best feature was a full pitch of continuous 5.7 climbing. We hiked out in a summer downpour. Our tent came afloat when a nearby lake overflowed into a meadow where we were camped.

FRED BECKEY

Canadian Rockies

Mounts Outram and Erasmus, North Faces. Tom Thomas and I ascended the Glacier Lake Trail, fording the river just downstream from the lake. An excellent goat trail led us to timberline and we followed the main north ridge extending from the east shoulder of Mount Outram to Glacier Lake. We camped at 7800 feet below the main ice chute on the north face. The route ascended this 55° ice for 1000 feet to a rocky section. About five pitches of solid rock and ice up the leftmost of two main couloirs in the band brought us to the summit of Mount Outram on September 5. We descended the east ridge. By bushwhacking and following game trails from the Glacier Lake Trail, we made our way up the Valley of Lakes to below the north cirque of Mount Erasmus. We climbed the main couloir for 1000 feet to a rock chimney. Three pitches of rotten rock followed: 1. a rock chimney to a sloping rock in the gully; 2. a wall angling up and right; 3. a traverse back left and up the main chimney to the upper ice. There were 12 pitches of 50° to 70° ice to the summit of Mount Erasmus. We skirted left on the face near the summit and bivouacked in an ice cave just below the lip of the summit. An early morning start up an ice chimney popped us onto the summit snow slopes on September 13. An eight-hour descent via the west side and skirting back around to the north cirque brought us back to our camp. The grade V ascent took us 14 hours from camp to the bivouac and two hours from the cave to the summit.

GIL MCCORMICK*, *Unaffiliated*

*Recipient of an American Alpine Club Mountaineering Fellowship Grant.

Dieppe Mountain, Roosevelt-Churchill-Stalin Group, Muskwa Range. After our previous visit (*A.A.J., 1986, page 184*), we were so enchanted with the region of many unclimbed peaks that we returned in 1987. The problem is the approach with ferrying food and equipment and crossing streams. On June 11, Barbara Pasenow-Zimmermann and I left the bus at Mile 442 on the Alaska Highway. We traveled for four days along the woodroad to the abandoned Davis Keays copper mine. After a rest day, we climbed a ridge that led to a pass to the Magnum Creek valley. Finally, after a seven-day approach, we placed Base Camp four kms east of Dieppe Mountain in a side valley. After reconnaissance, we decided on the long, steep east ridge. After bad weather, we set out on June 24 at six A.M. At ten o'clock we got to the beginning of the ridge proper beyond a minor peak. We had to traverse two 70-meter-high towers. In places we broke into deep snow up to our thighs. There were some cornices. Most of the rock was of 5.2 difficulty with a 90-meter section of 5.4. In lightly falling snow and wind, we climbed the corniced ridge to the summit, which we reached at 7:30 P.M. We bivouacked beyond the second tower on the descent. There are other interesting unclimbed peaks in the region, but we had no more time. It took us three days

PLATE 32

Photo by Barbara Pasenow-Zimmermann

Dieppe Mountain's East Ridge is the right skyline.

to take the same route back (no more double relaying of loads). We had to belay each other while crossing Yedhe Creek.

RALF ZIMMERMANN, *Deutscher Alpenverein*

Canadian Arctic

Auyuittuq National Park, Cumberland Peninsula, Baffin Island. This was a busy climbing season. Nine mountaineering groups totaling 39 people from five countries visited the park for climbing or skiing. Mountain climbers comprised 9.4% of the park's overnight visitation of 414. There were three successful ascents of the Swiss route of Asgard by Günter Zimmermann's German party, Jon Turk's American group and Howard Bentley's British expedition. Turk's group also climbed Freya via the southeast buttress, possibly a new variation of the Scott route. There were two unsuccessful attempts on the west face of the south tower of Asgard. Earl Redfern, Will McCarthy and John Middendorf climbed 225 meters of the route, about one-third of it, but they were hampered by logistical and weather problems. The Spanish Bohigas brothers were back to attempt the west face a second time. They got to only about the same height as the Americans, being hampered by very poor weather. They had only three good days during the 35 they were in the park. The Warden Service is trying to complete its record of past climbing done in the park and would welcome any detailed reports readers may have in their files.

TOM ELLIOT, *Chief Park Warden, Auyuittuq National Park Reserve*

Thorndike Peaks, Ellesmere Island, North West Territories. This expedition, sponsored by the Explorers Club (Flag #200), operated during May in the Thorndike Peaks, south of the entrance to Makinson Inlet, on the east coast of Ellesmere Island. This was the fourth in a series of our expeditions (1976, 1978, 1980 and 1987) aimed at exploration among the virtually unknown peaks bordering this large fjord, an ideal location for Arctic ski mountaineering. Base Camp was reached via Twin Otter from Resolute Bay on May 12 after several delays due to bad weather. Despite an additional four days lost to the weather, after reaching our 900-foot Base Camp at 77°10′N, 79°35′W, our six-man expedition completed the first circuit of the Thorndike Glacier system. During this 25-mile ski trip, we traversed two valleys from the sea to across the main divide. We also made the first ascents of four peaks in altitude from 2750 to 3700 feet. We returned to Resolute on May 25. We were C. Saville, S. Bull, C. Proctor, L. Scotton, T. Ferguson and I.

G.V.B. COCHRAN

**The unnamed pass between the
Sorgenfri and Christian IV Glacier
on the Gunnsbjørnfjeld expedition,
Greenland.**

GREENLAND

Gunnsbjørnsfjeld. Our expedition made the third ascent of Gunnsbjørns-fjeld, Greenland's highest mountain, on August 8. It lies in the Watkins Mountains of East Greenland, north of Kangerlugssuaq Fjord. The peak was first climbed in 1935 by a party that included Courtauld, Wager and Longland. The second ascent was made in 1971 by a party led by Alastair Allan. Our 1987 group consisted of Robin Illingwood, Rob Ferguson, Steve McCabe and me as leader. We landed in Sodalen, Mikis Fjord, on July 22. We spent two days carrying stores and sledges over two miles of moraine to the Sodalen Glacier, where we could use cross-country skis and man-haul sledges. The route was initially difficult, taking a line between the East Frederiksborg and Sorgenfri Glaciers. We lost and gained much height. We crossed the Black Cap Pass, named by Wager, and descended to the Sorgenfri Glacier and across it to the Christian IV Glacier via another high previously uncrossed pass, south of Wager's Icefall Glacier Pass, from which we had a 200-foot, much-crevassed descent. This glacier is some 100 miles long and 15 miles wide. We had been delayed for two days by icefalls on the Sorgenfri Glacier, but once beyond there we found better sledging. By August 4, we had crossed the Christian IV Glacier after some difficulty with melt streams and crevasses. The 1935 and 1971 expeditions ascended Gunnsbjørnfjeld via Gino's Glacier which flows north-northwest from the summit. We did it differently. We left a depot, including one of the Nansen sledges, at the foot of Gino's Glacier and then sledged around the flank of the Watkins Mountains until we could attempt the ascent via an unnamed glacier on the peak's northern side. We made a depot at the foot of the unnamed glacier and established a high camp on August 7. After a summit attempt that same day which was frustrated by lassitude and soft snow, on August 8 we all reached the summit, which we feel to be about 4000 meters (13,123 feet), but which appears on the official Danish maps as 3700 meters (12,139 feet). There were few technical problems and we made the greater part of the ascent on skis. At the base of the summit pyramid, we joined the 1971 route on the northwest ridge. The 1935 party had ascended the south ridge. The northwest ridge did include a 150-foot pitch with a 40-foot section of ice, directly under the summit. Time prevented further climbs, as we were due back on the coast by August 19 for the flight out. On the return, we crossed the Christian IV Glacier to the Sorgenfri by Windy Gap, used and named by the 1935 expedition on its return to the coast. We checked one of their depot sites at Dumpen, unvisited in 52 years. Pemmican and butter were in good order, albeit the tins were a little rusty. The prize find was a sealed tin with some 80 bars of chocolate, still in perfect condition. Because from the summit of Windy Gap we could see that the surface of the Sorgenfri Glacier had deteriorated badly, we deposited the sledges and other equipment and backpacked to Sodalen, arriving there on August 18 after a round-trip of just under 200 miles.

STAN WOOLLEY, *England*

Snehätten, West Greenland. On August 13, Egidio Bolis, Dario De Nigro, Andrea Farina, Amedeo and Margherita Gatti, Emilio Moreschi, Giovanna Nava and I climbed Snehätten (Nugatsiaup Qaqa; 1765 meters, 5791 feet), the culminating point of Qeqertarssuaq (Nugatsiaq) Island, 100 kilometers north of Umanak. The climb on ice was easy. We set out from 650 meters, went up the Akerte valley and climbed the south spur. We were unroped and used crampons only for the last 250 meters. The mountain was probably first climbed by Greenlanders centuries ago in a time of glacial recession. We found on the top a huge ancient construction, 80 cms across the base and two meters tall.

PIERO NAVA, *Club Alpino Italiano*

Ketil, South Greenland. A strong four-man Austrian team from Lienz under the leadership of Siegfried Girstmair spent three weeks in June and July on the Tasermiut Fjord area. In very fine weather they were able to repeat the 1974 Austrian route on the south face of Ketil Fjeld (2010 meters, 6595 feet) in two days of climbing (UIAA V to VI difficulty). They also made a new route on the east face of Kirkespiret on the western side of the fjord and a three-day ski trip onto the inland icecap.

DOLFI ROTOVNIK, *Dansk Bjergklub*

Ketil Attempt. During four weeks in July and August, three Danes, Sören Smid, Uffe Mortensen and I, and Swede Magnus Nilsson climbed in the granite section of Tasermiut Fjord. Our main objective was the smooth west face of Ketil Fjeld. We gave up a new route after 250 meters on the right of the face beside the 1984 Piola route because of dangerous loose flakes. We turned to a repetition of the 1984 Catalan route. Six ropes were fixed and two nights spent in portaledges before a major föhn storm struck. After a sitting bivouac 400 meters below the top, the weather forced a retreat first to the wrecked portaledge camp and then all the way down. The weather was never settled during our stay, in strong contrast to that of spring and early summer, which gave South Greenland the warmest, sunniest weather in decades.

MICHAEL HJORTH, *Dansk Bjergklub*

Stauning Alper. I have just (February) received information on a French expedition led by François Wolf with two others. They did 400 kilometers on skis and made three first ascents. They descended all the mountains by *parapente*, the first time this has been done in Greenland. Details are lacking.

DOLFI ROTOVNIK, *Dansk Bjergklub*

Lauper Bjerg Attempt, East Greenland. The British Tasilaq Expedition started with four members: Anthony Day, Stuart Raeburn, Nigel Topping and me. Unfortunately, Day had to leave the expedition early. Along with geological and glaciological studies, one of our major aims during our ten weeks in Greenland was to attempt the first British ascent of Lauper Bjerg (2580 meters, 8465 feet), first climbed by Swiss in 1938. After skiing 100 kilometers from Tasilaq Fjord, just south of the Arctic Circle, Raeburn, Topping and I reached the peak early on July 26. We decided to attempt a new route from the northeast, involving 1300 meters of ascent, long and committing, but technically straightforward. We skied to the foot of the climb that same day and made steady progress over mixed ground to the top of the subsidiary northeast spur, where I decided to return, allowing the other two to continue faster. Two abseils and scrambling down loose rock allowed Raeburn and Topping to work onto the northeast face. Unfortunately, when they were only 25 meters from the east ridge and a few hundred meters from the summit, they were were hit by an avalanche. Both had only minor bruises, but after twelve hours on the mountain, they decided to retreat. By August 4, we had safely returned to Base Camp on Tasilaq Fjord.

GRAHAM POOLE, *Cambridge University, England*

MEXICO

Cerro Blanco. Steve Grossman, Peter Noebels and I made a new route on the western portion of the broad south face of this gigantic rock formation on January 1. The peak can be seen from the rural town of Peñón Blanco. The pillar is to the left of the south promontory, very distinctive in shape and reddish in tone. The rock is superb with fine slab climbing and some interesting shallow face cracks. (III, 5.9.)

FRED BECKEY

SOUTH AMERICA

Ecuador

El Obispo, 1986. The first Venezuelan expedition to the Altar group was led by Luis Troconis. We shouldered supplies to the traditional Base Camp south of El Obispo. On December 25, 1986, we placed two tents at 4900 meters and the following morning we set out in two teams for the summit (5319 meters, 17,450 feet). C. Pernalete and N. Rojas made a new variant up the southwest ridge, while Troconis, Dora Ocanto and I made the second ascent of the Calvario variant on the normal route. An Ecuadorian team led by M. Purúncajas climbed our route right behind us. We did not reach our tents until six A.M. the next morning while the Ecuadorians bivouacked on the wall. On

December 27, Rojas and I climbed Monja Grande (5160 meters, 16,929 feet) by its exceedingly steep *canal de hielo* (ice gully), on the south face. Before leaving Ecuador, Ocanto, Rojas and Troconis climbed Chimborazo by its normal route.

José Betancourt, *Club Universitario de Andinismo y Excusionismo,*
Mérida, Venezuela

Chimborazo. Italian A. Campanile made what he feels was a new route to the right of the Direttissima to the summit of Cima Ventimilla. There were considerable difficulties in the ice of the upper part, especially below the final séracs, where the slope was of 75°.

Peru—Cordillera Blanca

Climbs in the Cordillera Blanca. Each year there is more climbing in the Cordillera Blanca. The first expedition in 1987 was composed of Colombians Fernando Pizzaro and Daniel Herrera, who climbed Tocllaraju on April 26. A few new routes were made. Italians Marco Schenone, Guido Ghigo and Enrico Tessera made the first ascent of the delicate mixed southeast face of Vallunaraju Sur on August 8. Slovenes (Yugoslavs) Marjan Freser, Milan Romih and Danilo Tič, climbed a difficult new route on the north face of Huandoy Norte; it ascends for 1445 meters up the great dihedral to the left of the big rock wall. Spaniards Chema Polanco, Manolo Oliviera, Eduardo de la Cal and Alejandro Madrid climbed a new route on the Torre de Parón (Sphinx), the south face (860 meters). Notable ascents included a repeat of the Australian 1985 route on the south face direct of Chacraraju Este. On July 25 Englishman Mick Dovie and Belgian Lars Vanhaelewyer and on July 30 New Zealander Brian Alder solo all were able to exit from the face directly over the cornice onto the summit; the Australians had had to traverse toward the east face and then climb to the summit from there. On July 26, Spanish Basques Pedro Sánchez, Francisco José Ruiz and Joan Cortejo repeated the Barrard route on the east face of Huascarán Norte. Caraz I was climbed by Yugoslavs Franc Čanžek and Ivanič Iztok on June 5, by Drago Praprotnik and Miha Uršič on June 6, and by Anton Pavlič, Andrej Grudnik, Erjavec Bošjan, Zdenko Cigljar, Miha Šorgelj and Victor Hribar on June 10. The west ridge of Huascarán Sur was climbed by members of the same group: Milan Jolič and Dušan Habolin on June 21, and by Praprotnik, Hribar, Uršič and Zdenko Zorič on June 23. Some of the expeditions climbed with incredible speed. On May 15, Swiss Jean-Claude Tondre and Pierre Dafflon climbed Pisco in 2½ hours and descended in an hour, Base Camp to summit and back. On May 22, they climbed the north face of Quitaraju in three hours and descended in 1½ hours. On May 23, they ascended the southwest-face (Ferrari) route of Alpamayo round trip in 3¾ hours. On May 30, it was Artesonraju's south face in three hours up and down. On June 7, joined by German Manfred Mehl, they took

PLATE 34

Photo by Milan Romih

**North Face of HUASCARÁN
NORTE, showing Slovene Route.
Bivouacs are marked.**

seven hours to climb Chopicalqui from the moraine camp and back again. The same three climbed Huascarán Sur in three hours from the Garganta and descended to there in 1½ hours. Italian Fabrizio Manoni on the southwest-face (French direct) route of Alpamayo in three hours and on July 15 the south face of Ocshapalca in 4½ hours. On June 3, Gladiz Diaz and I climbed Vallunaraju Norte in a single day from Huaraz. There were innumerable other ascents in the Cordillera Blanca, at least the number noted on the following: Alpamayo (15, mostly on the southwest face routes), Artesonraju (11), Tocllaraju (8), Huascarán Sur (6), Chopicalqui (6), Quitaraju (5), Pisco (4), Ranrapalca (4).

WALTER SILVERIO, *Asociación de Guías de Montaña del Perú*

Huascarán Norte, North Face. Danilo Tič, Marjan Freser and I first made four acclimatization climbs. We wanted to climb Huascarán's south face, but alternate snow and rain forced us to change our plans. We started for an unclimbed route on the north face of Huascarán Norte on June 29 and reached the steep part of the wall (UIAA difficulty V, 50° to 60° ice). The greatest threat there was rockfall and falling ice. We lost one rope. The next day we climbed five vertical pitches on brittle ice-covered rock (VI to VII−). We reached the ridge on the left of the face on the third day. The route was up a steep couloir at the top of which a sérac provided a bivouac site (VI+, 55° to 70° ice). The weather turned bad in the afternoon and it snowed all night. We got to the summit at ten A.M. on July 2 in falling snow and thick fog. Soaked and shivering with cold, we made a complicated descent starting down the standard route, which luckily Tič and I had climbed last year. We finally got back to the Llanganuco valley the next day.

MILAN ROMIH, *Alpinistični Odsek Impol, Yugoslavia*

Caraz III, South Face. On June 28, Haroon Khesghi and I climbed the south face of Caraz III (5720 meters, 18,767 feet). We started in a couloir that runs up just to the right of the summit. The climb was similar in length and difficulty to the southwest-face direct route on Alpamayo, involving eight pitches of snow and ice at about 55°. Then there were the final two pitches to the ridge with sections of ice up to 90°. The ridge was a knife-edged horror complete with several large holes; therefore we did not climb the last traversing pitch to the actual summit. After eight scary rappels in the dark, we reached the glacier.

GEORGE BELL, JR.

Pucaranra West Face. Several days of perfect weather were not enough to stabilize the snow at the base of Palcaraju and so Thor Kieser and I decided to try a line of the west face of Pucaranra across the Quebrada Cojup. There were several interesting lines that seemed as if they could avoid the overhanging ice

PLATE 35

Photo by George Bell, Jr.

South Face of CARAZ III.

blocks in the upper section of the face, especially steep ice couloirs on the north side of the face close to the ridge that connects Pucaranra and Palcaraju. We spent several hours on the afternoon of July 13 searching for the best route across the glacier. The next morning we left with rather heavy packs. The first section lay up an obvious avalanche chute that had us puffing to get to the safety of the bergschrund. Once above that obstacle, the face got significantly steeper. We came to the rock bands and had little difficulty with them. In the main couloir above, the angle steepened to 70° in places and the ice got harder. By midday the ice had begun to run water and ice screws were little more than a psychological protection. Finally at three P.M. we sighted a convenient cave at the top of the couloir and settled down for a long, cold night. On July 15 we continued to the top with a few exciting moments, such as dodging falling ice and crossing precarious snow bridges. We descended to the cave for a second bivouac and returned to Base Camp the following day. This line seems to be the same one that Spaniards were unable to complete in 1980 and may have been subsequently climbed by Poles in 1985.

ROGER GOCKING

Palcaraju and Santa Cruz. Between June 21 and July 21, fourteen Slovene climbers were active in the Cordillera Blanca. Aside from ascents on Artesonraju, Alpamayo and Huascarán, they made three new routes. On June 30, Emil Tratnik made the first traverse from Palcaraju to Palcaraju Sur, which was generally 50° to 60° with stretches of 80°. That same day Peter Poljanec and Žarko Trušnovec ascended the west ridge of Palcaraju, which was extremely difficult with very steep ice. The most important new route was on the south face of Santa Cruz, which Andrej Lužnik, Tratnik, Poljanec and Trušnovec ascended on July 7 and 8 in 18 hours of climbing. (See below.) This was Trušnovec's twelfth new route in the cordilleras of Peru.

FRANCI SAVENC, *Planinska Zveza Slovenije, Yugoslavia*

Santa Cruz South Face. On June 7 and 8, Emil Tratnik, Andrej Lužnik, Peter Poljanec and I climbed the 1200-meter-high south face of Santa Cruz. We had very bad snow conditions and had to bivouac when we gained the west ridge. In the last part there was a 150-meter section which was the most difficult part of the climb: a rock-and-ice barrier with rock of UIAA VI difficulty and ice of 90°. We descended the north face to the Los Cedros valley; it took us two days to return to the Cashapampa valley.

ŽARKO TRUŠNOVEC, *Idrija, Yugoslavia*

Torre de Parón. Four Spaniards from Madrid made an impressive new route on the 900-meter-high east buttress of the Torree de Parón, taking eight days and climbing UIAA difficulty of VI+, A3. The crux pitches were on the second quarter of the buttress. They climbed in two pairs, the first preparing the route and the second carrying the equipment. The summit was reached on August 20 by Manolo Olivera, Alejandro Madrid, Eduardo de la Cal and Chema Polanco. The route ascends left of the 1985 Bohorquez-García route. That pair made the first route on the face in ten days.

JÓZEF NYKA, *Editor, Taternik, Poland*

Peru—Other Ranges

Kikash, Huaman Hueque Group, Cordillera Huallanca, 1984 and 1986. In the Río Pativilca valley between the Cordilleras Blanca and Huayhuash is the little town of Aquia. Immediately to the east lies the Huaman Hueque group, a relatively virgin area. (Domingos Giobbi climbed farther to the north in 1968.) The group is dominated by a peak of 5338 meters (17,514 feet), referred to locally as Nevado Kikash, although the Kinzl-Schneider map calls it Pampash. Michael Stewart and I went into the area in July 1984 and, on a bad steer from a *campesino*, approached the peak from the southwest. On our first attempt we thrashed through an obstacle course of crags; our second attempt, further up the valley, was equally unsuccessful when we found ourselves confronted with steep slabs of wet rock. The third attempt got us past the ridge, but circling to the left of a rock buttress, we discovered another valley stretching out before us that we hadn't even known was there. The mountain was not the cone it had appeared from the distance but more like an unlucky horseshoe. We were well out to the side, blocked with insufficient rock gear by a buttress. Foiled again! We tried again, this time up a snow spur on the center right side of the valley and onto a hanging glacier. It went! We climbed up the glacier to the crest and then along 500 feet of knife-edged snow and ice to the summit tower, a single pitch of high-angle mixed climbing. We got to the top of the western of two pinnacles. The other one was 50 feet away and 15 feet higher. We didn't have the time or rock equipment to climb it. In the last weekend of August, I came back with Daniel Maldonado. We went into the Huaman Hueque valley and found an easier route onto the upper part of the mountain. The summit pyramid looked even more formidable, but looks were deceiving; we were able to reach the summit after half a pitch of exposed class 3. In 1986 Michael and I went back to the Huaman Hueque with John Dupuy and Chuck Watson. We followed the prominent trail that turned east over the pass into the next valley, crossed the scree slopes at its head and climbed the highest peak just south of the pass.

DOUGLAS RICE, *Unaffiliated*

Yerupajá and Jirishanca West Face. After arriving at Cajatambo by bus, Toni Ponholzer, Dr. Rolf Klett, Erich Grossegger, Mario Bürgen and I took four days to reach Base Camp at Jahuacocha. We then placed a camp at 5250 meters on the Yerupajá Glacier. On August 1, we started up Rasac for

PLATE 36

Photo by H. Adams Carter

JIRISHANCA from the West. The Austrian route is marked.

acclimatization but dangerous ice conditions forced us back at 5900 meters. On the 2nd we started up the west face of Yerupajá and bivouacked at 6200 meters at four P.M. in bad weather. We got to the summit the next morning. On August 4 we helped in the rescue of a climber who had fallen from the south summit of Yerupajá. On August 7, we placed a camp at 4950 meters on the Jirishanca Glacier. On August 8 and 9, Ponholzer and Bürger climbed the west face of Jirishanca. From their tent they ascended the very broken glacier for 1½ hours to the base of the wall. The lower part had mixed climbing. The first difficulty was a long traverse under the hanging glacier on 70° blue ice. From there they climbed straight up the fall-line to the summit. The slope became steeper as they ascended and was 80° near the summit. The rock sections near the top were of UIAA III to IV difficulty. The summit ridge was heavily corniced. They descended by the ascent route.

WALTER PETODNIG, *Österreichischer Alpenverein*

Huacratanca Traverse, Cordillera Urubamba. David Nicholson and I traversed the two peaks of Huacratanca from August 3 to 9. We went up the southwest glacier and up the west ridge. The northwest summit has been given as about 5200 meters and the east summit as 5000 meters. We descended the east ridge.

CARLOS BUHLER

Colque Cruz, Cordillera Vilcanota. An Italian expedition composed of Italo Bazzini, Mario Giacomelli, Livio Lanari and Roberto Manni climbed Colque Cruz, reaching the summit (6104 meters, 20,026 feet) on July 29. They had hoped to climb a direct route up the north ice face, but crevasses blocked the way and they had to deviate to the east. Their Base Camp was in the Muyoccocha valley at 4740 meters. After climbing slopes of 50° to 60°, they bivouacked at 5800 meters. From there they traversed up to the right. The last 150 meters were very steep, up to 80°. A photograph of their route appears in *Lo Scarpone* of December 16, 1987 on page 13.

Cordilleras Occidental (Volcánica) and Yauyos. Our 12-member Polish expedition first visited the Cordillera Occidental, establishing Base Camp at 4500 meters at Llullipampa, east of Ampato. On June 24 and 25, Kazimierz Głazek, Henryk Gawarecki, Kazimierz Pichlak and Jerzy Olech climbed the east summit of Ampato by the German southeast-face route. The ascent was later done by Kazimierz Sokołowski and me. From June 28 to 30, Kazimierz and Stanisław Głazek traversed all three summits of Nevado Ampato (6288 meters, 20,631 feet), having reached the southwest summit by a 40° to 55° ice couloir. On July 1, Wojciech Gala and Władysław Sarniak in eight hours completed a direct route on the southeast face of the northeast summit (6050 meters, 19,849 feet) on ice up to 70°. On June 30, during an attempt on the southeast face of Hualca Hualca (6025 meters, 19,767 feet) with Olech and Pichlak, Henryk Gawarecki was killed. He fell into a deep crevasse 150 meters from the top, carrying the party's only rope. The other two could make no contact with him and lacking a rope, could not descend into the crevasse. Five of the expedition then moved to the Huayllacancha valley of the Cordillera Yauyos. Jerzy Zontek and I climbed Padrecacca (5362 meters, 17,592 feet) by the east ridge on August 1. At the same time, the two Głazeks attempted the southeast ice face of Cotuní or Ticlla (5897 meters, 19,347 feet) and got to 5600 meters.

ANTONI SIDOROWICZ, *Klub Wysokogórski, Wrocław, Poland*

Bolivia

Mururata and Pico Schulze, Cordillera Real. Yugoslavs from Slovenia climbed in the Cordillera Real from May 9 to 31. Aside from climbs on Huayna Potosí and Illimani, they made three new routes. On May 18, Filip Bertoncelj, Bojan Počkar, Bojan Pograjc and Jernej Stritih took ten hours to climb the couloir on the south face of Mururata (5868 meters, 19,253 feet). The ascent rose for 540 meters from the glacier to a point just to the left of the summit. Two pitches were of 90° and much was between 60° and 70°. They made two new routes on Pico Schulze (5830 meters, 19,128 feet). On May 26, Pograjc and Počkar climbed the southeast face, while Stritih and Matjaž Vrtovec climbed the couloir in the southwest face. The latter route was extremely difficult.

FRANCI SAVENC, *Planinska Zveza Slovenije, Yugoslavia*

Chacacomani and Other Peaks, Cordillera Real, 1983. Our attention has just been called to a German expedition led by Georg Seifried and composed of Treuhard Hanke, Jürgen Bäumler, Peter Koch, Reinhold Siegel and Udo Knittel. Most of the mountains may be found on the 1:50,000 Bolivian IGM map 5945 IV, *Lago Khara Kkota.* All peaks which were not first ascents are noted. The Bavarians established Base Camp at 4440 meters in the Chacacomani valley on May 23, 1983. On May 24, Seifried and Hanke traversed from northeast to southwest all the seven summits of the group which lay south of Base Camp, from Jachcha Jokho (5192 meters) over Jachcha Kkollu (5298 meters) to Jayllahuaya Kunka (5300 meters) and climbed P 5260, an outlier to the west. Knittel and Siegel fell mountain sick and had to be temporarily evacuated. On May 26, Koch and Bäumler ascended a valley to the east side of the southeast outlier of Patapatani, which they climbed. Koch continued up the south ridge to the top of Patapatani (5452 meters) and Koch climbed the west face. This climb was repeated by Hanke the next day. Also on May 27, Seifried and Koch climbed Jachcha Thojo (5358 meters) by its east ridge. While Koch descended the south ridge, Seifried continued west over Wila

Wilani (5260 meters) and P 5250 before returning the same way to rejoin Koch. Together they traversed south over P 5270, P 5250 and Huarisepitaña (5314 meters). Seifried soloed Jankho Airi (5150 meters), the next peak to the east. On May 29, they established a high camp at 5100 meters southeast of Huari Umaña for climbs in the Chacacomani group. On May 30, Seifried, Koch, Bäumler and Hanke traveled northeast for four hours to the 5700-meter col between Chacacomani and Himaciña and continued up Himaciña's north ridge to the summit (5830 meters). On May 31, all four set out on the route of the previous day, climbed to the col between Chacacomani and its western outlier and on to the summit (5750 meters) of the latter by its east ridge. From the col Koch and Bäumler climbed Chacacomani Oeste (6045 meters) by its north face, while Seifried and Hanke traversed over the west ridge of Chacacomani Oeste, down the east ridge and onto the summit of Chacacomani Este (6066 meters). They believe that these were the third ascents of both the Chacacomani summits, but by new routes. On June 1, all four set out, hoping to climb Chearoco. They found that the glacial plateau dropped off from 5600 meters almost vertically for 600 meters to Chearoco Pass and so they turned to a 5810-meter snow dome northwest of Chacacomani, which they climbed by its south slope and east ridge. They then climbed Jakocire (5540 meters) by its north ridge. That same day, Seifried soloed Huari Umaña (5264 meters) by its south-southwest ridge. Meanwhile, Knittel and Siegel had recovered and set up camp at 4750 meters in the Huarca Jahuira valley, west of Potrero. On June 1, they climbed the north peak of Potrera (5100 meters) by its northwest face. On June 2, this pair climbed P 5225 from the north and continued south to the summit (5252 meters) of the right-hand of the two peaks given on the Bolivian IGM map 5945 IV as Cerro Himaciña and to P 5340. Not finding the others, this pair returned to La Paz. On June 3 the other four moved over the Himaciña Pass to establish a new Base Camp at 5240 meters. On June 4, they climbed by its west face and south ridge "Dambil Bamba" (5510 meters), which lies southeast of the pass; local people supplied them the name. They then began their withdrawal. On June 6, they camped below the Junka Laya Pass at 4900 meters and that same day all climbed by its northeast ridge Jalli Huaykunka (5392 meters) to the west of the pass. This was a second ascent. Seifried that day also crossed the valley, climbed the 5300-meter peak north of Cerro Janko Laya and traversed north over two more summits to Potrero (5150 meters). On June 7, Koch, Bächler and Hanke crossed the Mollo Pass and returned to La Paz. Seifried climbed to camp west of the pass. On June 8, he climbed P 5250 and P 5200 west of the pass, crossed over the top of the pass and climbed the north and main (5244 meters) peaks of Wila Llojeta. The latter two had been previously climbed. On June 10, Koch, Siegel and Knittel climbed Huayna Potosí. (We are grateful to Georg Seifried for this information.)

Chearoco and Other Peaks, Cordillera Real, and Sajama, 1985. After an acclimatization climb on May 25, 1985 of Colquejahui in the Hampaturi group, Bavarians Georg and Josef Seifried and Robert Wagner on May 26 placed Base Camp at 4650 meters a kilometer from the end of the Kellhuani valley. On May 27, they all climbed a 5000-meter peak north of Base Camp. On May 28, they ascended both peaks of the highest mountain north of Base Camp. They climbed the south buttress and southwest ridge of the lower western summit (c. 5420 meters) and traversed to the eastern summit (c. 5470 meters). On May 29, Georg Seifried soloed a number of peaks east of Base Camp. He ascended a valley that divides Thojo Loma from Patapatani, turned south over a foresummit to climb Thojo Loma (5174 meters) and continued southwest to another foresummit. From there he crossed the southeastern slopes of Thojo Loma to a 5050-meter col north of Patapatani. He climbed the east ridge of the peak west of the col (c. 5170 meters). He completed a long day by making the second ascent of Patapatani (5452 meters) by its north ridge. On June 1, Wagner climbed Thojo Loma and P 5170. That same day, the Seifried brothers ascended a peak (c. 5260 meters) north of Base Camp by its rather difficult southwest buttress. On June 2, the two Seifrieds made a new route, the southeast face and southeast ridge of Chearoco (6134 meters). This is probably the fourth different route on this peak. They climbed to the 5000-meter Chearoco Pass. After crossing a crevassed area, they gained the southeast ridge at 5500 meters. They then left the Cordillera Real and traveled to Sajama to camp at 5060 meters below the southwest ridge. On June 4, they all three climbed Sajama 6542 meters) by its east buttress. To reach the foot of the buttress at 4800 meters, they had a 3½ hour traverse. Nearly vertical ice at 5850 meters was the most difficult part. They feel this was a new route. They descended the south ridge. (We are also grateful to Georg Seifried for this report.)

Haucaña, Hancopiti and Illampu, Cordillera Real, 1986. Six Polish climbers led by Waldemar Zmurko made eleven alpine-style ascents in June 1986, including three new routes in the Ancohuma group: Haucaña (6206 meters, 20,360 feet) via 45° to 50° west face on June 12, 1986 by Lech Badzyński, Maciej Marczak, Adam Pierzyński and Zmurko; Hancopiti I (5867 meters, 19,249 feet) via the 55° to 60° center of the northwest face on June 13 by Marek Koszelak and Krzysztof Wesołek; and Illampu (6362 meters, 20,873 feet) via the 45° to 60° left side of the south face on June 16 and 17 by Marczak and Zmurko.

JÓZEF NYKA, *Editor, Taternik, Poland*

Araca and Choquetango Groups, Quimsa Cruz. This expedition of Germans was led by Hermann Wolf and composed of Rudi Bülter, Georg Fichtner, Christian Griesshammer, Peter Hacker, Karl-Heinz Hetz, Widukind Langenmaier, Michael Lentrodt, Michael Magerer, Gerhard Rebitzer, Georg tom Felde and Christof Wittmann. They also invited five Bolivians to join them full-time: Juan Carlos Andia, José Camarlinghi, José Miranda, Javier and José Thellaeche. With them for part of the expedition were Juan Bustamante,

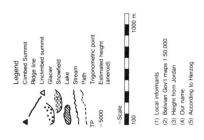

Legend

▲ Climbed Summit
△ Unclimbed summit
Ridge line
Glacier
Snowfield
Lake
Stream
Path
TP Trigonometric point
≈5000 Estimated height (aneroid)

Scale

≈100 1000 m

(1) Local informants
(2) Bolivian Gov't maps 1:50.000
(3) Height from Jordan
(4) Our name
(5) According to Herzog

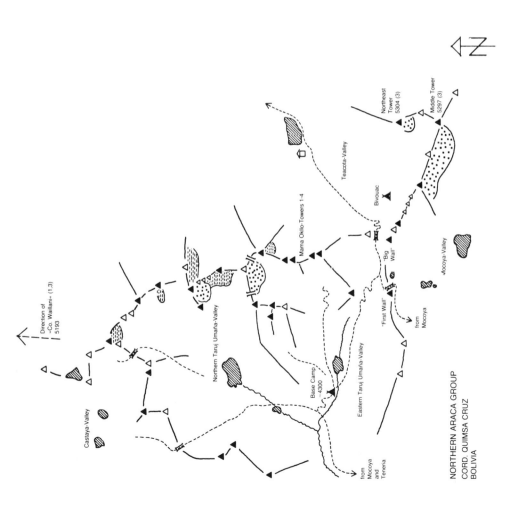

NORTHERN ARACA GROUP
CORD. QUIMSA CRUZ
BOLIVIA

Marcos Olivares and Rainer Müller. They were in Bolivia from May 24 to June 25. They were hosted by Hans Hesse, owner of the Hacienda Teneria, southeast of Illimani on the edge of the Quimsa Cruz range. There they divided into two groups. The larger party traveled by truck to Mocoya and then walked to Base Camp at 4300 meters in the eastern Taraj Umaña valley at the western end of the lake Chillhua (or Chilliwani) Kkota. They made a large number of climbs, most of them first ascents. These were in most cases difficult rock climbs on the excellent granodiorite of the region. The climbs follow: P 5050 (between P 5145 and P 5124 northwest of Mama Okllo) via north-south traverse by Hetz, J. Thellaeche, Wolf (also climbed via north ridge by Hacker, Miranda Bustamante, Olivares on June 10); Torrini Chico "First Wall" via west-east traverse (also climbed via west-northwest face by Lentrodt, Hacker on June 5) and "Big Wall" via northeast ridge by Bülter, Rebitzer, Lentrodt, Magerer, Olivares (also climbed via two different routes on northwest face by Hetz, Camarlinghi and Griesshammer, J. Tellaeche on June 2), both on May 31. 4th Mama Okllo Tower via west side by Camarlinghi, J. Thellaeche; Cerro Calsonani (5124 meters) via west face by Griesshammer, Hetz; Mama Okllu (5281 meters) via west side and south ridge by Bülter, Rebitzer (also climbed via northwest buttress by Griesshammer, Wittmann on June 10); P 5021 via southwest ice couloir by Lentrodt and via north ridge by Magerer, Wolf, all on June 1. Cerro Taruj Umaña (4852 meters) via northeast edge by Hetz, Andia, Wolf (also climbed via north-south traverse by Hacker on June 4); Cuernos de Diablo (5271 meters) via northwest side by Bülter, Rebitzer and via north-northwest face by Lentrodt, Magerer (also climbed via northwest face by Hetz, Camarlinghi, J. Thellaeche on June 4), all on June 3. P 5304 (northeast of the three towers) via west ridge by Bülter, Rebitzer on June 4. Cerro Torrini (5131 meters) via east face and southeast ridge by Hetz, Griesshammer; 2nd Mama Okllu Tower via northwest face by Lentrodt, Andia, Camarlinghi; P 5297 (middle of the three towers) via south side by Bülter, Rebitzer, Olivares; P 5110 via west ridge by Wolf, Hacker (also climbed via southwest face by Bülter, Griesshammer and via south face by Wolf, Hacker on June 8), all on June 6. Cerro Waillani (5193 meters) via southeast ice couloir by Lentrodt, Magerer, Rebitzer on June 9. 1st Mama Okllu Tower via north side by Bülter, tom Felde, Wolf; P 5104 (west of Mama Okllu) via north ridge by Hacker, Miranda, Bustamante, Olivares, both on June 10. 3rd Mama Okllu Tower via north side by Bülter, tom Felde, Wolf; P 5050 (south of P 5104) via west side by Magerer, Wolf and via north ridge by Bülter, Rebitzer; P 4800 (west of P 5050) via north ridge by Bülter, Rebitzer, all on June 11. The second group operated in the Choquetanga group. They established their Base Camp at the abandoned Carmen Rosa Mine south of the Abra San Enrique on the western end of the lake Kkota Khuchu. They apparently did not know that Japanese in 1968 had climbed both San Lorenzo and San Felipe. (The Japanese incorrectly identified the peaks and what they called San Lorenzo was actually San Felipe and vice versa.) The Germans made the following climbs: Nina Kkollu Chico (5199 meters) via west-north traverse by tom Felde, Wittmann on June 1. Nina

Kkollu Grande (5352 meters) via west ridge by tom Felde, Wittmann, Miranda, Bustamante, J. Thellaeche on June 2 and by Fichtner, Langenmaier on June 9. San Lorenzo (5508 meters) via south ridge by tom Felde, Wittmann, Miranda and via east side by Fichtner, Langenmaier, J. Tellaeche on June 4. San Felipe (5330 meters) via south side by tom Felde, Wittmann, Fichter, Langenmaier, Miranda, J. Tellaeche on June 6. San Pedro (5590 meters) via north ridge by Wittmann and via west ridge by tom Felde on June 7. After the climbing in the Quimsa Cruz, the members had their eyes on the Cordillera Real, just to the north. Lentrodt, Magerer, Rebitzer and Wittmann were joined by Rainer Müller in an attempt on the south face of Illimani. They moved to the foot of the face on the 16th and set out on the 17th up an ice couloir that was up to 70° in steepness. They bivouacked at 5700 meters. There was an abrupt change in the weather and it was snowing hard by eight P.M. During the night spindrift slides kept covering their tents, so much so that Rebitzer died, asphyxiated. During the descent on June 18, an ice axe from which he was rappelling pulled out and Müller fell 150 meters to his death. Not knowing of these tragedies, Hacker, Langenmaier and Miranda climbed the standard west-flank route on Illimani. An attempt on Illampu failed 700 meters from the summit. (We are grateful to Herr Hermann Wolf for this information.)

Chile

Mayra, Cordón de los Primos, Puna de Atacama. Ricardo Jara and Misael Alvial made the first ascent of Cerro Mayra (5300 meters, 17,389 feet) on January 21. They ascended from the mining camp Nevada at 3600 meters and climbed the granite south spur in 15 hours. (UIAA V+, A1.) This peak is located about 125 kilometers southeast of Vallenar, five or ten kilometers from the Argentine frontier.

IVÁN VIGOUROUX, *Federación de Andinismo de Chile*

Cerro Negro, Ice Cascade. The 250-meter-high ice cascade hanging on the south side of Cerro Negro, a peak northwest of Santiago, has long been a challenge to local climbers. C. Buracchio and I first climbed the mountain (4975 meters, 16,324 feet) by its north side to examine the ground. A few days later we placed a camp on the south side by the Glaciar Olivares Beta at 4600 meters. From there we descended to the foot of the cascade and climbed it on January 28. It varied in steepness from 60° to 90°.

CRISTIÁN THIELE, *Club Alemán Andino, Santiago, Chile*

Cerro Arenas, 1985. On December 29, 1985, Ricardo Jara made the first solo ascent of the 1200-meter rock south face of Cerro Arenas. He made the climb free without a rope or any belaying in eight hours. (UIAA V and VI.) (This climb was repeated in the Southern winter of 1986 by Cristián Thiele. —

Editor.) The peak is in the spur south extending from Cerro Placas, near Lo Valdés.

IVÁN VIGOUROUX, *Federación de Andinismo de Chile*

Volcán San José, Winter Ascent. A large group made the first winter ascent Volcán San José from September 12 to 17. After leaving Lo Valdés, they placed camps at 2900, 3250, 3900 and 4520 meters. The women climbers were A. Barrientos, M. Chiozza, V. Morales and C. Castillo and the men were C. Gálvez, N. Múñoz, L. Napolitano, F. Varela, C. Cancino, M. España, A. Mancini, C. Fuentes, J. Palma, R. Traub, F. Vito, M. Tapia, D. Rutland, J. Jaña, M. Quiroz, E. Garrido and I. This ascent took place during the most severe winter in the last 50 years.

IVÁN VIGOUROUX, *Federación de Andinismo de Chile*

Argentina

Mercedario, South Face. An Italian expedition originally had the west face of Mercedario as its objective. They were Alessandro Angelini, Giuseppe Angelotti, Carlo Barbolini, Gianluca Benedetti, Fabrizio Convalle, Bruno Nicolini, Giancarlo Polacci and Emilio Riccomini. The difficulties of the approach were considerable. They left Barreal, the last inhabited place, on January 10 but got to the foot of the south face at 3400 meters only on January 20. They reconnoitered to see if they could cross over the 5200-meter shoulder and descend 1000 meters on the other side to reach the foot of the west face but this would have been too arduous. They then headed for the left side of the icefall of the south face. On January 22 and 23 they carried to Advance Base at 4400 meters a half kilometer from the base of the face. Half of the group established Camp I at 5270 meters on January 26. After a snowstorm, while they moved up to Camp II at 6200 meters on January 28, the other half occupied Camp I. All were established at Camp II on a level spot below the foresummit on January 30. On the 31st Angelini, Barbolini and Benedetti reached the summit (6670 meters, 21,884 feet). There was no time for further summit climbs and the entire party withdrew.

Aconcagua, New Route on the Right Side of the South Face, 1986. Milan Romih and I made a trip to the Plaza de Francia in bad weather from February 9 to 11, 1986. We returned there on February 14. We were held back by bad weather until February 18 when we left the Plaza de Francia at noon. In the very region where we had wanted to climb, a sérac broke, causing an avalanche, and so we changed our route and started up the right side of the south face of Aconcagua. After climbing 200 meters of very rotten rock, we crossed to the left toward the icefall, where it was dripping and wet. We found the French Camp I and followed their route to the top of the southeast buttress and there we bivouacked. On February 19 we climbed the lower glacier up to under the séracs. First we tried to climb the left side of the séracs, but because of heavy cracking we retreated 200 meters, turned right and started up the séracs on that side, in the middle of which we had to bivouac. On the 20th we climbed to the top of the séracs, where the slopes had been in part 90° or overhanging. A storm caught us in the afternoon and forced a bivouac below the ridge, where in the night we were frequently covered by avalanches. On February 21 we climbed onto the ridge and dried our equipment. On the 22nd we ascended the last of the rock and then the long ridge. We bivouacked in bitter cold 200 meters below the summit. We got to the summit on the morning of February 23, 1986 and descended the normal route to the Nido de Cóndores with bad weather from the Berlin shelter on. We were back at Puente del Inca on February 25.

DANILO TIČ, *Alpinistični Odsek Impol, Yugoslavia*

Aconcagua. Aconcagua was the goal of a Polish group led by Andrzej Gardas. Of the 14 members, 13 reached the summit and eight got there twice. Piotr Konopka and Zbigniew Winiarski climbed the French route on the south face in just two days. Anna Skowrońska and Ewa Szcześniak made the first female ascent of the Argentine route up the Glaciar de los Polacos on January 25. The best success was the third ascent of the very difficult Slovene route on the left of the south face, done from January 25 to 31 by Leszek Cichy and Ryszard Kołakowski. Because of the cascades of water in the first 1000 meters, they had to make many variants. The rock was murderously rotten and both had minor rockfall injuries. There were UIAA difficulties up to V + and ice up to 90°. Five climbed to the summit and back from the Plaza de Mulas on the normal route in a single day, a difference of 2760 meters or 9055 feet; Cichy and Konopka did the round-trip in 13 hours. With so many ascents now being made of Aconcagua, there are many cases of high-altitude sickness and frostbite, leading in some cases to tragedy. Dr. Anna Skowrońska persuaded an American to turn back; he was suffering from obvious cerebral edema and yet was continuing to crawl toward the summit. On the summit lay the body of an Argentine whose German companion did make it down, but with severe freezing injuries. Expert climbers Spaniard Felix de Pablos and Frenchman Dominique Radique died on the south face on January 27.

JÓZEF NYKA, *Editor, Taternik, Poland*

Aconcagua, South Face, Winter Solo, 1986. Spaniard Fernando Ruiz made the second winter ascent of the south face of Aconcagua solo in alpine style. At the beginning of September, 1986, he made a first attempt with Antonio de Lorenzo, but they were turned back by the weather at 5000 meters. On September 8, he set out again solo on the 1954 French route with the Messner finish. After five-and-a-half days he reached the summit on September 13. The descent was a nightmare. He spent a frightful night in the Independencia Hut and seven nights in the Berlin Hut, awaiting better weather. He finally made it back to Puente del Inca on September 22, but with seriously frozen hands and feet.

Aconcagua South Face. From January 25 to 31 Leszek Cichy and I climbed the Yugoslav route on the left side of the south face of Aconcagua. Because of the lack of ice in the couloirs in the lower part, for the first 1000 meters we had to make a new variant to the right of the original route. It was difficult. We joined the original route under the sérac in the middle of the route.

RYSZARD KOŁAKOWSKI, *Klub Wysokogórski Warszawa, Poland*

Cerro Barauca. A large group of anthropologists, glaciologists and mountaineers from the Universidad Nacional de Cuyo explored the central part of the Cordillera del Tigre, near Mendoza, searching in the higher zones for ancient Indian occupancy. The Cordillera del Tigre runs north and south, east of Aconcagua and parallel to the Vacas valley, which gives access to the Polish route on that mountain. While they made findings on the lower slopes, no traces were located above the lake zone above 4400 meters or on the summits. F. Norton and F. Seufferheld made what is probably the seventh ascent of Cerro de los Tambillos (5570 meters, 18,275 feet) on February 9. Seufferheld and A. Rosell made the first ascent of Cerro Barauca (c. 5400 meters, 17,717 feet) on February 12. The expedition leader was Roberto Bárcena.

LUIS A. PARRA, *Club Andinista Mendoza, Argentina*

Tupungato, Southeast Face, 1986. Milan Romih and I approached the southeast face of Tupungato via Tupungato village and Fraile in four days. We bivouacked at 4800 meters on February 1, 1986 and climbed to the summit (6550 meters, 21,490 feet) on February 2. We descended the normal route, bivouacking the first night at 5200 meters and continuing on to reach Mendoza on February 4.

DANILO TIČ, *Alpinistični Odsek Impol, Yugoslavia*

Cerro Lomas Amarillas, South Face and Other Ascents. Because of its easy access by way of the Vallecito ski resort, the massif of Cerro de la Plata has had all of its peaks and most of its difficult faces climbed. In late 1987, M. Sánchez and C. Tejerina, from Mendoza, did two of the remaining rock routes. On November 10, they climbed the northwest face of Cerro Morro Chato (c. 4600 meters, 15,092 feet) and a month later, did the rockfall-threatened south face of Lomas Amarillas (4750 meters, 15,584 feet). In the last days of December, I led a group of three to prospect a new access route to the base of Cerro Santa María (5023 meters, 16,480 feet), southeast of Aconcagua and northeast of Puente del Inca. We wanted to verify the existence of the several 500-foot-high ice cascades hanging from the south face of Santa María, already noted in 1908 by Walther Schiller. The cascades are still there, but much thinner. One of our group, Evelio Echevarría, stayed behind and on December 31 made the first ascent of Cerro El Durazno (4597 meters, 15,083 feet), southwest of Santa María. Aconcagua was expecting a record number of expeditions. Already registered for the period from November 1, 1987 to January 31, 1988 were 136 expeditions, and more were expected later. Of this number 25 were American, 20 German, 19 Spanish, 16 Argentine and 10 Japanese. Seventeen other countries were also represented. A total of 421 men and 59 women were expected to participate.

FERNANDO GRAJALES, *Club Andinista Mendoza*

Argentine-Chilean Patagonia

San Lorenzo Attempt from Chile. John Hauf, Tom Walter and I went in from the Chilean side, an interesting and varied six-day trip: by bus from Puerto Montt to Quellón, ferry to Puerto Chacabuco, bus to Coihaique, plane to Cochrane, horses to Arroyo San Lorenzo and finally by foot to the De Agostini Base Camp site at the edge of the forest. To drive in from the Argentine side is obviously simpler, but one needs the proper vehicle, access problems have been reported with the owners of the *estancias*, and the scenery on the Pacific side is better than the pampas. Coihaique has all the food and supplies an expedition might need at typical Patagonian prices. Cochrane, a *very* isolated village of 3000 people, has some food but it is expensive and there is no gas. At Base Camp we spent a few days scouting routes. One line that looks good is the north-northeast face at the head of the glacier that drains into the Río de Oro, a large alpine ice gully that goes straight to the summit. This gully would require cold weather as we watched much ice and rock falling down it on a warm afternoon. Instead we chose a line on the north face, directly above Base Camp. This face gets raked by ice avalanches from the ice cliffs at the top, but after watching it, we thought we saw a route that would keep us safe. We began on a beautiful hot day, March 3. The following day started clear and we set out from a bivouac at 2000 meters. After an hour of exposed climbing through séracs, we crossed the bergschrund and relaxed, continuing up on ice through small buttresses. What made the rest of the route fairly safe was that we were not in the larger gullies that receive everything falling from above. Our crux was a 40-meter frozen cascade, 70° to 90° steep and only a meter wide, which took us through a rotten cliff. It led to a snow ridge which went directly to the top cliffs, full of icicle-hung overhangs. Some zigzags through them got us to the summit ridge at four P.M. The weather was deteriorating fast, with a lenticular cloud over the summit and clouds sweeping in from the west. For that reason, we did not continue east to the very top. For a brief period, the view was spectacular, from San Valentín, across the valley of the Río Baker, south to the peaks of the Southern Icecap. We didn't know how to get off the mountain quickly and without rappels, aware only that De Agostini's first-ascent route was somewhere on the west side, and so we staggered through the wind for a while before finding an icefall that looked good. We raced down it under lowering clouds. We spent that night in rain and snow perched on rocks somewhere on the west side and returned to Base Camp the following day, March 5. Since the weather stayed unstable after this, we hiked in the neighboring valleys. The adjacent Cadena Cochrane has some very nice climbing and one can be active there even when upper San Lorenzo is engulfed in storm. Rock quality is disappointing on the north and west sides of San Lorenzo. Clearly, the big routes are on the east or northeast of the peak.

TIMOTHY RAWSON, *National Outdoor Leadership School*

San Lorenzo, East Ridge. Casimiro Ferrari, Danilo Valsecchi, Annibale Borghetti and Maurizio Villa made the sixth ascent of San Lorenzo and the second ascent of the east ridge in January. Their route was somewhat more directly on the ridge than that of the South Africans.

SILVIA METZELTIN BUSCAINI, *Club Alpino Italiano*

Cerro Torre, First Female Ascent. Italians Maurizio Giordani and Rosanna Manfrini arrived in the early southern spring below Cerro Torre. Only ten days after their arrival the two completed the Maestri route on the peak, reaching the summit on October 29. The descent was difficult because of very stormy weather. This is the first time that this peak has been ascended by a woman.

Cerro Torre. Carlos Buhler and I set up Base Camp in the forest below Cerro Torre at the beginning of December. The weather in October and early November had been phenomenal and already over 20 persons had summited in 1987. With only a month in Patagonia, we decided on the Maestri bolt route. After an unsuccessful attempt, Carlos and I set out on December 16. We broke trail through deep, fresh snow up the southwest glacier to the five or six pitches below the col. We reached the col by late afternoon and bivouacked in an ice cave. The next morning we began to climb at three A.M. by headlamp. The climb is mostly ice and rock of only moderate difficulty with abundant fixed protection. The snow of the previous days still plastered the ridge and at times made route-finding difficult. The bolt ladders dominate the middle of the route. To save time, we moved together on those sections. By one A.M. we were one pitch below the summit on Maestri's compressor. Carlos' headlamp had died and we were forced to stop until daylight. At six A.M. we stood on the very summit. Later that day, three more teams also made it. Descent to the ice cave took ten hours as high winds on the first rappels played havoc with our ropes.

MARK RICHEY

Aguja de la S and St. Exupéry. After their successful ascent on the fourth try on December 3, 1986 of the Franco-Argentine route on Fitzroy, Austrians Hans Bärnthaler and Ewald Lidl returned to the region in late 1987. (Their companions Ernst Konzett and Reinhard Sperger had also completed the same climb four days later.) In 1987, Bärnthaler and Lidl made two new routes: the east face of the Aguja de la S (400 meters, UIAA VI−) and the south ridge of St. Exupéry (800 meters, VI, A2). Details are not yet available.

Aguja Guillaumet and Gorra Blanca. A seven-man, two-woman expedition of the Club Andino Bariloche, with Víctor Krajcirick as leader, entered the Chaltén (Fitzroy) massif by way of Piedra del Fraile, where they established Base Camp. Bad weather held them up for eleven days. On January 8, E. Gutiérrez and R. Garibotti set out for Aguja Guillaumet, which they climbed the next day by the Fonrouge route. Meanwhile D. Rodríguez and M. Joos ascended to the Continental Icecap by the Marconi Glacier. On January 9, they climbed Gorra Blanca (2920 meters, 9580 feet). The expedition stayed in the area another 20 days reconnoitering access to several peaks, but they had only 12 hours of good weather in that period.

VOJSLAV ARKO, *Club Andino Bariloche*

Guillaumet and Fitz Roy. At the end of September, Silvia FitzPatrick and I climbed the Aguja Guillaumet by the French couloir. For Silvia, this was her first Patagonian summit. We returned twice to Guillaumet and made a new variant on the northeast buttress of a route a friend and I had done in 1981 but we did not go to the summit. At the beginning of November, we climbed Fitz Roy by the Argentine route. This was the second ascent of the peak by a woman. The first was done in 1978 by Romy Druschke, who climbed the American route with her husband. A week later we attempted the Aguja Poincenot but were stopped by verglas two pitches from the summit. We climbed the Whillans route to the shoulder and then did a variant on the southeast spur. As on Fitz Roy, the descent was in very bad weather.

EDUARDO BRENNER, *Centro Andino Buenos Aires*

Aguja Poincenot, Northwest Buttress, 1986. Above a prominent pedestal to the left of the 1977 Carrington-Rouse route, the Italian route ascended some 2000 feet of sustained difficulties. The ascent was made between December 6 and 8, 1986 by Italians D. Bosisio, M. Panzeri, M. Della Santa and P. Vitali, members of the famous *Ragni* (Spiders) of Lecco.

Correction on Aguja Poincenot. On pages 212-215 of *A.A.J., 1987,* it incorrectly states that the climbers reached the summit of Aguja Poincenot.

They reached the 1962 Anglo-Irish route some 300 meters from the summit. They did not, however, continue all the way to the summit.

Paine South Tower, East Face, 1986. After their ascent of the Central Tower of Paine (*A.A.J.*, *1987*, page 216), Elio Orlandi, Maurizio Giarolli and Ermanno Salvaterra on November 20, 1986 were joined by Ginella Paganini to repeat the difficult 1963 Armando Aste route on the South Tower of Paine. Bad weather had forced them to wait a couple of weeks between their ascents. The weather was beautiful and they made fast progress. They reached the summit at nine o'clock on the second morning. Orlandi became the first person to climb all three of the Paine Towers.

Central Tower of Paine, South-Southwest Face, 1986. Italians climbed a new route on the south-southwest face of the Central Tower of Paine. The route, which rises from the col between the central and south towers, crosses the bottom of the Kearney-Knight route. The climb gained 800 meters on excellent, vertical granite. The difficulties were UIAA VI and A3. They made three attempts and spent five nights bivouacking on the wall. They finally got to the summit on December 24, 1986 and made another bivouac on the descent. The climbers were Dario Spreafico, Carlo Besana, Renato Da Pozzo, Marco Ballerini and Norberto Riva.

GASTÓN OYARZÚN, *Federación de Andinismo de Chile*

Torre Norte del Paine, South Spur, and Torre Sur, North Spur, Winter Ascents. Luca Leonardi and I left Italy on June 10 hoping to climb one of the Paine towers in winter. There had never been even a winter attempt before in the Paine group. On June 20, we got to Base Camp on the Río Ascensio. We decided on the south spur of the North Tower. After an unsuccessful attempt turned back by bad weather, on June 28 at four P.M. we got to the summit. Considering the little time we had left, we decided to try the highest of the three towers, the South Tower, by the Armando Aste route on the north spur. After carrying all our gear to the base and carving a snow hole, we fixed 200 meters of rope in two days. Seeing a definite improvement in the weather on July 10, we set out with full equipment. Toward evening, we got to the shoulder, where we could bivouac quite comfortably. The next day, July 11 at six P.M., we got to the summit. In the 40 days we were in the Paine Park, we had three good days, much wind and −25° C temperatures. There was not much snowfall.

MARIO MANICA, *Club Alpino Italiano*

Southern Summer Climbing Season in Patagonia, 1987-8. Just a few days ago (written on February 19, 1988), Sebastián de la Cruz returned from the

PLATE 37

Photo by Silvo Karo

**CERRO TORRE. Jeglič-Karo route
is left. Maestri bolt-route is right.**

South. He climbed Cerro Torre with Spaniards Ramón Portillo and Antonio Trabado from the snow cave at the base to the summit and back on December 19. On December 26, he soloed Adela Central and made an unsuccessful attempt on Stanhardt with Swiss Peter Lüthi at the end of January. Before he left, 36 climbers had ascended Cerro Torre, nearly all by the Maestri bolt route. The exceptions were the Slovenes Janez Jeglič and Silvo Karo, who climbed the vertical south face and on January 22, 1988 got to the Maestri route; they descended from there without going to the summit because of a frightful storm. Women climbed Cerro Torre for the first time. Italian Rosanna Manfrini with Maurizio Giordani got to the top a few days ahead of Ines Božič, accompanied by Janez Skok. Polish women, including Wanda Rutkiewicz, failed near the Maestri compressor. On January 29, 1988, American Kathy Cosley with Mark Houston became the third woman to reach Cerro Torre's summit. Argentine Silvia FitzPatrick, along with Eduardo Brenner, was the second woman to climb Fitz Roy.

VOJSLAV ARKO, *Club Andino Bariloche*

Tierra del Fuego

Monte Sarmiento, West Peak, 1986. Italians finally climbed the west peak of Monte Sarmiento. The east summit (2234 meters, 7730 feet) had been climbed by its south ridge on March 7, 1956 by Carlo Mauri and Clemente Maffei. Giuseppe Agnolotti led three expeditions, in 1969, 1971 and 1972, to try the west peak, but all were unsuccessful because of the frightful but typical weather and overhanging ice mushrooms. In early December of 1986, Daniele Bosisio, Marco Della Santa, Mario Panzeri and Paolo Vitali occupied Base Camp and carried loads to the foot of the climb despite very bad weather. On December 6, 1986, the four attacked the face, gaining 700 meters in a couloir and then climbed another 300 meters to the base of the west buttress. The weather was clear but the wind was strong and cold. After bivouacking on the spur, on December 8, 1986 they climbed the remaining 700 meters up the very difficult west buttress to the summit (2210 meters, 7251 feet).

ANTARCTICA

Mont Français, Anvers Island, Antarctic Peninsula. After a five-week passage through gales, fickle winds, heavy seas and finally a maze of sea ice in the mist, the steel ketch *Northanger*, specially designed as a mobile base in polar conditions, was secured in four feet of water, with her keel raised, away from drifting ice at Port Lockroy, Wiencke Island. Whilst New Zealander Tex Hendry and his French wife Joëlle stayed close to the boat, Englishman Rick Thomas, Australian Marguerite Tierney, and New Zealanders Greg Landreth and I set off to climb Mont Français (2822 meters, 9258 feet), the summit of

Photo by Vince Scully

PLATE 38

**On the way to Mont Français,
Antarctica.**

Anvers Island and the highest peak in the maritime peninsula. Skiing, we towed a sledge for three days along the flat piedmont to our route, Bull Ridge. We pushed progress for two days in poor light and bitter winds to camp at 6000 feet, roped up, as crevasses abounded on the ridge. With limited food, we headed for the summit in high winds. At least the snow conditions improved and we were no longer post-holing. The ridge merged with a steep face, too steep to solo; yet standing around to belay was out of the question. We kept moving to survive. We took a route under twenty three-story-high blocks. After innumerable false summits, at eleven A.M. on January 26, we revelled in victory on the summit. Graham Land lay before us, granite spires amid the waterway below.

VINCENT SCULLY, *New Zealand Alpine Club*

AFRICA

Egypt

Gebel Gharib. Gebel Gharib (1750 meters) is the highest of the northern Red Sea hills and rises a sheer 1500 meters from the gravel plains of the western Gulf of Suez. I made the first ascent of the south buttress solo on May 7. I found a lichen-covered cairn on the summit, probably erected by Bedouin ibex hunters. Two Nubian ibex were seen as I headed for the summit. There were exposed third- and fourth-class ledge systems, separated by easy fifth-class steps. The approach was made with a four-wheel vehicle up Wadi Kharm El Eyoun to a Bedouin camp about two hours' scramble from the base of the route. Its granite reminds one of that found on the Sinai Peninsula. Unfortunately, the rock is so shattered that potential routes on the sweeping arêtes and faces surrounding the summit would be somewhat tenuous. Slabs and domes on the lower nearby summits offer good prospects for solid fifth-class routes up to 500 meters in length.

DANA COFFIELD

ASIA

Italian Expedition to Tibet and Pakistan to Conduct Further Observations on the Altitude of Mount Everest and K2. (Professor Ardito Desio, who organized and was in overall charge of the group that undertook the new measurements, has kindly supplied the Editor with a report from which we print the following excerpts.) Renato Moro informed me that the Base Camp at 5300 meters on the Tibetan slope near the Rongbuk Monastery could actually be reached by motor vehicle. Therefore I decided to give precedence

PLATE 39

Photo by Dana Coffield

GEBEL GHARIB, Egypt.

to the measuring of Everest. On July 28 the expedition set off for Kathmandu. (It is assumed that the party traveled directly to the Everest Base Camp via the Kodari Road.—*Editor.*) The field party was made up as follows: Professor Alessandro Caporalli of the University of Padua in charge of geodesic measurements, Engineers Lionello Lavarini and Claudio Pigato, assistants to Caporalli, Dr. Attilio Bernini, physician, Dr. Mino Damato, journalist, Agostino Da Polenza, mountain guide, Kurt Diemberger, cine-photographer, Renato Moro, mountaineer, and Soro Dortei, mountain guide. I received no further news from them until on the tenth of August came the long-awaited telephone call informing me that the measurements of the height of Everest had been completed. All members were making preparations to leave for Pakistan. There was some difficulty in setting off for the Concordia Base Camp on the Baltoro Glacier. One of the helicopters managed to transport just the operators to near Urdokas and from there they continued on foot to Concordia. Professor Caporalli's team was able to complete measurements of K2 in only four days.

The equipment used consisted essentially of an electronic diastimeter theodolite and a pair of GPS (Global Positioning System) receivers of the latest generation. The theodolite allowed us to measure horizontal and vertical angles with the greatest of accuracy, allowing for atmospheric turbulence. The diastimeter with infra-red rays incorporated made it possible to calculate to a precision of some millimeters distances up to three or four kilometers. The new GPS technology is based on the use of the USA Navstar satellites, designed to provide a service for positioning in navigation. The satellites describe orbits at a height of 20,000 kilometers for periods of about 12 hours. These satellites transmit coded radio signals which, once they have been processed by the ground receiver, allow one to obtain, within a short time and from any point on the earth's surface, the exact location (longitude, latitude and altitude) of the instrument's antenna. When two of the receivers are used in conjunction, the accuracy of the measurements is far greater. The measuring is then done in two distinct phases. In the first phase, the altitude of the base in relation to the plane of reference is determined by observing the satellites. In the second, the altitude of the mountain's summit is determined by the theodolite, lining it up with different points. The absolute height of the peak is thus the sum of these two terms: the height determined by GPS and that obtained by theodolite, subject to appropriate corrections for the earth's curvature and atmospheric refraction. The most technologically innovative aspect of GPS lies in the fact that when two or more antennae operated at the same time, even at a relative distance of several kilometers, leveling and triangulation with precision become considerably more rapid and reliable than with traditional techniques.

It is time to let the figures speak for themselves. Let us begin with K2, which presents fewer problems. The height of K2, after various computer corrections, came to 8616 meters, plus or minus 7 meters. It is thus 5 meters more than the height obtained by Colonel Montgomerie of the Survey of India over a century ago. In addition to K2, our expedition measured another two peaks. Our figures are followed by the traditional figures in parentheses: Broad

Peak 8060m (8051m): Gasherbrum IV 7929m (7925m). As for Everest, the height arrived at from our measurements is 8872 meters, *plus or minus 20 meters*. This is 24 meters greater, therefore, than the figure previously considered the most valid.

ARDITO DESIO, *Italy*

First Ascents of Routes on Mount Everest, 1963-1987

COMPILED BY DEE MOLENAAR

Year	Date(s)	Route	Nationality	Climbers
1953	5/29	South Col, South Ridge	British, New Zealand, Indian	Edmund Hillary Tenzing Norgay
1960	5/25	Northeast Ridge	Chinese	Wang Fu-chou Chu Yin-hua Gonpa (Tibetan)
1963	5/22	West Ridge, Hornbein Couloir	American	Tom Hornbein Willi Unsoeld
1975	9/24	Southwest Face, ramp to above South Summit	British	Dougal Haston Doug Scott
	9/26			Peter Boardman Pertemba Mick Burke (?—disappeared)
1979	5/13	West Ridge Direct	Yugoslavian	Andrej Štremfelj Nejc Zaplotnik
	5/15	-ditto-	"	Stane Belax Stipe Božić Ang Phu (Sherpa)
1980	2/19	South Buttress	Polish	Andrzej Czok Jerzy Kukuczka
1980	5/10	Japanese Couloir, Hornbein Couloir	Japanese	Tsuneo Shigehiro Takashi Ozaki
1980	8/20	Upper North Face, Great Couloir	Italian Tirol	Reinhold Messner
1982	5/4	Southwest Buttress	U.S.S.R.	Eduard Myslovsky Vladimir Balyberdin
	5/4	-ditto-	"	Sergei Bershov Mikhail Turkevich
	5/5	-ditto-	"	Valentin Ivanov Sergei Ephimov
	5/8	-ditto-	"	Kazbek Valiev V. Khrishchaty
	5/9	-ditto-	"	Yuri Golodov Vladimir Puchkov Valery Khomutov
1983	10/8	Kangshung Face	American	Carlos Buhler Kim Momb Louis Reichardt

Year	Date(s)	Route	Nationality	Climbers
1983	10/9	Kangshung Face	American	Jay Cassell
				George Lowe
				Daniel Reid
1984	10/3	Great Couloir Direct from Rongbuk Glacier	Australian	Tim McCartney-Snape Greg Mortimer Andy Henderson (to 150 ft below top)
1984	10/20	Central North Face, Great Couloir	American	Phil Ershler

India—Sikkim

Kabru Dome, Forked Peak and Rathong. An Indian Army expedition led by Major K.V. Cherian climbed these three peaks in western Sikkim. After establishing two high camps, they climbed Kabru Dome (6600 meters, 21,655 feet) on May 15 and Forked Peak (6108 meters, 20,040 feet) on May 16. They then crossed the Rathong La to the Yalung Glacier and on May 24 climbed Rathong (6679 meters, 21,911 feet).

HARISH KAPADIA, *Himalayan Club*

Chomoyummo, 1986. As preparation for the 1987 Kangchenjunga expedition, the Indian Army Assam Rifles climbed Chomoyummo (6823 meters, 22,368 feet) in northern Sikkim. (The first ascent was made by Dr. Kellas in 1911. It was again climbed in 1945 by T.H. Tilly, but recently this region has not been open to foreign expeditions.) They put two officers, two women, Dikila Gyatso and Pempa Bhutia, and 35 soldiers onto the summit on October 29, 1986.

Kangchenjunga Ascent and Tragedy. A 62-member team from the Indian Army Assam Rifles, including three women, was led by Major General Prem Lal Kukrety. They left Gangtok on March 8, heading for the northeast face of Kangchenjunga, the route previously climbed by Colonel Narinder Kumar's expedition in 1977. Base Camp was established at Green Lake at 4690 meters on March 15 and Advance Base at 5000 meters on March 24. Camps I, II, III, IV and V were established at 5600, 6000, 6300, 6650 and 7250 meters on March 31, April 2, 20, 30 and May 16. Finally on May 22, loads were dumped at the site of Camp VI at 7750 meters, but during the return to Camp V the climbers were caught in a blizzard. They suffered frostbite, and eventually Havildar Phurba had to be evacuated by helicopter. Despite this setback, Phu Dorje, who had soloed Everest without oxygen, Naik Chorten Tsering and Phu Pu Bhutia occupied Camp VI on May 23. They headed for the summit on May 24. They lost radio contact with Base Camp in $-40°$ weather when their batteries went dead. It is presumed they reached the summit; Phu Dorje's prayer flag was found eight meters below the summit. They did not return and, despite an extensive search, their bodies were not found. Naik Chander Singh, Lance Naik Bhawan Singh, Rifleman Subhas Limboo, Havildar R.B. Ghale and Norden Lepcha set up Camp VII at 8180 meters and made a summit

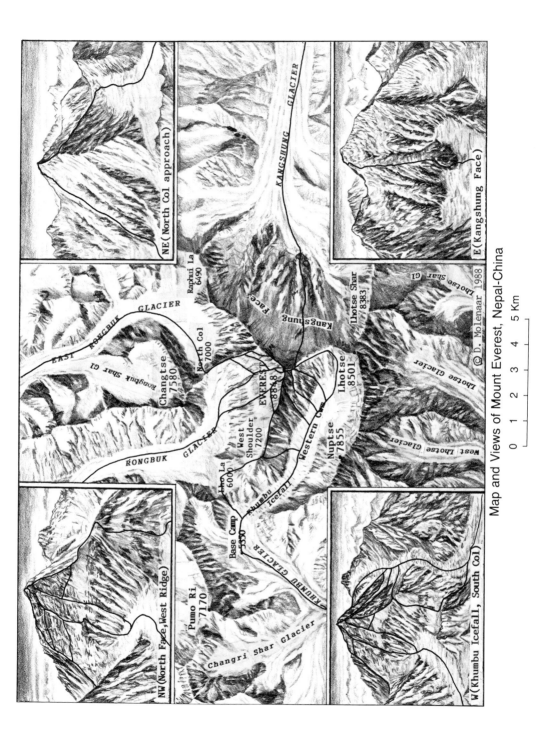

NE (North Col approach)

E (Kangshung Face)

KANGSHUNG GLACIER

Kangshung Face

Raphui La 6490

Lhotse Shar Gl

Lhotse Shar 8383

EAST RONGBUK GLACIER

Changtse 7580

Rongbuk Shar Gl

North Col 7000

Lhotse Glacier

EVEREST 8848

West Shoulder 7200

Western Cwm

Lhotse 8501

West Lhotse Glacier

RONGBUK GLACIER

Lho La 6000

Khumbu Icefall

Nuptse 7855

Base Camp 5350

KHUMBU GLACIER

NW (North Face, West Ridge)

Pumo Ri 7170

Changri Shar Glacier

W (Khumbu Icefall, South Col)

Map and Views of Mount Everest, Nepal-China

© D. Molenaar 1988

0   1   2   3   4   5 Km

attempt on May 30, which failed 100 feet from the summit in a severe snowstorm. Norden Lepcha fell and was injured; Ghale had to escort him off the mountain. The first three mentioned above made a second try on May 31 and gained the summit at two P.M. after a grueling 12-hour climb. On the way down, not far from the top, Chander Singh slipped and plunged down the Sikkim side of the mountain to his death.

KAMAL K. GUHA, *Editor, Himavanta, India*

Nepal

Himalayan Fatalities, 1986. I have read with considerable interest the pages devoted to the Himalaya. On the basis of these reports, there seem to have been 44 deaths in 1986. That in itself may not seem noteworthy related to the overall number of climbers involved. What has changed over the past decade is the leading cause. Falls account for 13 deaths (36.6%). Avalanches are the second most important cause with 13 deaths (31.7%). High-altitude oedema comes next, accounting for 12.25% of all deaths. Exhaustion and "other" causes make up the rest. Germans (6) and Japanese (5) top the list of fatalities, followed by Poland and Switzerland with 4 each.

TREVOR BRAHAM, *Alpine Club*

Corrections of "Classification of the Himalaya" in A.A.J., 1985. Thanks to a very thorough study by Michael Westmacott while he was working on the indexing project of the Alpine Club, we must report further corrections, mostly typographic errors or errors in converting meters and feet.

page 113 Gimmigela: 24,114 feet (not 24,144)
     114 Taple Shikar: 20,804 feet (not 21,000)
          Simvo East: 6771 meters (not 6671)
     115 P 6754: 22,160 feet (not 22,170)
          Sharpu: 20,788 feet (not 20,460)
     121 Lang Dak: 20,788 feet (not 20,460)
     123 Changbu: 22,247 feet (not 21,919)
     124 Salasungo: Latitude 28° (not 25°)
     126 P 6933: 22,747 feet (not 22,727)
          P 6932: 22,743 feet (not 22,723)
     127 Bhrikuti Shail: 20,880 feet (not 20,870)
     129 P 7010: 23,000 feet (not 23,300)
     130 P 6998 (incorrectly listed as P 6698)
     134 Changla: 21,533 feet (not 21,523)
          The *Yoka Pahar Subsection* lies west (not east) of the Seti.
     137 Mrigthuni: 22,490 feet (not 22,940)
     138 P 6651: 21,821 feet (not 21,815)
     139 P 6805: 22,326 feet (not 22,330)

Kangchenjunga, North Face Solo Attempt. Frenchman Eric Monier hoped to climb the north face of Kangchenjunga solo. He set out from Camp I at 5900 meters where the only other member of the party stayed. On April 24, the third day after leaving Camp I, he started from his bivouac at 6850 meters. At 7350 meters two toes became seriously frostbitten and he had to abandon his attempt. He began on the German route and then went over to the 1980 Japanese route.

MICHAEL J. CHENEY, *Himalayan Club,* and ELIZABETH HAWLEY

Kangchenjunga. On October 10, Australians Michael Groom and John Coulton went to the summit of Kangchenjunga by the southwest face in semi-alpine-style without Sherpas and artificial oxygen and with four bivouacs. However, on the descent their vision became blurred and their thinking ability badly affected, with the result that they could not mentally cope with the fact that an avalanche had wiped out their track and they could not see their tent at 7900 meters. Groom fell into a crevasse which they had not seen, but no harm came of it. Indeed it provided shelter for them from the wind that night. They bivouacked there at nearly 8000 meters. Their hands and feet were seriously frozen and both men will lose parts of fingers and toes.

MICHAEL J. CHENEY, *Himalayan Club,* and ELIZABETH HAWLEY

Kangchenjunga, North Face Attempt. Terry Tremble, Dr. Carol Brand-Maher and I attempted to climb the north face of Kangchenjunga. Dr. Brand-Maher had no prior experience in mountaineering. The walk-in from Hille to Pang Pema with 33 porters took 15 days. We arrived at Base Camp on August 31. Camp I was a temporary one on the glacier. Camp II was in the usual place. From there Tremble and I climbed between the north ridge and the north face, fixing 100 meters of rope on the ice cliffs below Camp III. We fixed another 500 meters above to the ridge where the site of Camp IV was reached on September 30. Our first summit attempt was called off on October 10 at 7500 meters below the rock step on the north ridge when Tremble developed altitude sickness. We returned safely. A second try was aborted on October 17 with the arrival of the huge storm. Thereafter there was very deep snow and high winds. Our third attempt failed at the base of the ice cliffs where an avalanche had wrecked our fixed ropes and we had no equipment left to reclimb the cliffs. We left Base Camp on October 26. While at Base Camp, we made serial measurements of blood viscosities. The rise was much greater than had been predicted. We retrieved an ice axe with the name of Günter Dyhrenfurth on the head and the remains of a short person in prewar clothing, who we assume to be the Sherpa who died in the 1930 attempt.

JAMES VAN GELDER, *Australia*

Kangchenjunga South Attempt. The leader of three Belgians and a Nepalese on the southwest face of Kangchenjunga, Alain Hubert, reached

8000 meters on October 14 in a solo bid for the summit of Kangchenjunga South. He was forced to bivouac there by strong winds and a heavy pack. On the second summit bid, Hubert went alone on October 22 to the site of Camp II at 7200 meters on the Great Shelf and could find no trace of the camp. A huge storm had intervened on October 19 and 20. The camp was either buried under very deep snow or it had blown away. All his down clothing for the climb and all the food were lost and so the climb was finished. He had intended to descend from above the Great Shelf by paraglider, but that too had been lost at Camp II.

MICHAEL J. CHENEY, *Himalayan Club,* and ELIZABETH HAWLEY

Kangchenjunga Winter Ascent, 1988. A South Korean expedition led by Jung Sang-Moo made a winter ascent of the southwest face of Kangchenjunga. Lee Jeong-Chel made the 24th ascent of the mountain on January 2, 1988. On the way to Base Camp, a member and a porter died of illness. Further details are still not available.

ELIZABETH HAWLEY

Yalung Kang Attempt. I had originally hoped to climb Yalung Kang by the normal southeast-face route with a small alpine-style team. When the members of my original team could not come and I could find no others, I decided to attempt it alone with a support team of John and Charlie Smith and Dana Welch. In the end, one of the original members, Jim Farkas, could come. Because of my commitment to climb alone, we agreed to hire a high-altitude porter to go with Jim. We would still climb alpine-style and without oxygen. We left Kathmandu on August 10, but severe flooding in eastern Nepal complicated the approach. We finally arrived at Base Camp at 5400 meters up the Yalung Glacier on August 30. There we realized that we were missing three weeks of food. That meant we had to work together and climb fast. By September 15, Camp I was established at the top of the lower icefield at 6200 meters. On September 20, Camp II was placed at 6400 meters so that it could be reached in a day from Base Camp. It was a third of the way up the second icefield. On October 3, the support group left for Kathmandu. Camp I was eliminated and Camp II was the only permanent camp. After a couple of days of snow, the weather cleared and on the 7th we left Base Camp for the first summit attempt. We made Camp III at 7000 meters near the top of the second icefield. On the way to Camp IV, I was putting my down jacket into my pack when a gust of wind blew it into a crevasse. I went down to try to retrieve it, but since I was alone and without rope, there was nothing I could do. I spent the night at Camp IV, hoping to borrow a jacket later, but that did not work out. Jim tried for the summit from Camp IV on two consecutive days. On October 11, with porter Ong Chu and sirdar Narayan, they found the snow too soft. Ong Chu went down, complaining of a headache. The following day, Jim

PLATE 41

Photo by Magda King

**YALUNG KANG (left) and
KANGCHENJUNGA.**

and Narayan tried again, but just over 8000 meters, Jim fell several hundred feet. Narayan lost his ice axe and they abandoned the climb. Jim was shaken by his fall and I stayed with him and Narayan on the way down. Near Camp II, I went ahead to melt snow. Narayan arrived shortly, saying that Jim was on the last part of the fixed rope and would soon be with us. As time passed, we grew concerned and at nine P.M. we went out to look for him. Our batteries were weak and by 11:30 we realized we could not find him until daytime.The following morning we found him nearby. He had fallen but spent the night in his sleeping bag. We helped him to Camp II. The next day, Ong Chu came up with the news that there were only two days of food in Base Camp. He and Narayan descended to get porters for the walk out. I would go down with Jim the next day. However, we got caught by a snowstorm at the site of the Belgian Camp I at 6200 meters. The first night we stayed in the Belgian tent but by morning it was completely destroyed. I put up my tent. It snowed constantly for three nights and two days with a total accumulation of five feet. It was not until the sixth day that we could move. At some time, Jim had frostbitten his toes and several fingers. From Base Camp it was another eight days of painful walking for Jim to reach Yamphuding, where we were met by a helicopter that took us to Kathmandu.

MAGDA KING, *Colorado Mountain Club*

Kumbhakarna (Jannu) Attempt. Beverly Boynton*, Randal Harrington, Evan Kaplan, Chuck Schaap, James Springer, Callum MacKay (our only Briton) and I as leader left Kathmandu on March 23, hoping to climb the French route on the south ridge of Kumbhakarna. We established Base Camp at 15,000 feet on April 6. Numerous load carries mixed with periods of bad weather finally led to placing Camp I at 17,500 feet. An easy snow gully, a corniced ridge and a small icefall put us in a spectacular cirque at Camp II at 19,500 feet. Springer and Schaap had to return to Base Camp to recover from flu. Daily snowstorms covered our tracks and we had to break trail in new snow every day. Because of delays and shortage of time and fuel, we decided to make an alpine-style attempt from Camp II. Bev Boynton dropped out to allow the formation of two 2-man teams. Kaplan, Harrington, MacKay and I set out on April 26 as the bad weather continued. After climbing 700 feet of fixed ropes, we kept on along the difficult corniced ridge in a mild blizzard. Five pitches of thin climbing ended on easier snow slopes below the first tower on the south ridge (Tête du Butoir). Though the bad weather continued, the night at the first bivouac at 20,400 feet was starry. On April 27 a short pitch of névé ice and steep snow led to a plateau below the Tête du Butoir. In a blizzard with no visibility, we tried to traverse to the second tower (Tête de Dentelle) above a 4000-foot drop to the Yamatari Glacier. Moving in sometimes hip-deep snow

*Recipient of a Vera Watson-Alison Chadwick Onyszkiewicz Memorial Fund Grant.

across the steep face, we could see that the avalanche danger was rapidly increasing. We returned to the plateau below the Tête du Butoir, camped at 21,000 feet and listened to the blizzard. The morning of April 28 was sunny with signs of another storm forming. With supplies running out and the terrible weather, we gave up our try. We believe this was the second American attempt and the 18th attempt in all on the mountain.

HOOMAN APRIN

Kumbhakarna, North Face. Ascent and Tragedy. Our expedition consisted of Ger Friele, Edmond Öfner, Ferry van Wilgenburg, Rudolf de Koning, Dr. Ingo Doornenbal and me as leader. With 55 porters we set out from Hille on September 5. Base Camp was at 4600 meters on the northern moraine of the Jannu Glacier, a beautiful spot with a small stream. After reconnaissance, we decided to repeat the route pioneered in 1975 by New Zealanders and finally climbed by Japanese in 1976. We abandoned the idea of climbing the very demanding pillar left of the route. From September 21 to 25, we fixed rope on the lower buttress to the snow plateau at 5500 meters. The weather was bad and the climbing up to UIAA V difficulty. Camp I was at the top of the buttress. After a few days of rest, we fixed rope on the "Wall of Shadows," 600 meters of technically very difficult climbing with three pitches of vertical ice couloirs. Camp II was at the top of this at 6100 meters. On October 9, Öfner and I started from Camp II for the summit alpine-style. The first part above Camp II had some difficult vertical rock and a vertical ice couloir. Afterwards we came onto the large snowfield and difficulties diminished. We bivouacked at 6700 meters and again a second night on the summit ridge at 7250 meters. There I discovered I had frostbitten feet. Öfner left the bivouac at midnight and reached the summit at 6:30. At 11:30 he was back and together we descended, still on October 11, to our third bivouac at 6600 meters. Meanwhile, Friele and de Koning had bivouacked at 6400 and 7100 meters. While Öfner and I descended to Base Camp on the 12th, they reached their third bivouac at 7250 meters. They got to the summit at 1:30 P.M. on October 13 and returned to 7250 meters. The next day they were returning to Camp II and at six P.M. made radio contact from 60 meters above camp. From then on, we heard nothing and could not see them. On the 15th, van Wilgenburg went to look for them and discovered their bodies at the foot of the "Wall of Shadows." They must have been struck by falling ice while descending the last 60 meters to Camp II. Van Hilgenburg buried the two bodies in a crevasse on the snow plateau.

GERARD C. VAN SPRANG, *Koninklijke Nederlandse Alpen Vereniging*

Kumbhakarna (Jannu) North Face. Erik Decamp, François Marsigny, Spaniard Juan Tomás and I arrived at Base Camp on September 23. Since Eric was coming from Mustagh Ata and I from Everest, we two were well acclimatized. We first had planned to climb the steep ramp between the

Japanese route and the huge rock wall. The first buttress was fixed by the Dutch with their ropes and ours. We placed Camp I at 5400 meters on the glacier below the big wall. From October 6 to 11 we climbed on the ramp, although threatening séracs at 6700 meters made us hesitate. At last, after two days searching for a passage, we climbed it and went on. After so much time we were short on food, gas and equipment. Cold was exhausting as the sun hit our route only one hour before dusk. We backed off, deciding to return to the face via the Japanese ramp. The Netherlanders were better off there. After the accident to them, Marsigny and Tomás left the expedition. On October 19 a terrible storm destroyed Base Camp, Deposit Camp and Camp I, and we lost much equipment. Then the weather turned clear, but windy and cold. From October 21 to 25, we climbed the face, using the Dutch ropes for the first 100 meters. Above that we went alpine-style. Bivouacs were at 6000, 6600 and 7200 meters. Luckily the wind stopped for the summit climb. The last ridge took us only four hours with incredible views. We were on the summit at 12:30 P.M. In two days we were in the valley and in five in Kathmandu.

PIERRE BEGHIN, *Groupe de Haute Montagne*

Kumbhakarna (Jannu). Our team was made up of Elizabeth Julliard, Marion Gaillard, Gérard Auger, Jean-Robert Grasso, Mario Paffumi, Frédéric Vallet, Michel Vincent and me. We trekked for eleven days from Shidua to Ghunsa. After the storm, which left much snow up high, we went with yaks and porters from Ghunsa to Base Camp I at 4500 meters, the same site as that used by the French expedition in 1962. We set up Base Camp II in the middle of the Yamatari Glacier on October 23. On October 23 and 24, we established Camp I up the glacier at 5300 meters below the Eperon des Jeunes (Youngsters' Spur). A south-facing ice couloir rose above Camp I to the middle of the spur. It was some 45°, but in places up to 60°. On the 25th and 26th, Julliard, Vallet, Vincent and I climbed the couloir and went along the ridge on mixed terrain for several rope-lengths. The ridge above was so snow-covered and corniced that it would have taken many days to fix. On October 27, we continued up the glacier to place Camp II at 6000 meters. There was some danger in séracs and one vertical passage. We occupied Camp II on October 29. We climbed to the crest of the Eperon des Jeunes to a col above our previous high point and along the ridge to under the Tête du Butoir. After some rope was fixed, Camp III was installed there at 6400 meters. On November 3, Julliard, Vallet, Vincent and I left Camp II on our summit attempt. We slept at Camp III. On the 4th, we quickly crossed the Tête du Butoir and continued to the foot of the Arête de la Dentelle (Lace Ridge), where we bivouacked. On November 5, we climbed the Lace Ridge and crossed the Throne Glacier to 7000 meters, where we set up Camp IV. On November 6, we started directly for the summit, possibly a little late in the morning. We climbed the ice slope to where the 1962 French Camp VI had been. Above this, at 7400 meters on the very narrow ridge Julliard and I turned back. It was two P.M. and we were beginning to get frostbitten. Vallet and Vincent continued on to the summit. They came back at night and reached Camp IV at eleven P.M. We were all back in Base Camp II on November 8.

HENRI SIGAYRET, *Groupe de Haute Montagne*

Makalu Attempt. This five-man expedition from the Netherlands hoped to climb the Yugoslavian route on the south face of Makalu. After establishing three high camps, leader Edewin van Nieuwkerk and Joost Ubbink reached 7600 meters on May 4. Exhaustion from combatting fierce winds and lack of manpower defeated this team.

MICHAEL J. CHENEY, *Himalayan Club,* and ELIZABETH HAWLEY

Swiss Makalu Attempt. Two of the three team members, Daniel Anker and Martin Fischer, reached their high point of 7600 meters on the southeast ridge of Makalu on October 13. After they went back to Base Camp for a rest, they were struck by the blizzard of October 18 to 20. They tried to resume their climb on the 22nd, but the winds were too strong and gave no signs of abating. They abandoned the climb.

MICHAEL J. CHENEY, *Himalayan Club,* and ELIZABETH HAWLEY

Austrian Makalu Attempt. This five-man Austrian expedition led by Wilfried Studer ended with a permit for the west-pillar route on Makalu. They began climbing the normal northwest route for acclimatization before tackling the pillar. A French-American team, which had permission for the normal route, arrived and demanded that the Austrians leave the route. Soon afterwards, a big snowstorm came. The Austrians did not want to try the pillar with so much snow and they abandoned the climb. Four members had gone to 6500 meters on October 13 and 17 on the normal route.

MICHAEL J. CHENEY, *Himalayan Club,* and ELIZABETH HAWLEY

Makalu Attempt. The 1987 Franco-American Makalu Expedition consisted of Michel Fauquet, leader; Americans Michael Crosset, Fred Phinney, Barry Rosenbaum, Jay Sieger and me; Canadian Bill Clifford; and French Denis Pivot, Annie Pivot and Christian Fournier, ably supported by Patrick Sance, Kathleen Pope, and Sherpas Kikeme, Pemba and Lhakpa. The attempt was by the normal route. After a 14-day trek, Base Camp and Camp I were established on September 17 and 21 at 5200 and 6100 meters. In continuing good post-monsoon weather, Camp II was fully established on October 1 at 6700 meters at the foot of the pitch to the Makalu La. Fixed ropes were placed to the right of the usual couloir to the col because of avalanche danger and Camp III, the high point, was established on the summit ridge on October 16. Sanse and

Fauquet survived without serious injury a ride on a wind-slab avalanche while fixing rope. High winds prevented immediate advance and the team regrouped for summit bids starting from Base on October 18. On October 19, a large unseasonal storm struck, halting all activity in the region. Base Camp was buried by four feet of snow, and Camp II was demolished by nine feet of snow and wind-slab avalanches. Camp III could not be revisited because of extreme avalanche danger. Fortunately, Camps II and III were unoccupied during the storm. Crossett escaped from Camp I with snow shovels strapped to his feet the following day. After a week of attempting to rescue gear, we descended. Morale, esprit and friendship were strong features of the expedition.

JAMES F. FRIES

Makalu Winter Attempt. Our expedition was composed of Poles Andrzej Machnik, leader, Grzegorz Fliegel, Julian Kobowicz, Wojciech Jedlinski, Zbigniew Terlikowski and Dr. Krzysztof Witkowski, Thomaz Brandolin of Brazil and me from the United States. Our objective was the winter ascent of Makalu via a variation of the northwest ridge. We arrived at Base Camp at 4850 meters on December 8, having left Kathmandu on November 24. Jedlinski, Machnik, Terlikowski and I established Advance Base on December 10 at the mouth of the Chago Glacier at 5200 meters. We then placed Camps I, II and III at 5820, 6430 and 6850 meters on December 16, 20 and 31, the latter two being snow caves. Then attrition and illness took their toll, leaving only Machnik, Terlikowski and me to stock the higher camps and fix the route to Makalu La. Brandolin was the only other climber to reach Camp III in January. Dangerously high winds kept us below Makalu La until January 19, 1988, when I alone reached 7500 meters while trying to site Camp IV. I recorded −15° F with winds in excess of 60 mph. The consistently severe weather and fatigue led us to abandon our attempt on January 21, after 44 days. Machnik, Terlikowski and I cleaned the mountain to Advance Base unassisted by January 25.

ANDREW EVANS

Kangchungtse (Makalu II) Attempt. Swiss climbers Wilma Simonetta and Claudio Righeschi intended to climb the normal route on Kangchungtse. They established two camps and reached Makalu La at 7400 meters on April 29 before retreating to Base Camp for a rest. They never got to this point again. Righeschi reached Camp II at 6800 meters on May 4 while Simonetta, weak from intestinal illness, turned back at 6000 meters. On May 5 there was heavy snowfall and they decided to abandon the attempt. The other two members of the party made no real effort to climb.

MICHAEL J. CHENEY, *Himalayan Club,* and ELIZABETH HAWLEY

Kangchungtse (Makalu II) Attempt and Tragedy. A ten-member French expedition led by Louis Dollo attempted Kangchungtse by the normal south-ridge route. The big snowstorm put an end to this team's climb as it did to many others this season. The highest point reached was 6800 meters on October 13 by the leader's brother Pierre Dollo, François Duthil, Mlle Hélène Hardy and Mlle Aline Paneboeuf. A second summit bid to 6550 meters turned back on the 18th when the storm loomed. Two members left Base Camp on October 15 because one was ill and Jacques Saint-Martin was exhausted. They were trekking from Base Camp when the storm hit. They became separated. Two porters and Saint-Martin died of exposure and exhaustion.

MICHAEL J. CHENEY, *Himalayan Club,* and ELIZABETH HAWLEY

Chamlang East Attempt. Jon Deak and I, one of four regular members and founder and life president respectively of the Juilliard Mountain Club (and both professional double bass players), set up "Bass" Camp near the lower Barun Glacier in mid May. To reach our high camp was wild and dangerous with two major avalanche tracks to cross and falling rocks to dodge. Easy scrambling turned into gripping, exposed free climbing when wet gloppy snow fell in the afternoon as it invariably did after we had left the ropes in the cache above. We had all our stuff at 18,500 feet after a week and set out on April 30 up the north face. We think we were to the left of Doug Scott's route as we went up a snow gully that topped out with a few pitches of vertical, snow-covered, frozen rock and a little steep ice. We gained the ridge well to the left of the saddle. After bivouacking in a small crevasse at 22,000 feet for 36 hours, we headed for the summit on May 2. At dawn a major storm appeared when we were level with the saddle at 22,500 feet but on the east side of the horn. We retreated to Camp I in the storm. After waiting a couple of days there, we went back to Bass Camp. Jon's toes, frostbitten in the bivouac, became terribly painful. We gave up thoughts of another summit attempt, retrieved our high camp and walked out to Tumlingtar despite the intense pain Jon was suffering. After this stimulating sight-reading, we shall probably go back to try for a complete performance on this spectacular mountain.

RICHARD (DOBBS) HARTSHORNE

Baruntse Attempt. A French expedition led by André Mathis failed to climb the northeast face and north ridge of Baruntse. Still short of the ridge, on October 17 all four members got to 6000 meters, where they had placed Camp II. Then came the big blizzard of October 19 and 20. During the night of the 19th, the two still in Camp II took down the tents that were being buried in continuing snowfall and cleared Camp II. Climbing was finished.

MICHAEL J. CHENEY, *Himalayan Club,* and ELIZABETH HAWLEY

Ama Dablam. Nelson Max, Bruce Cox, Dave Karl, Ron Norton, Chip Kamin and I arrived at 15,000 feet at the normal Ama Dablam Base Camp

above Mingbo on March 26. Though the weather had been clear for a week, it began a predictable pattern of clear mornings and foggy or snowy afternoons. After a rest day, we spent until April 2 carrying our gear without Sherpa help to 18,000 feet. Although exhausting, it was good for acclimatization. At this time, the Greek National Team arrived in Base Camp. With the help of yaks, the next day they moved camp to 18,000 feet and tried to occupy it, but a day later they were back in Base Camp, sick. With the approval of our liaison officer, we moved Base Camp to a small bench lake at 16,400 feet, which saved us three or four hours round trip. From there we were able to make quick progress and established Camp I on the southwest ridge on April 4. The tent platforms were encased in several feet of ice. It took two days of work to establish reasonably level tents. Our overall strategy was to fix the route to Camp III at 20,900 feet and then go alpine-style to the summit. From April 4 to 8 we stocked Camp I and began to lead on up the narrow ridge to Camp II. The rock was sound and the climbing enjoyable. On the evening of April 8 a storm began which put down a foot of snow. We descended to our new Base Camp, where we waited for two days. On April 11, just to get back to Camp I took eight hours, double the previous time. We attempted to go on to Camp II but were stopped 500 feet from the Yellow Tower by darkness and difficult ground. What had been an easy friction traverse became positively treacherous. Ice had filled good rock handholds. We established Camp II above the Yellow Tower on the 13th. Only three of us stayed, the other three relaying loads from Camp I. We realized we could not all make the summit. Several of the Greeks had used our fixed line and were being supplied by one hard-working Sherpa. Three of them and Sherpa Tenzing joined us. The route was out of condition. The overhanging crack at the first step was completely filled with ice. Up to there, the route had been stripped of all fixed rope; suddenly it exploded with line and gear, resembling a mountaineering museum. On April 16, Kamin, Karl and Max made it to Camp III at 20,500 feet, accompanied by the three Greeks and Tenzing. At five A.M. on April 17, all seven set out and reached the summit at four P.M. A long, cold night of rappels brought them back to Camp III and then to Camp II. Kamin suffered superficial frostbite of the fingers and toes. On the night of the 18th a storm set in. The two-day descent and stripping of the route, in which the other three assisted, was incredibly laborious.

JOHN IACOVINO

Ama Dablam. The first Greek ascent of any Himalayan or Karakoram peak was achieved on April 17 when Mike Tsoukias, Christos Lambris, Konstaninos Manalis and Sherpa Tenzing went to the top of Ama Dablam with the successful Americans. The Greeks and Americans camped at the same limited campsites on the ascent, went to the summit and returned to Camp III together.

MICHAEL J. CHENEY, *Himalayan Club,* and ELIZABETH HAWLEY

Ama Dablam South Ridge Attempt. After a 13-day walk-in, we arrived at Base Camp on September 17. Four members succumbed to illness. Ian Barton suffered a retinal hemorrhage, leader Martin Mandel contracted glandular fever, Mac Battersby was debilitated from giardia and Dave Green had such severe food poisoning that he had to be stretchered rapidly to the valley. On September 28, Andy Cave, Henry Todd, Bert Simmonds and I left an 18,800-foot bivouac and climbed the granite rock ridge to 19,500 feet. The following day Cave and I climbed to a third bivouac at 20,500 feet, while Todd and Simmons rested at 19,500 feet. On the 30th, Cave and I climbed to 21,000 feet but found bad snow conditions at the sérac line on the upper snowfield. We retreated in threatening weather. The other two turned back at 20,000 feet. Pete Swift and Jane Richmond climbed to 19,000 feet but descended with Todd and Simmons. Todd and I again reached 20,000 feet on October 13 with deteriorating snow conditions.

ANDREW PERKINS, *Alpine Climbing Group*

Ama Dablam, North Ridge Attempt. Steven Davis, Charles "Mick" Holt, Jeffery Alzner and I attempted the north ridge of Ama Dablam. After some delay in getting our baggage because of the continuing monsoon, we established Base Camp on September 25 at 16,400 feet at the end of the lateral moraine of the Ama Dablam Glacier just under the end of the north ridge. The initial section of our route ascended a spur that forms the right side of a large rock triangle at the base of the ridge. We made an equipment dump at a 17,300-foot col at the base of the spur. Above there we made extensive use of fixed rope. Camp I at 19,300 feet was on the corniced ridge above the apex of the triangle. Conditions had varied from mixed rock and snow to 75° unconsolidated snow. On the remaining ridge we generally climbed on the eastern side just under the large overhanging double cornices on the crest. We often had to carve around and through them. We also had pitches of steep or overhanging ice as well as 5.10 rock. On October 13, Davis retreated to Base Camp with pleurisy. Two days later, Holt joined him suffering from exhaustion and bronchitis. Alzner and I with the help of Tsering Lakhpa Sherpa reached our high point at a shoulder at 20,900 feet on October 17 and left equipment for Camp II. Two more climbing days should have put us on the summit. Unfortunately it began to snow and we descended to wait out the bad weather in Camp I. Heavy snow fell for two days, destroying our Camp I tents. In a whiteout, we began to retreat. Alzner was caught unroped in an avalanche but miraculously stopped himself without injury. After hours of post-holing, we found Base Camp under five feet of new snow. Only two of the seven tents were usable. After three days of sun, the deep snow finally consolidated enough to let us evacuate Base Camp.

FREDERICK ZIEL, *M.D.*

Ama Dablam Attempt. A British-American expedition led by Englishman William O'Connor had hoped to climb Ama Dablam's normal route, the south ridge. They were defeated by the heavy snowfall of October 18 to 20. All five members reached the high point of 5700 meters on October 17 and then retreated in the face of the storm. When two members and a Sherpa went back up to this point, where they had placed Camp I, they found not only a destroyed tent but also extremely dangerous snow conditions. It was getting colder too and so they abandoned the climb.

MICHAEL J. CHENEY, *Himalayan Club,* and ELIZABETH HAWLEY

Bulgarian Ama Dablam Attempt. This Bulgarian expedition led by Venelin Petrov had hoped to climb a new route, the northwest ridge to the west face. They were badly delayed because cargo by truck from Bulgaria failed to arrive on time and they had been on the mountain only for four days when the big October blizzard struck. Valeri Gueorguiev Peltekov and Nicolai Apostolov Proev reached 5600 meters on October 23 and then the climb was abandoned because of dangerous snow conditions.

MICHAEL J. CHENEY, *Himalayan Club,* and ELIZABETH HAWLEY

Ama Dablam. An American team led by Annie Whitehouse had planned to attempt Tawoche first and then Ama Dablam, but when they reached Tawoche, they decided against trying it. Deep unconsolidated snow lay at its base and the couloir they had thought to climb was bare rock rather than the ice they had expected. They went immediately to Ama Dablam, made Base Camp there on November 18 and climbed to the summit by the normal south ridge in three waves, all before the official beginning of the winter season, which starts on December 1; they informed the Nepalese authorities that they climbed earlier than their permission had been granted for because of threatening weather. Sandy Stewart and Eric Reynolds went to the summit on November 23, Annie Whitehouse and Clay Waldman on the 26th. Todd Bibler made a fast solo ascent and was on top later on the 26th. They had three camps above Base Camp. Because they climbed before the official beginning of the winter season, the Nepalese authorities on February 22, 1988 announced that all five summiters are banned from climbing any Nepalese mountain for the next five years.

MICHAEL J. CHENEY, *Himalayan Club,* and ELIZABETH HAWLEY

Correction on Ama Dablam Ascent. On page 238 of *A.A.J., 1987,* the climb made by the Yugoslavs was on the south face of Ama Dablam and not on Pumori.

Tawoche Attempt. Ten Britons and Americans were led by Scott Mal Duff on a guided climb on the southwest face to the southeast ridge of Tawoche. None of the clients got higher than 6100 meters, but after they left, on October

2 Duff and the other guide, Andy Black, ascended to 6350 meters, about 150 vertical meters below the summit. They did not climb to the top because of dangerous snow slabs. They descended and moved Advance Base for an attempt on the unclimbed east face, but they were forced to give up because of Duff's ill health.

MICHAEL J. CHENEY, *Himalayan Club,* and ELIZABETH HAWLEY

Lhotse Shar Attempt. The members of our expedition were Filip Bence, Janez Benkovič, Vincenc Berčič, Tomo Česen, Milan Gladek, Silvo Karo, Radivoj Nadvešnik, Janez Plevel, Marko Prezelj, Andrej Štremfelj, Janez Šušteršič, Dr. Peter Panjtar and I as leader. Hoping to climb the Austrian route, which ascends the southwest ridge from the col with Island Peak to 7200 meters and continues up the southeast ridge, we established Base Camp on March 14. Despite alternating high winds and heavy snowfalls, we fixed the route to 7200 meters and established three camps on the route. We were very surprised when on April 11 the leader of the French expedition and one other came to our Base Camp, proposing to climb the same route. Later it proved that they had permission for the east ridge. They established their Base Camp on the other side of Island Peak. We met them a few days later on our route, fixing ropes to 6600 meters and from there on proceeding only on our ropes. We found this behavior most extraordinary. After having been on the mountain for 60 days in miserable weather, food supplies were running low and the climbers were exhausted. The attempt was abandoned on May 12 although the weather was improving. The high point, which was to have been the site for Camp IV, was reached on April 20 by Bence.

VINCENC GRILJC, *Planinska Zveza Slovenije, Yugoslavia*

Lhotse Shar. Our expedition was composed of Guy Donzey, Dr. Xavier Bigard, Pierre Royer, Lionel Mailly, Yves Tedeschi, Eric Gramond, Philippe Renard, Robert Flematti, Daniel Semblanet, French, Nima Norbu, Nepalese, and Rajeev Sharma, Indian. We climbed the southwest ridge to 7200 meters and then the southeast ridge to the summit. Base Camp was established at the foot of the south face on April 12. On April 15 Camp I was placed at 5800 meters on the little col between the southwest ridge and Island Peak. Camps II and III were set up on April 27 and May 1 at 6200 and 7000 meters. We had planned for a Camp IV at 7600 meters, but weather conditions prevented this. On May 20 Tedeschi, Sherpa Senge, Royer and I set out from Camp III. Royer and I turned back at 7600 meters because we began to suffer from frostbite. Senge stopped at 8250 meters. Tedeschi reached the summit of Lhotse Shar at ten A.M., having been climbing for ten hours. He did not continue on the traverse to Lhotse as had been the original hope. The climbing was mainly on ice. On May 8 Gramond and I flew with a two-place *parapente* from Camp III at 7000 meters to the Lhotse Shar Glacier at 5300 meters.

ALAIN ESTÈVE, *Captain, Groupe Militaire de Haute Montagne*

Lhotse Shar, East Ridge Attempt. Alan Burgess, Joe Frank, Dick Jackson and I had hoped to traverse from Lhotse Shar to Lhotse via Lhotse Middle. We arrived at Base Camp on August 28 and established staging camp at 19,000 feet from where we could fix a small amount of rope on steep ridges above. The rope began at 20,000 feet and led to easy ground at 21,700 feet. From there the southeast flank of the mountain consisted of wide open slopes averaging 40° interspersed with short but steeper séracs. On September 27, at 23,000 feet we triggered a five-foot-thick avalanche. With great luck we were carried only 30 feet and stopped at the edge of an ice cliff. However, the avalanching snow stripped the entire slope we had just climbed. We descended, carefully. A week later, we tried again, but snow conditions were even worse with the whole of this side of the mountain covered by vast areas of slab. We abandoned this route on October 8. We then changed to the south spur from which a Spanish team had recently withdrawn because of four avalanche fatalities. Unfortunately, the time taken in changing the permit lost us so much time that we were hit by the big storm of October 19. Four feet of snow fell in Base Camp and two avalanches destroyed two of our tents with direct hits. I was in one of them, but the snow stopped six inches from my shoulder.

ADRIAN BURGESS, *A.A.C. and Alpine Climbing Group*

Lhotse Shar Tragedy. On September 27, four of the Spanish Catalan expedition that was trying to repeat the Austrian route on Lhotse Shar left Camp IV at 7350 meters on the southeast ridge, intending to set up Camp V at 7850 meters. At noon they failed to establish radio contact with their four companions at Base Camp. The following day, the latter went to search for the missing climbers and eventually saw the bodies on the glacier at 6000 meters. A collective fall of some 1500 meters is suggested. The unfortunate victims are leader Toni Sors, Sergio Escalera, Francesc Porras and Antonio Quiñones. The highest point by any of the expedition was 7800 meters, reached by three other members of the expedition searching for their companions on September 29. One of the searchers was María Mercedes Macía, who thus set an altitude record for Spanish women.

XAVIER EGUSKITZA, *Pyrenaica, Bilboa, Spain*

Lhotse Attempt. Frenchmen Eric Escoffier and Eric Bellin and Swiss Stéphane Schaffter acclimatized on Island Peak and Lhotse Shar before heading on April 16 for their objective, the south face of Lhotse. The good weather didn't come. Every afternoon there was new snow and every morning the face avalanched. On April 27 they gave up.

MICHAEL J. CHENEY, *Himalayan Club,* and ELIZABETH HAWLEY

Lhotse South Face Attempt. An International expedition to the still unclimbed south face of Lhotse was led by Krzysztof Wielicki. The climbing team had eight Poles, two South Tiroleans, one Briton and two Mexicans, some of whom joined the expedition after the successful Shisha Pangma expedition. They followed basically the 1985 Polish route and managed to get only 50 meters higher. On September 15, Dr. Czesław Jakiel was killed by an avalanche that fell from high above. Walenty Fiut broke his femur. They were both swept down 150 meters. Tirolean Alois Brugger jumped into a crevasse and was unhurt. Fiut was carried to Base Camp and evacuated by helicopter. Brugger also left the expedition. The other Tirolean Kurt Walde and Poles Mirosław Dasal, Piotr Konopka, Maciej Pawlikowski, Andrzej Osika and Wielicki were joined by Mexicans Carlos Carsolio and Elsa Avila, Pole Artur Hajzer and Englishman Alan Hinkes, who had been on Shisha Pangma. The big storm of October 19 and 20 caused great difficulties. The highest point reached, 8300 meters, was gained by leader Wielicki and Artur Hajzer on October 29 and then the wind defeated them.

MICHAEL J. CHENEY, *Himalayan Club,* and ELIZABETH HAWLEY

Czechoslovakian Everest Attempt. A Czechoslovakian expedition of 23 climbers was led by Ivan Gálfy. They had hoped to make two new routes on the southwest face of Everest but early on it was decided not to attempt them because four of the strongest climbers had permission to try an alpine-style ascent of Bonington's 1975 route, many climbers had got sick and it was important for the leader to have a successful climb because of sports politics in Czechoslovakia. While the four tried the 1975 route, the main party concentrated on the 1972 Bonington route and a few joined the Spanish-Italian team on the south pillar. None reached the summit. The four-man alpine-style team got to 7900 meters, the main party on the 1972 route reached 8250 meters and one of those who went to the south pillar traversed to the South Col but went no higher. The causes of failure were terrible winds and the lack of Sherpa support. The load-carrying Czechs got exhausted. Only one of the three Sherpas who went above Base Camp got as high as Camp II. This expedition took place in the pre-monsoon period.

MICHAEL J. CHENEY, *Himalayan Club,* and ELIZABETH HAWLEY

Everest Attempt. Our expedition was composed of 13 Spaniards and two Italians. We set up Base Camp on April 3. Camps I, II, III and IV were established at 5950, 6400, 7400 and 7900 meters on April 5, 8, 26 and May 19. We were able to set up the first three camps so rapidly since we were following in the steps of the Czechoslovakian expedition. We were slowed terribly above there by fierce winds, which twice completely destroyed Camp III. I cannot tell with exactitude what happened above Camp IV, which we placed on the Polish South Pillar route. Spaniard José Carlos Tamayo, Italian Fausto De Stefani, Czech Miroslav Šmid, Sherpas Ang Phurba and Pemba and I ascended to Camp IV on May 19. I scarcely remember a thing from the next three-and-a-half days. I do know that Tamayo and I climbed to 8200 meters, where we set up a bivouac in a comodious bergschrund protected from the wind. I also remember that we got up at four A.M. on May 21 to head for the summit. Tamayo set out a little ahead of me and immediately returned, telling that there was furious wind and that it was frigidly cold. We had to go back to the tent. After that, my mind is a complete blank until we got to Camp II, except that I am aware that Ramón Portillo and Antonio Trabado helped us down to Camp II. Tamayo had severe frostbite and I was mentally completely confused, probably from cerebral edema. Another summit attempt on May 27 failed at 7900 meters.

JUANJO SAN SEBASTIÁN, *Federación Vasca de Montaña*

Everest Attempt. In the post-monsoon 31 climbers attempted Everest from the Western Cwm. All but four climbers were on the permits of Austrian Hanns Schell and all used his route through the icefall and cwm. Murray Rice and I were a two-man expedition from the Northwest attempting the South Col route and the northwest face of Lhotse without Sherpas and without supplementary oxygen. We helicoptered to Lukla and arrived at Base Camp at 5400 meters on September 1. We spent eight days acclimatizing and carrying loads through the icefall before moving to Camp I at 6000 meters on September 9. We acclimatized there during a five-day storm, carried to Camp II at 6500 meters on the 14th and moved up the next day. On the 16th we descended to our single-tent Base Camp for the last of our gear. Fearful of hepatitis and infectious diarrheas, both present in Base Camp, we moved up again to Camp I (our fifth carry) and to Camp II on the 18th (our third carry). We now had food and fuel in Camp II for a month. I set up Camp III on the 20th at 7300 meters on the Lhotse Face. Three days later we both moved up to the higher camp with heavy loads. I felt wasted on arrival. During dinner, eating competed with breathing and in order to chew and swallow, we first had to hyperventilate. This was difficult with a respiratory rate of 60 already. My breathing was stimulated partly by acetazolomide, but Murray's only by his very brisk ventilatory drive. During the night I noticed the now familiar sensations of wet cough and sweet-tasting fluid of pulmonary edema. At first light we began an eight-hour descent to Base Camp. The Lhotse Face had wind-blown snow varying from ankle to thigh deep. The lower cwm had a half meter of new snow. The heavily laden west shoulder unloaded an avalanche across our tracks an hour after we hurried by. The "Golden Gate" bridge below Camp I had been extended to six ladder-lengths as the crevasses widened and the séracs in the mid section of the icefall collapsed. Uneasy about climbing soon above 8000 meters without oxygen, I left Base Camp on the 26th to join the Polish expedition on the south face of Lhotse as physician. Murray returned that same day to Camp II and continued climbing with French Bernard Muller and Laurence de la Ferrière and Austrian Rüdiger Lang. With them he reached the South Col on September 29. When the tent threatened to disintegrate in the high winds, they descended the next morning to Camp II and several days later all the way to Base. Murray made another trip to Camp II and two more attempts as far as Camp III before descending for good on October 17, just in time to clear out our camps before the blizzard on October 18.

STEVEN BOYER

Everest Attempts. The "expedition" organized by Hanns Schell was actually a group of teams. It included the American Snowbird Expedition as well as Steve Boyer and Murray Rice whose efforts are given above. In all there were 5 Austrians, 5 Germans, 1 Italian, 2 French and 13 Americans. They all attempted the South-Col route and none were successful. The highest any of them got was 8400 meters reached by South Tirolean Reinhard Patscheider and Austrian Thomas Schlicher on October 2. They were turned back primarily by wind. The French couple Bernard Muller and Laurence de la Ferrière and Austrian Rüdiger Lang spent the night of September 29 on the South Col.

MICHAEL J. CHENEY, *Himalayan Club,* and ELIZABETH HAWLEY

Everest Attempt. The Snowbird Everest expedition began with a casual visit to Nepal's Ministry of Tourism and then a letter to Austrian Hanns Schell, Everest's permit-holder for the post-monsoon season. Karen Fellerhoff gained from Schell the admission of a cadre of Americans to join his group on the classic South-Col route. Our climbing group was composed of Fellerhoff, Sally McCoy, Mary Kay Brewster, Kelly Rhoads, Steve Fossett, Renny Jackson, Robert Link, Christopher Noble, Peter Whittaker and me as well as journalist Elizabeth Kaufmann and film-maker Marjorie Lester. From Namche Bazar we quickly made our way to 17,800-foot Everest Base Camp, arriving on September 6. We were preceded by the Austrian team, who had agreed to establish the icefall route. For safety reasons, we traveled through the icefall during the colder periods of the day, usually arising at three A.M. each day. With the assistance of our able Sherpas, we established Camps I and II (Advance Base) at 20,000 and 21,800 feet. From there we placed Camp III at 23,500 feet on the Lhotse Face and Camp IV on the South Col at 26,000 feet. With the exception of one major storm and the odd morning or afternoon snow, the weather proved amenable. By September 27, we were ready to send our first summit team from Base Camp with the hopes of summitting on October 2. Those plans were not to materialize; nor were the next series of summit attempts. High winds above Camp III would prevent us, the Austrians and all other expeditions on the mountain, in Tibet as well as Nepal, from reaching the top. Finally Peter Whittaker and Christopher Noble were climbing above Camp IV on October 9, but unfortunately they were thwarted by wind not far from Camp IV. They made a stalwart attempt to wait out the winds in the cwm, even after the exodus of the Austrian team on October 15. Everest administered the *coup de grace* on October 19, 20 and 21 with gale-force winds down to 7000 meters and snow accumulations of more than a meter of snow in Base Camp. Camps II, III and IV were virtually destroyed by burial or wind. Seven members departed for lower climes shortly after the storm, leaving Fellerhoff, Rhoads, Jackson and me with our Sherpas to continue. Weeks of work and illness had taken their toll.Two Sherpas and I were the last to ascend to Camp II. Our intention was to clear the mountain of valuables other than what we might need for one last attempt, which was scheduled to begin on October 26. We began the laborious ascent of the Lhotse Face with great hopes. The wind seemed to have abated slightly. From Camp III on, these hopes were dashed. The plumes on Everest, Lhotse and Nuptse were greater than ever and the wind coming from Tibet heralded winter. We retrieved supplies from Camp III and turned our back on the mountain for good. Two days later, we had completed our clean-up and descended to Base. Everest has now not been climbed from Nepal for two years.

PETER ATHANS

Everest attempt. Raging winds brought progress on our four-man attempt on the south pillar of Everest to a standstill as the jet stream lowered prematurely. Despite our 70-day vigil at 5500 meters and over, the outrageous winds never abated and those who ventured high invariably returned unsuccessful and with frostbite. We established Base Camp on August 23. At the time of our first summit bid, in late September, the jet stream lashed the mountain ferociously, catching the first pair, New Zealander Kim Logan and Australian Mike Rheinberger, in their bivouac at 8075 meters. After a horrifying night when they used their bodies to prevent their tent from being demolished by the extreme winds, they began their long descent via the South Col to the Western Cwm. As they crossed the wind-swept col, they were both blown off their feet successive times and it was certainly then that they began to develop frostbite. Their cold injuries ended the expedition for them. Australian Jon Muir and I continued our attempt alone for another six weeks. Three times we ascended the icefall from Base Camp to Camp II in the Western Cwm, where we waited for a week or more each time for the wind to abate. On numerous occasions we got ready to depart when the weather again deteriorated. The frightful blizzard starting on October 19 all but ended the effort for all. A week later Jon Muir and I reascended the icefall to our destroyed advance camp. For two more days we remained on the mountain completely alone, ever hoping for a break in the weather which never came. We had been high too long and both of us felt seriously deteriorated. On the last day of October, we packed up our tiny camp and headed down the glacier. In the icefall, suddenly all hell broke loose. With a crack, an area 100 by 200 meters in size lurched violently. Huge crevasses opened around us and other chasms snapped shut. The snow-covered ice buckled like the rise and fall of surf on a wild coastline. After five seconds all movement ceased as quickly as it had started. Lugging heavy packs, we negotiated the collapsed section, climbing vertical steps where there had been none and ambling past horizontal ladders which had previously been vertical. It was dark before we stumbled into Base Camp, exhausted.

PETER HILLARY, *New Zealand Alpine Club*

Everest. A Korean expedition led by Hahm Tak-Young successfully climbed Everest by the South Col. Heo Young-Ho and Ang Rita Sherpa reached the summit on December 22. Heo used oxygen while sleeping at Camp IV on the South Col, where he spent three nights, and above while climbing and bivouacking, but Ang Rita used none at any time. They left Camp IV at half past midnight and arrived on the summit at 2:20 P.M., having had trouble finding the route past numerous crevasses. They began their descent at three P.M. and near the south summit made an unprepared bivouac. Heo had fallen 15 meters down the east face when a cornice collapsed under him. He was unhurt. He and Ang Rita were roped and the Sherpa held the fall. They were only slightly frostbitten. This was Ang Rita's fourth ascent of Everest, making him the second man atop Everest four times (following Sundare Sherpa). He claims to have made all ascents without artificial oxygen. This would make him the first to make four ascents without bottled oxygen, including the only winter ascent without it.

MICHAEL J. CHENEY, *Himalayan Club,* and ELIZABETH HAWLEY

Nuptse Attempt. On October 10, after four bivouacs, the two members, Italians Enrico Rosso and Fabrizio Manoni, reached 6700 meters on the south spur of Nuptse, previously attempted twice by Jeff Lowe. They abandoned the climb because of bad snow conditions.

MICHAEL J. CHENEY, *Himalayan Club,* and ELIZABETH HAWLEY

Nuptse Attempt. Like the Italian team this season, Americans Rob Newsom and his companion wanted to climb the south spur of Nuptse, attempted previously by Jeff Lowe. This pair never even got onto the spur. They waited for the Italians to finish their attempt and acclimatized themselves. Then they went to the base of the south face on October 12. They got no higher than 400 meters above Base Camp at 5640 meters that day and turned back when they saw a storm approaching. They thought they would have to wait only a couple of days for improved weather but the big blizzard buried their gear at Base Camp and left unconsolidated powder snow. The climb was over.

MICHAEL J. CHENEY, *Himalayan Club,* and ELIZABETH HAWLEY

Pumori Attempt. The two Dutch climbing members, leader Joost Pielage and Bart Jordans, never really got onto the mountain in their attempt on the east face of Pumori. On May 7 they went to the foot of the face and decided that the danger of falling séracs was too great. The next day they left Base Camp.

MICHAEL J. CHENEY, *Himalayan Club,* and ELIZABETH HAWLEY

Pumori, East Face. On October 25, Sherpas Sundare, Ang Dorje and Nima and I got to the top of Pumori. We made the climb directly from Base Camp. With five Sherpas, I had fixed 1500 meters of rope for my seven clients, but not one of them could get beyond 6300 meters.

MARC BATARD, *Club Alpin Français*

Pumori, Japanese Southwest Ridge Ascent. This large expedition marched up the mountain in true Himalayan style with four camps, 3000 meters of fixed rope and four Nepalis accompanying them. The result was that eight Japanese and a Nepali got to the summit just before the big snowstorm. The summiters were Etsuji Ksaneko, Tomihira Tsakeda and Arjun Tamang on October 12, Fumiaki Goto, Fumihiko Kogure and Yoji Ogama on October 13 and leader Yoshiio Ohashi, Hisao Hoshino and Toru Yamato on October 14.

MICHAEL J. CHENEY, *Himalayan Club,* and ELIZABETH HAWLEY

Pumori, German Southwest Ridge Ascent. All four members reached the summit. On October 24, the successful climbers were leader Jürgen Knappe and brothers Peter and Rainer Bolesch. Two days later South Tirolean Josef Anton Holzer, who had been ill at the time of his teammates' ascent, climbed to the top. They had two camps above Base Camp. The Japanese were difficult people to share the route with. In fact, according to them, the Japanese had been given permission for a different ridge but were on the southwest ridge by the time this team arrived at Base Camp. They fixed a vast amount of rope, but they cut out small sections before leaving the mountain. At Base Camp, they opened unused gas cylinders, which caused fumes to enter the Europeans' tents and made them sick.

MICHAEL J. CHENEY, *Himalayan Club,* and ELIZABETH HAWLEY

Ngojumba Kang II. The members of our expedition were Edin Alikalfić, Zdenko Anić, Mario Bago, Nives Boršić, Davor Butković, Željko Gobec, Jerko Kirigin, Boris Kovačević, Branko Ognančević, Branko Puzak, Mario Rodeš, Branko Šeparović, Vojislav Vusić and I as leader. We climbed the south face and south ridge. We established Base Camp on October 15 at 5200 meters on the lateral moraine of the Lungsampa Glacier. The next day we improvised a cable lift to raise equipment 200 meters up onto the glacier. On October 17, Advance Base was placed at 5350 meters seven kilometers up on the edge of the Ngojumba icefall. That night a snowstorm began which lasted

PLATE 43

Photo by Darko Berljak

Ngojumba Kang II.

till October 20 and dumped a meter and a half of snow at Base Camp. On October 27, Camp I was set up at 5950 meters. We had fixed 200 meters of rope on the rock below the camp. The weather was beautiful, but the wind and deep snow caused difficulties and it was not until November 2 that we placed Camp II at 6500 meters. Camp III was established at 6950 meters on November 7. Progress was slowed by huge crevasses below the final face. On November 10, Kovačević and Puzak climbed the face both in deep snow and on hard ice, which was of 50° to 65°. They set up Camp IV at 7200 meters. On the 11th, they reached the summit of Ngojumba II (7743 meters, 25,403 feet). From the same camp on November 13, Butković and Alikalfić got to the top while Ognančević gave up at 7500 meters. (The Croatian climbers thought they had made the first ascent. They did make a new route and the second ascent. The first ascent was made by Japanese in the pre-monsoon period of 1965, when they first thought they had climbed Ngojumba Kang I. They later acknowledged they had gone to the slightly lower summit, Ngojumba Kang II.—*Editor.*)

DARKO BERLJAK, *Planinarski Savez Zagreba, Yugoslavia*

Cho Oyu Attempt. Matt Baker, Ney Grant, Ron Reno, Kirk Swanson, Dr. Rich Gerhauser and I as leader, accompanied by Base Camp helpers Sue Baker, John Bell and Mona Livingston, attempted the so-called traditional "southwest" ridge route from Nepal, which is in actual fact the northwest ridge. Only one high-altitude Sherpa was employed above Base Camp. We established Base Camp at Kangchung (5200 meters) on April 12. Advance Base at 5950 meters was occupied on April 22, close by the Chilean camp. A commercial expedition from Europe with over 20 members, which had approached from the Tibetan side, was also there. Camps I, II, III and IV were established at 6400, 6800, 7200 and 7600 meters on April 25, 27, 29 and 30. At Camp IV, Swanson and Grant were joined by two Chileans; another Chilean pair had reached the summit a couple of days earlier. Bad weather stopped a summit attempt on May 1 and continued bad weather forced a descent to Camp II on May 2 and to Base Camp on May 4. No subsequent summit attempt was made since most of our supplies had been removed from Advance Base on the Tibetan side by unknown persons. On April 25, having carried to Camp I, I was confronted by Chinese army and police officials, who confiscated the Nepalese climbing permit and my passport and prevented me from climbing higher. I descended to Base Camp to report on the political border difficulties now developing over the route. Apparently a border re-alignment moved the border south to the Nangpa La and the natural drainage divide between the two countries. This puts the original ascent route and the Messner variation in Tibet. Future climbing parties attempting the mountain from Nepal via the Thame valley and the Nangpa Glacier may experience similar difficulties. It is also possible that a Chinese customs post is being constructed at or near Dzapama and the border may be patrolled during the climbing season. Possibly an agreement could be reached with climbing authorities in Beijing, permitting an expedition to approach the mountain from Nepal and to cross over into Tibet for the actual ascent on the upper reaches of the mountain.

ROBERT WATTERS, *Unaffiliated*

Cho Oyu. Alejandro Izquierdo, Italo Valle, Rodrigo Mújica and I established Base Camp at 5200 meters on April 3 and Camp I at 5600 meters. In order to reach Camp II at 5850 meters on the normal (Tichy) route on Cho Oyu, we had to cross either the Nangpa La or the Senta-ghu pass; we did it both ways. Camps III and IV were at 6600 and 7200 meters. On April 28 we set up two tents at Camp V at 7600 meters. After six hours on April 29, Valle, Ang Rita, Ang Phuri and I reached the summit. Swiss Fredy Graf and Josef Wangeler arrived just five minutes after us. (See Cho Oyu from Tibet.— *Editor.*) This was one of the only three sunny days we had on the expedition. Izquierdo and Mújica got to Camp V in a second summit try but could not continue because of bad weather. Ang Rita has one of the best records of the Sherpas. He has now climbed to the summits of ten 8000ers: Dhaulagiri (4), Everest (3), Cho Oyu (2), Kangchenjunga (1).

MAURICIO PURTO, *Chilean Section of the Club Alpino Italiano*

Cho Oyu, Illegal Ascent. Two Polish climbers, Tadeusz Karolczak and Aleksander Lwow, made an unauthorized climb of Cho Oyu, reaching the summit on September 30. They climbed the northwest face after crossing into Tibet from Nepal.

Swiss Cho Oyu Attempt. Leader Norbert Joos, Peter Alig and Louis Deuber were defeated by dangerous snow conditions on this attempt on Cho Oyu's southeast face. They reached 7600 meters on September 20 but were forced to retreat. They had had four bivouacs in their alpine-style attempt. On October 1, they got only to 7100 meters. Waist-deep powder snow and fierce winds meant great avalanche danger.

MICHAEL J. CHENEY, *Himalayan Club,* and ELIZABETH HAWLEY

German Cho Oyu Attempt. This four-man expedition dwindled to just one member before arrival at Base Camp; two went to Lhotse first and never went on to Cho Oyu and the third got sick before getting to Base Camp and left Nepal. That left Hans Eitel to climb alone, which he did. There were constant avalanches on his intended southeast-face route and so he changed his plans and tried the south ridge, the eastern one of the two lines attempted by Mark Udall's team. Eitel got to 7400 meters on October 23 before giving up. The route was too difficult and long for him alone.

MICHAEL J. CHENEY, *Himalayan Club,* and ELIZABETH HAWLEY

Cho Oyu, West-Southwest Ridge Attempt. Our team was composed of Bill Roos, Wally Berg, Frank Coffey, Dr. Chuck Coffey, Alan Roberts, Ted Keresote, Rob Gustke, Scott Thorburn, Brad Udall and me as leader. Our approach march started from Jiri on September 4 and on the 12th we reached Namche Bazar. On September 19, Base Camp was established at 16,900 feet in the upper Thame valley, three hours above Sumna Phug in a beautiful meadow on the east side of the Sumna Glacier. While the monsoon continued, we acclimatized by carrying to a dump at 17,700 feet locating Camp I at 19,000 feet. When the weather became clear on the 25th, we turned our attention to the "arête." Our goal was to climb a 2000-foot steep snow-and-rock arête to reach the Nangpai Gossum plateau, to follow the plateau to the upper sections of the west-southwest ridge at 23,000 feet and to climb the ridge to the summit. After ten days of fixing rope on the steep terrain of the arête, we found an exposed knife-edge, over a quarter mile in length, between us and the plateau. After deciding on October 5 that fixing ropes and carrying loads over this section was not worth the risk, time or energy, we moved to the "Sumna Spur," a prominent 4500-foot-high rib just west of the arête. On October 14, Gustke and Frank Coffey established Camp I at 20,400 feet on the spur. To get there, we climbed 2000 feet of ice, snow and rock up to 65°. We fixed 300 meters of rope in the upper sections. Gustke, F. Coffee and I reached 22,000 feet on October 17 but were stymied by an unstable knife-edge that led to the base of a 200-foot-high ice cliff. Above the cliff, the way was clear to the Nangpai Gossum plateau. Unfortunately, the massive storm that commenced on October 17 and lasted until the 20th precluded further attempts. Base Camp was evacuated with much difficulty because of deep snow. We reached Namche on November 2.

MARK UDALL

Cho Oyu Solo Winter Ascent, 1988. Until early this year, only six men had climbed an 8000er alone, none in wintertime. Spaniard Fernando Garrido took five days for his lonely ascent, beginning on February 2, 1988 from a camp at 5850 meters near the foot of Cho Oyu's western slopes. On February 6 at six P.M., in cold and windy weather, when daylight was fading fast, he stood on the summit. He describes the top of Cho Oyu as looking like the rim of a volcanic crater and to make sure he had reached the highest point, he says he went all around the rim before descending that night to 7600 meters, where he had left his sleeping bag. Two days later, Garrido was safely back in his glacier camp. (The route was said to be the west ridge-west face route.—*Editor.*)

ELIZABETH HAWLEY

Ngojumba Kang Winter Ascent, 1988. Under the leadership of Chung Jin-Yang, South Koreans Yu Wang-Yul and Choi Mi-Ho made the third ascent and the first winter ascent of Ngojumba Kang on February 11, 1988. They had hoped to continue on along the east ridge of Cho Oyu, but they did not progress very far along that.

ELIZABETH HAWLEY

Khatang. An expedition of 14 Swiss and a Liechtensteiner (Helmut Kindle) was led by Karl Kobler. They climbed the northeast ridge and placed 14 climbers on the summit (6782 meters, 22,250 feet). They had two high camps. The summit was reached on October 14 by leader Kobler, Christoph Pfistner, Miss Parvine Eva Bähler and Helmut Kindle, on October 15 by Jan Messerli, Lucien Criblez, Philippe Arnold and Reto Schild, on October 16 by Martin Schürch, Walter Bähler, Stefan Aebersold and Samuel Melchior Anderegg and on October 17 by Felix Stampfli, Max Fahrni and by Kindle for a second time.

MICHAEL J. CHENEY, *Himalayan Club,* and ELIZABETH HAWLEY

Loenpo Gang. Our expedition consisted of Dr. Cho Suk-Phil, Dr. Kwon Hyeon, Hong Woon-Ki, Lee Jeong-Hoon, Kim Soo-Hyeon and me as leader. We climbed Loenpo Gang by a new route, the west face and southwest ridge, and made the third ascent of the peak. After leaving Kathmandu on August 26, we traveled up the Trisuli and Langtang valleys to establish Base Camp at 4750 meters on the Langshisha Glacier on September 3. Bad weather held us up for a week. On September 10, we set up Advance Base at 5000 meters and the next day Deposit Camp at 5250 meters. The constantly clear weather helped speed up establishing Camps I and II at 5750 and 6200 meters on September 18 and 21. Between Deposit Camp and Camp I there was a very steep snow wall where we fixed 500 meters of rope. Lee and Sherpas Da Gombu and Ang Temba fixed 600 meters of rope between Camps I and II on a steep ridge which looked difficult but avoided avalanche dangers. After snowy weather, climbers fixed 300 meters of rope in the knife-edged southwest ridge and set up Camp III at 6680 meters. The summit (6969 meters, 22,897 feet) was reached at 8:15 A.M. on September 27 by Lee Jeong-Hoon, Kim Soo-Hyeon and Sherpas Da Gombu and Ang Temba. On the route to the summit, there were many crevasses, but the slope was not too steep. Due to the very steep ridge between Deposit Camp and Camp II, we gave up a second summit attempt.

RYONG YOON-JAE, M.D., *Chonnam University Medical School, Korea*

Langtang Lirung Winter Ascent, 1988. A 12-man Polish expedition led by Wojciech Masłowski made a winter ascent of Langtang Lirung by the southeast ridge when on January 3, 1988 Kazimierz Kiszka, Adam Potoczek and Mikołaj Czyzewski reached the summit for the eighth ascent of the peak.

ELIZABETH HAWLEY

Langtang Ri. Only three expeditions have ever attempted Langtang Ri and all three have been Japanese and successful. All have climbed the same route, the southwest ridge. The recent expedition established three high camps. Yuzo Ichinose, Mitsuru Yamamoto and Sherpas Nima Wanchu and Ajiba reached the summit on April 17, followed by leader Katsuyuki Fukuzawa, Keiji Maryyamo, Daizo Yamamoto and Ajiba on April 18. Ajiba waited in Camp III before making his second trip to the summit.

MICHAEL J. CHENEY, *Himalayan Club,* and ELIZABETH HAWLEY

Langshisha Ri Southwest Summit. Leader Mirosław Gradzielewski, Anna Bruzdowicz-Dudek and Jolanta Patynowska of a seven-person Polish expedition reached the southwest summit of Langshisha Ri (c.6145 meters, 20,160 feet) by its southeast ridge on October 24. The climb ended there because two others were sick, one had already left for home and the others had little time left.

MICHAEL J. CHENEY, *Himalayan Club,* and ELIZABETH HAWLEY

Ganesh V. The first autumn attempt on Ganesh V was successful when Koji Shibuya and Yasuhiro Matsuda and Sherpas Kusang Lama and his brother Dorje reached the top (6986 meters, 22,919 feet) on October 4 by a previously untried route, the south ridge. Our five-man expedition also included S. Ishikawa, Yasuhiro Yahara and me as leader. We established Base Camp, Advance Base, Camps I, II, III and IV at 4300, 4900, 5150, 5550, 5850 and 6300 meters on September 9, 10, 14, 20, 27 and October 1. The weather was almost always fine although it was cloudy on the day of the ascent. From Base Camp to Camp I was easy. From Camps I to IV we followed the ridge. The face above Camp IV was mixed snow and ice and 70° ice. This was the third ascent of the mountain.

HARUO MAKINO, *Fukui Alpine Club, Japan*

Manaslu Attempt. Both Catalan members, Enric Bassas and Francisco Barcelona, with sirdar Nima Dorje Tamang and Gyalgen Sherpa, pitched Camp at 5600 meters above Naike Col on April 8. That is as high as they got on the standard route. A heavy snowstorm drove them down to Base Camp with frostnipped toes. They stayed in Base Camp to let their toes recover and then returned to the site of Camp II on April 21. An even heavier snowstorm on April 18 had so deeply buried their camp that they could find no signs of it; they retreated that same day to Base Camp. That was the end of the attempt.

MICHAEL J. CHENEY, *Himalayan Club,* and ELIZABETH HAWLEY

Manaslu Attempt. Only the Poles Krzysztof Pankiewicz and Ludwik Wilczyński did any serious climbing. The expedition leader was the Pole

Wojciech Szymański and there were also two Czechoslovaks and a German doctor. The Polish climbers first made acclimatization climbs on the normal northeast face route and on the third climb got to 7100 meters. They then turned their attention to a new route on the southeast face in what they hoped would be an extremely light, brief, alpine-style climb. The enormous difficulty of the line they tried and the snow conditions forced them on May 20 to abandon the attempt after three days at 6800 meters. They then thought of an ascent of the northeast face, but a big snowstorm blew up on May 21 and lasted for three days, by which time their supplies were nearly used up and the climb was over. They are convinced that their new route can be climbed but it would be best done in the winter when avalanche danger is minimal.

MICHAEL J. CHENEY, *Himalayan Club,* and ELIZABETH HAWLEY

Manaslu. A 10-member Austrian expedition led by Arthur Haid climbed Manaslu by the normal northeast-face route. On October 7, from Camp IV Johann Etschmayer, Walter Hauser and Sonam Lhakpa Sherpa reached the summit.

MICHAEL J. CHENEY, *Himalayan Club,* and ELIZABETH HAWLEY

Manaslu Attempt and Tragedy. A 15-member Japanese expedition to the east ridge of Manaslu was led by Seigo Matsushima. On October 27, Shinja Furukawa, Hiroshi Kokub, Hitoshi Kudo and Ichigi Kudo reached 6500 meters and descended. The next day Ichigi Kudo suddenly toppled over while eating supper at Base Camp. He was unconscious and died three hours later. His death and the great difficulty of the route above 6500 meters on the big rock pinnacle led the team to decide to abandon the climb.

MICHAEL J. CHENEY, *Himalayan Club,* and ELIZABETH HAWLEY

Himlung Himal Attempt. Our party consisted of Steve Tenney, Bob Rosso, Kirk Bachman and me as leader. We had little information about the peak, knowing only that the summit had been reached once, by Japanese via the east ridge from the glacier above the Larkya La in 1984. Two other attempts, one in winter, were by the same route. Our attempt was by the south ridge. We left Kathmandu on April 3 and reached Base Camp at 13,700 feet on the Himlung Glacier on April 11. Fresh snow made moving up the glacier to the foot of the south face difficult. We cached food and fuel at Advance Base at 14,400 feet on April 15. We then explored the Ratna Icefall and left equipment and fuel at 16,400 feet. On April 18, we climbed back through the icefall and bivouacked at 17,000 feet on the south ridge. After a heavy snowfall we determined that the ridge would require more time and gear than we had and so we moved left to the "Wishbone Couloir." After spending all day climbing the couloir, at dark we still had not found a suitable bivouac site. We climbed a few pitches in the dark to reach the western spur of the south ridge and pitched camp at 18,500 feet. April 20 was spent fixing lines over a very difficult traverse. We spent a second night at a pinnacle bivouac and the following day climbed to the top of the western spur. The climbing on cold, brittle ice and steep rock was of high standard. The next morning we reached the actual south ridge. Because of the difficulty and the condition of one of the members, we descended from a high point of 20,050 feet. It took two days to get back to Base Camp on April 23. We hope to return to finish this beautiful route next year.

KEVIN SWIGERT

Chulu West, Southwest Face. On October 14, Dawa Lama Sherpa and I climbed the southwest face of Chulu West by a *direttissima*. From a camp at 4300 meters, we made a reconnaissance toward the glacier at the base of the face. We found the glacier full of séracs and open crevasses that could hardly be crossed. The only alternative was to cross the face from right to left above the glacier. Delayed by morning fog, we did not set out until three A.M., crossing first easy but unstable scree, then mixed terrain and finally 50° firm snow and somewhat spongy ice. The first two-thirds was subject to rockfall. At 6100 meters the slope lessened to 45°. Then at 6300 meters, as we climbed up the right of the sérac wall, the angle steepened to 70° or 80° for some 30 meters before it eased so that we could walk to the summit (6419 meters, 21,059 feet). We arrived at four P.M. The descent was complicated by the wind on the steep east-northeast ridge and then at the foot of the summit pyramid until we found a couloir sheltered from the wind.

CARLO STRATTA, *Club Alpino Italiano*

Annapurna II Attempt. This two-man Japanese team, Kunihiko Kondo and Kazuo Yamamoto, attempted the south face of Annapurna II with no fixed camps or Sherpas. They gave up on October 13 at 7500 meters because of the dangers of the route, which included falling ice, and strong winds.

MICHAEL J. CHENEY, *Himalayan Club*, and ELIZABETH HAWLEY

Annapurna IV Attempt. An expedition of three Swiss, two Germans and an Austrian, led by Austrian Harald Navé, got no higher than 5700 meters on the normal route, the northwest ridge and northwest face, of Annapurna IV. Heavy snowfall resulted in severe wind-slab avalanche danger. Navé and the three Swiss, Fridolin Herger, Daniel Schaer and Heinz Inderwildi, reached the expedition's high point on April 23 and then descended to Base Camp the next morning when a new snowstorm began, thus ending the climb.

MICHAEL J. CHENEY, *Himalayan Club*, and ELIZABETH HAWLEY

Annapurna IV, North Ridge Attempt. Our expedition was composed of Curt Hewitt, Bob Wilson, Craig John, Ken Bures, Jean Ellis, Al Chambard,

Richard Wright, Charles Peck, Dan Holle, LaVerne Woods, Jeff Shropshire, Paul Slota, Jan Cover, Bill Thompson and me as leader. We established Base Camp on September 29 at 15,500 feet after hiking in from Dumre. We were accompanied by a Nepalese cook staff but no Sherpas. The route to Camp I at 17,200 feet required 1000 feet of fixed rope on steep loose rock. Camps II and III were at 18,200 and 20,500 feet. We fixed another 1000 feet of rope above Camp I. We spent eight days at Camp III trying to get to our Camp IV site but were unable to do so due to continuous high winds, often over 70 mph. The high point was 21,500 feet. A severe storm hit us from October 17 to 19, which forced us to an epic retreat. It took two full days of plowing down the steep and deep snow to reach the valley, a trip that normally took three hours. Over six feet of snow fell at Base Camp. We had to wait twelve days before we could return to Base Camp to recover the equipment we had left behind there, a trip that took 18 hours in waist-deep snow.

ERIC SIMONSON

Annapurna IV, Central Rib of the North Face. Our climbing team consisted of John Collett, Doug Kosty, Tim Schinhofen and me as leader, with Sherpas Pemba Norbu, sirdar, Dawa Onchu, Ang Dorje and Lhakpa Temba. In support were Dan Bridges, Bill Dailey and Karl Herrmann. Base Camp at 15,500 feet was reached on September 16 after an eight-day approach up the lush and beautiful Marsyandi valley, into the lower Manang valley with the route following the Subje Khola from Ombre. The route we had planned was on the prominent rib nearest Annapurna II. However, almost continuous avalanches convinced us to concentrate on the central rib, which leads to the upper snowfields just west of our original route. After two days of acclimatizing, we started load carries across a mile of moraine into the lower section of the central icefall, where we established a dump at 16,500 feet. On October 1, Schinhofen, Pemba, Dawa and I occupied Camp I amidst many crevasses at 17,300 feet. The main difficulties started between Camps I and II at 18,000 feet. The route snaked around, across and into crevasses. Several séracs had to be ascended on the way to the rock wall at the base of the central rib. We fixed line up the steep rock wall to a point where it joined a long steep snowfield. The search for a location for Camp II was even more challenging, as the route was on sheer faces of granite or narrow ledges of loose rock. Finally, after pushing the route to 19,500 feet, the advance team spotted a site for Camp II. On October 3, we all went down to Base Camp for a rest, returning on the 5th. Schinhofen, Pemba and Dawa resumed developing the route and on October 6 occupied Camp II on a narrow ledge at the base of a large granite wall. Kosty, who was not feeling well, went back to Base, accompanied by Herrmann, while I stayed on at Camp I, moving up to Camp II on the 8th. As I arrived, Schinhofen, Pemba and Dawa rappelled the last pitch into camp. During the night, I showed signs of altitude problems but with my condition better the next day, Schinhofen and Pemba started up to occupy Camp III. Pemba led some

PLATE 44

Photo by Karl Hermann

Central Rib Route on the North Face of ANNAPURNA IV.

bold sections, fixing line along a zig-zag route atop the rib crest which took them to a 100-foot vertical ice wall. This was the last barrier to the upper snowfields and the summit plateau. After ascending two steep snowfields, they placed Camp III at 22,800 feet. On October 10, I was feeling better and with Dawa Onchu moved up to Camp III. The incredibly exposed route clung to the side of a narrow crest that dropped away, in places, 5000 feet nearly vertically to the icefall below. We arrived at 3:30 to a completely deserted camp. Tim Schinhofen and Pemba Norbu had set out to place Camp IV higher up. At dark, there was no sign of the climbers. We called Base Camp by radio to find that they had spotted the duo just below the summit at 2:30. At 7:30 we heard voices and within seconds our friends were standing in front of the tent, totally exhausted. In hoarse voices, they told us of the climb. At 3:15, with Pemba Norbu, Tim Schinhofen became the first American to ascend to the summit of Annapurna IV (7525 meters, 24,688 feet). This was also by a new route. During the night, I had difficulty with a fluid build-up in my lungs and realized I could not proceed to the summit. We four started down toward Base Camp. Tim and I spent the night in Camp II while the Sherpas continued down to Base. A second summit team of John Collett and Doug Kosty moved to Camp I, but there was no route through the now much changed icefall.

STEVEN BRIMMER

Gangapurna Attempt. An Icelandic expedition of five, led by Gudmundur Petursson, hoped to attempt Gangapurna by its east ridge from the col between Annapurna III and Gangapurna. However, they did not reach the col but abandoned the climb at 5500 meters after two days of a three-day electrical storm that deposited 50 centimeters of snow daily and caused serious avalanche danger. They got to 5500 meters twice. On April 28 Torfi Hjaltason, Anna Lara Friariksdotter, Jon Geirsson, Porsteinn Gudjonsson and Chawang Rinzin Sherpa put a tent there for Camp III and on May 1 and 2 the four Icelanders occupied the camp for two nights.

MICHAEL J. CHENEY, *Himalayan Club,* and ELIZABETH HAWLEY

Annapurna Attempt. A New Zealand-Australian-American expedition of four was led by New Zealander Robert Hall. They had got no higher than 5600 meters on the north face of Annapurna and were still establishing their second high camp when, on April 7, Hall fell about ten meters while taking photographs in the Base Camp area. He broke a kneecap and an ankle and suffered deep cuts on both hands. The climb was abandoned.

MICHAEL J. CHENEY, *Himalayan Club,* and ELIZABETH HAWLEY

Annapurna Attempt and Tragedy. A ten-man Spanish expedition to the north face of Annapurna was led by Juan Maldonado. The climb came to an abrupt halt when Andrés Ferrer died from head injuries received in a 300-meter fall. He fell while rappelling from Camp III at 6800 meters on May 23 after having spent a bad night suffering from the altitude. He died the next day while being carried down to Camp I. After the accident, they abandoned the climb. The highest point, 6850 meters, was reached on May 23 by leader Maldonado and Daniel Villa, who, with Ferrer, would have made up the summit-attack party.

MICHAEL J. CHENEY, *Himalayan Club,* and ELIZABETH HAWLEY

Annapurna. The first Spaniards to reach the main summit of Annapurna were two members of this eight-member expedition, leader Josep María Maixe and Rafael López, who went to the top on October 8. They climbed the north face east of the Dutch rib, the 1980 German route toward the central summit and then the French 1950 route, which was a new variation of north-face routes. The same route was followed by the other Spanish expedition, which sent two members and a Sherpa to the summit three days later. They had five camps above Base Camp.

MICHAEL J. CHENEY, *Himalayan Club,* and ELIZABETH HAWLEY

Annapurna. Our expedition was composed of Francisco José Pérez, Kaji Sherpa and me. We climbed Annapurna alpine-style by the north face using the Dutch rib. We set out from Pokhara on September 16 and got to Base Camp at 4500 meters up the Miristi Khola on the 24th. We established Camps I and II at 5200 and 5800 meters on September 27 and 29, before returning for a rest at Base Camp. On October 2 we ascended to help one of the Tarragona expedition down to Base Camp; he had suffered a cerebral edema. We were back in Camps I and II on October 5 and 6. On the 7th, we ascended the buttress to bivouac at 6250 meters. At the end of the ridge, where the technical difficulties cease, we set up Bivouac IV at 6700 meters. On October 9, we ascended the long sloping plateau to bivouac at 7250 meters. We continued the next day to Bivouac VI at 7650 meters. On October 11, we three left our tent at six A.M. in cold, windy weather and reached the summit of Annapurna at one P.M. We descended to the site of Bivouac V. On the 12th, we returned to Base Camp, where our friends from the Tarragona expedition looked out for our seriously frozen toes and fingers. We shall suffer the loss of some fingers and toes. We were evacuated by helicopter to Kathmandu.

JUAN CARLOS GÓMEZ, *Centre Excursionista de Valencia, Spain*

Annapurna Winter Attempt. Two Japanese climbers, Yoshitomi Okura and Masaaki Kukushima, found in their attempt on the French 1950 route on Annapurna that climbing alone without a fixed rope was more than they could manage on difficult ground swept clear of snow, leaving very hard ice, and punctuated by several dozen big crevasses. They gave up the attempt on December 5 at 6100 meters.

MICHAEL J. CHENEY, *Himalayan Club*, and ELIZABETH HAWLEY

Annapurna Winter Attempt. Our Canadian-American expedition was an unsuccessful attempt to make the second winter ascent of Annapurna by a new route on the eastern end of the south face. We were Ken Reville, Julien Marceau, Steve and Don Adamson, J.C. Laverne, Emilie Seneult, Dan Walsh, Pemba Norbu Sherpa and me. We reached Base Camp on November 15 but could not officially begin climbing until December 1. We spent these first days acclimatizing on Tent Peak (5663 meters, 18,580 feet), sorting gear and reconnoitering Annapurna's south glacier. On November 20, we established an Advance Base. Our route required going up the center of the glacier to an icefall that gave access to the wall directly below the east ridge of Khangsar Kang or Roc Noir (7485 meters, 24,556 feet), which is part of the east ridge of Annapurna. We then proposed to traverse the east ridge to the summit. Reville, Pemba Norbu and I did most of the climbing, reaching Camp II at 20,000 feet on the wall on December 7. On December 11, we retreated in a storm to Advance Base and the next day to Base Camp. While going down, Reville, Steve Adamson, Laverne and Pemba were avalanched but were able to extract themselves with little trouble. It was decided to abandon the climb because of the weather conditions, diminishing resources and a lack of commitment by most of the members. The difficulties up to the high point were objective dangers in the icefall, 5.6 rock and grade-3 ice.

JAMES CUNNINGHAM

Annapurna South Face Ascent and Tragedy. On December 20, Noboru Yamada, Yasuhira Saito, Teruo Saegusa and Toshiyuki Kobayashi reached the summit of Annapurna, completing the first winter ascent of the south face and the first ascent of the mountain by Japanese in the winter. This was the seventh 8000er for Yamada. During the descent, two fell to their deaths, Kobayashi at 7900 meters and Saito just 20 meters above Camp IV, their highest camp at 7400 meters. It seems likely that their falls were caused by fatigue. They had followed more or less the 1970 Bonington route. A second summit bid planned for December 22 was cancelled after their teammates' falls.

MICHAEL J. CHENEY, *Himalayan Club*, and ELIZABETH HAWLEY

Hiunchuli, Southeast Face, Winter Ascent, 1986. Chris Watts and I departed a tea lodge at 10,800 feet on December 3, 1986 and toiled for five hours up steep grass slopes to set up camp on the moraine at 13,500 feet. True Camps I and II were placed below the rock band of the north glacier at 15,500 and 17,500 feet on the 4th and 5th. On December 6 we set up Camp III at

18,500 feet in a crevasse to avoid being hit by tottering séracs. We departed Camp III at one A.M. and reached the summit (6441 meters, 21,133 feet) at ten A.M. by traversing first under the sérac zone and then directly up it. This avoided the deep snow and trail-breaking of previous expeditions but gave steepish climbing and one very serious 90° ice pitch at 21,000 feet.

LINDSAY ABBOTTS, *Alpine Club*

Annapurna Dakshin Women's Attempt. Our Yugoslav women's expedition attempted the nearly five-kilometer-long southwest ridge of Annapurna Dakshin (Annapurna South), which was first climbed in the autumn of 1978 by Japanese after their unsuccessful attempt in 1974. Our members were Vlasta Kunaver, Maja Dolenc, Ana Mažar, Sanja Vranac, Irena Komprej, Nives Boršič, Mira Uršič, Danica Mlinar and I as leader. We placed Base Camp, Advance Base, Camp I and Camp II at 4050, 4800, 5700 and 5850 meters on April 16, 20 and 24 and May 9. We reached our high point of 6100 meters on May 13 and 22 before the expedition was abandoned. Our greatest problem was the weather. Of 42 days, we had only four days without snowfall and storm. There was lightning danger and high wind. The length of the ridge was also a problem. We fixed 3500 meters of rope. We carried all our loads without Sherpa help.

MARIJA FRANTAR, *Planinska Zveza Slovenije, Yugoslavia*

Annapurna Dakshin Attempt. A French expedition led by Philippe Berger failed to climb the southwest ridge of Annapurna Dakshin (South). The other three members, Vincent Couttet, Eric Fauret and Denis Leroy, reached their highest point of 6300 meters on November 12 and 13, but both times they were driven back by high winds. To have continued would have been difficult on the knife-edged ridge and there was danger of falling rock. In addition, food supplies in Camp II at 6200 meters were now exhausted and the Nepalese government's designated end of the autumn climbing season, November 15, was very near. So the climb was over.

MICHAEL J. CHENEY, *Himalayan Club,* and ELIZABETH HAWLEY

Annapurna Dakshin Winter Attempt. A seven-man Japanese expedition led by Masami Yamagata hoped to climb the south face of Annapurna Dakshin (South). They tried the south face for only one day. Because a huge avalanche came crashing down the face, they switched to the southwest ridge. There they fixed 3000 meters of rope, but they abandoned the climb at 5880 meters on December 21 when they had exhausted their supply of rope. They estimated that they needed 3000 more meters because of the numerous big rock pinnacles they had to go up, over and down. The highest point was reached by leader Yamagata and Hideo Tateno. They had three camps above Base Camp.

MICHAEL J. CHENEY, *Himalayan Club,* and ELIZABETH HAWLEY

Tilitso Attempt. Our expedition was composed of Dr. Josep Barrachina, Francesc Albera, Lluis López, Conrad López and me as leader. We left Dumre on March 10 with 40 porters. Seven days later we got to Kangsar and to Base Camp on March 28 at 4910 meters after crossing the frozen lake. Advance Base was set up two days later at 5100 meters. We started up the French route, the north spur, on Tilitso on April 7. Camp I was established the next day at 6100 meters. On the 9th Barrachina and Tashi Sherpa set out for the summit and got to within 100 meters of it, but the weather was so bad that they turned back. Strong winds destroyed Camp I and Advance Base. It was difficult to get back to Base Camp and we lost much material. We waited for a week but the weather continued bad. On April 14 we crossed the Messo Kanto Pass and descended to the Kali Gandaki valley.

JORDI COLOMER, *Unió Excursionista de Catalunya, Spain*

Tilitso Attempt. Swiss climbers, Bruno Zaugg and Marco Battaglia, climbed for only two days on Tilitso's northeast spur, carrying supplies up from Base Camp to 5800 meters. On October 3, they decided that the snow conditions were too unsafe to continue.

MICHAEL J. CHENEY, *Himalayan Club,* and ELIZABETH HAWLEY

Tukuche. Three members of this Spanish Catalan team, Pere Giro, José María Jane and leader Lluis Gómez, reached the summit on October 4. They believe they were the first to ski a part of their ascent and descent of Tukuche. They skied from Camp I at 5520 meters to Camp II at 6120 meters and down again. This was done by all 11 members and their Sherpa sirdar. There was no snow at Base Camp and above Camp II the terrain was too difficult for skiing. They climbed the northwest ridge.

MICHAEL J. CHENEY, *Himalayan Club,* and ELIZABETH HAWLEY

Sita Chuchura (Tukuche West) Attempt. Eric Delcasso led this eight-man French expedition. Three climbers and the sirdar ascended nearby 6000-meter summits and then four climbers and the sirdar devoted their attention to Sita Chuchura while the other members stayed at lower altitudes because of some altitude illness and deep snow between the Dhampus and French Passes. Jean-François Rouys and Kami Tenzing Sherpa got to 6000 meters on Sita Chuchura's south-ridge-to-east-ridge route on October 29, but they decided that it was impossible to climb the final sérac on the last ice face without fixing rope; they had no rope and gear for fixing.

MICHAEL J. CHENEY, *Himalayan Club,* and ELIZABETH HAWLEY

Dhaulagiri Attempt. A nine-man Japanese expedition led by Masakatsu Nakamura attempted the normal northeast ridge of Dhaulagiri. Strong winds and deep soft snow defeated the first summit attack on May 10 when Haruo Mizukoshi, Seiichi Sekiya, Ang Phurba Sherpa and Kunga Sherpa got to 7955 meters from Camp V. Another summit party, moving up behind the first, did not go higher than Camp IV because a storm was approaching on May 11 that could mean a long spell of bad weather. Food and fuel were running out and so they decided to abandon the climb.

MICHAEL J. CHENEY, *Himalayan Club,* and ELIZABETH HAWLEY

Dhaulagiri. The American Dhaulagiri Expedition got permission to climb the east face. The team, Matt and John Culberson, Colin Grissom and I, arrived at Base Camp on September 9. Advance Base was established at the col on September 21. We then got permission from the Japanese to climb the northeast ridge up to 7500 meters in order to leave a cache and to acclimatize. On September 27, Camp I was placed at 6500 meters. At 6700 meters on the 30th, we were caught in an avalanche which carried us 150 meters down the north face before we were stopped by the Japanese fixed lines. We descended to Base Camp for five days to recuperate. On October 6, we returned to the col. Because the avalanche had set us back physically and mentally and because the lower third of the east face was exposed rock with running water, we decided to climb the northeast ridge. We returned to Camp I on October 8. At 6800 meters, Matt Culberson was concerned about avalanche danger and went down. John Culberson, Colin Grissom and I made Camps II and III at 7000 and 7500 meters on October 13 and 15. We summited on October 16 and returned on October 18. The climb was done without Sherpas or supplementary oxygen.

KITTY CALHOUN

Spanish Dhaulagiri Attempt. A four-man Spanish team led by Miguel Díaz had hoped to climb the east face of Dhaulagiri to the northeast ridge, but this was too dangerous because of big falling ice slabs and they turned to the northeast ridge. Rafael Hernández and Juan Luis Terradez got to 8000 meters on October 13 but Hernández was hit by a falling block of ice and fell 50 meters. Although his fall was stopped by Terradez and he was not injured, they decided to give up because of this and because two days earlier they had both had frostnip. The other two members were not well and so the climb was over.

MICHAEL J. CHENEY, *Himalayan Club,* and ELIZABETH HAWLEY

Japanese Dhaulagiri Attempt. On October 6, leader Tatsuhisa Mitoma, Koji Hayashi and Nuru Zambu Sherpa gained the team's highest point of 7050 meters on the normal northeast-ridge route of Dhaulagiri. When they tried again after a rest, they found a snow bridge had broken, much of their fixed rope was gone and they had no time left.

MICHAEL J. CHENEY, *Himalayan Club,*'and ELIZABETH HAWLEY

Dhaulagiri South Face Solo Attempt. The unclimbed south face of Dhaulagiri remains unclimbed. Hiroshi Aota made his Base Camp and then Advance Base at the bottom of the glacier at 4300 meters. He then did some acclimatization climbing on P 6620. Eleven days after arriving at Base Camp, he concluded that the face was too dangerous to attempt. Two or three big avalanches and uncounted numbers of smaller ones were coming down the face every day. He thinks that the winter might be a safer time to try this notoriously avalanching face.

MICHAEL J. CHENEY, *Himalayan Club,* and ELIZABETH HAWLEY

Dhaulagiri Winter Ascent. Our expedition was composed of Louis Audoubert, François Poissonier, Patrick Marcelot, Lionel André, Paul Vuillard, Annie Dubois and me. On December 1, Sundare Sherpa and I left Base Camp at 4700 meters and got to 7100 meters at six P.M. We left our bivouac at 5:30 A.M. and got to the top at 12:30. With a wind gauge on the summit ridge, I recorded a wind of 150 kilometers per hour.

MARC BATARD, *Club Alpin Français*

Dhaulagiri Winter Ascent. Our Slovene expedition consisted of Dr. Iztok Tomazin, Marjan Kregar, Pavel Kozjek and me as leader. We established Base Camp at Hiangdi Chuli at 4100 meters on November 27. We planned to climb the mountain by a combination of routes, the east face to the northeast ridge at 6000 meters. Snow on the mountain had melted abnormally in three weeks of sunny weather, which caused us difficulty in the rocky bottom part of 1800 meters. The snow conditions on the upper 2300 meters above the plateau were reasonably good. Our main difficulty was the lack of acclimatization. On December 1, we began the ascent at eight A.M. By eleven A.M. we crossed a dangerous icefall and got to 5600 meters to bivouac. We were on the east face on the route Kregar and I already knew. On December 2, I descended to 5100 meters to get some pitons and a hammer we had left there. I climbed back up to the bivouac and we four continued up the very rotten rock and then up the tongue of a hanging glacier to a plateau at 5860 meters. By evening we had crossed the plateau and bivouacked in a big crevasse at the foot of the northeast ridge. On December 3, we climbed solid snow in high winds to 6600 meters, where we set up our tent at three P.M. That night, just before midnight, Kozjek, Kregar and Tomazin set out; I followed at two A.M. We climbed for the whole of the next day and night. Tomazin reached the summit at five P.M. and Kregar at 5:20 in winds so strong that they could not stand upright. Because of the conditions, Kozjek and I returned from 8050 meters. The latter bivouacked at 8000 meters without bivouac gear. I waited for Tomazin at 7100 meters in a snow hole for nine hours. On December 5, Tomazin and I reached the tent in the crevasse at 6400 meters at 3:30 A.M. Kregar returned at 8:30 and Kozjek at five P.M. We all bivouacked together. Kregar and Tomazin descended during the next two days. Meanwhile, Kozjek and I set out for another summit attempt. We began at nine P.M. and by dawn were at 7450 meters. The wind was strengthening and Kozjek was showing signs of pulmonary edema. By night we had descended to 5100 meters and continued to Base Camp on December 8.

STANE BELAK, *Planinska Zveza Slovenije, Yugoslavia*

Dhaulagiri V Attempt. Four Spaniards hoped to climb Dhaulagiri V by the southeast ridge via White Peak, the route climbed by Japanese in 1979. Camp II was at 6400 meters on the summit of White Peak. Leader Angel Sierra and Xavier Robiro reached 7080 meters on October 6 and turned back because it was snowing. Bad weather continued. The ridge became dangerous without fixed rope, but their rope supply had been exhausted lower on the mountain. They abandoned the climb.

MICHAEL J. CHENEY, *Himalayan Club,* and ELIZABETH HAWLEY

Churen Himal East Peak Attempt. An eight-man Korean expedition led by Do Chang-Ho attempted to climb the east peak of Churen Himal by its southeast ridge but they found the final summit ridge too difficult. It was very sharp, knife-edged, steep ice. By the time they got there, the weather was deteriorating again and the climbers were tired, having been on the mountain for a month. Their highest point was 7200 meters gained on May 11 by Kim Eun-Chang and Dawa Wangchu Sherpa.

MICHAEL J. CHENEY, *Himalayan Club,* and ELIZABETH HAWLEY

Saipal Attempt. On October 24, Austrians Franz Kröll, Fritz Mross and Ang Chhepal Sherpa reached 6630 meters on the west ridge of Saipal, at a point called "Firnkopf" by Austrians in 1954. They then turned back. They estimated it would have taken them two weeks more to reach Saipal's summit.

MICHAEL J. CHENEY, *Himalayan Club,* and ELIZABETH HAWLEY

India—Kumaon

Tharkot, 1986, and Laspa Dhura, 1987. Our two Kumaon expeditions were joint ventures between the Indian Himalaya's Beckon Club of Calcutta and British teams. In 1986 we travelled up the Sundardhunga valley and ascended Tharkot (6099 meters, 20,010 feet) by the southeastern ridge. The summit was reached on September 15, 1986 by Alison Worcester, Carl Schaschke, Keven Gheen and me and on September 16 by Rob Neath, Bivujit Mukhoty and Narayan Mitra. We established Base Camp at Sukram on September 2. Camps I, II and III were placed at 15,000, 17,000 and 19,000 feet on September 5, 7 and 14. In 1987 we followed the track to Pindari "O" built by Mr. Traill, the First Commissioner of Kumaon, in 1830. From there, we explored access to Changuch (6322 meters, 20,740 feet). We gained the upper Kafni Glacier from the col at the head of the Shal Changuch Glacier. From a camp there, Laspa Dhura (5913 meters, 19,400 feet) received its first ascent via the north ridge; descent was by the west ridge. The summit was reached on September 1 by John McKeever, Aqil Chaudary, Duncan Hornby and Jonathan Preston and on the 2nd by Bivujit Mukhoty and me.

GEOFFREY M. HORNBY, *Comford Wheeltappers and Shunters Club, England*

Bamba Dhura. Bamba Dhura is so remote and difficult of access that it took us 20 days to have our first glimpse of the peak. Munsiari was the last bus station, reached via Almora. From there it took us four days to get to Base Camp at 13,200 feet on the moraine of the Sankalpa Glacier. We went on for endless miles with Advance Base, Camps I, II and III at 15,800, 17,200, 18,500 and 19,500 feet. Although we left Munsiari on August 5, we established Camp III only on the 26th. After reconnaissance and the acclimatization climb of P 20,260, we had to descend to Advance Base for three days of bad weather. On September 2, Shirish Joshi, Lama Tashi and I reached Camp II and on the 3rd at 4:25 P.M. got to the summit (6334 meters, 20,780 feet) via the west ridge, a new route. Other members were Vasant Ghag, Nandu Agashe, Pramod Joshi and Satish Ranade.

SHRINIVAS DATAR, *Bharat Outward Bound Pioneers, Pune, India*

Nanda Kot. A joint Indo-Japanese expedition led by Kosuke Ota was composed of seven Japanese and two Indians. On October 17, Masaki Nomura, Tsuyoshi Takeda, Hiroaki Takeishi, Akira Tomita and two Sherpas reached the summit (6861 meters, 22,510 feet), followed the next day by the leader and Mitsumasa Ushikubo. The Japanese were all graduates or students of Rikkyo University; it was an expedition of Rikkyo University that made the first ascent of Nanda Kot in 1936.

Trisul. A Spanish expedition led by Jaime Izquierdo made the ascent of Trisul. Details are not yet available.

India—Garhwal

Kamet and Abi Gamin. An expedition of the Indian Border Security Force was led by Deputy Commander Chhering Ram. Bogged down by bad weather, landslides, road blocks and deep snow, they got to Base Camp only on May 17. Their last camp, Camp V at 7150 meters on Meade's Col, was set up on May 25. The first summit attempt was made on June 1. When 200 meters from the top in a blinding snowstorm, one climber slipped and pulled off his partner.

They fell 100 meters but escaped without injury. The attempt was given up. A second try was made on June 3 by Sub-Inspector Habib Ullah, Lance Naiks T.R. Angdoo and T. Dorji, Constable Jamuna Prasad and Head Constable Jagat Singh. After a gruelling 11-hour climb in bad weather and poor visibility, they gained the summit (7756 meters, 25,447 feet) at 12:30 P.M. On June 15, Deputy Commandant S.C. Negi, Angdoo, Habib Ullah and Dharam Singh climbed to the summit in fine weather, Habib Ullah and Angdoo for the second time. Also on June 15, Jumma Khan, Dilawar Singh and Mahavir Singh climbed Abi Gamin (7355 meters, 24,130 feet) from Camp V. On the descent, Khan slipped and fell 100 meters, carrying Mahavir with him. Khan was badly injured and had to be carried down to Base Camp to be evacuated by air.

KAMAL K. GUHA, *Editor, Himavanta, India*

Kamet and Abi Gamin. Two Indian expeditions are said to have successfully climbed Kamet and Abi Gamin. The leaders were Flight Lieutenant A. Choudhary and Dr. D.T. Kulkarni. Details are lacking.

Purbi Dunagiri Attempt. Our 12-man expedition established Base Camp on the Bagini Glacier at 4640 meters on August 23. Camps I, II and III were set up on the Bagini Glacier at 5000, 5250 and 5740 meters on August 26, 28 and 30. Camp III was beneath the south face of Purbi Dunagiri (6489 meters, 21,290 feet). Camp IV was placed on the south buttress at 6120 meters on September 1. The high point of 6250 meters was reached on September 4, but the climb was abandoned because of excessive rockfall.

JIBAN KRISHNA PAUL, *Diganta, Calcutta, India*

Chaukhamba. A 38-man team from the Indo-Tibetan Border Police was led by Assistant Commandant Vinod K. Dandona. Despite very deep snow, they established Base Camp at 4725 meters on the Bhagirath Kharak Glacier on May 22. Camp II was set up on May 27. On the 29th, Base Camp was flattened by a rolling snow mass. That same day, the first summit attempt was led by Company Commander Nafe Singh. When they were only 400 feet from the summit, two climbers fell into a crevasse but were held by a third. That attempt was given up. The summit (7138 meters, 23,410 feet) was finally gained by six members and two Bhotia dogs on May 31. The climbers were Sub-Inspectors Dawa Renzing, Neema Dorjee and Kanhaiya Lal, Havildars Thondup Sherpa and Agar Singh, and Constable Bachan Singh. Five of them skied down from the summit, but it took the sixth member three days to reach Base Camp.

KAMAL K. GUHA, *Editor, Himavanta, India*

Shri Kailas. A joint 11-member Indo-French expedition climbed Shri Kailas (6932 meters, 22,742 feet). After leaving Gangotri on June 26, they established Base Camp on the Raktvarn Glacier on the 28th. Camps I and II were placed on the Shyamvarn Glacier. The French decided at that time to abandon the climb. Camps III, IV and V were set up on August 2, 3 and 5. The first summit try was turned back by bad weather on August 7, but on the 8th, Ram Samir and Tej Bahadur reached the summit. The leader was Mrityunjoy Biswas and the deputy was Dominique Mathieux Goudier.

KAMAL K. GUHA, *Editor, Himavanta, India*

P 6210, Chaturangi Massif, Gangotri. The team, consisting of Jayant Tulpule, Bharati Kale, Bipin Raje, Vajaya Gadre, Devendra Rana and me as leader, camped at Nandanban on May 18, went up the Chaturangi Glacier and camped at Vasuki Nala on the 24th. We crossed the Chaturangi Glacier near where the Sundar Glacier meets the Chaturangi. P 6210 lies north of the Chaturangi Glacier and south of P 6407 on the same ridge. We established Camp I at 5500 meters near a frozen lake and ascended a snow slope to the col between P 6407 and P 6210, placing Camp II at 5800 meters on the ridge. The summit of P 6210 (20,374 feet) was reached on May 29 by Rana, Kale and Raje. The summit is of triangular shape and lies above a snowfield. It was approached from the west and finally the north.

USHA PAGE, *Giripremi, Pune, India*

Satopanth, Kedarnath and Kedarnath Dome. There were successful climbs of Satopanth (7075 meters, 23,212 feet) by Germans, by Italians under the leadership of G. Federico and Swiss led by Wolfgang Stefan. Australians led by John Robert Muir and Italians under the leadership of Arturo Bergamaschi climbed both Kedarnath (6940 meters. 22,770 feet) and Kedarnath Dome (6831 meters, 22,410 feet). Kedarnath Dome was climbed by Poles led by Daviusz Kubik and by three Indian groups led by Dr. T. Venkatesh, Captain A.K. Vaid and P.K. Chatterjee.

P 6561 Attempt. Greg Collum, Steve Mascioli and I attempted the first ascent of P 6561 (21,525 feet), which might be called the western summit of Santopanth. We tried the south ridge, the same route attempted by the British in 1985. We established Base Camp at Nandanban on May 27 and reached the glacial basin below the southwest face at 17,000 feet on June 7, but storm kept us there until June 10. On the 11th, we climbed the broad snow couloir to a spectacular bivouac at the 19,000-foot col on the south ridge. The next day, insecure mixed pitches led left and up to a bivouac at 19,700 feet, directly below a steep rock buttress. Since a direct line through the rock proved impossible, we traversed several hundred feet left and climbed frozen cascades and mixed ground to bivouac at 20,000 feet back on the ridge crest. June 14 dawned clear and cold. As Steve was not well, he elected to stay at the bivy, urging Greg and me to continue. We climbed two hard pitches to the central icefield. We followed the ice to steepening mixed terrain and a very exposed bivouac at 20,500 feet. The next morning we left bivy gear behind and climbed several excellent, difficult mixed pitches to just below the summit ridge. There the rock turned back from granite to shale, covered by a foot or more of unconsolidated snow. We were climbing too slowly and at 21,000 feet we retreated, bivouacking with Steve at 20,000 feet that night. We continued the descent in deteriorating weather the next day and reached Nandanban on the 17th in a wet snowstorm.

DANIEL CAUTHORN

Bhagirathi II. A 9-member Indian team led by Narayan Chandra Pramanik climbed Bhagirathi II. They set up two high camps. Prokash Kujur and high-altitude porters Rajendra Singh and Sher Singh from Lata reached the summit on August 8.

KAMAL K. GUHA, *Editor, Himavanta, India*

Bhagirathi II. We established Base Camp at Nandanban on August 24, Camp I at 16,650 feet on August 30 and Camp II at 19,020 feet on the southeast ridge on September 1. On September 3, Swapan Kumar Ghosh, Sher Singh Rawat, Ashok Ghosh, high-altitude porters Joy Singh and Puran Singh and I climb the rock face above Camp II for 500 feet, traversed east toward the shoulder of the ridge. We turned westward to reach the midpoint of the ridge that connects the lower peak and the main summit. We moved along the narrow ridge northward to the summit wall. We climbed the southeast face to the summit.

NIDHIR KUMAR PAL, *Durgapur Mountaineers, India*

Bhagirathi II. Japanese climbed Bhagirathi II by its east face. On October 16, leader Yoshiki Yamanaka, Masaki Hayashi, Yoko Mihara, Yuki Sato, Hitoshi Tsuge and a porter reached the summit (6512 meters, 21,364 feet) from Camp III. They had to bivouac on the summit and returned the next day.

P 6721. A North Irish-English expedition led by Dr. Simon Wheeler made the successful ascent of P 6721 (22,050 feet) above the Swachand Bamak in the Gangotri region. Details are missing.

Kharchakund, North Ridge. Bobby Gilbert, Rob Tresidder, Pete Scott and I made the first ascent alpine-style of the north ridge of Kharchakund (6612 meters, 21,695 feet). It was the third ascent of the peak, which had previously been climbed twice by the west ridge, the route by which we descended. The summit was reached on September 18 after a one-day approach from Base Camp at Sundanban and a 5½ -day ascent. The first difficulties were to reach and traverse a group of five pinnacles, which had turned back previous unsuccessful attempts. The pinnacles provided excellent rock climbing. The route above there was of consistent high quality. Other pinnacles and towers proved significant obstacles between relatively easy snow-and-ice walls and arêtes. The hardest climbing was a bold rock pitch to gain the summit of the Great North Tower, where we made the sixth and highest bivouac at 6085 meters. Since some difficult diagonal and overhanging abseils were made, we left 120 meters of rope to facilitate retreat along the ridge if it had been necessary.

ROBIN BEADLE, *Oread Mountaineering Club, England*

Kedarnath Dome. After installing Base Camp, Camp I and Camp II at 4700, 5700 and 6300 meters on August 11, 17 and 20, the following climbed to the summit of Kedarnath Dome: on August 22, Ettore Nanni, Libero Pelotti, Roberta Faldella, Fabrizio Desco; on August 23, Cristina Carantoni, Luciano Pasuali, liaison officer Kumar Das; on August 24, Eliana Palazzi, Rossalio Patuelli; on August 25, Rodolfo Baraldini, Angela Montanari. On August 28, Nanni, Palazzi, Pelotti and Patuelli climbed Baby Shivling (5500 meters, 18,045 feet) by a 400-meter-high rock route of UIAA V to V+ difficulty.

ARTURO BERGAMASCHI, *Club Alpino Italiano*

Bharte Khunta. This peak was climbed on June 19 by a team from Delhi led by C.S. Pande.

KAMAL K. GUHA, *Editor, Himavanta, India*

Bharte Khunta. We set up Base Camp at Topovan on September 18. Once acclimatized and having set up Camp I on the Kirti Bamak at 4630 meters, we made a cache higher. On September 26, we occupied Camp II at 5640 meters. On the 27th, Toni Bou, Kiko Colo, Josep Ximenis and I climbed to the summit of Bharte Khunta (6578 meters, 21,580 feet). The mountain is more dangerous than difficult because of crevasses and threatening séracs. The ice is from 45° to 60°.

JOAN SALA, *Club de Esquí de La Molina, Girona, Spain*

Shivling Attempt. Our expedition was composed of geologists and climbers: Tony Rex, Mike Norry, Paul Metcalf, Nick Groves, Alan Newby, Jill Peacegood, Jon Tinker, Mark Miller, Simon Nathan and me, United Kingdom; Maryrose Fowlie, New Zealand; Patrick LeFort, Arnaud Pecher, and Jacques Dardel, France; and Bruno Scaillet, Belgium. We spent from April 1 to May

28 around the Gangotri Glacier and side valleys with two objectives: to conduct a regional geological survey involving mapping, sample collecting for geo-chemistry, mineral chemistry, radiometric dating and fission track geochro-nology and to climb new routes on Shivling and Bhagirathi I. Base Camp was established at Tapovan on April 4. We spent a week exploring the Chaturangi Glacier and the northwestern flanks of the Bhagirathi group. Without skis and snowshoes, movement would have been impossible the whole time we were in the Gangotri region. Four big snowstorms each deposited about two meters of snow and there was more snow when we left than when we arrived. Local climbers said it was the heaviest snowfall and the worst pre-monsoon season in 30 years. We made three attempts to climb two new routes on Shivling: the northwest face, about 200 meters left of the original Indo-Tibetan Border Police route, and the north face. The first two attempts failed when avalanches buried lower camps and bad weather set in. A second try on the north face from May 16 to 20 by Tinker and Miller reached 5800 meters at the funnel below the upper icefield. Newby, Rex and I reached 6250 meters on the northwest face after a tremendously exposed bivouac clipped into ice screws on a 70° face. The final summit ridge would have been in a frightening unstable condition. We were also suffering from mild frostbite. On May 19 we abseiled ten rope-lengths down the mixed ridge bounding the right side of the north face.

MICHAEL SEARLE, *Leicester University, England*

Shivling Attempt. During the summer of 1987, a Norwegian team com-posed of Jan Westerby, Thornbjørn Envold, Magnar Osnes and Aril Meyer hoped to climb the north buttress of Shivling. Unstable weather hindered progress. Some 500 meters below the summit they got stopped where the ridge is of steep and difficult rock. Climbing difficulties, lack of equipment and illness of one of the members forced them to retreat.

JUSTYNA KOLSTØ, *Oslo, Norway*

Shivling North Face Ascent and West Ridge Tragedy. Our joint expedition had 15 Czechoslovakian and three German climbers. From Gangotri we set out with 10 porters and 15 horses and got to Base Camp at Tapovan a day later. To acclimatize, we decided to climb Shivling by the normal west-ridge route, hoping to get all members up that route before attempting the unclimbed north face. To our sorrow, two of our group were too much in a hurry and used no camps or fixed ropes. Karel Jakeš and German Erik Henseleit reached the summit (6543 meters, 21,467 feet) on August 26. On the descent, Henseleit used an old fixed rope that was in place on the upper part of the rock buttress, which broke, and he fell to his death. The expedition was interrupted for some time. The other two Germans, Knut Burgdorf and Christian Dirjack, went back home. On September 4, the summit of Shivling was reached via the west ridge

PLATE 45

Photo by Tomás Kysilka

SHIVLING's Northeast and North Faces. Yugoslav route on left and Czech route on right.

by Branislav Adamec, Tibor Jánoš, Robert Kukučka, Jiří Švejda and me and two days later, by Richard Kašták, Jiří Pelikán, Pavel Rajf, Josef Rybička, Stanislav Šilhán and Jiří Vodrážka. Then we rested a couple of days, spending some time rock climbing on a nearby 80-meter-high rock wall. From September 12 to 16 the north face was successfully climbed. Branislav Adamec tells their story: "According to our information, the only virgin face of this beautiful mountain was the north face. Its fantastic shape attracted us strongly. We could see right off that there was very difficult ice, mixed and rock climbing there. Our first attempt had been stopped by bad weather. Švejda, Rajf and I set out again on September 12. The access to the wall led up an avalanche-threatened ice couloir. By noon we approached a small cave at the top of the first icefield, where we had cached equipment on the first try. We continued on for some time and returned to the cave for the night. The difficulty on this first day was 70° ice and UIAA IV + rock. On the 13th we ascended the ropes fixed the day before. Then the first problem on the wall awaited us: the ice couloir that led to the second icefield. There we found some pitons with runners left behind on previous attempts. There were parts of the couloir that were of 80°. Above, we had two pitches of 65° on the snowfield and one more on the buttress. Finally we could find a bivouac site. On September 14, after we climbed 65° to 70° ice in the icefield, we came to the next problem: a huge rock-and-ice step. We climbed this in an 85° water-ice groove. Darkness overtook us when we were still two rope-lengths from the summit chimney. We dug tiny platforms in the ice, placing our feet in rucksacks for the night. The route continued on for two lengths of water-ice of 75° to 80° and then a terrible rotten chimney encrusted with snow and ice, which took the lead climber three hours. During the next pitches, the rock got better. With the light of our headlamps, we got to a fine bivouac spot, but either chopping ice or cooking, we didn't finish until midnight. On September 16, we first had a pitch of 80° water-ice, then mixed pitches of IV + and 70°. We finally climbed the ice slope below the summit and at 2:30 P.M. reached the summit. We spent one more cold bivouac on the descent. A day later we were back in Base Camp, drinking beer with our friends and celebrating our beautiful and difficult route." The other members of the expedition were Arnošt Holub, Jan Krch and Jiří Slavík.

TOMÁS KYSILKA, *Czechoslovakia*

Shivling, West Ridge and Northeast Face. Boštjan Kekec, Rupar Uroš, Damjan Vidmar, Aco Pepelnik and I got to Base Camp at Tapovan on September 3, but on the 7th I left for New Delhi. I returned with food on September 13. Meanwhile Uroš and Kekec had climbed the west ridge of Shivling. Pepelnik, Vidmar and I started up the northeast face of Shivling on September 17. It took us three days to climb the lower part of the face, first rock and then mixed climbing. On the fourth day it was mostly snow and ice. We got to the Scott ridge on the fifth day. The sixth bivouac was in the séracs just below the summit. We reached the summit on the morning of September 23 and were back in Base Camp that night. The greatest difficulties were in the lower half of the lower wall and near the top of Shivling.

DANILO TIČ, *Alpinistični Odsek Impol, Yugoslavia*

Shivling Attempt and Satopanth North Ridge. Our expedition operated in two groups, Andreas Walder, Willi Wehinger, Walter Bell and I in the first and Dieter Blümel, Egon Haselwanter, Kurt Wolf, Gottfried Mayr and Traudl Stauder in the second. We are all Austrian except for Walder, who is Swiss. We established Base Camp at Tapovan on September 20. We acclimatized on Kedarnath Dome on September 26. Walder and I headed for the west ridge of Shivling. We placed Camps I, II and III at 5000, 5400 and 6100 meters on September 29, 30 and October 1. On the 2nd, we got to the summit ridge at 6400 meters but turned back because of bad weather and lack of time. We then went to camp at Vasuki Lake on October 5 and to a glacier camp north of Satopanth at 5500 meters the next day. Camp II was at 6000 meters on a col in the north ridge and Camp IV above a difficult ridge section at 6400 meters. We climbed to the summit on October 9. Because Group II's objective, a new route on the east face of Shivling had just been climbed by Yugoslavs, they changed their objective to the west ridge. Blümel and Mayr got to 6100 meters.

WOLFGANG STEFAN, *Österreichischer Alpenverein*

Thalay Sagar. Our expedition made the fifth ascent of Thalay Sagar, the second by the first-ascent route on the northwest couloir and ridge made in 1979 by the Anglo-American party led by John Thackray. The other three ascents have been by the northeast buttress. Before our ascent, there had been 14 unsuccessful attempts. We were Jaume Altadill, Oscar Cadiach, Jordi Camprubí, Xavier Pérez Gil and I as leader. Our three-day approach brought us to Base Camp at 4600 meters on August 13. We placed Advance Base and Camps I and II at 4800, 5600 and 6200 meters on August 14, 20 and 23. The glacier up to Camp I was of moderate difficulty. The 900-meter-high couloir was up to 60°. On August 25, Cadiach, Camprubí and Pérez Gil bivouacked at 6600 meters, climbed to the summit (6904 meters, 22,770 feet) on the 26th and descended to Camp II. The rock in the last 400 meters was rotten and up to UIAA difficulty of V.

JERÓNIMO LÓPEZ, *Club Alpino Guadarrama, Madrid, Spain*

Thalay Sagar Attempt. Paolo Pezzolato and I were driven back from the final part of the south face of Thalay Sagar by a terrible snowstorm. After reaching 6300 meters, we had to turn back, Pezzolato with a dislocated knee and I with frostbitten feet.

FRANCO PERLOTTO, *Club Alpino Italiano*

PLATE 46

Photo by Spanish Thalay Sagar Expedition

THALAY SAGAR from Northwest. Route ascended snow on right to rock.

COLOR PLATE 10

Photo by Gottfried Mayr

SHIVLING's Northeast Face, showing Yugoslav route.

Bhrigupanth, West Buttress. In September, I led an expedition to the Kedar valley of the Gangotri region. From September 18 to 20, Zbigniew Krośkiewicz and I made a new route, the west buttress of Bhrigupanth (6772 meters, 22,220 feet). The route more or less followed the crest of the buttress till the last great upswing of the face. Because of rotten rock and rockfall, we veered to the right onto the south face. The climb gained 1800 vertical meters. It had ten pitches of UIAA IV to V, two of VI-, ice of 45°. Up to the beginning of the greater difficulties, in the first 500 meters, we found old fixed ropes and then no more signs of any previous attempt. We descended the normal route. Tomasz Kopyś and Zbigniew Skierski climbed 800 meters of the east face of Thalay Sagar (VI, A2). Unfortunately they did not complete the route to the summit because one of the climbers had a fall. They descended their ascent route. Michał Nowski and Jerzy Barszczewski also climbed Bhrigupanth by the normal route. While we were in the Kedar valley from September 3 to October 3, the weather was beautiful and sunny.

RYSZARD KOŁAKOWSKI, *Klub Wysokogórski Warszawa, Poland*

Jogin I. Walt Kaskel, Joseph Mazzotta, Dick Osborn, Dick Painter, Ron Rickman and I as leader began the two-day trek up the Kedar Ganga from Gangotri on May 30 and placed Base Camp just above the lake, Kedar Tal, at 15,000 feet. After walking on the lateral moraines east of the lake, we placed Camp I at 17,500 feet on June 3. Camp II was established at 18,500 feet after climbing the right side of the icefall and then toward a saddle between Jogin I and III. It was on a bench below the saddle. On June 6, we left Camp II and plowed through knee-deep snow to the col. Once there, the snow became firmer and we arrived at the summit of Jogin I (6465 meters, 21,210 feet).

TONY LEWIS

Bandarpunch Group. Indian climbers were active in the Bandarpunch group. Kala Nag (6387 meters, 20,956 feet) was climbed by Shyamar Krishna Karag's and by Sanat Ghosh's expeditions. Bandarpunch I (6302 meters, 20,676 feet) was ascended by climbers led by Rajendra Bardoloi. On June 16, Swagarohini II (6247 meters, 20,496 feet) was climbed by both the ONGC Himalayan Association and A.C. Shelat's expedition.

India—Himachal Pradesh

Climbs in the Lingti Valley, Spiti. The Lingti valley lies northeast of Kaza, west of Tibet's Pare Chu valley and south of Ladakh's Rupshu district. Without a trade route to Tibet or Rupshu, local villagers do not venture into this valley. In 1983 we penetrated halfway through the valley and climbed four peaks, the first mountaineers to do so. After leaving Bombay on June 6, we finally reached Lalung village after a long bus trip on July 17. With 12 yaks we

trekked for nine days over Zingu Top (4510 meters), Sisbang Top (5060 meters), crossed the Lingti at Phiphuk, over Kuli La (4880 meters) to Chaksachan La (5230 meters). The locals had no knowledge beyond this point. We ferried our baggage to the banks of the Lingti at 4280 meters. The Lingti river, springing from the border of Rupshu, flows southeast and makes a huge turn to the southwest after meeting Chaksachan Lungpa. We first hoped to descend the river to this junction and proceed north to the base of Gya (6794 meters), the highest peak in Himachal Pradesh. At the end of three days and six difficult river crossings, we were back where we had started. The Lingti cut through a deep gorge near the junction which was not fordable at that time. We turned upstream and in two days were at 4940 meters near the upper watershed. On July 4, Dhiren Toolsidas and I headed north for a high pass leading to Rupshu, camping at 5470 and 6000 meters. On July 5, we had crossed a new pass, the Yangzi Diwan (5890 meters), and climbed the pass peak, Lama Kyent (6040 meters). On July 6, we descended 250 meters and climbed steep scree and snow to the summit of Parilungbi (6166 meters), above the Rupshu plains. This was the only peak we climbed which was not a first ascent. We returned by the same route to Base Camp in one long day. At the same time Muslim H. Contractor and porter Har Singh had entered the Lhakhang Nala to the west, but Har Singh had felt sick and they returned from 5720 meters without climbing Lhakhang (6250 meters), the highest peak in the upper valley. We entered another valley leading westwards to the base of the legendary Shilla. We failed to reach the north col of Shilla because of dangerous snow. On July 12 we got to Shilla's east col but conditions ahead were thought too dangerous. We turned southwards along the ridge and climbed Labrang (c. 5900 meters). A valley farther south leads east to the base of Gyagar, which has a high ridge running to the northwest with six peaks on it. After a steep, exposed climb, we placed three camps at 4880, 5340 and 5970 meters, the latter between Runse and Geling. On July 18, Contractor, Toolsidas and I reached the summit of Runse (6175 meters). We probed toward Gyagar (c. 6400 meters), but a rock buttress and cornices made us realize that we needed more time and support for the climb. On July 19, we climbed Geling (6100 meters) and traversed to the northwest to the summit of Gyadung (6160 meters). With four porters we ferried our loads out. We returned via Chaksachan La and Kuli La to Shelatse and then went west over Syarma La (5040 meters), crossed the turbulent Syarma and passed across the Shilla Jot (5850 meters), reaching Kaza on July 30.

HARISH KAPADIA, *Himalayan Club*

Chau Chau Kang Nilda. Nine climbers from Calcutta set up Base Camp at 5300 meters on June 28. On July 1, Bibhas Das, climbing leader, Swapan Banerjee, Goutam Chatterjee, Apruna Ganguly, Probir Nandan and high-altitude porter Dhan Singh gained the summit.

KAMAL K. GUHA, *Editor, Himavanta, India*

Shigri Parbat Ascent and Tragedy. An 18-man expedition from the Indian Army Corps of Engineers was led by Major M.P. Yadev. They made the second ascent of Shigri Parbat (6526 meters, 21,410 feet). The only previous ascent was by a British team on August 27 and 28, 1961. The Indians could not cross the Rohtang Pass until May 15 due to blizzards and heavy snowfall. After wading through waist-deep snow, the advance group and a few porters reached Chhota Dhara on May 22. Since most of the porters had deserted the expedition, they decided to make an alpine-style ascent from Advance Base at 16,000 feet. On May 30, Captains Sudhir Mittal and G.K. Sharma set out. After a third bivouac, on June 2 they reached the summit. On that same day, a group was moving from Base Camp to Advance Base with supplies. While crossing the improvised bridge over the Chandra River, Captain Kishore Papola fell midstream into the river. He was entangled in ropes and died when his head hit a boulder. Captain B. Bhutani, who was standing on the bank, moved swiftly and tried to hold the rope. He slipped on the ice overhanging the river and was carried away by the current. His body was never found.

KAMAL K. GUHA, *Editor, Himavanta, India*

CB 46, CB 47 and CB 49. Toru Takahashi, Isao Ogane and I established Base Camp in the Kulti valley at 3600 meters on July 23. We then set up Camps I and II at 4250 and 5000 meters. On August 7 all three climbed CB 49 (Tila Ka Lahr; 5964 meters, 19,567 feet). On the 13th, Ogane and I climbed CB 46 (Akela Qila; 6005 meters, 19,701 feet) and CB 47 (5900 meters, 19,357 feet).

JUN'ICHI SHINOZAKI, *Nagoya University Alpine Club, Japan*

Peaks in Himachal Pradesh. Snow Cone (6335 meters, 20,456 feet) was ascended by a six-member team from Calcutta. They set up Base Camp at 5000 meters on the Bara Shigri Glacier on August 22. Camp II was set up between P 20,078 and Snow Dome. On August 24, Soumitra Bannerjee, Borun Ganguly, and high-altitude porters Gopi Chand and Jog Raj reached the summit of P 20,078 and on August 25, of Snow Dome. Nearby, another Calcutta group of 12 led by Shyamal Dey set up Camp II at 5900 meters below Kulu Pumori. On August 7, Sankar Bhadra, Indra Nath Datta, Kanak Ghosh and high-altitude porters Alam Chand Thakur and Bikram Thakur reached the summit of P 6185 (20,292 feet). Stimit Srimany's Young Explorers climbed Milang 7 (6340 meters, 20,800 feet) in July, while Kiron Mukherjee led a group that climbed the same peak on August 17. Climbers from Bombay led by Vinay Hegde climbed CB 53 (6095 meters, 19,996 feet) and another group from Calcutta led by Dhiren Pain climbed the same peak in September. Japanese led by Yuichi Sasaki ascended KR 4 (6340 meters, 20,800 feet).

KAMAL K. GUHA, *Editor, Himavanta, India*

India—Kashmir and Jammu

Nun, Kun and White Needle. Many expeditions now successfully climb the peaks in the Nun and Kun Group. Nun (7135 meters, 23,410 feet) was climbed by French led by François Chantran, Austrians led by G. Steinmair, Poles led by Wacław Otreba, Spaniards led by José Antonio Masio, Japanese ladies led by Miss Hiroshi Kinoshita and other Poles led by Jan Kwiatoń, Spanish Catalan Jordi Magrinyà climbed solo to within 150 meters of the summit on the north ridge in July but turned back because of avalanche danger. Kun (7077 meters, 23,220 feet) was ascended by French led by Georges Tsao, Germans led by Ekkart Gudelach and other French led by Philippe Alibert. Five of six members of an Austrian expedition perished on the night of October 13/14 when an avalanche swept over Camp I. The White Needle (6500 meters, 21,325 feet) was climbed by French led by André Latuier. On September 17, four women, Naseem Akhter, Ghirishangpui, Changthang Jami and Mayrujyoti Sakia with C.S. Bhattarcharya and R.P. Gantam reached White Needle's summit. These were the first Indian women to make the climb.

Nun. Two Polish expeditions climbed Nun in 1987. Starting from the Shafat Glacier, they established four camps at 5300, 6150, 6550 and 6800 meters. On August 12, the summit was reached by leader Wacław Otreba, Andrzej Rykaczewski, Bozena Bruzdowicz, Marek Kaźmierowski, Jacek Kiełbratowski, Waldemar Soroka and Edward Taylor. The autumn expedition ascended from the northwest side. Camps were set up at 5400 and 6300 meters. The summit was reached by Marek Grochowski, and Zbigniew Kacuga on September 30, by Wojciech Jedliński and leader Jan Kwiatoń on October 4 and by Andrzej Perepeczko and Jerzy Tillak on October 6. Despite the many expeditions, the campsites were clean.

JÓZEF NYKA, *Editor, Taternik, Poland*

Nun, East Ridge Attempt. In September the weather was fine and we climbed a number of peaks in Kashmir. By early October there was much unsettled cold weather. We reached 21,000 feet on the east ridge of Nun and bivouacked there for three days in a storm that dumped much snow. An epic descent followed. We left the area when the major storm began that killed five Austrian on Nun and stranded thousands in Ladakh.

GRAEME DINGLE, *New Zealand Alpine Club*

Hagshu Tragedy, 1986. A four-man British team, Stephen Biggs, Ian Kerr, David Woolbridge and Ian Fox, passed a police post on September 25, 1986, headed for Hagshu. They have not been seen since and are presumed dead.

KAMAL K. GUHA, *Editor, Himavanta, India*

India—Eastern Karakoram

Saser Kangri I, West Ridge, and Saser IV. In 1973, an Indo-Tibetan Border Police team climbed Saser Kangri from the eastern or Shyok River approach. Four unsuccessful attempts were later made from the west. Saser II and III were also climbed by Indo-Japanese and Indo-Tibetan Border Police teams in 1985 and 1986 respectively. Saser IV alone remained unclimbed. A joint Indo-British Army expedition under my leadership composed of 36 Indians and 19 British reached Leh on April 7. The British leader was Colonel Ivar Hellberg. The joint team acclimatized in the Zanskar region south of Leh. We established Base Camp at 4950 meters at the snout of the Phukpoche Glacier, a day's trek from Panamik in the Nubra valley. We made a two-pronged attempt on Saser Kangri I, via the northwest ridge along the North Phukpoche Glacier and the west ridge along the South Phukpoche Glacier, the latter being the main effort. Seven Indians and four British climbed P 6640 (21,785 feet) on the northwest ridge during May and June. In the meantime, the team on the west ridge fixed twenty rope-lengths, made excellent progress and climbed virgin Saser IV (7410 meters, 24,310 feet) in two parties. The first, consisting of Martin Bazire, Dave Howie, Thakur Dass, Devi Singh and Lalit Negi, reached the summit at two P.M. on June 6. The British pair climbed a snow gully on the west face and took nearly eight hours from Camp III, while the three Indians first carried out six hours of route fixing on the summit ridge of Saser Kangri I; they then astonished everyone by making it to the summit of Saser IV in one-and-a-half hours on their return journey, following the south ridge from the col. A second party, Jodh Dhillon, Dave Orange and Dave Torrington, reached the summit at nine A.M. on June 7. After the success on Saser IV, the weather suddenly deteriorated. Indians got to the western foresummit of Saser Kangri I on June 7 and 8. No further progress was made for a fortnight thereafter. We withdrew to Base Camp. The weather improved slightly on June 24. Two teams were poised at Camp II (Advance Base) at 5800 meters and at Camp III at 6500 meters. On June 25, Lopsang, Tshering, Umed Singh, Devi, Somnath, Anchuk and Sandop left Camp III at nine A.M. and were on the summit at noon. In a most remarkable feat, ND Sherpa, Sonam and Magan Bissa climbed to the top of Saser Kangri I from Advance Base. They climbed 6000 feet in nine hours and descended to Camp I at 5450 meters that same evening. Two days later the team was at the roadhead at Panamik.

D.K. KHULLAR, *Brigadier, Indian Army*

Pakistan

K2 Attempt. The 1987 season on K2 was markedly different from that of 1986. No successful ascents were made, as opposed to 27 in 1986; the death toll was one, as opposed to 13 in 1986. The lack of success was due to a pattern of almost constant storm. Heavy winter snows lay on the mountains.

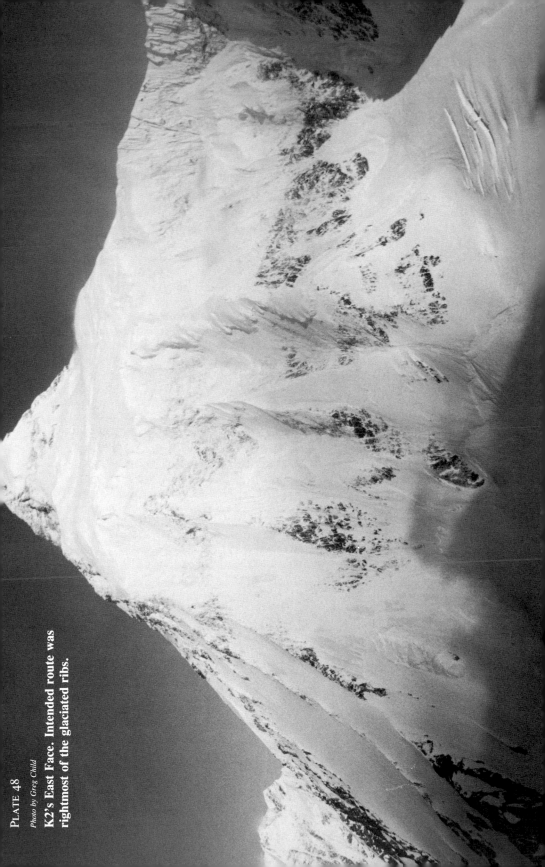

PLATE 48

Photo by Greg Child

K2's East Face. Intended route was rightmost of the glaciated ribs.

Hurricane-force winds blew above 7000 meters. Our expedition was comprised of Americans Phil Ershler and Steve Swenson, British Doug and Michael Scott, and Australians Tim Macartney-Snape and me. We were assisted by Carolyn Gunn as Base Camp manager and medic. We arrived beneath K2 on July 1. There, amid a vast sea of rubbish mostly of Korean origin, the various K2 expeditions assembled. We intended to investigate the unclimbed east face of K2 but were willing to settle for any route that could be climbed alpine-style. From July 1 to 18 we skied on the Godwin Austen Glacier below the east face up to 6500 meters. Unstable snow made continuing higher unviable. It became clear that our proposed route on the east face was suicidal. We had planned to follow the prominent glaciated rib left of the American northeast ridge. From the flattish plateau at 7300 meters we would either follow an independent line up the summit pyramid via the line attempted by the Poles in 1976 or traverse left toward the Abruzzi Ridge to join it at 7900 meters. We abandoned this route when we saw large séracs obstructing the rib itself and huge avalanches pouring from the ice cliffs at 7200 meters and from the great plateau. From July 21 to 23, Ershler, Swenson, Macartney-Snape and I climbed to 6800 meters on Broad Peak, bivouacking twice at 6500 meters, but again, dangerous snow sent us down. During our foray on Broad Peak we met Norman Croucher and his companion. Croucher, who has no legs from the knees down and climbs with special crutches, doggedly persisted and bivouacked at or above 6500 meters for some two weeks before giving up. At that same time, the Japanese-Pakistani team discovered the body of Dobrosława Miodowicz-Wolf, between Camps II and III on a steep section, clipped into a Jümar with the fixed rope wrapped around her wrist. (Kurt Diemberger has pointed out an error on page 13 of *A.A.J., 1987*. It stated that Przwysław Piasecki and Michael Messner "climbed to 7100 meters, where she was last seen." Actually, according to Krystyna Palmowska, they went only to the tent at 6900 or 7000 meters, below the big ladder, and looked in. Not finding her, they could well assume she was dead; nobody could have survived outside. Her body was just above the big ladder, much below where Diemberger had last seen her.—*Editor*.) With the help of other climbers, they carried her down and buried her at the foot of the Abruzzi Ridge. From July 25 to 27, Ershler, Swenson and I spent two stormy nights at Japanese Camp II at 6900 meters on the Abruzzi Ridge. On July 29, Macartney-Snape, who had personal business to attend to at home, left. The next day, after two nights on Broad Peak at 6500 meters, the Scotts did likewise. Doug had broken eight ribs falling off a horse a few weeks before the expedition and was still suffering from his injuries. Michael had a lung infection, which hampered acclimatization. That left Ershler, Swenson and me. On August 10, it cleared and we left Base Camp at midnight, heading for the rib on the south face climbed by Kukuczka and Piotrowski in 1986. With light packs, we made rapid progress up to a technically difficult knife-edge. There we found old fixed ropes. Twelve hours after leaving camp we were at 6900 meters, bivouacking nervously under the big ice cliffs that span the south face. It was our plan to traverse rightwards

across a ramp beneath the threatening cliffs to join the route the Basques were working on. After an uneasy night, we awoke to storm and gladly descended through bad snow, glissading into Base Camp at noon. Our final attempt began on August 13. Joining forces with the Basques, we jümared up their lines to 7100 meters in 13 hours. Bivouacking near Juanjo San Sebastián and his high-altitude Balti porter Karim, we planned to continue to the shoulder the next day and to the summit on the third day. This was not to be. Storm and wind up high set in. We were all in Base Camp on August 14. On August 15, our group left K2.

GREG CHILD

K2 Attempt. Our expedition of French guides consisted of Francis Chaud, Alain Hantz, Titou Sagot, my husband Jean-Jacques Rolland, Dr. Bernard Hostein and me as leader. Having arrived at Base Camp on June 4, the whole team got to 7000 meters on June 18 but could not continue because of bad weather. Sagot and I descended by *parapente* from 6000 meters. During a second attempt, my hand was seriously hurt by a falling rock but I was able to get back to Base Camp thanks to my companions. After the complete destruction of Camp I at 7000 meters, the rest of the team gave up the attempt since the bad weather persisted.

MARTINE ROLLAND, *Club Alpin Français*

K2 Attempt. Swiss Jean Troillet and I arrived at the traditional K2 Base Camp at 5000 meters on June 16. Erhard Loretan had had to drop out of the team when in February he was swept down by an avalanche on the Mönch and suffered serious back injuries. We hoped to make a new alpine-style route on K2's west face via a line we call the "Sickle," which follows clockwise the series of snowfields and rock barriers to the left of the distinct central rock "pear." The weather conditions were the worst I have ever seen in the area. Of the 56 days after reaching Base Camp, we did not have a single really clear day. Acclimatization up to 7000 meters was a harassing task. First we walked to Savoia Pass on June 23 and 24. Snowfall forced us down from 6700 meters on the Abruzzi Ridge, where we climbed on July 1 and 2, and from 6400 meters on Summa Ri on July 5 and 6. On July 15, we climbed in a single push from 4800 to 7200 meters and after spending the night at 7200 meters, we decided our acclimatization was sufficient. We then turned to the west face of K2. We started up it twice, on July 25 and August 8, but each time we were forced to return to the base of the face from 6400 meters by big snowfalls.

WOJCIECH KURTYKA, *Klub Wysokogórski, Kraków, Poland*

K2 Attempt and Tragedy. Our joint expedition was led by Japanese Kenshiro Otaki with Pakistani Sher Khan as deputy. Other members were

Japanese Takeo Ishiwatari, Akiro Suzuki, Kaoru Nagaota, Fumihide Saito, Tetuei Hanzawa, Akihiko Sugawara, Hiroshi Kawasaki, Touru Kurusawa and I as doctor, and Pakistanis Ikram, Rahat Ali and Tufail Ibrahim. We hoped to climb the Abruzzi Ridge. We established Base Camp, Advance Base and Camps I, II, III, and IV at 5200, 5500, 6300, 6900, 7500 and 7900 meters on July 1, 2, 3, 19, August 1 and 22. At the start we maintained a good pace until July 10, but after that the weather was bad for a month. By the end of August four of the six expeditions to K2 had left. During the ascent, some members found the body of Dobrosława Miodowicz-Wolf, the Polish woman who had disappeared during the descent in August 1986. She was on a ledge at the end of a fixed rope section, apparently having died of exhaustion. On August 21, the weather seemed better and so five members left Base Camp on a summit try. Suguwara and Kawasaki left Camp IV on August 23 but they suffered from deep snow and at 8300 meters returned to Camp III. The next day, Suzuki, Sher Khan and Saito also left Camp IV, but at two P.M. it was snowing so heavily that they turned back. Only two got back to Camp IV. No one saw Suzuki fall, but after an eleven-day search, we found him dead at 5300 meters on the south face. He apparently slipped from 8200 meters. We left Base Camp on September 9.

TAKEHIKO YOKOMIZO, *M.D., Toyo University, Japan*

K2 Attempt. A Japanese expedition led by Haruyuki Endo of the High Altitude Research Institute reached 7400 meters on the Abruzzi Ridge, but after the leader had difficulties apparently from the altitude at 5800 meters, the expedition was called off.

K2, South-Southeast Spur Attempt. Jaime Alonso, Txema Cámera, Ramón Portilla, Juanjo Sebastián, Koldo Tapia, Martín Zabaleta, Sirdar Abdul Karin and I set up Base Camp on the Godwin Austen Glacier at the foot of the south face of K2 on July 14. We attacked K2 by the rocky south-southeast spur (the route pioneered by Yugoslav Tomo Česen in 1987). Because of the steepness of the route, we could not establish the next camp until we got to 7200 meters, where we dug a snow cave. We fixed rope up to this Camp I. Hampered by bad weather, we remained stuck in Base Camp for several weeks. From Camp I we continued alpine-style to the shoulder, where our route joined the Abruzzi Ridge. We placed two tents for Camp II at 7900 meters, where we were joined by members of the Japanese-Pakistani expedition, which had been climbing the Abruzzi Ridge. August 23 dawned clear. Eight of us, San Sebastián, Zabaleta, Portilla, Abdul Karim and I of our expedition and Pakistani Sher Khan and Japanese Akira Suzuki and Fumihide Saito set out and climbed the Bottleneck to 8350 meters. Suddenly it clouded in and we were enveloped in a storm of wind and snow. We turned back and groped our way back down to Camp II, where we became painfully aware that Suzuki had disappeared on the

PLATE 49

Photo by H. Adams Carter

K2. The corrected Polish route is indicated.

descent. Two of our group descended the Abruzzi Ridge to Base Camp that same day. The rest of us bivouacked, but since the weather was no better in the morning, we all descended to Base Camp. Suzuki's body was found days later at the foot of the south-southeast face.

ALBERTO POSADA, *Orhi Mendi, Federación Vasca de Montaña, Spain*

K2 Winter Attempt, 1988. A winter ascent led by Pole Andrzej Zawada with members from Poland, Britain and Canada failed at 7300 meters, Camp III. Maciej Berbeka made the first winter ascent of Broad Peak on March 6, 1988.

K2 Photo Correction. The line of the Polish route on the south face of K2 on Plate 1 of *A.A.J., 1987* on page 5 was carelessly drawn. A more accurate line appears on Plate 49 in this Journal.

Gasherbrum I (Hidden Peak) Attempts and Tragedy. A Pakistani Army expedition was high above the Gasherbrum La, following the Japanese couloir. Four members were trying to establish Camp III above 7000 meters when one of them became ill and another suffered frostbite. They all turned back on July 29, and while moving slowly through a dangerous section, there was a fall that triggered an avalanche in which they were all dragged down for about 500 meters. Rescue groups from the various expeditions on the spot failed to find any survivors. The attempt was abandoned. Three other expeditions joined together after this accident. After helping in the search for the missing Pakistanis, all three expeditions decided on the 1975 Messner line which starts up the face from below the Gasherbrum La and appeared safer. There was a mixed group from New Zealand led by Craig Strobo. A Basque team led by Juan Ignacio Lorente had had permission to attempt the French route on the south face but, in view of the difficulties, they switched to the north side of the mountain. A Japanese expedition organized by Masaki Matsumoto also had had permission for the south face but it was reduced by illness to only two members. Then Tamio Hitachi and another climber moved to the north side. Ropes were fixed from Camp II at 6500 meters up to 7000 meters, but the difficult conditions encountered forced them to turn back on August 13, first the Japanese pair, then from 7100 meters New Zealanders Steve Bruce and Hugh Van Noorden and the Basques. Members of the last two expeditions decided to attempt Gasherbrum II after descending to Camp I, which was common to both peaks. (See Gasherbrum II.)

XAVIER EGUSKITZA, *Pyrenaica, Bilbao, Spain*

Gasherbrum I (Hidden Peak) Correction. On page 278 of *A.A.J., 1987,* it was omitted that Rüdiger Lang had climbed solo to the summit on August 17, 1986, the day before his companions.

Gasherbrum II Ascent and Tragedy. There were a number of ascents of Gasherbrum II. An American group climbed the standard route. On June 28, Malachi Miller, leader, Phil Powers and Michael Collins were among those who reached the summit. That same day Germans Sigi Hupfauer and his wife Gabi climbed to the top of their second 8000er together. (They had climbed Broad Peak in 1986.) On July 10, Michael Dacher and Dr. Ulrich Schmidt got to the summit. This was Dacher's tenth 8000er and Sigi Hupfauer's sixth. These Germans were part of an expedition led by Hans Henning Seym. Members of a combined British-New Zealand-Swiss expedition led by Englishman Roger Payne managed to reach the summit on the same dates as the German team. On June 28, Englishman Richard Thorne and Swiss Jean-Pierre Hefti got to the top with the previously mentioned climbers. The next day, while descending on skis, Hefti deviated from the route and fell to his death from 6700 meters. A second group, Scots Iain Peters and Donald Stewart and New Zealander Guy Halliburton, also reached the summit on July 10. Payne and his New Zealander wife, Julie Ann Clyma, got to 7500 meters before they were forced to give up when Payne fell ill. Luxembourger Eugène Berger (leader) and Italians Sergio Martini, Fausto De Stefani and Maurizio Giordani of a five-person expedition completed the ascent on August 8. This was the fifth 8000er for both Martini and De Stefani. The leader's fiancée, Pascale Noël, had reached 6600 meters on July 30 but was forced to withdraw because she was suffering from an edema. Six of the climbers of the New Zealand and Basque expeditions who had just given up on Hidden Peak decided to try an alpine-style ascent of Gasherbrum II. Having left Camp I on August 14, Brigitte Muir gave up at Camp II at 6400 meters while the others continued the ascent. On August 16, Basques Juan Oyarzábal and Atxo Apellániz, Australian Geoff Little, and New Zealanders Carol McDermott and Lydia Brady reached the summit. This was the second 8000er for the Basques. Brady is the first New Zealand woman to climb an 8000er. A large French group led by mountain guide Claude Jager abandoned its attempt on August 11 after reaching Camp III at 7000 meters. A Spanish team was reduced to three members when leader Manuel Amat fell ill and had to return, accompanied by one climber. Just before arriving at Base Camp, their 60-year-old liaison officer suffered a severe edema and had to be evacuated by helicopter. The three remaining climbers, Francisco Amat, Pascual Castillo and José-Luis Clavel, were the last group to leave the area. After a month of trying, they had to give up their attempt.

XAVIER EGUSKITZA, *Pyrenaica, Bilboa, Spain*

Gasherbrum II. Our expedition was composed of Mike Collins, Dan Heilig, Rob Hess, Phil Powers and me. We climbed Gasherbrum II by the normal southwest ridge. We left Dassu on May 11, but a very bad storm on the ninth day of the approach trapped us at Goro, some 30 miles from Base Camp. We had to dismiss our badly clad porters. Luckily we could rehire 19 porters from a returning Japanese expedition on May 29 and made it to Base Camp on

May 31. We established Advance Base on June 7, but that night a huge avalanche plunged down from Gasherbrum I, two miles distant. The air blast flattened out tents and carried equipment away. We were unhurt, could patch a tent and retrieve much of the gear. We moved camp to a safer location. Camp I was set up at 5900 meters on June 13. We next had to carry loads up to the southwest ridge for Camp II at 6450 meters. Bad weather slowed us down and we established Camp II only on June 23. We placed Camp III at 7000 meters on June 27. All five of us set out for the summit at 5:15 on the morning of June 28. That day was one of the most difficult any of us had ever attempted. Every step required a conscious effort. At 7400 meters Hess and Collins were too tired to continue and turned back. Heilig, Powers and I struggled on. Between 2:00 and 2:30 we reached the summit. The next day we descended to Base Camp and were back in Skardu a week later.

MALACHI MILLER, *National Outdoor Leadership School*

Broad Peak. Aside from the Swiss team led by Bruno Honneger and the Catalans led by Josep Estuch, no other expedition to Broad Peak was successful in 1987. The following expeditions had to abandon their attempts, mostly because of bad weather and excessive snow. From a four-man British group led by Mark Hallam, Richard Foley reached 7300 meters. They were accompanied by Norman Croucher, who has no legs from the knee down and climbs with special crutches. Four Yugoslavs led by Slavko Cankar had little time left to make the climb after their ascent in the Trango Towers. Franc Knez got to 7500 meters. A French group led by Louis Audoubert reached 7200 meters. A Mexican expedition led by Antonio Cortés had permission for the middle peak, but they ascended only to 7000 meters on the common route to both peaks. A Norwegian team of six climbers was led by Ragnhild Amundsen, the widow of Hans Christian Doseth, who was killed in 1984 on the Trango Towers. On July 20, she and other members established Camp III at 6900 meters but could go no higher than 7000 meters. However, that is an altitude record for Norwegian women. In 1983 she nearly climbed Bhrigupanth (6772 meters). A few days later, Haavard Nesheim reached 7300 meters before turning back. Older climbers from France led by Pierre Mazeaud, who is 59, were reported to have reached 7300 meters. The five-man Swiss team led by Bruno Honegger made the only solo ascent of the year. Norbert Joos made a two-day solo climb, reaching the summit on May 29, having depended on no one else for trail breaking, food, gear or anything else. It was his fifth 8000er. On June 7, Honegger and Ernst Müller also reached the summit. The Spanish Catalan expedition led by Josep Estruch is reported on below.

XAVIER EGUSKITZA, *Pyrenaica, Bilbao, Spain*

Broad Peak. Our expedition was composed of Francesc Domínguez, Lluis Vandellós, Genis Rodríguez, Manuel Belmonte, Josep Graño and I as leader.

PLATE 50

Photo by Jean-Etienne Hénault

CHOGOLISA from the Northwest.

We set up Base Camp on the Godwin Austin Glacier at 4950 meters on August 10. On the 12th, we set up Camp II at 6250 meters, leaving a cache at 5750, which would become Camp I. After bad weather, on August 13 we set up Camp III at 6800 meters. On the 28th, Vandellós and I climbed to 7500 meters, where we found we could find shelter in a half buried French tent. We continued on the morning of August 29 to arrive with bad snow conditions at the col at one P.M. At 2:30 P.M. we two reached the foresummit.

JOSEP ESTRUCH, *Catalonia, Spain*

Chogalisa from the Northwest, Third Ascent. Our expedition was composed of Françoise Hénault, Pascal Poizat, Christian LaVergne, Philippe Arnaud, Christine Da Ronch and me. Our approach march was from July 18 to 27. Base Camp was at 4950 meters on the Vigne Glacier, five kilometers above the confluence of the Vigne and Baltoro Glaciers. From July 28 to August 2, we established Camp I at 5500 meters eight kilometers higher on the east branch of the glacier at the foot of a rocky triangular spur 1000 meters in height at the top of which we would place Camp II. We fixed 500 meters of rope on mixed terrain and steep snow on the spur. Camp II was occupied on August 10 at 6500 meters. On the 11th, we made the first attempt. My wife Françoise, Poizat and I reached 7300 meters in deep snow; Arnaud gave up at 6800 meters. Poizat and I remained in Camp II for another attempt two days later. The north ice face of Chogolisa averages 35° with a few places of 45°. There are few crevasses and little ice. At one P.M. on August 13, Poizat and I reached the summit (7665 meters, 25,148 feet) in dense fog. We struck Base Camp on August 15.

JEAN-ETIENNE HÉNAULT, *Club Alpin Français*

Nameless Tower, Western Buttress, Trango Towers. Right after our attempt on the south face of Lhotse, Frenchman Michel Fouquet and I joined Swiss Michel Piola and Frenchman Patrick Delale in Skardu on May 24. With mountain bicycles, we got to Base Camp at 5000 meters beside the Uli Biaho Glacier. After completing our acclimatization by carrying supplies to the foot of the western buttress, we were ready on June 3 for the attack. For the next two weeks our two rope teams alternated fixing ropes on the first half up to the only ledge that permitted the installation of a small wall tent. The sustained very steep climbing, slowed by terribly bad weather, obliged this kind of ascent. A first summit attempt lasted for six days and let us reach 5900 meters. Battered by daily snow flurries and short of food, we were forced back to Base Camp. After a two A.M. departure on June 22, we reascended to the bivouac, where we rested a couple of hours. We then ascended the fixed lines we had installed on our previous retreat. The snow forced us to bivouac another night before reaching the fantastic summit (6237 meters, 20,463 feet) at five P.M. We had had to fix another 100 meters of rope, without which the descent would have been impossible. It took three of us two days to descend, removing the fixed ropes, while Fouquet descended to Base Camp in eleven minutes by *parapente*. He made a very exposed, windless take-off only a few meters from the abyss. We rate the climb as 6c, A4 with no let-up on any of the 30 rope-lengths. (The Nameless Tower was climbed by British climbers, including Joe Brown, in 1976 by a difficult route on the southwest face, to the right of this route. Another British group in 1984 climbed a route between the present route and the first-ascent route, but had to give up 100 meters from the summit.—*Editor*.)

STÉPHANE SCHAFFTER, *Guide, Switzerland*

Nameless Tower, Trango Towers, Second Ascent. A six-man Yugoslav team from Celje, Slovenia, led by Slavko Cankar, climbed the 1200-meter-high south-southeast face of the Nameless Tower on a new route to the left of the Polish-Japanese and American attempts of 1986. For six days they fixed rope on the lower 900 meters. The crux was a nearly vertical section just above the snow ledge 300 meters up the wall. They were ready to attack the summit in early June, but bad weather drove them back to Base Camp. The final push started during the night of June 15. The pitches above the previous high point were climbed in icy cold. The summit was reached by Cankar, Franc Knez and Bojan Šrot. During the descent, the weather worsened again and it snowed. The expedition then moved to Broad Peak but was unsuccessful there.

JÓZEF NYKA, *Editor, Taternik, Poland*

P 5753, Trango Towers. A Japanese expedition led by Reiji Nonaka ascended P 5753 (18,875 feet). Also on the expedition were the leader's wife Yukiko, Toshikazu Fujita, Takao Sasaki and Masahiro Oto. They climbed 63 pitches on the east face and southeast buttress, a difficult route (VI+, A2), which took them 15 days. They reached the summit on September 8. This foresummit of the great Trango Tower was tried unsuccessfully by two Japanese expeditions in 1986.

Latok I Attempt. Our expedition was composed of Remy Martin, Roger Laot and me. We hoped to climb the Lowe route on Latok I. It took us seven days from Dassu to reach Base Camp on the Choktoi Glacier on July 11. We fixed rope on the first 600 meters. The climb was particularly difficult because there was a lot of snow covering the rock. Moreover, the weather was very bad in the Karakoram this summer. Martin became sick. Laot and I made a summit attempt and on August 1 reached about 6000 meters.

LAURENT TERRAY, *Club Alpin Français*

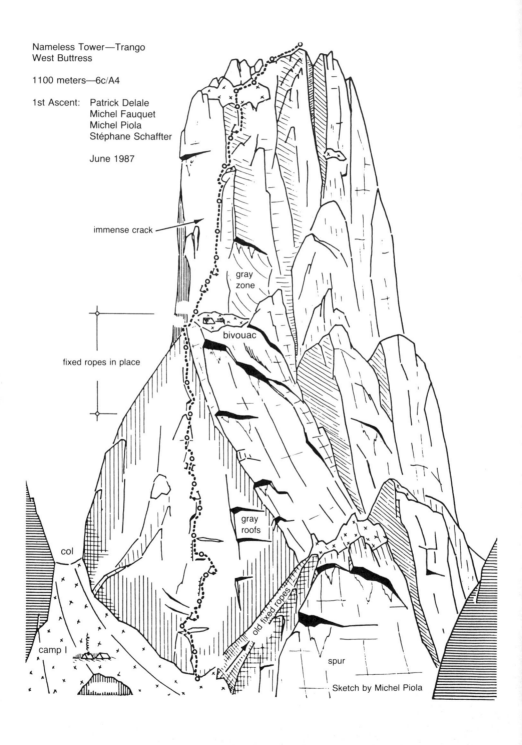

Nameless Tower—Trango
West Buttress

1100 meters—6c/A4

1st Ascent: Patrick Delale
              Michel Fauquet
              Michel Piola
              Stéphane Schaffter

              June 1987

immense crack

gray
zone

bivouac

fixed ropes in place

gray
roofs

col

old fixed ropes

camp I

spur

Sketch by Michel Piola

PLATE 52

Photo by Stéphane Schaffter

NAMELESS TOWER, Trango Towers.

Latok II Attempt. Because of very bad snow conditions when, seven days after leaving Dassu, Paul de Mengel, Dr. John Hancock, Brian Mullen and I as leader reached the Uzzam Brakk Glacier, the porters were unable to reach our intended Base Camp. We had to settle for being about 1½ hours short. We paid the porters off and made an enforced camp where we stood in the deep snow. The following week was spent ferrying 1.3 tons of gear as far as we could, still just short of where we had intended to place Base Camp. On June 21, Paul Nunn, Bill Barker, Joe Brown and Mo Anthoine arrived at Base Camp, bringing the full complement of eight team members together. We forced a passage across the Uzun Brakk Glacier and up the subsidiary glacier leading to the west ridge of Latok II. We established Advance Base at 17,500 feet on June 23. The ridge flank was climbed in five days to Camp I at 20,000 feet. Five more days were spent pushing along the ridge to what we called Camp I½. This was used to overcome a difficult rock-and-ice section. After ropes were fixed, Camp I½ was not used. After much hard work in poor weather, Camp II was established at 22,000 feet on July 8. On July 10, Brown and de Mengel reached a high point of 22,500 feet. A storm started that evening and lasted for three days. Concern was expressed about our being able to get *off* the mountain, never mind getting *up* it! Avalanches swept away fixed ropes. Food was running short. On July 14, the descent began. Despite extremely dangerous conditions, the evacuation was completed safely. In spite of a multiplicity of attempts, no summit in this range has ever been reached more than once. Italians climbed Latok II from the south in 1978. The Pakistani official altitudes are 7145 meters for Latok I and 7108 for Latok II. Yet there are doubts about their height. This led Arturo Bergamaschi's 1978 Italian expedition to resurvey and renumber the peaks, but as this has not been accepted in Pakistan, it would be best to keep the old ordering to avoid confusion.

EDWARD HOWARD, *Minute Climbing Club, England*

Peaks Above the Biafo Glacier. Matthew Powell, Robert Rider and I of Cambridge University and Bruce Hubbard from St. Andrews University spent 3½ weeks climbing peaks above the Biafo Glacier in July and August. We made three first ascents and carried out a scientific programme for the St. Andrews Botany Department. All were alpine-style, single-day, snow-and-ice climbs. Base Camp was at Ho Bluk at 13,500 feet on the southwest bank of the Biafo. Our first peak, Ho Bluk (5364 meters, 17,600 feet; 35°50′N, 75°42′E) was traversed by its northeast and north ridges on July 30. A short section of mixed climbing on the north ridge added interest to an otherwise easy route. P 18,600 (5669 meters; 35°54′N, 75°43′E) was right under the Ogre. Our route followed a 3000-foot gully up the south end of the Biafo side before taking the southeast ridge to the summit. The 5000-foot route was climbed in 12 hours on August 5. Our main objective, Ghur, (5796 meters, 19,010 feet; 35°52′N, 75°37′E) was climbed from an Advance Base at the junction of the Ghur

Struan Gray at 19,000 feet on first ascent of GHUR.

Glacier tongue and the Biafo. Powell, Hubbard and I took 23 hours on August 11 to climb the north face and descend over a subsidiary peak to the northwest. The descent involved a 1500-foot detour down the south face to avoid dreadful snow conditions on the corniced northwest ridge.

STRUAN M. GRAY, *Cambridge University*

Kunyang Chhish Tragedy. A Japanese expedition led by Seichi Wada tried unsuccessfully to climb Kunyang Chhish. On July 19 Takumi Onuma fell and was killed after his rope was cut by a falling block of ice. Further details are not available.

Rakaposhi Attempt. Twelve climbers from Črna in northern Slovenia attempted to make the second ascent of Rakaposhi's north ridge, which was first climbed by Japanese in 1979. We established Base Camp, Camp I and Camp II at 3600, 4300 and 5350 meters on June 23, 27 and 28. On July 4, we reached a high point of 5700 meters. We just could not establish Camp III because of deep snow. The members were Zdenko Žagar, Karlo Ritonja, Milan Savelli, Milan Plesec, Tomo Jeseničnik Jure Mavrič, Ivan Štornik, Alojz Keup, Zdenko Razbornik, Miro Jelen, Dr. Janez Gorjanc and I as leader.

IGOR RADOVIČ, *Planinsko Društvo Črna, Yugoslavia*

Rakaposhi Attempt. A Japanese expedition from Meiji University was composed of Munehiko Yamamoto, leader, Atsushi Yamamoto and Hiroshi Ohishi. They attempted the east ridge, also tried by Edi Koblmüller in 1985, who got only to the east peak. After establishing four camps and fixing ropes, they got to the east peak on July 3, but gave up because of the difficulties above.

Rakaposhi Attempt. We had hoped to make the first ascent of the east ridge of Rakaposhi. In 1985, Austrians led by Edi Koblmüller climbed to the east summit (7010 meters, 23,000 feet) via the north spur. Before we arrived, Japanese attempted the climb in siege-style with four camps and fixed ropes to 6700 meters. On July 3, the Japanese got to the east summit and turned back despite excellent weather. They told us that traversing the ridge to the summit of the east ridge (c. 7300 meters) seemed too difficult. Our expedition was composed of Arnfried Braun, Ulrich Calmbach, Hans Jakobi, Felix Haas and me as leader. On July 1, we got to Base Camp at 3470 meters, two days distant from Pisan on the Karakoram Highway. We acclimatized for ten days and on July 11, the weather turned bad for a week. We started an alpine-style attempt on July 17, but got only to 5100 meters before being driven back down by the weather. We made a second try starting on July 22. The next day we got to 5700 meters, but the route from 5100 meters on was very dangerous from

PLATE 54

Photo by Stephen Venables

P 5979 on the Biafo-Solu Divide. Main Peak is on the right. The Central Icefield was reached by a hidden glacial ramp.

falling ice and threatening avalanches. We pulled back to Base Camp on the 24th. After more bad weather, we left Base Camp on July 29.

HUBERT BLEICHER, *Deutscher Alpenverein*

Traverse from Dassu to Pasu and P 5979. In July, Phil Bartlett, Duncan Tunstall and I spent four weeks walking from Dassu to Pasu, a journey of over 200 kilometers. We used porters to Base Camp at the head of the Biafo Glacier. A break in generally bad weather allowed Tunstall and me to climb a fine route to the south summit of P 5957, a granite tower on the Biafo-Solu divide, just south of the Hispar Pass. After ten days in the area, we continued toward Shimshal, taking eleven days to cross Snow Lake, the Khurdopin Pass (c. 5750 meters), the Khurdopin Glacier and Shimshal village to Pasu. I returned in August to Snow Lake with Steve Razetti, approaching via the Hispar Glacier. I climbed another route on P 5957, this time taking the northeast face to the main summit (19,617 feet), probably for the first ascent. We walked out to Skardu via the Sokha La, Sokha Glacier and Bashar valley.

STEPHEN VENABLES, *Alpine Climbing Group*

Batura Attempt. Our expedition set out from Hasanabad for Batura on July 2. We walked for three days through an inhospitable land to 3800 meters, where the porters refused to go on, frightened by the glacier crossing. We had to ferry our loads from there to Base Camp at 4100 meters. After the establishment of Base Camp, the weather turned bad and the mountain became so loaded with new snow that it would have taken days for it to be safe. We gave up on the route, which had been climbed by Edi Koblmüller's expedition some years ago, having got no higher than 5000 meters. We warn others that the porters do not stick by the "Rules and Regulations" and demand much higher wages. The liaison officer also demanded much more than was stipulated.

THEODOR KUBICKA, *Österreichischer Alpenverein*

P 5735 and P 6090, Batura Glacier Area. My wife Sue and I enjoyed two weeks in the Batura Glacier area. We left Pasu on August 12 with two porters who carried to Guichisam in three days and then on to the Yoksugoz Glacier, where we pitched Base Camp at 4000 meters on the 16th. The porters left us there. After exploration of the southwest branch of the Yoksugoz, on August 20 we climbed P 5735, prominently seen from Guichisam and the culminating point of a long ridge that runs east from Kuksar. We joined the narrow attractive southeast ridge by climbing southwestwards up a flowery hillside three kilometers up the Yoksugoz. We carried big loads back down the Batura for two days but early on the 24th, just beyond Yashpirt, we made an unpremeditated decision to climb P 6090, the first prominent peak on the south side of the Batura. We crossed the glacier to Wudmul and climbed the steep vegetated hillside to bivouac at 4400 meters. This we left at 12:30 A.M. on August 25 and followed an easy ridge to reach the main east-west ridge of the Batura massif. After going over subsidiary humps, we reached a short harder mixed section below the final snow comb. Near the top of this, Sue waited while I continued to the summit. We regained our bivouac at 7:30 P.M. We were back in Pasu on the 27th.

GEOFFREY COHEN, *Scottish Mountaineering Club*

Peaks near Pasu. Although the weather was not particularly good, we did climb some lovely 5000ers. On June 13, Robert Gruber ascended solo Sost Sar (c. 5200 meters, 17,061 feet) by its rocky south face. The peak lies north of Sost, a village just east of the junction of the Khunjerab and Chapsuran Rivers. On June 16, Gruber and I climbed Khudabad Sar (5230 meters, 17,159 feet) by its northwest side. The next day we ascended the next peak to the west, Borumter Sar (5480 meters, 17,979 feet) by its 60° east face. The two peaks lie at the head of the next valley west of the Kar Purar valley. On July 17, Christine Schmid, Gruber and I made the first ascent of Ambarin Sar (6175 meters, 20,260 feet). We traveled for three days from Pasu up the Shimshal valley to Ambarin Base Camp. We camped at 5000 meters on the ascent and at 5800 meters on the descent of the south ridge. The peak lies south of the village of Zyara and east of the Momhil Glacier.

KURT LAPUCH, *Österreichischer Alpenverein*

Peak Above Khurdopin Glacier. Andrew Bradley, Richard Osborne, John DeBank, Paul Simpkin, Tony Briggs, Dr. Luke Hughes-Davis and I journeyed up the Karakoram Highway to Pasu. There we engaged 15 porters and a cook for the walk to Base Camp. From the roadhead, a three-day walk to Shimshal remained. After a rest day in Shimshal, two further days' walk were undertaken before the porters were paid off. Our intended Base Camp was still another day's walk across the moraine of the Yukshin and Khurdopin Glaciers. We finally established Base Camp at 12,000 feet just above the snout of the Khurdopin Glacier. Due to the distance of the mountain we originally hoped to climb, Bradley, DeBank, Simpkin and Briggs carried climbing equipment while Osborne and I each carried 28 kilograms of food and fuel for them. After three days, this food was dumped and we two returned to Base Camp. A brief reconnaissance showed the original objective, P 6240, was out of range from our Base Camp, though a worthy objective. From the gear dump, the four moved east following a hanging glacier to its head at 16,000 feet. They climbed the highest peak attainable from that glacier. The unnamed peak was about 19,000 feet high. Meanwhile, Osborne and I made an unsuccessful attempt on an 18,500-foot peak close to Base Camp. The following day the whole party was reunited at Base Camp. We decided that no more climbing was possible due to the rotten rock near Base Camp and the distance to the mountains with greater snow cover.

GARY MURTON, *Plymouth Polytechnic, England*

Momhil Sar Attempt. The members of our expedition were Heiko Irmisch, Rolf Steffens, Roland Köhler and I as leader. We hoped to make the second ascent of Momhil Sar (7343 meters, 24,092 feet) by the east ridge, the route by which Austrians made the first ascent in 1964. We approached our 4600-meter Base Camp via the Trivor Glacier in five days from Nagar with 32 porters. We got to our highest point, 6600 meters, on July 8. While descending to Camp III at 6350 meters, three of us were caught in an avalanche from which luckily we could free ourselves. Since it snowed each day, avalanches were constant, the east ridge seemed to us under the present conditions unclimbable and any other route out of the question, we decided to abandon the expedition.

GÜNTER SCHULZ, *Deutscher Alpenverein*

Yazghil Sar. Between August 15 and September 26, a team of six led by me visited the remote Shimshal valley. We successfully made the first ascents of both the north and south summits of Yazghil Sar, an isolated snow-and-ice peak which lies between the Yukshin Gardan and Yazghil Glaciers, some 10 kilometers north of Yakshin Gardan Sar. Yazghil Sar should not be confused with much higher Yazghil North and South Domes, which are due east of Disteghil Sar at the head of the Yazghil Glacier. Pete and Claire Foster reached the north summit on September 7 via the northwest face and north ridge. They made the climb in three days from Base Camp at 3600 meters on a lateral moraine next to the Yazghil Glacier. It had taken four days prior to the ascent to reconnoiter the peak and stock an advanced camp. The south summit (5933 meters, 19,465 feet), which is about 100 meters higher than the north summit, was reached on September 8 by Ernie McGlashan, Jack Brindle and John O'Reilly. They used the same approach and climbed the interconnecting ridge between the summits. Again the route took three days of climbing, using the high camp on the northwest slopes at 4670 meters and a bivouac ledge hacked out of the ice on the north ridge at 5180 meters.

ROY LINDSAY, *Alpine Club*

Tupopdan. Our expedition made the first ascent of Tupopdan (or Tlipobdan) in the Markhun valley of the Karun Koh region of the northern Karakoram. We were Andy Cave, Tom Richardson, John Stevenson, Joe Simpson and I as leader. We established Base Camp under the north face at 4000 meters on June 14 and a snow cave on the col at the foot of the northeast ridge at 5180 meters on June 28. Further visits to the col had to be abandoned because of snow

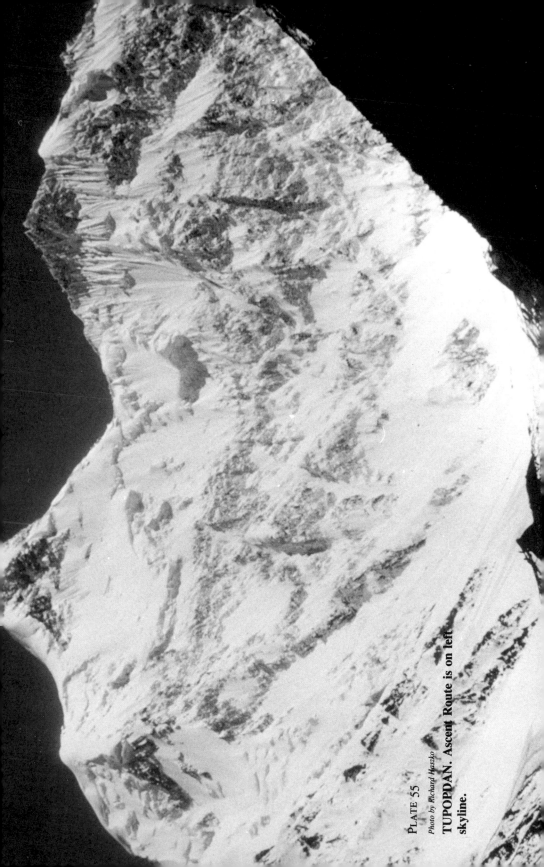

PLATE 55

Photo by Richard Haszko

TUPOPDAN. Ascent Route is on left skyline.

conditions and a new approach was made via a parallel valley. On July 4, Cave and Stevenson reached the col for the summit attempt. They climbed the ridge above with a bivouac on a rock buttress at 5500 meters and reached the summit (6125 meters, 20,095 feet) at 10:15 on July 6. (The Editor suspects that this peak and the one reported on immediately below may well be the same mountain.)

RICHARD HASZKO, *England*

Tlipobdan. On June 24, most of our group started the drive to Pakistan. They were Bernhard Juptner, Stefan Oberhauser, Christian Schimanek, Beatrix Meyer, Christine Fegerl, Robert Klapps and Andreas Ranet. En route, they climbed Ararat in Turkey and Damavand in Iran. One month later they arrived in Islamabad. Leader Harry Grün and I flew from Vienna. We all had six weeks in Pakistan. The first three weeks we trekked and acclimatized. On August 17, we arrived at Markhun. Tlipobdan is 100 kilometers south of the Khunjerab Pass to China. Base Camp at 4000 meters was an eight-hour hike from the Karakoram Highway. We ascended the Markhun River to get there. The porters charged 3¾ days' pay and collected 410 rupees for the route. We ascended the glacial moraine to the col at the base of Tlipobdan's northeast shoulder. A rock outcrop breaks the shoulder midway. Above the shoulder the route crossed the northwest face to the summit. A first alpine-style attempt was abandoned three hours after sunrise. Snow conditions indicated acute avalanche danger. Since the snow froze overnight, we decided to climb the ridge at night. Grün, Schimanek and Klapps spent two nights fixing all the rope we had, 450 meters. Using these, Juptner, Meyer, Ranet and Oberhauser established Camp II at 5800 meters before eleven A.M. on August 31. All climbing was done on snow with rock belays where possible. On September 1, they reached the summit (6106 meters, 20,033 feet). The snow prevented belays. Deep loose snow was broken by thin layers of ice. The next day, Grün, Schimanek, Fergl, Klapps and I started from Camp I. Schimanek turned back due to illness and Fergl went with him. After five weeks of unbroken sunshine, September 3 dawned foggy. In light of the conditions, Grün and I waited at 6050 meters while Klapps went on alone. The fog cleared shortly before he reached the summit. The view from Camp II that evening was unbroken by clouds. The weather remained good while we cleared Base Camp. By September 15, we had the truck packed for the 10,000-kilometer journey home.

MARGARET KERR, *Österreichischer Alpenverein*

Nanga Parbat, Diamir Face. After the successes on Gasherbrum I and II in 1985 and Broad Peak and K2 in 1986, the Quota 8000 climbers turned in the summer of 1987 to the 1962 German route on the Diamir face of Nanga Parbat. We were Italians leader Agostino Da Polenza, Gianni Calcagno, Soro Dorotei,

Dr. Giovanna Gaffuri and I, Frenchman Benoît Chamoux, and Austrians Kurt Diemberger (cameraman) and Hildegard Diemberger (sound). We got to Base Camp on June 20. The weather for an entire week was terribly snowy. Even so, we set up Camp I at 6110 meters and Camp II at 6750 meters, from which we hoped to climb to the summit. On June 29, our summit attempt at 7300 meters failed in the Bazhin Basin when deep snow and threatening weather forced us back to Base Camp. On July 3, the weather turned fine and we returned to Camp I and the next day to Camp II. At 2:30 P.M. on July 5, despite deep snow, wind and cold, Dorotei, Calcagno and I stood on the summit after a 12-hour climb. Giovanna Gaffuri had to give up at 7500 meters. That same day Benoît Chamoux left Base Camp and climbed to the summit of Nanga Parbat in 23 hours. We were all back in Base Camp on July 6.

TULLIO VIDONI, *Club Alpino Italiano*

Nanga Parbat, Diamir Face. We established Base Camp at 4200 meters at the foot of the Diamir Face on July 6. We climbed the Kinshofer or Schell route. We placed Camps I and II at 5000 and 6200 meters. Because of bad weather we were unable to set up Camps III and IV at 6800 and 7200 meters until the first week of August. On August 9, Sergeants Pedro Expósito and Domingo Hernández and civilians Pedro Martínez and Fernando Alvarez reached the summit. The other members of the expedition were Captains José María Jayme, Alfonso Juez, Francisco Gan and Dr. César Alforo, Sergeants Pedro Aceradillo and Juan Orta and civilians Carlos Soria and Pedro Nicolás.

SANTIAGO ARRIBAS, *Major, Escuela Militar de Montaña, Spain*

Nanga Parbat Attempt. Todd Bibler, Harry Kent, Andy Lapkass and I attempted to climb Nanga Parbat from the Rupal valley. Our objective was to try the central pillar of the Rupal Face in as close to alpine-style as possible. We spent from July 5 to 22 acclimatizing on the smaller peaks south of Nanga Parbat. Among other unnamed peaks, our ascents included Middle Rupal Peak (18,000 feet) and Shagiri Peak (20,000 feet). We also climbed to 21,000 feet on the west ridge of Nanga Parbat above Mazeno Pass. While our acclimatization went well, the snow conditions above 20,000 feet were abysmal. This, combined with a period of unsettled weather, provoked us to abandon the central pillar and focus on the Schell route, which ascends the southwest ridge and crosses over onto the Diamir Face. We made a carry to 17,500 feet on July 27. Our first serious attempt came on August 1. However, a storm which brought 14 inches of new snow forced us to retreat from our first camp. After waiting for the snow to set up, we made our next attempt on August 7. We moved rapidly to 20,000 feet, but above we encountered knee- to waist-deep snow. After leaving a cache at 23,000 feet, we descended to Base Camp. Three of us elected to give up the climb because of the conditions and the extreme avalanche danger. Andy Lapkass continued. He returned to the route alone on

August 15. Using the food and equipment we had left, he fought his way for the next seven days to the rock step on the Diamir side above 25,000 feet before giving up and descending. He cleaned the route of all but 300 feet of fixed rope.

MARK HESSE

Nanga Parbat, Southwest Ridge (Kinshofer or Schell Route). We set up the following camps: Base Camp, and Camps I, II, III, IV and V at 4500, 5000, 6180, 6800, 7200 and 7300 meters on July 28, 29, August 5, 7, 9 and 11. Camp IV was just below the Bazhin Gap and Camp V was in it. On August 12, Koji Matsui, Ryoichi Okabayashi and Hitoshi Yamaguchi tried for the summit. Yamaguchi had mountain sickness and suffered frostbite. In the terrible weather they couldn't find the route and gave up. On August 15, Taisaku Tamura and I suffered from mountain sickness and we turned back. A third attempt by Matsui and Okabayashi on August 17 failed. On August 19 Matsui and Okabayashi set out at 5:30 A.M. and reached the summit at 7:42 P.M. They bivouacked for four hours on the descent and were back in Camp V at eight A.M. They returned to Base Camp on the 22nd. The summit day was the only good day we had on the mountain. It rained or snowed in Base Camp every day except for that. The snow above 7000 meters was always deep, averaging 70 cms. Of our seven members, six had trained in a low-pressure laboratory, but three suffered from mountain sickness. Four were frostbitten. The two summit climbers had second or third-degree frostbite. We set up fixed ropes on the lower part of the ice slope between Camps I and II. We used the Spanish fixed rope on the upper part. Above that we dug up and used fixed ropes that past expeditions had left. But every time we climbed, we had to free the fixed ropes from newly fallen snow. Osami Nakazima and Hitoshi Ohtani were also members of the expedition.

TADAKIYO SAKAHARA, *Kawasaki City Teachers' Expedition, Japan*

Nanga Parbat Attempts. There were two other expeditions to Nanga Parbat in 1987, both unsuccessful. Spaniards led by Javier Bermejo were on the Diamir Face and Japanese under the leadership of Hitoshi Tamada attempted the Rupal Face.

Shahan Dok Attempt, Hindu Raj. Saburo Hiroshima, Makoto Nebuka, Fumio Okitsu, Masatoshi Sato, Mitsutaka Kudo and I as leader got to Base Camp at Horgojit at 4000 meters on July 22. We had hoped to climb Shahan Dok (6320 meters, 20,735 feet) via the Shahan Dok Glacier, but dangerous conditions persuaded us to try the ridge running from Shahan Dok II to the main peak. Bad weather and severe route complications stopped our try after establishing Camp II at 5400 meters. We had reached the lowest col of the main ridge. We hope to complete the climb in 1988.

KATUITI HONDA, *Japan*

Istor-o-Nal North I. We climbed Istor-o-Nal North I on the 1967 Lapuch's Austrian route, which was repeated in 1976 by Naar's Dutch expedition. We were Horst-Jürgen Stierle, Klaus-Jürgen Cramer, Norbert Kraus, Anita Burkhardt and I as leader. We started from Islamabad for Shagrom in the Tirich valley on August 4. Base Camp was placed at Babu at 4900 meters on the 10th. Camps I, II and III were set up at 5630, 6050 and 6680 meters on August 15, 18 and 21. We varied the route between Camp I and II from the earlier climbs, climbing the northern tongue of the Nobaison Glacier to avoid objective dangers. Between Camps I and III we had to climb some dangerous icefalls and ice up to 60°. On August 25 Stierle and I climbed to the summit, (7373 meters, 24,190 feet). On the 28th, Cramer and Kraus were successful. We were back in Shagrom on September 2. For the last two years there has been a road from Reshun to Shagrom. It is no longer necessary to cross the Zani An.

ALFRED FENDT, *Deutscher Alpenverein*

Southeast China

Yulong Shan. Phil Peralta-Ramos, John Warfield, Marty Gollery and I as leader and five trekkers headed for China's Yunnan province in April. We threaded through pony carts, rotor-tiller machines, bicycles and honey wagons for two days from Kunming to Lijiang. A two-hour truck ride from Lijiang brought us to the Base Camp used by unsuccessful Japanese in 1984 and Americans in 1985 and 1986. Racing a tight schedule, we set up Base Camp, loaded packs and headed up a forested cow trail for snowline, trying to establish Advance Base all on the first day. Unfortunately the Naxi porters got drunk on rice wine, lost the trail and mired the team in a dense bamboo jungle. We established Advance Base the next day. Good weather allowed rapid progress and the swift establishment of Glacier Camp at 16,000 feet. Then altitude problems struck. Gollery descended to Base Camp and Peralta-Ramos holed up at Advance Base. A two-day storm dropped 18 inches of snow and gave us a chance to rest. Previous attempts had tried a rock gully and a long, twisting ridge. This time we took a more direct line that could be completed in one long day. Warfield, a freshly-recovered Peralta-Ramos and I left Glacier Camp at first light on May 8. We threaded up snow gullies and scrambled up snow-splattered limestone headwalls. Avalanche danger was high and protection sparse. The ice was too rotten to hold a screw. Ice axes crashed through and hooked on limestone edges. Technical difficulty reached 5.7, not easy in plastic boots and crampons. The "Jade Dragon's" usual horrific weather held steady. We pulled onto the ridge at 18,000 feet at two P.M. Warfield was exhausted and chose to sit tight. Peralta-Ramos and I pushed up the three-foot-wide ridge, groveling through steep, loose snow. The weather stayed clear for another ten minutes and then the clouds closed in and never lifted. We reached the summit (5596 meters, 18,360 feet) at 3:45 P.M.

ERIC S. PERLMAN

Anye Maqin IX. On September 5, Martin Hampar, Michael and Catherine Pettipher, Ben Williams and I established Base Camp at 4200 meters in the main valley about a quarter mile beyond the large stream descending from the east face of Anye Maqin I. On the 7th, we placed Camp I at 4800 meters on the highest end of the north moraine of the Harlon II Glacier. Our attempt to find a route up the right bay, recommended by the Chinese, was halted by a series of complex icefalls. A reconnaissance of the Japanese route of 1981 via a spur between the two bays revealed why they had fixed 1000 feet of rope. Having neither the resources nor the time for this, we switched our attention to the relatively straightforward unclimbed summit of Anye Maqin III (6090 meters). Williams and I reached 5200 meters on the east ridge before running out of steam. On September 18, Williams and Mike Pettipher established a camp at 4700 meters on the east side of the northern glacier of Anye Maqin IX, the prominent southern outlier of the range clearly seen from Snow Mountain Commune. On September 20, after having been turned back the previous day by snow squalls, they made the first ascent of this peak (5690 meters, 18,668 feet) by the northern glacier and the col on its west side. Like the Australians in 1981, we deplore the environmental damage left by the 1981 Japanese Joetsu expedition.

JOHN TOWER, *Alpine Club*

Tibet

Everest, Hornbein Couloir, Winter Attempt, 1985-6. An expedition to Mount Everest in the winter of 1985-6 was not reported in the *A.A.J.* Under the leadership of Mrs. Michiko Takahashi, Japanese attempted to climb the mountain via the Hornbein Couloir. Despite a good team of Sherpas led by Sirdar Lhakpa Tenzing, fierce wind and cold drove them back. On December 15, 1985, two members got to the head of the couloir at 8450 meters before having to retreat.

XAVIER EGUSKITZA, *Pyrenaica, Bilbao, Spain*

Everest Attempt via the Great Couloir. Our expedition was composed of Jack Allsup, leader, Ann Smith, Bob East, Bob Allison, George Dunn, Greg Wilson, Craig Van Hoy, Ed Viesturs, Bonnie Nobori, Dr. John Baumeister, Travis Cannon and me as climbing leader. Four went via Beijing and Lhasa. The rest traveled via Kathmandu, where we were joined by five Nepalese Sherpas and a cook. We met at Xigare, Tibet, and reached the Rongbuk Base Camp at 16,800 feet on March 17. Very good weather prevailed for the next few weeks. Advance Base was established on the Central Rongbuk Glacier at 18,300 feet on March 23. Yaks carried 90 loads there in nine days. At this point Allison and Dr. Baumeister became ill and returned to the United States. The remaining Americans and the Sherpas made rapid progress, establishing Camp I at 20,400 feet at the base of the north face on March 26 and Camp II at 22,000 feet at the foot of the technical climbing on March 31. Instead of a direct approach up the face, we continued eastward between the flanks of Changtse and the north face to 23,000 feet. On April 17 Camp III was placed at 25,000 feet at the bottom of the Great Couloir. Storms, high winds and illness prevented Camp IV from being established at 26,800 feet until May 14. Between Camps II and IV we fixed 9500 feet of rope because of icy spring conditions. Camp IV was stocked for four summit attempts. On May 17 Dunn and Wilson made the first try, using oxygen, but were slowed by difficult rock in the Yellow Band, where they fixed 500 feet of rope. While descending from their high point of 27,500 feet, Wilson fell 40 feet when his rappel piton pulled out but was held by Dunn. On May 21 Viesturs and I ascended rapidly through the Yellow Band on the previous team's rope and then fixed 500 more feet in the Grey Band above on 50° to 60° ice and mixed ground. We climbed straight out of the top of the Great Couloir rather than traversing right above the Yellow Band, the route followed by the Australians and Ershler in the post-monsoon period of 1984, when there was more snow. Upon reaching the final summit snowfield, we traversed to the west ridge. Using oxygen, I reached 28,700 feet stopping below a steep rock step. Without a rope and unsure of getting down without a rappel, I turned back. Viesturs, who was climbing without oxygen, descended with me from 28,600 feet. That same day, a Swede, who had traversed across from the northeast ridge, turned back below the Grey Band, and Roger Marshall fell to his death from the Japanese Couloir during his solo attempt. The third summit attempt was to take place on May 27, but after spending the night at Camp IV, they did not leave because Dunn was not feeling well. A fourth attempt on May 29 by Allsup, Smith and Sherpas Nuru and Pasang Tsering failed to get higher than 25,500 feet.

ERIC SIMONSON

Swedish Everest Attempt. We are still waiting for details about a large Swedish expedition led by Ebbe Wahlund that attempted the North-Col route on Everest. They established Camp IV on the North Col late in April and Camp V at 7500 meters. We do have a few details about their summit attempt. On May 20, Lasse Cronlund and Daniel Bindner crossed to the Great Couloir to establish Camp VI at 8000 meters. That night Bindner did not feel well and descended the next morning, May 21. Cronlund set out at 4:30 and after passing through the American camp, caught up with Ed Viesturs and Eric Simonson on the Yellow Band. Cronlund led much of this. Above was a snowfield where the Americans had left a fixed rope on a previous attempt. All three climbed separately. Simonson and Cronlund were climbing with oxygen, but Cronlund used up his supply at about 8650 meters. He felt he would not be strong enough to continue on without it and still be able to descend. For that reason he turned back. What the Americans did is covered in their report.

Everest Attempt. Josema Casimiro and I shared the route on the north side of Everest with a large Swedish expedition. We followed the classic route on the East Rongbuk Glacier and on May 20 climbed to the North Col some 300 meters to the left of the usual route among seracs, where we found fixed ropes. From a bivouac at 6990 meters just below the col, we followed the north ridge to 7500 meters to a point 100 meters below the usual Camp V on May 21. From there we traversed diagonally on a strip of snow to the Great Couloir at 8100 meters. Despite theoretical protection we should have had from the sides of the couloir, the violent wind raked us for two nights and a day as we waited in vain for an improvement in the weather. On May 24, we gave up the attempt because of the wind and descended.

MARI ABREGO, *Orhi Mendi, Federación Vasca de Montaña, Spain*

Everest Tragedy. On June 19 Roger Marshall set out with the hope of making a solo ascent of Mount Everest via the Japanese and Hornbein Couloirs. He made good progress and, at the end of the second day, he was at the foot of the Hornbein Couloir. However something must have been amiss since he was observed by his friend Ruth DeCew to begin on the morning of June 21 to descend. On very hard ice in the Japanese Couloir he slipped and fell to his death. Marshall was born in 1942 in England and moved to Canada in 1967. During the past few years he had lived in Boulder, Colorado. In 1984 he soloed Kangchenjunga. It had been his ambition to solo the five highest mountains of the world.

Everest, Hornbein Couloir from the North Face Attempt. Our expedition was composed of Luis Fraga, Luis Bárcenas, Juan Agustín Casillas, Iñigo Mauleon, Pedro Holst, Bicen Itxaso, Cristóbal Salas, Fernando Garrido and me, all from different regions of Spain. We were also joined in part by Frenchman Pierre Beghin. We crossed from Nepal to Tibet by way of Kodari on June 20. We established Base Camp on July 5 at 5150 meters, somewhat higher than usual. On July 8, we put Advance Base at 5500 meters in the splendid place the Australians had used. On July 14, Camp I was set up at the foot of the north face on a great plateau at 6050 meters. The weather turned bad for a long time and left the face in bad condition, but on August 6, we placed Camp II at 6900 meters. We used a route this far which was to the right of the Japanese route and to the left of the one used by Loretan and Troillet; we feel that this was safer from avalanches than the Japanese. Camp III was established on August 9 at 7350 meters on a rocky spur. Beyond Camp II we were also on new ground until we reached the Hornbein Couloir to the left of the route used by the Japanese and by the Swiss Loretan and Troillet. On August 25 Fraga and I made the first summit attempt from Camp IV at 7900 meters, but we were driven back by the weather from 8000 meters in the Hornbein Couloir. Our retreat was problematical in the deep snow that fell. On August 27, a second summit try failed due to Sherpa misunderstanding and bad weather. On September 2, Bárcenas, Fraga, Garrido and Beghin set up two small tents at 8200 meters and on September 3, Garrido and Beghin got to 8700 meters. They had to deviate to the right to emerge on the upper part of the west ridge, but the deep snow turned them back. Without a bivouac, they could not have reached the top.

ANTONIO RAMOS VILLAR, *Tenerife, Spain*

Everest Attempt. Between August 13 and 17 our team arrived at the Rongbuk Base Camp at 17,000 feet, hoping to climb the traditional East Rongbuk-North Col route. Base Camp had the appearance of an international camp with teams from Australia, Britain, Ireland, Japan and Spain also in residence. Our expedition consisted of Americans Paul Briggs, Michael Flynn, Dr. Brack Hattler, Peter Jamieson, Steve Matous, Dr. Tom McCullough, Dave Nettle, Greg Sapp, Steven Strain, Base-Camp Manager Rod Willard, Canadian Geoff Creighton, Sherpas Ang Rita and Chuldim Dorje and me as leader. For two weeks we stocked Camp I at 19,500 feet on the East Rongbuk Glacier and Advance Base at 21,300 feet with the help of 21 yaks. By August 29, Advance Base was completely stocked. Camp III was established on the North Col at 23,000 feet on September 3. We fixed 2500 feet of 8mm rope below the col, the only section that was fixed. The weather was still excellent and we talked of the summit in two weeks. The next three weeks saw intermittent periods of heavy snowfall, making the route to the North Col extremely dangerous; there were high winds. Greg Sapp was hit by an avalanche while ascending the fixed ropes but fortunately escaped with only bruised ribs and a torn climbing harness. Camp IV was finally established at 25,500 feet on September 23. For several weeks winds frequently over 100 mph slowed progress and hampered efforts to stock this camp. Camp IV, including five bottles of oxygen, was blown away. On October 9, Camp IV was reestablished by Flynn, Ang Rita, Sapp and me. We dug a snow cave instead of setting up tents. On October 12, Camp V at 26,500 feet was established by Strain, Ang Rita and Jamieson. The latter was forced to descend because bitter cold was causing his feet, frostbitten in 1983 on Everest, considerable pain. Strain spent the night alone at Camp V and left for the summit at five A.M. Using oxygen and climbing in high winds and −40° temperatures, he reached the First Step after seven hours. The winds increased and he was blown off his feet three times. Since the wind did not let up, he had to descend. No further attempts were made due to wind, exhaustion, illness and Tibet's worst snowstorm in 40 years that from October 19 to 21 left four feet of snow at Advance Base.

STEVE VAN METER

Everest, North Face Attempt. Our team was composed of five women: Stacy Allison, Evelyn Lees, Liz Nichols, Melly Reuling and Mimi Stone*, and ten men: Q. Belk, Dr. David Black, Peter Goldman, Michael Graber, Wes

---

* All five received Vera Watson-Alison Chadwick Onyszkiewicz Memorial Fund Grants.

Krause, Bob McConnell, George Schunk, Ben Toland, Rick Wyatt and me as leader. On August 6, after struggling against landslides and flooding rivers, we arrived at Base Camp at 17,000 feet on the remote Tibetan side of Mount Everest and were ready to attempt the Australian route on the north face. Well in advance of the post-monsoon period, we intended to stock four camps by October. Supplies were carried to Advance Base at 18,400 feet with the help of yaks. In continuing beautiful weather, we established Camp I at 19,200 feet on the Rongbuk Glacier by August 17. The climbing between Camps I and II was the steepest on the route. We ascended on a snow-and-ice spur, often at night, to avoid avalanches and ice and rockfall. The crux was a nearly vertical rock pitch. Camp II was a well-stocked snow cave. From there we intended to launch our summit assault. Camp III at 25,000 feet was also a snow cave, dug into what the Australians called White Limbo, an ominous snowfield which stretches across the entire north face. Camp IV, at 26,600 feet in the Great Couloir, was stocked with tent, stove, fuel and oxygen. After two months, the weather changed from summer to what soon would be winter. Michael Graber and Mimi Stone made the first summit attempt on October 15. They were turned back at 28,000 feet by strong wind. Mimi now holds the American women's altitude record. A second summit-attempt team consisted of Wesley Krause, Q. Belk, Stacy Allison and me. A fierce blizzard hit us on October 20 when we were climbing White Limbo. We were forced to retreat to Camp II for three days. When the snowstorm ended, we climbed to Camp III and spent three more days waiting for the wind to abate. The storm complicated our descent off the mountain and delayed our departure from Everest by two weeks.

SCOTT FISCHER

Everest Northeast Ridge Attempt. Our expedition arrived at Base Camp at 5000 meters on September 3. We were British climbers Doug Scott and Rick Allen, co-leaders, Nick Kekus, Michael Scott, and I, Austrian Robert Schauer, American Steve Sustad and Sharu Prabhu, who was the first Indian mountaineer to represent her country in China. Our route was the unclimbed northeast ridge and we were attempting it without oxygen and in lightweight style. We established snow caves at 7090 and 8000 meters. Doug Scott, Allen, Schauer, Kekus and I set out from Advance Base to try for the summit in very windy conditions. I turned back that same day, convinced that good weather was not to come. Kekus and Schauer retreated the following day with frostbitten toes. Scott and Allen got to 8100 meters in 100 mile-per-hour winds. We had ideas of another attempt, but heavy snowfall in the second week of October prevented this. Also, our Nepali cook, Nima Mangal Sing Tamang was caught in an avalanche near Base Camp. His body was later cremated at the Rongbuk Monastery. Other expeditions on the north side abounded and all had problems clearing Base Camps due to the depth of the snow.

SANDY ALLAN, *Alpine Climbing Group*

PLATE 56

Photo by Joss Lynam

CHANGTSE from the Lho La. The South Ridge is on the right.

Everest Attempt. In September, the Iranian, Mischa Saleki, who lives in Germany, reached the North Col of Everest from the East Rongbuk Glacier with two Sherpas but did not go higher.

Everest Tragedy. The Defense Academy Team led by Takashi Kawakami comprised 10 members. They hoped to climb Everest by the west ridge via the Rongbuk Glacier. The climbing leader, Masashi Yokoyama, was drowned when he failed to jump across a glacial stream between Base Camp and Camp I. In spite of the tragedy, the team continued to attempt the mountain but had to give up at 8000 meters in the last week of October.

SADAO TAMBE, *A.A.C. and Himalayan Association of Japan*

Everest. A Japanese expedition is attempting Mount Everest from Tibet during the winter, as reported in January of 1988. The leader Tsuneo Hasegawa is accompanied by his wife and two others. They had hoped to make their climb in the autumn but were prevented by the big October snowstorm from getting to the mountain. They did get to Base Camp on December 9 with permission to continue their attack until February. On January 5 they established Camp III at 7500 meters, apparently in the great couloir. Further details are not yet available.

Everest Photo Correction. The photograph in Plate 79 of *A.A.J., 1987* on page 303 was printed backwards.

Changtse. We were R. Turner, G. Nash, D. Hunter, C. Gordon, J. Smart and I as leader. We established Base Camp at 5100 meters on September 5. Camps I and II were at the traditional sites on the East Rongbuk Glacier at 5400 and 5800 meters. Advance Base was at 6000 meters at the junction of the Changtse and East Rongbuk Glaciers. We spent two weeks acclimatizing. Two routes were attempted: 1) a central couloir to the left of the north-face icefall, climbed by a Japanese team in 1986 in the pre-monsoon, tried by Nash and Turner; 2) an objectively safer route farther east which led to the ridgeline and thence to the summit, attempted by Hunter, Smart, Gordon and me. We on the second team reached 7100 meters after three bivouacs at 6400, 7000 and 7100 meters. Gordon and I turned back there, while Smart and Hunter went on to 7200 meters before turning back two days later. The first team, Nash and Turner, reached the summit (7580 meters, 24,869 feet) on September 29 after bivouacs at 6200, 6500, 6650 and 6900 meters despite high winds, two avalanche incidents and a fall into a schrund.

LOUIS A. WHITTON, *Australia*

Changtse Attempt. Our expedition was composed of Mike Barry, Richard Fry, Sarah Gillam, Leslie Lawrence, Shay Nolan, Donal O'Murchu, Danny

PLATE 57

Photo by Michiko Takahashi

CHO OYU from the North.

and Geraldine Osborne, Dermot Somers, Phil Thomas and me as leader. We had hoped to ascend the southwest ridge and descend the north ridge. In the snow conditions prevailing, the southeast ridge was unclimbable, as was the north ridge from the *Main* Rongbuk Glacier. (The Australians were on the *East* Rongbuk side.) We turned to the south ridge running up from Everest's North Col. Two summit attempts were made from camp on the col. The first was frustrated by a heavy snowfall, leading to an epic retreat down the east side of the col to the East Rongbuk. The second party, Nugent and Thomas, were stopped by avalanche conditions at 7250 meters. Like other expeditions in the Everest region, we had difficulty getting out to the main road after the heavy snowfall of late October.

JOSS LYNAM, *Federation of Mountaineering Clubs of Ireland*

Cho Oyu from Tibet. Our group from five nations under my leadership placed 13 climbers on the summit of Cho Oyu via the northwest side, the same as has normally been climbed after crossing from the Nepalese side. We approached from Kathmandu by way of Kodari-Zhangmu through Tingri in Tibet. Ours was the first foreign expedition to make our entire approach from the Tibetan side. Base Camp and Camps I, II, III and IV were at 5700, 6400, 6800, 7200 and 7600 feet. Our summit climbs took place between April 29 and May 12 with temperatures as low as −35° C. We used no artificial oxygen and had no high altitude porters. The following reached the summit: Swiss Fredy Graf and Josef Wangeler on April 29 (along with two Chileans and two Sherpas who had come from the Nepalese side); Austrians Peter Wörgötter, Helmut Wagner and Oswald Gassler on May 5; German Karl Wimmer on May 6; Swiss Robert Hofer on May 7; Austrian Robert Strouhal on May 8; Austrians Wastl Wörgötter, Kurt Hecher and Hanns Pree on May 9; Netherlander Bart Vos on May 12. Vos tried unsuccessfully to climb a new route on the northwest face and reached 6700 meters before switching to the standard route.

MARCUS SCHMUCK, *Österreichischer Alpenverein*

Cho Oyu Ascent and Paraglider Descent. After seven Sherpas joined us on August 25, we settled Base Camp that same day at the tongue of the Gyabrag Glacier at 4950 meters. We were Kazuyuki Takahashi, Akio Hayakawa, Kenji Kondo, Tomoji Kato, co-leaders Yoshitomi Ohkura and I, and a Asahi Newspaper and Television team consisting of Junichiro Ohkei, Houei Ohtani, Taijiro Maeda and Shinji Kobayashi. On September 5, Camp I was placed at 6350 meters on the north-northwest side of Cho Oyu. In the following bad weather, we carried loads to Camp I. On the 15th, Camp II was established at 7200 meters. The route to there went around the right end of the icefall. Camp III was put at the bottom of the rock band at 7700 meters on September 18. On September 20, after a 4½-hour climb from Camp III, Hayakawa and Kondo reached the summit without supplementary oxygen. They had climbed to the southern side of the vast summit snowfield in knee-deep snow. Suddenly Everest and Lhotse appeared through a rift in the dense fog. On September 21, Ohkura, K. Takahashi, Kato,Ohtani and Sherpas Nima Dorje and Ang Dawa reached the top. (They were accompanied by Frenchman Tierry Renard, who apparently was not authorized to make the climb—*Editor.*) Takahashi descended in ten minutes from the summit some 2600 vertical meters to Base Camp by paraglider. It took him five tries to take off. This is the record for the highest take-off. This is all the more remarkable when you consider that he had to run some distance on the flat mountain top to be able to take off. On September 22, Kobayashi, Sherpas Lhakpa Tenzing, Ang Phurba and Mingma Tenzing and I gained the summit. We withdrew from Base Camp on September 26 and were in Lhasa on the 29th.

MRS. MICHIKO TAKAHASHI, *Kamoshika Alpine Club, Japan*

Menlungtse Attempt. Our team was composed of Norwegians Odd Eliassen, Bjørn Myrer-Lund, Torgeir Fosse and Helge Ringdal and Britons Jim Fotheringham and me. Getting to Base Camp was an adventure. We had originally planned on five days to reach there from the Nepalese-Tibetan frontier at Kodari, but it took us over a fortnight. We made a difficult trip by lorry over the 17,500-foot Lalung Leh pass to Tingri. There our liaison officer, Wang Ja Ren, told us that the pass that led back south was still blocked by snow but that he had ordered yaks to carry our gear over it. Life was further complicated by altitude sickness which afflicted for the time being three of the Norwegians. We finally made it to the northern foot of the Nangpa La. We swung to the right from the route over the Nangpa La, climbed a steep ridge and crossed a 17,500-foot pass and, despite reluctance on the part of the yak drivers, descended to Chang Bu Jian, the district headquarters. After much bargaining, we got yaks and porters to continue in the narrow valley with its lush green vegetation in contrast with the dry Tibetan plateau. We set out on March 22, walking down an incredibly beautiful gorge. An hour's walk took us to the confluence with the Menlung valley. We climbed steeply up the valley and on March 25 found a perfect site for our Base Camp at 13,400 feet, ten days behind schedule. On our first reconnaissance on March 27, we looked at the north side of the mountain, walking up a long moraine towering above the glacier, but there was no hope from that side. The following day we set out to explore the southern aspect. The four ridges dropping from the high ramparts all appeared difficult and steep, but the route that gave the greatest chance was more of a buttress than a ridge. Three days later, on April 2, we were at 17,200 feet at the foot of the buttress, although the approach had been frightening. We decided to use fixed rope to make it safer for the descent and to give us a higher jumping-off point for our alpine-style push for the summit. We ran out some rope-lengths before dropping down to Advance Base in the valley. The following day we returned with tents and food, but we still had rope to fix. On

PLATE 58

Photo by Peter Boardman

MENLUNGTSE's South Face from East Face of Gaurishankar. The Central Buttress was attempted.

PLATE 59

Photo by Chris Bonington

MENLUNGTSE from the North.

April 5, we put the rest of the rope in place. This took us to the rocky crest of the buttress but what had looked like solid rock from a distance turned out to be a terrifying pile of shattered blocks. There was the constant threat of dislodging one of the huge rocks, which all weighed several tons. Eventually the difficulties eased and the rock was marginally more sound. We climbed another four or five rope-lengths until we had used up our fixed line and our four climbing ropes before dropping back to our camp at the foot of the ridge. Now it was time for our alpine-style summit attempt. Heavily laden with six days of food and gear, by late afternoon we had reached the top of the fixed ropes and picked up our climbing ropes. Odd Eliassen and Bjørn Myrer-Lund camped a few meters above us shouted down that the way ahead looked clear. The following day we made faster progress, but at three P.M. clouds swirled in. Jim and I were digging into the crest of the steep, narrow snow ridge when I was aware of a high-pitched buzz. Jim collapsed onto his knees. "I've been struck," he muttered. It was lightning. There was nothing we could do and we had to camp there. The next morning the wind was as fierce as ever. Bjørn and Odd's tent had been torn to shreds. We had to retreat. This was no easy matter. We were nine rope-lengths above the top of the fixed ropes. I began to fall as I clipped badly into the abseil rope, but I just managed to grab the rope, which tore my hands, and I held on. It was late afternoon when we reached the camp at the foot of the ridge. Without discussion, we stripped the site and carried everything down to the valley, 3000 feet below. We hadn't really examined the southeast ridge, which led straight to the summit. Four of us walked below the southeast ridge and realised it would be even more difficult and time-consuming than the buttress. We decided to try our original route, fixing the remainder of our rope so that we could have a higher jumping-off point. We returned to the fray on April 16, spent two days reclimbing the difficult section and leaving a line of fixed rope behind us. At the end of the second day we were hit by another thunderstorm and retreated all the way to Base Camp. The next morning the weather seemed to improve and we rushed straight back, going from Base at 13,400 feet to Camp I at 17,200 feet in a single day and on the following one, April 22, climbed the fixed ropes to the previous high point of 20,000 feet. We had plenty of food and fuel and felt well set for a push to the summit. That evening it began to snow and blow. The next afternoon Odd and Bjørn decided to go down. Jim and I sat out one more night, hoping for an improvement. It started snowing ten minutes after they left and by dark the wind had built up into a crescendo of terrifying force. The following morning, shaken and exhausted, we fled as the weather deteriorated even more.

CHRISTIAN BONINGTON

Labuche Kang Reconnaissance, 1986. From September 1 to October 5, 1986, a joint Chinese-Japanese expedition made a reconnaissance of Labuche Kang (7367 meters, 24,170 feet). The peak lies between Cho Oyu and Shisha Pangma. The Chinese were Cheng Tian Lian, leader, and Lee Wang, and the

Japanese were Yasuhei Saito and Masashi Kumada. They made Base Camp at Longoro village at 4500 meters on September 9, 1986 and Advance Base at Tsolongma at 5300 meters on September 17. On September 18, they climbed P 6140 (20,145 feet) and spotted a possible but not too easy route. From a new Advance Base they ascended a lateral moraine and located a suitable Camp I site at 5650 meters. From there, they climbed to a 6200-meter col and found a reasonable route on the west ridge. The north face and north ridge were deemed unsuitable.

SADAO TAMBE, *A.A.C. and Himalayan Association of Japan*

Labuche Kang. Labuche Kang lies between Cho Oyu and Shishapangma. The joint expedition of the Tibetan Mountaineering Association and the Himalayan Association of Japan was led by Cheng Tian Liang with deputy leader Ken'ichi Yamamori. There were nine members from each association. On September 16, we established Base Camp at 4500 meters near Langgoloz village. On the 20th we placed Advance Base 21 kilometers up the valley at 5300 meters. On September 28 we pitched Camp I on a snow plateau at 5600 meters. Camp II was established on October 6 at 6150 meters on the hanging glacier on the northwest face. We fixed 20 ropes to gain the west ridge. The blizzard from October 17 to 19 left heavy snow. Camp I was buried by a snow slide but no members were hurt. Camp III was placed on the west ridge on October 25. On October 26, Japanese Hidekatsu Furukawa, Keiichi Sudo, Osamu Tanabe and I and Tibetans Wanjia, Diaqiog, Gyala and Lhaji climbed to the summit (7367 meters, 24,170 feet), having fixed 14 more ropes. On October 27, Japanese Sadao Ogawa, Yasuhiro Hashimoto and Toshiya Takahashi and Tibetans Lhaba, Pupu, Akapu and Tonglu also got to the summit. Tonglu and Lhaji are ladies. Lhaji is only 17 years old.

ATARU DEUCHI, *Himalayan Association of Japan*

Shisha Pangma Attempt. Our climbing party consisted of Chuck Huss. Ken Nolan, John Pelner, Art Porter and me. We arrived at Base Camp at 16,000 feet by truck on April 12, anticipating a straightforward climb on the normal route from the north. With 15 yaks, we moved toward the head of the valley in two days. There the yak drivers refused to proceed, reluctant because of the unusually deep snow cover from the heavy winter snows. We continued ferrying loads for the next ten days, but a variety of illnesses and minor injuries caused one after the other to drop out. We abandoned the climb on April 24.

RICHARD DIETZ, *Colorado Mountain Club*

Shisha Pangma. New Zealanders Steve Bruce and Dick Price reached the summit of Shisha Pangma by the standard route on May 16, followed on May 20 by leader Mike Perry and Mark Whetu, who descended on skis. The latter is a Maori. A nine-man Austro-Swiss expedition, organized by Hanns Schell and led by Stefan Wörner, climbed the standard route. The lower central summit was reached by Swiss Alfred Meyer and West Germans Otto Huber, Klaus Solbach and Peter Blank. Poles Wanda Rutkiewicz and Ryszard Warecki, Mexicans Elsa Avila and Carlos Carsolio and Ecuadorian Ramiro Navarrete, all members of a Polish expedition, got to the main summit. A seven-man commercial expedition led by Oreste Forno abandoned its attempt on the standard route on September 10 after having reached Camp I at 6400 meters in bad weather with huge accumulations of snow.

XAVIER EGUSKITZA, *Pyrenaica, Bilbao, Spain*

Shisha Pangma and Kukuczka's 14th 8000er. Polish climber Jerzy Kukuczka became the second person after Reinhold Messner to scale the world's 14 highest mountains when he completed his ascent of Shisha Pangma. The 13-member international team, which he led, established Base Camp on August 22 at 5800 meters. To acclimatize, Kukuczka and Artur Hajzer climbed virgin P 7365, north of the Shisha Pangma massif. Bad weather with much snow delayed progress, but three camps were established at 6400, 6800 and 7000 meters. By mid September the skies cleared and the final attack could begin. On September 18 at five P.M., Kukuczka and Hajzer reached the summit, having ascended the unclimbed west ridge. The climb was made in three days alpine-style, starting from Camp Ia. On the way they made the first ascent of the western peak (c. 7966 meters, 26,083 feet). At the same time, Mexicans Elsa Avila and Carlos Carsolio, Ecuadorian Ramiro Navarrete, and Poles Wanda Rutkiewicz and Ryszard Warecki arrived on top. The following day, Englishman Alan Hinkes and American Steve Untch attained the summit via another new route, the central couloir of the north face. After a bivouac, Kukuczka skied down from the summit. On September 24, they left Base Camp. A total of nine climbers reached the summit, two of them ladies. They made two impressive new routes, the third and fourth on Shisha Pangma. Two virgin peaks were ascended. Elsa Avila is the first Latin-American women to top an 8000er. Wanda Rutkiewicz became the first and only woman to have climbed four 8000ers, which include Everest and K2. The most remarkable success, however, is that of Kukuczka. In nine years, he climbed all fourteen 8000ers, outclassing Messner in the style of his ascents. While the famous Tirolean made some of his climbs by the standard routes and with Sherpa help, Kukuczka climbed all except Lhotse by new routes or in winter. Cho Oyu, Kangchenjunga and Annapurna were first winter ascents.

JÓZEF NYKA, *Editor, Taternik, Poland*

Shisha Pangma. Our nine-member Hungarian team climbed Shisha Pangma by the original route. We had a difficult journey to the mountain and back: Budapest-Moscow-Tashkent-Delhi-Kathmandu-Base Camp-Lhasa-Golmud-

PLATE 60

Photo by Stephen Venables

Nyanang Ri, Pangpa Ri and Shisha Pangma (summit hidden).

Beijing-Ulan Bator-Moscow-Budapest, half of it on the surface to manage it by the cheapest way. From Base Camp at 5000 meters, we reconnoitered on September 11 for a site for Advance Base at 5850 meters. With six yaks and two drivers, we walked the 30 kilometers to Advance Base from September 18 to 20. Camps I and II were placed at 6400 and 6950 meters. On the 25th we had to return to Advance Base because Peter Dékány had fallen seriously ill. After two days' rest, three of us set out again and made Camp III on the very windy northeast ridge at 7400 meters. On October 1, Attila Ozsváth and I got to the top. When Zoltán Balaton, Lászlo Vörös, József Csíkos and Lászlo Várkonyi got to Camp III, they had to dig a snow cave because the tent had been blown off by the wind. On October 8, they also reached the summit. These were the 25th and 26th ascents of Shisha Pangma.

SÁNDOR NAGY, *Magyar Hegymászó Klub, Hungary*

Pungpa Ri Second Ascent and Shisha Pangma Attempt. Our expedition was a joint civilian and military operation with a 17-member climbing team led by Lieutenant Colonel Henry Day and a 12-member scientific team led by Colonel John Blashford-Snell. The climbing objective was to make the first ascent of Shisha Pangma from the east, by the unexplored Phola Glacier. Base Camp was established at 4950 meters near the snout of the glacier on October 21, but due to illness and yak transport difficulties it was another two weeks before all the climbers and supplies were installed. From a close look at the mountain, we decided that the main east face was too dangerous and opted for a circuitous route via the southeast face of Pungpa Ri. Advance Base was at 5100 meters on the Phola Glacier. A complex icefall, where we fixed short sections of rope, led to Camp I at 5850 meters. An easier section of glacier brought us to Camp II at the head of the cwm between Nyanang Ri and Pungpa Ri. The 60-meter-high 50° ice-and-mixed face was fixed with rope and on October 16 Camp III, a four-man snow hole, was dug into the col between the two peaks. So far, the weather had been fine. On October 17, the Everest region was hit by a big 2½-day storm. Most of the tents were destroyed and a large equipment cache at Camp II was lost in an avalanche. After the storm resources were limited but the weather was perfect. Luke Hughes and I set off on October 21 with food and gear for a summit attempt. John Vlasto and Kate Phillips accompanied us to Camp II. Snowshoes were essential to break trail from Camp I to II. The fixed ropes on the headwall were intact but often buried. On October 25, we two continued from Camp III up the south ridge of Pungpa Ri, joining the final part of the Scott-McIntyre-Baxter-Jones route of 1982. We reached the summit (7486 meters, 24,561 feet) at two P.M. We camped just below the summit and on the 26th continued toward the three-kilometer connecting ridge to Shisha Pangma, carrying just a shovel, food and a gas stove for an emergency bivouac. We traversed across the south face of Pungpa Ri to the Pungpa Ri-Shisha Pangma col. A fairly firm wind crust provided good conditions, but knife-edged bumps were time-consuming and by four P.M. we had reached only 7650 meters. With a big cloud build-up we decided to dig a snow hole and to try for the summit in the morning. After a cold night without sleeping bags, we left at dawn on the 27th but after 50 meters had to descend because of strong winds. At the tent on Pungpa Ri, Hughes discovered that several fingers were frostbitten. On October 28, we descended to Camp II. Nigel Williams and John Vlasto had come up to investigate and, finding we needed no help, they were able to repeat the ascent of Pungpa Ri. The whole climbing team reassembled at Base Camp on October 29. There were hopes of another summit attempt, but a radio message from the Tibetan Mountaineering Association and the local government forbade this and ordered us down to Nyalam. That same day, 18 Tibetans arrived at Base Camp, announcing that they were not porters but a "rescue party" sent to escort us down. It seems likely that the liaison officer and the interpreter, anxious to get home, played a part in having us removed from the mountain. It seems that although the CMA and TMA are charging ever more exorbitant rates, they no longer provide the efficient service of a few years ago.

STEPHEN VENABLES, *Alpine Climbing Group*

Minor Peaks around Shisha Pangma. In addition to the attempt on Shisha Pangma described above, we made climbs of other peaks. P 5900, east of Phola Ganchen and north of the lake Kung Tso, was probably first climbed by the 1984 reconnaissance party; it was ascended this year by Brian Davidson and me on separate occasions. P 5750 immediately east of P 5900 was also climbed by Davidson and me. P 5850, on the long ridge flanking the east side of the Kung Tso, was also probably first ascended by the reconnaissance party; its summit was reached by Chung Kin Man and Robert Durran and later by me, when I also ascended P 5625 and P 5800 on the same ridge.

LINDSAY GRIFFIN, *Alpine Climbing Group*

Nianqintanggula Correction, A.A.J., 1987. On page 299 of *A.A.J.,1987,* the Editor admitted that he did not know of the location of the peak. This information has been supplied by Xavier Eguskitza. It lies about 90 kilometers northwest of Lhasa in the middle of a long range west-southwest to east-northeast. The coordinates of this 7088-meter peak are 30°23'N, 90°35'E.

Dolmalari. While making two pilgrimage circumabulations of unclimbed Kailas in western Tibet, I made an apparent first ascent of a non-technical peak above the Dolma La, a pass shown as 18,600 feet on most maps. Although my altimeter readings were within 100 feet of most ground references, both times I climbed the pass my altimeter indicated about 18,150 feet. Since the peak was an indicated 900 feet above the pass, I have chosen an altitude of 19,050 feet. Since Tibetans are likely to leave evidence of their passage on peaks, with no sign of human presence I assume that it had not previously been ascended. The peak is a mile northwest of the pass and affords a fantastic view of the north face of Kailas as well as of Gurla Mandhata and Nanda Devi in the distance. On the east side of the pass I attempted a spectacular granite spire, locally called "Thari" ("shovel" in Tibetan) because it is shaped like an upside-down shovel. Its narrow spire culminates in a wildly overhanging flake of granite. I got to within 15 vertical feet of the summit but could not solo the exceedingly exposed 5.11 final block. The highest point, however, is behind and to the left of the prominent shovel blade seen from the pass. This I ascended after several tries via 5.9 climbing on the north side. My altimeter read 18,100 feet. Both climbs were on June 16.

GALEN ROWELL

Tamchok Kambab Kangri. While exploring the source of the Brahmaputra River for the National Geographic Society, I made a solo first ascent of the peak immediately above the two source glaciers about 60 miles southeast of Kailas. Tamchok Kambab means "the horse's mouth," an allusion to the appearance of the source of the river where the two glaciers form the horse's ears and the peak behind them is the face of the horse. The two glaciers are completely separated by the knife-edged west ridge of the peak. My one-day ascent began by headlamp on June 20 from a camp beside the river at 16,300 feet, which we had reached by driving 30 miles overland in Land Cruisers from the southern road to Kailas and then by walking for two days. The peak lies seven miles from the Tibetan-Nepalese border just north of Dolpo. At the point where the Tamchok Kambab Glacier produces the Chemayungdung River (the true source of the Brahmaputra), I found a herd of 17 wild yaks, the ancestor of the domestic yak. At over 17,000 feet, I found herds of Tibetan wild asses, as well as wolves, gazelles and antelope in the lower valleys. Because of mountaineering gear lost during my first leg of air travel from Oakland to Los Angeles, my equipment for the ascent was limited: high-topped trekking boots and adjustable ski poles. They served well as I walked by the edge of the glacier, scrambled up mixed snow and rock and traversed up a snow slope to the summit ridge at 20,000 feet. To my consternation, the true summit was a mile away along a corniced ridge, interrupted by rock turrets. By a combination of step-kicking and crawling, I traversed the ridge to a final 5.6 rock tower, where a 15-foot headwall of crumbling gneiss put me on the virgin summit (6285 meters, 20,620 feet). I dreaded descending the corniced ridge without crampons and ice axe and so I chose a route down a 50° snowfield that was perfect for stepkicking. A thousand feet below, the snowfield merged with rock walls dripping with water and festooned with icicles and verglas. The descent took almost as long as the ascent, and I finally made it back to camp at five in the afternoon.

GALEN ROWELL

PLATE 61

Photo by Ryozo Yamamoto

The Crown (Huang Guan Shan).

Western China

Bodga Shan. Located in the eastern Tien Shan Mountains, Bogda Shan (5445 meters, 17,864 feet) was first climbed in 1981 by Japanese climbers. Canadian Evan Price and I, a Scot, reached the summit on August 13 at six P.M. before descending to our tent at 4600 meters at one A.M. on the 14th. We think that ours was the first ascent of the peak by Western mountaineers. It is a fantastic region to climb in. We found the people in the area and the Chinese Mountaineering Association staff in Urumchi most friendly and helpful.

SANDY ALLAN, *Alpine Climbing Group*

The Crown (Huang Guan Shan) Attempt. Our 14-man expedition was composed of Y. Hirose, N. Kondo, R. Tateyama, H. Shimizu, N. Shimizu, M. Ochiai, M. Hoshino, R. Okamoto, K. Uchiyama, T. Sakurai, T. Yamamoto, T. Mizuno, J. Tayama and me as leader. We had permission to try the Crown (7292 meters, 23,924 feet), 15 miles northwest of K2, and Chiring (7090 meters, 23,262 feet). On July 18, we arrived with camels at Base Camp at 3900 meters near the end of the Skamri Glacier via the Aghil Pass and Skaksgam River from Mazan-Dara. Advance Base was established on July 21 at 4410 meters near the junction of the Skamri and Crown Glaciers and Camp I on July 29 at 5100 meters below the southeast ridge of the Crown. We climbed a steep rock band and a snow face to Camp II on the ridge at 5800 meters and to Camp III at 6500 meters. Camp III was made on August 17. We then traversed for 200 meters on the steep snow east face and climbed 500 meters directly upward to 7000 meters. An A-shaped rock wall rises for 100 meters from there. We tried a chimney but could not complete it because of dangerous conditions. Our highest point of 7050 meters was reached on August 23. After that, Captain Henry Morgan and a British team of six came to our Base Camp on September 1. Morgan's subsequent letter to me says that they also could not get to the summit for lack of time. They got to within 75 meters of the top. We could not try Chiring because we had no time.

RYOZO YAMAMOTO, *Academic Alpine Club of Shizuoka, Japan*

Koshi Toshi Attempt, Kunlun Mountains. An eight-member expedition under the leadership of Hisahiro Moro'oka attempted Koshi Toshi Mustagh (6699 meters, 21,979 feet). They had a difficult approach and got to Base Camp west of the peak at 3800 meters on August 1. Hoping to reach the north ridge, they placed Camps I and II at 4100 and 5090 meters on August 5 and 11. The next day Matsunaga, Antoku and Takazu climbed P 5740, followed on August 13 by Miss Katsuko Takahashi and Ikuto Ota. They decided against continuing this approach. Miss Takahashi and Matsunaga then set out with five days' food on a more southerly approach from the west to reach the north ridge. After bivouacs at 4200 and 5200 meters, they got to 5970 meters on the north ridge but were stopped by a gap in the ridge.

Mustagh Ata Ascent and Mustagh Ata North Attempt. The NOK Mustagh Ata International Friendship Expedition successfully climbed Mustagh Ata (7546 meters, 24,757 feet). On August 8, British Anthony and Victoria Willoughby and Frenchman Didier Gaillard reached the summit. On August 11, British Dick Renshaw, Japanese Keiichi Ozaki and Hiro Sasao and Americans Marti Martin Kuntz and I got to the top. Previously we had made an unsuccessful attempt on Mustagh Ata North (7427 meters, 24,367 feet). This is in fact not a sub-peak but a completely separate mountain cut off from Mustagh Ata by the Yambulak Glacier which gouges a 3000-foot cliff-lined chasm between the two from summit to base. Its windy north ridge was climbed by four Japanese in 1981, the only ascent of the peak. (On August 7, 1981, leader Tadakio Sakahara and Koji Matsui reached the summit, followed on August 14 by Takao Hayashida and Junichi Takahashi.) Our plan was to see how high we could reach on the same ridge on skis in preparation for our quick, nonstop ski ascent and descent of Mustagh Ata. We approached the ridge from the southwest flank as opposed to the Japanese, who had reached it via a northeast spur. The ridge itself essentially begins at 20,000 feet. We set up Base Camp at 15,700 feet on the south side of the Chodomak Glacier. The glacier led into a giant amphitheater flanked by the north and northwest ridges. We climbed a headwall and, after a third carry, camped at 18,570 feet on a protected shoulder just below the main north ridge. Renshaw and I both were struck by the first symptoms of altitude sickness and descended the next morning, along with Gaillard, who was snow-blind. The others continued their ascent of North Mustagh, reaching 20,500 feet on the north ridge before storm conditions and persistent high winds drove them back down.

MICHAEL JARDINE

Mustagh Ata North. Horst Schindelbacher, Hans Sauseng, Thomas Hois, Manfred Wydra and I as leader climbed Mustagh Ata North in September. We went up the Chodomak Glacier on skis but where the Yambulak and Chodomak Glaciers meet at about 7000 meters, we saw two summits. Instead of repeating the ascent of the main summit of Mustagh Ata, we climbed to the lower summit, which is divided from the main peak by a glacial valley.

BRUNO BAUMANN, *Österreichischer Alpenverein*

Mustagh Ata. Our Franco-Italian ski expedition climbed the normal route on the Mustagh Ata. We arrived at Base Camp on August 6 from Pakistan via the Kunjerab Pass. On August 16, Marc Chauvet, Paolo Henry, Pierre Gaillot, Françoise Walter, André Lequêque and I reached the summit. On August 22,

Chauvet and I accompanied Guy Luce to the top. We had excellent snow conditions and good, clear weather during the second half of August.

ERIK DECAMP, *Club Alpin Français*

USSR

Khan Tengri, North Face, 1986. One of the most notable Soviet climbs of 1986 was the new route on the 2800-meter-high, very difficult north face of Khan Tengri (6995 meters, 22,950 feet) in the central Tien Shan. Eight climbers from Moscow, led by V. Koroteev, began on August 8. They bivouacked at 5350, 5725, 6100, 6350, 6550 and 6850 meters. The last bivouac was close to the summit. At 4900, 5000 and 5400 meters nearly vertical rock barriers were climbed. At 6500 meters, a 70°, 180-meter-high chimney led to the summit cone. The summit was reached on August 21, 1986. The rock was somewhat rotten. In 1974, Soviet teams led by Boris Studentin and Eduard Myslovski each climbed routes in the central part of the north face.

JÓZEF NYKA, *Editor, Taternik, Poland*

USSR Pamir Camp. The 1987 season was wet and snowy, worse than the 1986 season. Pik Lenina saw the brunt of the activity, especially in early August. Lenina's Lipkin Cliffs route was skied by a French group from Lyon. However, they lost skis and axes in an avalanche. I got to the summit of Pik Lenina on August 15 with four Soviet climbers. One of them had climbed Denali in 1986 and had been above 6000 meters forty times. Pik Korzhenevskoy was climbed by several groups, but many were turned back by heavy snow above Camps II and III. Pik Kommunizma had few ascents, mostly by Soviets, because of weather and few clear breaks. Only one Soviet team made a crossing of the Firn-Plateau via the Fortambek approach. The Borodkin route via Pik Dushanbe was never open due to wind-slab avalanche hazard. On July 31, Czech Jon Ladislav made the first ski descent of Kommunizma on short skis. His side-slip track down the summit pyramid was wild, being 60° and knife-edged above a rock overhanging abyss! He finished via the slabby Dushanbe face. On August 1, Germans Christof Schork and Herman Rieschl and I accompanied 18 Eastern European climbers to the summit of Pik Kommunizma. There were 14 fatal accidents in the range in 1987. Five Soviet climbers were killed in an avalanche on Pik Kommunizma and some others on Pik Klara Zetkin. There were four other American groups, all on Pik Lenina. The Soviets are studying construction of an annual international camp in the Tien Shan to complement their excellent Pamir and Caucasus operations.

JOHN REHMER

P 5684, Pamir Mountains. A seven-man Bulgarian party led by Todor Batkov ascended a previously unclimbed, unnamed peak northeast of Pik

Korzhenevskoy, between the Mushketov and Ayu-Dzhilga Glaciers. They reached the summit (5684 meters, 18,648 feet) on August 4 from Camp I at 4600 meters in the upper Ayu-Dzhilga valley. To commemorate the 150th birthday of a Bulgarian national hero, Vasil Levski (1837-1873), who organized fighting against the Turks, they named the mountain for him and fixed a plaque on the rocks below the summit. The party was accompanied by a Soviet instructor, Leonid Troshchinenko, a member of the Soviet Everest expedition.

JÓZEF NYKA, *Editor, Taternik, Poland*

Fanskiye Gory and Turkestanski Ranges. Nine Americans climbed in two mountain ranges in the Soviet Union in 1987. Carla Firey, Tom Hargis, Matt Kerns, Frith Maier, Jim McCarthy, Dan McNerthney, Jim Phillips and Bill Sumner from Seattle and I from Boulder were invited to climb in the Fanskiye Gory and the Turkestanski ranges of the Pamir Alai as the first half of a Seattle-Tashkent sister city mountaineering exchange. Nine Soviet climbers will visit Seattle climbers in the Northwest in 1988. The Fanskiye Gory is in Tadjikistan, just west of the Pamir Alai, and the Turkestanski is in Kirghizistan about 100 miles north of the Afghan border. In the Fanskiye Gory we climbed Energia (5200 meters, 17,061 feet) and Tschimtarga (5480 meters, 17,979 feet) with our Soviet hosts. Hargis, Kerns and Sumner then did the second ascent on the northeast face of Soan. All these peaks are in the Sindon valley, on the other side of the mountains from where the 1976 exchange was located. We then traveled to Leninabad, via bus and truck, into the Turkestanski mountains where we had Base Camp at a large Soviet camp. This range was only recently opened for any climbers, including Soviets. We were the first Westerners invited to climb there. We established a higher camp near the base of 14,500-foot Observation. Hargis, Kerns and McNerthney attempted the east ridge of Ak-Su (5200 meters, 17,061 feet). They spent over three days and were turned back at about 4800 meters because of continuous bad weather and winter snow conditions. Firey, McCarthy and I tried Iskander Mal and retreated because of rockfall from a dozen Soviets jümaring above us. We then attempted Pik Aleksandra Bloka, the second highest in the region, but were forced to turn back when a severe storm struck us at a bivouac at the top of an ice couloir. Maier, Phillips and Sumner climbed two previously unclimbed peaks, Atabekovoi (4700 meters, 15,420 feet) and an unnamed peak in an adjoining valley. The mountains are the most spectacular I have ever climbed in, reminiscent of Patagonia.

SIBYLLE HECHTEL

Book Reviews

EDITED BY JOHN THACKRAY

Clouds from Both Sides. Autobiography by Julie Tullis with final chapter by
  Peter Gillman. Foreword by Arlene Blum. Sierra Club Books, San Francisco, 1987. 322 pages. 8 pages black & white photographs. Maps. $17.95.

K2, Triumph and Tragedy. Jim Curran. The Mountaineers, Seattle, 1988. 219
  pages. 42 color photographs, diagram and map. $22.95.

K2. John Barry. The Oxford Illustrated Press, Yeovil, Somerset, England,
  1987. 187 pages. 30 pages color plates. Map. $15.00

To one who remembers approaching K2 when there were no routes on it, and
the last attempt on the mountain had been by the Duke of the Abruzzi 29 years
before, the focus of attention on K2 today seems extraordinary. The three
books reviewed below are all by people who were on K2 in the summer of
1986; that terrible summer when 27 climbers from nine different nations
reached the summit but 13 died, including Julie Tullis, England's outstanding
woman climber.

Clouds from Both Sides, Julie Tullis' autobiography (with a final chapter by
Peter Gillman), takes us through her lifetime of climbing, starting with her
meeting Terry Tullis and beginning to rock climb with him. They married, had
two children and began a life that included running a climbing area and
climbing school in England. Julie also became interested in martial arts, whose
physical and mental discipline had a great influence on her. She began teaching
it, along with climbing, to handicapped children whose horizons it helped to
expand. In 1977, in her first overseas expedition, she helped a legless man to
climb Huascarán in Peru. She and Terry had long worked in film, and two
years later they were sent to Trento as British representatives to the Mountain
Film Festival. Here they met Kurt Diemberger, an outstanding Austrian
climber and cameraman of mountain films. That changed her life.

In 1980 she climbed in Yosemite, and two years later went to Nanga Parbat
as Diemberger's assistant to film a French expedition. The expedition had its
troubles, but Kurt and Julie climbed high, establishing themselves as an
outstanding professional team. In the next years they were hired again and
again to make expedition films. In 1983 they were with an Italian party that
climbed K2 from the Chinese side. I met Kurt and Julie in Urumchi on their
way back, sad that bad weather had stopped them at 26,000 feet and kept them

from the summit. Next year they were on K2 again, with a Swiss team, on the Pakistan side. Bad weather stopped the expedition, but afterward Kurt and Julie climbed Broad Peak, an 8000-meter mountain, where they were nearly killed by avalanches during the descent. Next came expeditions to Everest, Nanga Parbat (where again they almost reached the top), and K2 in 1986 to film an Italian expedition. Though Kurt was 53 and Julie 47, they were eager to reach the summit, and on August 4 they did, but at great cost. They had a fall, were forced to bivouac very high and descended in storm. Though they reached their high tents, Julie died during the storm, and afterward Kurt was barely able to stagger down to Base Camp. This book is likely to become a mountaineering classic on the development of an international woman climber.

Triumph and Tragedy by Jim Curran, is the definitive story in English of what happened on K2 in the summer of 1986. Jim was cameraman for a British expedition, led by his good friend Alan Rouse, an experienced climber. They were stopped on the northwest ridge. During the summer he met and photographed most of the men and women from ten different countries, whose triumphs and tragedies he records. There were plenty of both. Wanda Rutkiewicz, a Pole, became the first woman to reach the summit of K2, followed an hour or two later by Liliane Barrard, a French woman, and six weeks later by Julie Tullis—all by the Abruzzi Ridge—but only Wanda came back alive. New routes were made on the south face and the south-southwest ridge; also at great cost. The other ascents (nineteen) were all by the Abruzzi Ridge, but there were nine casualties on this route alone. Not a good average! Only the Korean team used oxygen and established a line of stocked camps on the mountain. It is significant that members of this team climbed the mountain and returned safely, and that their tents and supplies helped to save the lives of other climbers. The most astonishing triumph was by a Frenchman, Benoît Chamoux, who climbed the ropes and ladders of the Abruzzi Ridge, went on to the summit, then descended to Base Camp, all solo and in 23 hours. The book has good color pictures and most interesting appendices, including an interview with Willi Bauer, and accounts by Wanda Rutkiewicz and Benoît Chamoux of their ascents.

Jim Curran gives his opinion of what happened on the big mountain, but others may not entirely agree. Diemberger and Bauer, who were at the high camp together, disagree on details. Kurt Diemberger is understandably upset with Curran's book and has expressed his displeasure to the editor of this journal. After Diemberger's return to Europe, he offered to go over details with Curran but was rebuffed. He states that in many cases Curran has taken Bauer's account as the full truth and disregarded what Diemberger has to say. As an example, Bauer (and Curran) state that Diemberger and Tullis reached the summit at seven P.M. and should have turned back sooner. Diemberger put the summit hour no later than 5:30. A photograph in possession of the editor taken by Bauer at 3:15 looking down from the summit shows the pair 150 meters from the top. Diemberger knows it did not take them almost four hours to cover that distance. There are many other discrepencies in what the two survivors have to say. An interview with Bauer is given as an appendix. Might it not have been more objective if Diemberger had also been allowed to express the facts as he remembered them?

During the summer there seemed little regard for the dangers of descending from high on the mountain during a storm; trail markers, placed higher above the Abruzzi Ridge, for example, might have saved lives. Some things, however, are certain. Whether climbers were urged on by competition or by the thought that there is safety in numbers, I don't know, but the accepted level of risk was very high. People apparently did not always look out for one another very well, and some depended on using tents and food that others had carried up. Possibly, also, physical and mental deterioration at great heights is worse than generally believed. For many years to come, Curran's book will be sober reading for climbers.

K2 by John Barry is a very different book. Barry was co-leader with Alan Rouse of the British expedition to climb the northwest ridge. They made a good attempt, but after the expedition was stopped by prolonged bad weather, Barry departed for home. Rouse stayed on, eventually climbed the Abruzzi Ridge and went on to the summit, but he died at Camp IV during the big storm. The book is sometimes amusingly written and there are lovely color plates, but it takes 96 pages to get to the mountain. Much of what Barry writes is good for those who know little or nothing about how expeditions are put together, but less so for others. The second half of the book concerns the northwest ridge team. There is little about the other expeditions that were on K2 at the same time.

ROBERT H. BATES

Nanda Devi The Tragic Expedition. John Roskelley. Stackpole Books, Harrisburg, PA, 1987. 239 pages, illustrated. $16.95.

A full accounting of the events on the 1976 Indo-American expedition described in John Roskelley's new book *Nanda Devi The Tragic Expedition*, if it is understood anywhere, is inscribed deep in the hearts of the climbers who survived that troubled ascent.

What then is Roskelley's book about, if not a review of the climb? He was, after all, a member of the expedition. And not just on it. Notably, he and two others reached the summit, but not merely by his efforts as he suggests. At first glance, this seems to be the full story of the events. The background data, if a bit lurid, sounds authentic. Roskelley recounts what he sensed to be controversy and conflicting goals in the climbing party. We feel privy to a rising drama. We get numerous snatches of dialogue, retained either by a remarkable memory or constructed by a vivid imagination. And it's here we begin to think some of what we're being told is approximate or biased—or both.

Still, we are drawn into a thickening plot. He considers the factors contributing to the dire evacuation of an ailing Marty Hoey. He describes the events and, though confusing in detail, the route leading to the summit success, just before the sad death of Unsoeld's daughter, Nanda Devi, on the mountain for which she was named.

There is a lot of "I" in this book. Too much of it for me. Though if that were all—too much ego, the book could still hold its own. And there is the rub. The same single-mindedness that served Roskelley well on the mountain and allowed him, Lou Reichardt and Jim States to push a new route up through the difficult North Buttress here gets in the way and throws the scale out of balance. This is a partial telling, partial both to Roskelley himself and to his closest allies on the climb. There are lengthy accounts of why he was right about events and others were wrong. Most notably, he implies that he alone understood the reason for Hoey's illness and Devi Unsoeld's death. All too often the "I" in the book becomes, "I told you so." That is where it suffers.

And that is where it is doubly partial. Not only do we come away feeling we are reading a story partial to Roskelley, we are reading only his part of the story. There's no evidence he consulted other expedition members for their version of events. If an "A and B team" really existed on this climb, as he claims, one can only wonder what the B team, whose objective abilities were certainly equal, thinks of this decidedly singular point of view.

Any controversy about the expedition will hardly be laid to rest because of this book. It's too bad, really. For there is drama here. As with any good literature of adventure, the potential is present not so much for a book about mountaineering as a book about human frailty juxtaposed with feats of endurance. And surely those elements form the basis of Roskelley's narrative.

There is intrigue and mis-communication. There is stealth. Subterfuge. Romance. There is the love of the mountains, and expecially the love of this particular mountain.

Yet the book fails to translate the great power of events into great literature. It fails through lack of perspective. The description of other points of view are needed as a counterweight to the ever-present author. And it suffers from inattention to detail. Lots of little things add up to distracting neglect. Conflicting statistics, for example. All that verbiage about rope: 4000 feet is all that's to be allowed. Roskelley wants 8000. But as the packs are loaded in New Delhi, there's 10,000 feet, and some is left behind. Confusing.

Not that one asks for an encyclopedic account of the climb. Or for Shakespeare. But more attention to detail would have helped here, along with some editing of the hyperbole and sophomoric writing. All those "awestruck" reactions at the first sight of Nanda Devi. And the melodramatic summations: "This is what we had come so far to attempt."

Only detail is the flaw here. It is insufficient art. The book has the flavor of drama without poetry. It has the feel of history without all the facts. The elements of a powerful human documentary do not hold together for lack of these things.

Even so, there is pathos in the events. Despite Roskelley's self-righteous reminders of his many successes, we are inevitably drawn into his version of this now well known expedition. How painful this process of recall can be is evidenced by the fact that he felt compelled to have the account published at all. With well over a decade to work through the emotions and polish the document, there is precious little peace about the whole affair.

ERIK S. HANSEN

Überlebt—Alle 14 Achttausender. Reinhold Messner. BLV Verlagsgesell-
schaft, Munich, 1987. 247 pages. Many photographs, mostly in color,
route paintings.

On October 16, 1986 with the ascent of Lhotse, Reinhold Messner became the first to climb all the 8000-meter peaks. In this big, beautiful book, he describes how he accomplished this remarkable feat.

A separate chapter is devoted to each mountain. Each begins with a short history of the peak and a painting on which his routes are clearly marked. There follows the tale of his attempts and successful ascents. Interesting and apt accounts by other eminent mountaineers are interlarded. The text concludes with valuable appendices which give fascinating statistics. The very numerous beautiful photographs make this large-format book worth owning even for one who does not read German. The gorgeous pictures, taken by Messner himself or by his companions, have been beautifully reproduced.

ADAMS CARTER

Patagonia: Terra magica per alpinisti e viaggiatori. Gino Buscaini and Silvia
Metzeltin. Dall'Oglio, Milano, 1987. 272 pages, 73 color photographs, 76
black-and-white photographs, 11 maps, topos, route sketches, drawings.
Lire 50,000.

This magnificent volume is doubtless the most important book yet published on Patagonia. The English-speaking reader should not be put off by the text being in Italian. Of course, it is better to be able to read every word, but this is a book for everyone. For the beauty of its many illustrations, it ranks with the best of the "coffee-table" books. For a student of the area, it has a wealth of information about all aspects of Patagonia. The mountain historian can find the most complete data here on what has been climbed in this fascinating region. Anyone planning an expedition would be foolish not to consult it.

The authors, Gino Buscaini and his wife Silvia Metzeltin, are highly qualified to write this book. Gino Buscaini has written excellent guidebooks and has edited mountain books for the Club Alpino Italiano. Silvia Metzeltin is an author with advanced degrees in geology. Until recently, she was the chairman of the UIAA Expeditions Committee. Together, they have made a large number of expeditions to their beloved Patagonia.

The book opens with a general description of Patagonia. There follow sections on the geography, climate, geology, fauna and flora. Man's influence on the region is shown both in pre-history and by tracing early exploration. We learn about Reichert, Padre De Agostini and even as recent explorers as Ferrari and Fonrouge. The origin of many of the names of the area is given. Patagonian legends are recorded. The last third of the book is devoted to a complete history of Patagonian climbing. Just about *all* climbs well into 1987 with references as to where further information is available have been accurately recorded with meticulous care. Maps show the location of peaks and glaciers. Topos and route sketches give details.

To many the book will appeal because of its sheer beauty. The photographs were mostly taken by Gino Buscaini, but both historic and scenic pictures by others are included. The color photographs are reproduced with striking accuracy. Gino Buscaini is a skilled artist as well, and his drawings enhance the volume. This is a book I recommend heartily to anyone who loves the mountains.

ADAMS CARTER

El enigma de los santuarios indígenas de alta montaña. Antonio Beorchia Nigris. Universidad Nacional de San Juan, San Juan, Argentina, 1987. 414 pages, 211 black & white photos, 74 maps, tables and diagrams.

Risking being accused of gross exaggeration, I will start by declaring that this is one of the most important mountaineering books of the century. For one reason: it will force chroniclers to move the standard "Chapter One" in the history of world alpinism to a second place and have it preceded by another, which will have to be drawn from this work. And the impact of this book may not even stop there. Hopefully it will also force historians of our sport to delve into whatever records can be found to identify other peoples in other mountain lands who, like Beorchia's Incas, went to the summits before Mont Blanc was won.

This work is indeed the fifth bulletin, now issued in book format, by the Centro de Investigaciones Arqueológicas de Alta (high) Montaña, based at San Juan, Argentina, of which Beorchia is the president. It is a record of the pre-Columbian ascents in the Andes, carried out by the Incas and their subjects from around 1400 to near 1800 and mostly for religious purposes. It is divided into two major parts. The first surveys in alphabetical order a total of 113 peaks from 4700 to 6739 meters. Full description and evaluation of findings, together with information about modern climbs, are given. The second part is a photographic collection that illustrates such findings and the mountains where they occurred. The last 25 pages are devoted to conclusions about the incredible mountaineering activity of the ancient Andeans. Incidentally, it will please many to learn that Beorchia regards American anthropologist-climber Johan Reinhard as one of the great collaborators he was fortunate to have in his enterprises and studies.

The old concept that mountaineering was born in 1786 will have to be set aside. World alpinism, as we have known it, is now more than 200 years old and deserves better researched chronicles. Beorchia, even if only dealing with the Andes, with this remarkable work has pointed to the obligation that lies ahead: dig out records of ancient mountaineering wherever it may have occurred (Atlas? Central America? Rocky Mountains? Persia? Simyen?) and rewrite the history of climbing. It is a debt that we owe to the unknown highlanders that preceded us in the high places. It is available from CIADAM, República de Libano 2621, 5423 San Juan, Argentina.

EVELIO ECHEVARRÍA

Mountain People. Michael Tobias, editor. University of Oklahoma Press, Norman, 1986. 219 pages, black-and-white and color photographs, maps. $29.95.

For the past several years I have been looking forward to the Christmas season. Just about that time I have been receiving, annually, an offensive book to review for the *American Alpine Journal.* Into the gloom that usually descends onto the Holidays, there has, until this year, arrived from the club, a carefully wrapped festive package containing that year's bad book. It had become sort of a tradition and I had gotten to depend on it.

This year, the usual package arrived but, *mirabile dictu,* it turned out to contain an incredibly good book. Not only is *Mountain People* a good book, but I think especially interesting for the readers of this journal, a very important one. It consists of 24 essays, one written by Michael Tobias, who edited the collection, about the status of mountain people all over the world. There is nothing sterile or academic about these essays. They are an extraordinarily moving testimony to the fact that the mountain communities of the world are disappearing—or at least altering beyond recognition—like melting snow. Furthermore, we, the mountain-traveling readers of this journal, bear much of the responsibility for this. It is all too easy, as we trek through Nepal or Ladakh, or even the Alps, to lose sight of the local mountain people as people and to think of them at best as another aspect of the scenery.

It is all too easy as we trek through Nepal or Ladakh, or even the Alps, to lose sight of the local mountain people, as people, and to think of them, at best, as another aspect of the scenery. I will never forget, a few years after the tunnel under Mont Blanc opened, watching the annual parade, which takes place on August 15, of the Chamonix guides to the local cemetery where a service is held for any of the guides who has died that year. The guides are dressed folklorically and parade in a small knot, a hundred, or so, through the center of town. I watched that year as the tourists in cars honked at the parade, since it was impeding their route to the tunnel. The guides looked as if they didn't belong there.

Some of the essays in this book are unforgetable. I do not think it is possible to think of the Nepalese hill people in quite the same way having once read Broughton Coburn's magnificent essay entitled "Gurung Shepherds of the Nepal Himalaya." The shepherds are the social outcasts of the community.

They live a life that would kill most of us in short order. But they take a crazy pride in it. The Gurungs, the tribe that produced most of the Gurkhas, are moving south out of the hills to take up subsistence agriculture. How much longer will the shepherds be willing to put up with the life they are required to lead and if they disappear, what should be our feelings about that? This is one of the deep questions this book raises. One cannot have the kind of "progress" that, say, modern medicine has brought to a country like Nepal, something with which many readers of this journal have had a hand in, without the rest of the infrastructure of a modern society. Who would wish the ten-year reduction in life span that would result if modern medicine were to disappear from Nepal and the situation returned to what it was prior to 1960? But part of the price is having former Gurung shepherds working as bellhops and bartenders at the Hotel Everest Sheraton.

I have had, as it happens, the opportunity to watch the evolution of a Sherpa family. When I first went trekking in Nepal in 1967, climbing had been stopped, largely due to the irresponsible border crossings of people like Woodrow Wilson Sayre. If it had not been for trekking, the Sherpa communities would have been in serious difficulty. Since there was no climbing, the likes of us could have as sirdar a Sherpa like Ila Tsering, who had distinguished himself on the Everest West Ridge expedition. Ila was extraordinarily intelligent, but illiterate. He was never able, for example, to read the brief profile I wrote of him in the *New Yorker*. We lost touch. This past year, to my great surprise, I received a letter from one of his sons who was studying medicine in the Middle West. He later told me he was planning to return to Nepal to practice medicine in Namche. When I went to Nepal last spring, I ran into a second son who was in the trekking business. (A third son is becoming a monk.) He told me both of the family's new opportunities and regrets. His children, who live in Kathmandu, do not want to speak Sherpa and he goes back to Namche only in the summer, when there are no tourists, to recapture his own tradition. Is this evolution a triumph or a tragedy?

Reading these essays, this question keeps asserting itself. What is one to feel, for example, towards the wonderful Bimin-Kuskumin people of Papua, New Guinea? They are described in a heart-breaking essay by FitzJohn Porter Poole. These forest people worshipped oil—the semen of their god Afek— which was seeping out of the ground. It does not take much imagination to divine what happened to them once the news of the oil got out.

Each of the essays is marvelous in its own way. The book has been beautifully constructed with splendid photographs. It might well be a coffee-table item from the way it looks. The issues it raises do not have any easy resolution.

Jeremy Bernstein

H.W. Tilman, The Eight Sailing/Mountain-Exploration Books by H.W.
   Tilman. Published simultaneously in the U.K. and the USA by Diadem
   Books, London and The Mountaineers, Seattle. 1967. 16 pages of color
   photos, maps. 995 pages. $36.

Tilman must be the most eccentric, stubborn, bull-headedly romantic, and
plain cussed a fellow ever to put to sea and write about it. He's the grinch of
the high latitudes. Climbing and sailing are similar pursuits, he says, having
quit the mountains for the sea in his fifties, both concerned with elemental
things "which from time to time demand from men who practice those arts
whatever self-reliance, prudence and endurance they may have. An essential
difference is that the mountaineer usually accepts the challenge on his own terms,
whereas once at sea, the sailor has no say in the matter and in consequence may
suffer more often the salutary and humbling emotion of fear."

If he ever suffered fear, he neglected to mention it, though he sailed some
of the most frightful coasts in the world. Between 1954 and 1977 he voyaged
to and went ashore on Patagonia, Crozet Islands, east and west Greenland,
Iceland, Baffin Island, Kerguelen Island, the South Shetlands, Jan Mayen, and
Spitsbergen. He conceived these as seaborne climbing expeditions, but
invariably the climbing part didn't come off, or proved disapppointing. In the
Crozets, the target mountain even turned out not to exist. Tilman and his
various crew did, however, manage to traverse the Patagonian Icecap, climb
two 6000-foot peaks in Greenland and Mount Raleigh on Baffin Island.

This is cruising, not climbing, literature. And, it is unique. Small-boat
sailors seldom visit the high northern latitudes, and most of those who sail
southern latitudes are just passing through. Tilman describes voyages of
exploration in the old sense of the word—the dangerous approach to an
unknown coast after a long outward passage, and then the expedition ashore,
all in total self-sufficiency. His models are the great Elizabethan sailor/
explorers like Drake, Raleigh, and Tilman's hero John Davis. Like them,
Tilman *had* to explore. Their excuse was the Northwest Passage; Tilman's is
the unclimbed peak—even if it doesn't exist.

Tilman seems to have been a naturally talented seat-of-the-pants sailor, but
he must have been hell to sail with. His views are outrageous—and freely
expressed. The scope of his prejudices is global. Sometimes one thinks he must
be kidding; he can't possibly believe *that*. Not a single voyage goes by without
crew problems, which Tilman seems to attribute to the general decline to
decadence of today's masculinity. Commenting on his first trip where he had
a mutiny, the disillusioned Skipper can't understand why it's hard to fit young
men (women need not apply) ready to sail 14,000 miles in an old wooden boat,
nip across the old icecap and return in a year and a half, if all goes well. About
a crewman who desserts, Tilman says, "His real grievance was that we had no
distress signals and carried no liferaft. In my view every herring should hang
by its own tail. Anyone venturing into unfrequented and dangerous waters does
so with his eyes open . . . and should neither expect nor ask for help. The

confidence that is placed in being rescued fosters carelessness or even foolishness, and condones ignorance."

He can be maddening when he goes on like that, especially in view of the boat his crew should have been ready to go down with. *Mischief* was a Bristol Channel pilot cutter built of wood in 1906, with cement in her bilge, inside ballast, and cumbersome, ill-shaped canvas sails. Tilman insists she was a well-designed sea boat, despite the fact that she was deathly slow and un-weatherly. She lacked halyard and sheet winches because the Skipper thought winches were for wimps. He actually says so. Self-steering devices and dacron sails go unmentioned, no doubt because Tilman considered them to indicate a state of nautical debasement near that of women aboard. As for conditions below, Eric the Red probably lived better at sea. Though she was 45 feet in length, *Mischief* seems not to have had standing headroom, and her primitive galley was located forward, the worst possible place, where the motion at sea must have been dreadful. Several prospective crew, Tilman gleefully reports, took a gander below and suddenly felt some pressing career obligations ashore.

The Skipper liked to do it the hard way. He made those magnificent voyages despite his boat, not because of it. He insists on discomfort even at the expense of his own objective. *Mischief*'s optimum crew was nine—*ten* guys crammed into a 45-foot hull. In a proper sea boat, he could have made the same voyages with a crew of three (plus climbers, who wouldn't need to work themselves into a stupor before they reach the mountain) in half the time as the lumbering *Mischief*, which needed five guys to hoist the main.

Yet the pages of this book speed by. Tilman, as a character, is fascinating. One comes to care about him, not exactly to like him—he's too tightly closed for that—but to hope for his success. Tough as he is, he seems to need protection. He's such a dreamer and a romantic, so maladjusted to life ashore that he could never have survived it. One comes to hope, therefore, that his own prejudices won't cause him failure in the wilderness.

Ironically, he died on another man's boat, a better boat than he ever captained. An ex-crewman of Tilman's, Simon Richardson refit and ice-strengthened a boat called *En Avant* in which he meant to visit Smith Island in the South Shetlands for a Tilman-style expedition. Richardson invited Tilman, at 79, to serve in the crew which, Tilman wrote from Rio, was "a better lot than any I have sailed with." *En Avant* headed south in November, 1977. She was never seen again. Tilman had hoped to celebrate his 80th birthday in Antarctica.

To that small audience who cares about cruising literature, this book should become a classic. Tilman belongs in that old tradition of small-boat cranks—Slocum, Tristan Jones, Blondie Hasler, Chichester, others—all complicated misfits who sailed to the ends of the earth and wrote about it. Tilman's prose, intelligent and erudite, is better than theirs, and his scope is broader. He is more than a deep water sailor, he is an explorer, and his book arrives at a time of swelling interest in high-latitude cruising.

DALLAS MURPHY

The Everest Years: A Climber's Life. Chris Bonington. Viking, New York, 1987.
   256 pages, 160 photographs in color and black-and-white, maps. $24.95.

Chris Bonington has done it again. *The Everest years: A Climber's Life* is his
tenth book and his third autobiographical story. And as always, Chris has written
a book that the reader cannot set down. The reviewer picked the volume up and
did not stop reading until he had gone through the whole in one sitting.

The Everest Years covers a fifteen-year period, from 1972 on when Chris'
party first attempted the southwest face of Everest. It covers the successful but
tragic climb three years later when Mick Burke kept on alone toward the summit,
never to be seen again, and the 1982 expedition to the incredibly difficult
northeast ridge when Joe Tasker and Peter Boardman were lost. His final Everest
expedition was a Norwegian one, which he joined, not in his usual role as leader.
At the age of fifty, he finally reached the summit of Everest and held the record
for the oldest man to get to the top until Dick Bass broke it a week later.

As for me, I was easily as interested in his other climbs. There was the
breathtaking drama of the Ogre, where Doug Scott broke both his legs descending the first pitch below the summit and had to crawl off the peak, heroically
assisted by his companions. Bonington had a nearly fatal fall, broke a number
of ribs and suffered pneumonia during the harrowing six-day descent in a raging
blizzard. The tragedy of the west-face K2 expedition, the Kongur success and
the ascent of the highest point of Antarctica, the Vinson Massif, all come vividly
to life in these pages. The reviewer was naturally interested to read about the
first ascent of the southwest summit of formidable Shivling since he was of the
party that accompanied Chris and Jim Fotheringham to Base Camp. His personal
and family life and climbs on British crags are not slighted.

The book is amply illustrated by some 160 photographs in color and
black-and-white. The color pictures and most of the others are beautifully
reproduced, but for some reason, the photos showing routes are invariably
washed out. The fault obviously did not lie with the originals (one of the
reviewer's photos is shown and the original is clear-cut), but this is a small
quibble in this magnificent and fascinating book.

ADAMS CARTER

*Norman Collie: A Life in Two Worlds—Mountain Explorer and Scientist,
   1859–1942.* Christine Mill. Aberdeen University Press, Aberdeen, 1987.
   XIII+197 pages, black-and-white photographs, maps, appendices. £14.90.

In *Norman Collie: A Life in Two Worlds*, Christine Mill gives a measured
account of the dual career of John Norman Collie, distinguished mountaineer
and scientist. A chemist by profession, he both taught and conducted research
at a time when chemistry was not held in particularly high esteem in academic
circles. After a brief stint teaching at Cheltenham Ladies' college, in 1887 he
moved on to University College, London, where (except for a period of six
years) he spent the rest of his professional life, becoming the first Professor of

Organic Chemistry.

A man of many parts, Collie was also a collector. His jade was the envy of many a museum. He was fascinated by gemstones. His interest in color led him to be among the first to take up color photography. In 1896, he took the first X-ray to be used for surgical purposes. He also blew his own laboratory vessels. He was attracted to the mystical and the magical, believing "emphatically in the Loch Ness monster" and proposed Aleister Crowley for membership in the Alpine Club in 1895.

His climbing career, which began in 1886 on the island of Skye, took him to the far reaches of the globe in the company of such mountaineering luminaries as Alexander Mitchell Kellas, Albert Frederick Mummery, William Cecil Slingsby and Hugh E.M. Stutfield. With Kellas, to whom he suggested the possibilities of the Himalaya, he climbed in Scotland. With Mummery, he first climbed in the Alps; in 1895, they went to Nanga Parbat. Although Mummery died on the mountain, their extensive reconnaissance of the peak would serve subsequent expeditions well. With Slingsby, the "father of Norwegian mountaineering," he climbed on Lofoten Island in 1903 and 1904; together they made numerous first ascents. He may be best known, however, for his exploration of Canada's then unknown Rocky Mountains. Between 1897 and 1911, he made a total of six trips, two of them (1898 and 1902) with Stutfield.

He was the author of two books, *Climbing on the Himalaya and Other Mountain Ranges*, published in 1902, and *Climbs and Exploration in the Canadian Rockies*, which he wrote with Stutfield, in 1903. His love for the mountains continued until his death, in 1942, on his beloved Skye.

In this book, Christine Mill provides a sensitive and thoughtful assessment of the life of John Norman Collie—a pioneer in two worlds. She has written a biography that both holds one's attention and enriches one's knowledge.

PATRICIA A. FLETCHER

A Dream of White Horses. Edwin Drummond. Diadem Books, Cheshire (England), 1987. 224 pages, black-and-white photographs. £10.95.

Once in a while something happens that takes your breath away. A stunning physical attraction, a taste of exquisitely prepared food, a blend of classical stringed instruments, an unclimbed route of heroic proportions, a plunge into ice-cold waters, hot sex. Ed Drummond's *A Dream of White Horses* is all of these, and more.

Combining previously published pieces with new work, this collection of autobiographical writings reduces the readers to grains of sand on a beach, alternately pounded by the passion of Drummond's high tide and caressed by his ebb. There aren't many works of which this can be said, especially in climbing literature.

These are "autobiographical writings" in the broadest sense. Drummond's work isn't easily categorized by the genre, except for the poetry. The autobiographical nature of the pieces is unquestionable, but so too is the strength of the fictional character. Even the essays are unmistakably Drummond. Fictohagiography?

White Horses is divided into three parts, "Mirror, Mirror," "Terrorist Minerals" and "Do they Reach." Amalgamated loosely in chronological order, they reveal the development of Drummond as person, climber and writer.

"Mirror, Mirror" asks a lot of questions. The opening poem, "The Heretic," rejects man-made, organized religion and, by association, organized climbing. Yet, it acknowledges the existence of inner spirit and possibility of omniscience. The next piece, "Proud," briefly details Drummond's early years, the confusion of adolescence and sexuality, spreading one's wings through various activities and testing the waters of a religious calling. Other pieces recount some of his climbing exploits.

"Terrorist Minerals" includes material from Drummond's family life and his struggles to free his hostage self from the rocks which held him. Perhaps, in a way, some of the pieces are an apology for his obsession with vertical events that led him up, up and away so many times. The middle part contains poignant observations about the difficult life of a climber.

The end part, "Do they Reach?," is named after a line from his poetry performance's title piece, "Between a Rock and a Soft Place," where Drummond ponders several questions, whose literal application and metaphor is whether his ropes reach the ground.

When Ed Drummond's work first appeared in America, climbing was in its modern infancy. Hard aid was still as popular as free climbing, 5.11 was the limit and our sport was about to undergo an incredible transformation. Drummond was there, part of it, taking the lead. He put up several true horror shows. His prose from that time, most of which is in "Mirror, Mirror," reflected the upheaval climbing was experiencing. Brash, direct, vibrant with image and word, that's Drummond's early writing.

Take "Great Wall." Written about the fifth ascent of Cloggy's Great Wall, it is a masterpiece. Cloggy glooms dark and grey above a misty, cold valley. It's always wet. The Great Wall, a blank slab in the middle, has always been a British climber's Grail. Peter Crew's ascent of it was a giant step; it was talked of for months. Drummond manages in two short pages vividly to relive his ascent.

Abruptly, Drummond more or less disappeared from the limelight in the mid seventies. It was over this time that the material for "Terrorist Minerals" is taken. Having left Britain for California, he took up residence in the Bay area. What a change from quiet England! The multiple distractions and opportunities in California were pursued with gusto. Although he continued to climb, it is clear from these pieces that there were personal crises to be dealt with, that relationships with his family were frequently rockier than his sport. Most of the writing is about climbing, and yet some of the best is not. The constant in Drummond's family life is his devotion to a seldom seen son, Haworth. At the end of "A Grace Period," the last piece in this section, Drummond has just left a tumultuous expedition to Makalu in which team members spent much time and energy examining their climbing motives and personal values.

Throughout the last section, Drummond devotes his pen almost exclusively to answering human questions. The first piece, "Nelson Mandela's Column," pertains to one of his protest climbs. He spent much time during his U.S. habitation climbing buildings and monuments to protest social ills. In this piece, he climbs Nelson's Column, centerpiece of Trafalgar Square, to protest Barclay Bank's involvement in South Africa. As he clearly becomes more concerned about the world condition, one wonders if this heretofore wild and seemingly irresponsible person has taken on some semblance of responsibility to others.

"Jimlove Menwords" deals with human frailties and the need for climbers to address issues beyond simple climbing ethics. Drummond's view is that Jim Perrin's biography of Menlove Edwards missed the central element in Menlove's miserably lonely life and death: that Menlove wasn't driven by society to suicide. Drummond believes that glorifying Menlove as Perrin does is a disservice both to the man and ourselves because it places value on introspection and emotional avoidance rather than on the nurturing posture that Drummond feels should be the real goal of life. This is a major change from the earlier Drummond. The ultimate lay-it-on-the-line soloist now calls for human interaction and responsibility!

Poetry is the perfect medium for Drummond to work in, for he is good at capturing the essence of activity and feeling. Try reading his work aloud. The words vibrate with rhythm and excitement and elicit aural connections that work less well when read silently.

My copy of *A Dream of White Horses* is already thumbworn. This is literature that I will read again and again because the writing is challenging, exciting and the most consistently excellent climbing literature I know. Finishing the book is like coming up for air at the end of a long dream. Grab a copy, settle in and enjoy.

STUART PREGNALL

Degrees of Difficulty. Vladimir Shatayev. Translated from the Russian by Deborah Piranian. Foreword by Pete Schoening. The Mountaineers, Seattle, 1987. 194 pages, 13 black-and-white photographs. $10.95 (paper).

In this book the great Soviet climber, Vladimir Shatayev, has developed his ideals allegorically, through tales of a life centered around mountaineering. Through climbing, he learned discipline and independence; he accepted fear; he exceeded thresholds; he found love and experienced tragedy. And with artistic measure he has poured into his book just enough of his mountaineering experiences to reveal a lot about the development of his own character. He accomplishes this mainly by the straightforward method of recounting emotional dialogues between climbers during poignant moments of crisis and debate.

Thus this book is more a psychological autobiography than a conventional description of the mountaineering feats of a master climber. It is an intelligent, sensitive, self-searching attempt to address the age-old question of "why mountaineering?" and to extend his answers to all human endeavor.

For the western reader Shatayev's book offers special insights of another kind. It is an unvarnished account of how a single individual pursued his personal goals and developed his own community of peers within, but distinct from, the larger context of Soviet society. Shatayev's mountaineering community is no safe haven from the bureaucratization of that society, though. It too suffers from the battles over rank, turf and authority, as well as from personal jealousies and prejudices. His depiction of how and why these battles occur and the human motivations behind them exposes a fascinating slice of Soviet society. These unfamiliar characteristics and obstacles of Soviet mountaineering, such as their rigidly hierarchical organization of the sport and a certain "peak-bagging" approach to meeting out climbing permits according to rank, will impress many readers almost as much as the fact that Shatayev overcame them.

Readers may be surprised by Shatayev's frank account of his own early prejudices against women in mountaineering. The emotional core of his story relates how his own wife gained his grudging respect as a true mountaineering leader before her entire team of eight women tragically perished in 1974, while descending Pik Lenin in a hurricane. His wife's unprecedented 1971-72 climbs on all-women teams of Ushba in the Caucasus and Pik Korzhenevskaya in the Pamirs had "shaken his opinion" just before her tragic death in 1974. Since the book ends with his moving account of his personal reaction to that accident, he never adequately resolves the question of how much he had actually changed his earlier, strongly expressed prejudices. In fact, my own impression from extensive climbing in the Soviet Union is that the legendary death of "The Eight," as the Soviet public refers to them, reinforced a widespread prejudice against women mountaineers in the Soviet Union. Fewer permits are given for all-women expeditions to the more difficult peaks.

But it is only by virtue of the unfailing honesty of his dialogues that Shatayev lays himself open to criticism for his treatment of women in mountaineering. To his credit he does not simply set up "straw women" to act as foils in this arresting debate. He allows his wife and other super-achieving Soviet women climbers to eloquently defend their own objectives and special capabilities. Honesty and uncanny recollection of psychological nuances even better serve him, though, when he reveals the internal dialogues during his pivotal mountaineering experiences with external danger and human failings.

WILLIAM GARNER

Yosemite Climbs. George Meyers & Don Reid. Chockstone Press, Inc., Denver, 1987. 433 pages, monochrome photos, line drawings, maps. $22.00 (paper).

Yosemite Valley has some of the best granite rock climbing in the world. It also has crime, poverty, disease, despair, and frequent natural disasters. Local culture is warped by a small town mentality compressed to urban densities. Low-rent crag cowboys curse it as a dusty ditch, yet never leave. Above it all, the Clone Ranger keeps a watchful eye on the status quo.

To compile the climber's guide to Yosemite Valley is the ultimate Sisyphean task. George Meyers took on the project back in the 70s with the original *Yosemite Climbs*, a loose leaf set of route topos. Communicating route information visually, line drawing topos advanced guidebook standards by a couple of grades. Of course, it was some Brits who published the first set of climbing topos to the Valley, but Meyers' guide set new standards for clarity and accuracy.

Knowledge is power, and the dissemination of route information only accelerated new developments. The guide was hardly off the press before it was out of date. Technology, technique, and training sent the standards skyrocketing while every Joe Sunday scoured the remotest reaches of the obscure in search of the next classic crack. After years of waiting for someone else to step forward and tackle the challenge of an update, Meyers once again cranked it out.

The second edition of *Yosemite Climbs*, the "Yellow Bible," was a trend-setting tome. To condense such an immense quantity of reliable route information into a portable package was incredible, but to communicate it so well to such a functionally illiterate populace was truly amazing. Guidebook standards ratcheted up another notch, and the masses thronged to the crags. Life in the Valley got trickier and the scams more refined. Eurodogs came and went, as did pins and bolts. Slander filled the night while fresh faces took the places of those who couldn't sweat out the summer swelter of Camp 4. In the meantime, new lines multiplied like lemmings as informed visionaries discovered realities where none had gazed before.

Doomed, yet not resigned to a tormented fate as editor-for-life, Meyers recruited local guide Don Reid to help out with the latest and third edition of *Yosemite Climbs*. With professionalism based upon years of experience, Meyers and Reid have produced one of the finest guidebooks to some of the finest climbing in the world. The design is clean, the organization straightforward, the scope mindboggling, and the details accurate, and the construction bombproof. *Yosemite Climbs* weighs less than a pair of sticky boots, a set of Jümars, or an apron rack. The information density is high enough to get you out of those challenging situations it will lure you into. Yosemite Valley finally has a guidebook to match its stature in the climbing world.

The bulk of the volume is devoted to route topos in a basic left to right circuit of the Valley, starting at the western end. Photodiagrams are liberally interspersed amidst the drawings. Historic photographs provide random inspiration, linking past to present with a continuous evolution of techniques. Photo quality is high throughout the book, with dramatic cross-lighting to reveal the features of the faces.

Approach descriptions in prose highlight the beginning of each section, and a few critical descents have rappel topos. Given the graphic nature of the guidebook, it seems odd that approach and descent information wasn't sketched in on maps and photographs.

Rack lists are appropriate for the free climbs, but overdone for the big walls. The topo for "Lurking Fear" on El Capitan recommends a rack of fifty pitons, yet this route has been done clean and hammerless. A rule of thumb for the big walls would be to cut the piton list in half, then throw in the latest tech-nut tricks and custom hooks. You'll be less destructive, and have less to haul.

Efficiency and compact style, notable traits of many Yosemite routes, are reflected in the introductory text. The section on "Staying In The Park" clearly details the logistics and cultural nuances unique to living in Yosemite Valley. The rules have changed in recent years, and staying legally on a low budget for an extended period of time can be more challenging than climbing the routes. It would be nice to see a sample budget for lean living that outlined the cash and other costs of staying in Yosemite for a week, a month, or a season.

John Dill's analysis of Yosemite climbing accidents should be required reading for all Yosemite climbers. It presents a number of little details and considerations inherent to safe practice of the sport of rock climbing. You can learn from other climbers' mistakes. Follow the climbing advice presented and you'll probably leave Yosemite alive and unhurt.

The book's history of Yosemite climbing is patched together from climbing guidebooks of various periods. The recent history presents most of the modern trends and their protagonists, analyzed through the rose-tinted spectacles of a Nouveau Traditionalist.

The new "Free Climbing Styles and Ethics" section outlines the bounds of intolerance for Yosemite. Anything goes, except littering, chiselling, or placing pins and bolts on anything except unrehearsed, unpreviewed first ascents established from the ground up and personally approved by God. There seems to be a curious attitude that runouts are unfair unless established in rigid ignorance, in which case they're OK because they're bold. Fortunately, most free climbers in the Valley don't carry a hammer, a bolt kit, or even dream of doing new routes, so they may climb secure in the knowledge that their worst risk is stylistic slander back in the campground.

For aid-climbing styles and ethics, anything goes except bothering the Peregrine falcons on El Capitan during certain seasons, and hurling objects (yourself included) from the heights. Don't send your excrement flying down the walls in plastic bags; it greases up the holds on the free routes at the bottom.

The evolution of the Yosemite Decimal System of rating free climbs is discussed with an attempt to resolve the difference between move ratings and continuity ratings. A move rating describes a pitch by the difficulty of the hardest single move, while a continuity rating says that if the whole pitch has a lot of equally hard moves, it's probably harder. A proposal to apply both ratings to each climb seems doomed to confusion. Aid ratings follow the definitions used in prior editions, an aid pitch being A5 if you take a monster fall and get mangled. In practice, there are only two aid ratings: it sticks or you fly. Anything on the topos rated A4 or harder requires engineering genius, not much love of life, and a wizard's bag of tricks.

The back of the book is a gold mine for climbing historians and rock stars alike. The graded list of selected routes is indispensable in setting up a day's climbing circuit. Harder routes (5.9 and up) are categorized by the predominant type of climbing, from faces to cracks to chimneys. All that's missing are little boxes to tick off your conquests.

First ascent parties are listed in fine print after the route lists. Some climbers feel this information doesn't belong in a guidebook. They suspect that the ego trip of being listed is the only rationale for establishing new routes. This view ignores the historical continuity buried within the first ascent list. It overrates the value of a name in microscopic type. A number of routes are found in the first ascent listings but not in the topos. Where are the more recent wall climbs by Warren Harding? Who got the FFA on the "Stigma?" Did Tom Rohrer solo a new route on the Lost Arrow? There's more to history than what gets printed, and first ascent listings provide clues to what really happened.

The index in the back of the book is a great shortcut to locating a particular route. It is also a wild collection of the bad puns, obscure references, monuments to posterity, and dull cliches that Yosemite climbers use to mark their territory. If you're into establishing new routes, the index will help you avoid the *faux pas* of an unoriginal name.

The last few pages contain reproductions from the U.S.G.S. topographic map of Yosemite Valley. Gone are the excellent line maps that graced the front and back of the previous edition. This is a loss, since they put the cliffs in context and would complement the topographic maps.

In effectively communicating the critical aspects of more routes than anybody could ever hope to climb in a lifetime, *Yosemite Climbs* succeeds beyond all expectations. It's only a matter of time before the next edition comes along, but until then, *Yosemite Climbs* sets a guidebook standard to which other climbing guides may aspire.

ALAN NELSON

Rock Climbs in the White Mountains of New Hampshire. Second Edition. Ed Webster. Mountain Imagery (PO Box 210, Eldorado Springs, Colorado 80025), 1987. 564 pages, 85 black-and-white photographs, 2 color photographs (on cover), 5 maps, bibliography. $21.95 (paper).

Once again, Ed Webster has produced one of the finest guidebooks in the country. This second edition of *Rock Climbs in the White Mountains of New Hampshire* far surpasses the 1982 guide, in both accuracy and quality. The quantity and clarity of the action photos is excellent. Not only do they show the current activists on some of the newer routes, but there are also a host of historically significant pictures taken during first ascents, or first free ascents. The historical photos should give some of the younger set food for thought. Try leading *Crack in the Woods* without Friends (page 314), or *Interloper* without "sticky shoes" (page 145) . . . I can't do them that way!

My criticisms are few and far between. A detailed map to Band M Ledge would be helpful, as would a map of the Crawford Notch crags. Since reviewers are allowed to quibble, here are the inevitable gripes about ratings. *Birch Tree Crack* (Whitehorse) *has* to be harder than 5.10; *Lookout Crack & Little Feat* (Cathedral) *must* both be easier than 5.9; and finally, *Science Friction Wall* (Whitehorse) sure *felt* like 5.10 rather than 5.11.

For those of you that still haven't made it to New Hampshire, it's time to buy this newest guide, and go. You'll be in good hands with Webster!

TODD SWAIN

Extreme Rock: Great British Rock Climbs. Ken Wilson and Bernard Newman. Diadem Books, London, 1987. 296 pages, color photographs, line drawings, bibliography. £27.95.

This colorful and exciting book gives us an insider's view of the contemporary British rock-climbing scene. But more than that, because rock climbing today is so international, with the best climbers visiting the hot crags wherever they may be, it is a look at the sport in general. The format is similar to that employed in Ken Wilson's other books in the series such as *Hard Rock:* a region-by-region approach with different authors writing about their experience on one or more routes. This approach naturally leads to a considerable variety of writing skills. Some of the articles are excellent, conveying a sense of being there with the author on the crag, and setting the climbs in an historical perspective, while others are more pedestrian in nature. Nonetheless a very good picture of the top players and their motives emerges.

While the writing may be uneven, the pictures are generally excellent. Drawn from many sources, here are surely some of the finest action pictures of contemporary rock climbers. It is apparent that the photographers were not just present by chance, but took great pains to position themselves for the really telling shot. With these photographs we can almost feel the effort involved in getting to grips with this intimidating terrain.

Almost two-thirds of the photographs are in color, and this sets up the interesting thought that the balance of black and whites are from an earlier era. An inspection reveals that a few of the black and whites are indeed older, but in general they appear to be conversions from color. The result is that while the color pictures are crisp and dramatic, the black and whites are often washed out, lacking in detail, and thus appear dated. This perception brings to mind a talk by the producer of a documentary film of the Kennedy years. Taken for the most part from the news footage, the resulting color film caused people to question its authenticity and suggest it had been re-enacted. Viewers recalled the TV news of that era in black and white, as most people then still had black and white TVs. In order for the film to be accepted the makers had to convert it to black and white!

This disturbing contrast in the feel of the pictures in *Extreme Rock* took me back to two earlier books, John Cleare's *Rock Climbers in Action in Snowdonia* (1966) and Ken Wilson's *Hard Rock* (1974). Spaced about a decade apart, the three books reveal a fascinating change in the sport. In Cleare's book those two sixties pioneers Peter Crew and Barry Ingle are very much the stars. We see the first primitive nut protection, real machine nuts threaded onto the laid-nylon rope slings of the day; waist tie-ins; piton hammers and a couple of pitons dangling from the leader; knickers or long pants and heavy sweaters; and routes that by today's standards seem generously supplied with holds. The crags themselves appear cold and dark; the prevailing mood is somber.

By the mid seventies the field of play covered in *Hard Rock* has expanded to include all manner of outcrops and sea cliffs, but the mountain crags of Snowdonia and the Lake District still look just as dank and the climbers are still bundled up against the elements. Hard hats are now pretty much in vogue; the protection nuts are the early custom-made stoppers and the hex's; climbing harnesses are beginning to appear; piton hammers are still seen; some of the pictures show other parties on adjacent routes; and the walls are steeper and the holds are smaller.

As revealed in *Extreme Rock,* today's clothing runs to tights and shorts; hard hats and piton hammers have pretty much been gone; protection devices such as Friends are far more sophisticated; the crags are getting crowded; and the routes look steep and difficult. All these changes are quite understandable. More puzzling is the apparent change in the weather; what do these climbers in shorts and muscle shirts know that the earlier generations did not? The contrast is strikingly made in *Extreme Rock* by the wonderful picture of Peter Crew and Al Harris in 1964, bundled up in parkas and festooned with ropes, and the pictures on the very next pages of bare-chested athletes powering their way up the very same crag. And, *mirabile dictu,* the sun now seems to be shining in Snowdonia. What accounts for the apparent change in Britain's notorious weather? In part the different appearance of crag and climber may be due to the fact that the climbers of yesteryear were off in the Alps or someplace else during Britain's brief summer and so not available to be photographed; today's top performers cannot afford, in Joe Brown's words, to go "traipsing about with a bloody ice axe." The competition is too intense.

Another reason has to do with the self-perception of the participants. The sixties climbers still looked to the Alps and saw themselves in the mountaineer mold. By the eighties we have more specialists, whose self-perception is not as an alpinist but as an athlete and rock jock. Serious athletes cannot perform in cast-off clothing. The sport has evolved from an eccentric activity for oddballs, to a mainstream activity for athletes: no wonder that the standards of difficulty are shooting up.

But there is disquiet in the land. The book ends with a timely observation about "the French style of pre-placing fixed protection and practising hard routes exhaustively on top ropes before attempting an elegant free lead," and goes on to say "If seductive continental styles of unrestricted bolt protection become the norm, all existing poorly protected routes would eventually be threatened, and the whole adventurous and ethical edifice built up over the years would be critically weakened, in favor of a safer, clinical and no doubt gymnastically superior activity." If that happens, Ken Wilson's next book on difficult British rock climbing will have yet another interesting story to tell.

CHRISTOPHER JONES

Pure and Perpetual Snow: Two climbs in the Andes of Peru. David Mazel. The Free Solo Press, Alamosa, Colorado, 1987. 136 pages, 22 black-and-white photographs, 1 illustration, bibliography. $10.95 (paper).

I enjoyed Mazel's small but personable book about climbing Alpamayo and Ausangate in Peru's Cordilleras Blanca and Vilcanota. The text alternates between experiences on his own guided climbs and extensive research about the history and culture of Peru's mountains and people. A rough map would have been useful.

In the last ten years, not many books in English have been written on Peru's Andes. The two that come to mind are John Ricker's *Yuraq Janka,* guide to the Cordillera Blanca, and Jim Bartle's *Trails of the Cordilleras Blanca and Huayhuash of Peru.* Mazel adds a short, fun work to this list. On a month's journey, the author joined the American Alpine Institute's guided itinerary but failed in ascending the southwest face of 19,100-foot Alpamayo. However, he succeeded in climbing the less visited 20,945-foot Ausangate in the Cordillera Vilcanota.

Mazel gives a fascinating account of the history of Andean climbing, focusing on such pioneers as Annie Peck, Georges and Claude Kogan. But he does not omit the climbs of the ancient Indians, who built structures for religious observances at 20,000 feet. He covers the disastrous earthquake of 1970, which killed 67,000 people in the Callejón de Huaylas below the Cordillera Blanca.

The author discovers, as many do, that the joys of the Andes lie not only in the ascent itself, but in the valleys, villages and ruins below the mountains. Peter Getzel, a wonderful American anthropological researcher, who has made the Andes his life work, and archeologist Johan Reinhard help convey some enlightening religious relationships that Peru's people had to the white ranges.

JOHN A. REHMER

Angels of Light. Jeff Long. William Morrow, 298 pages. $18.95.

Jeff Long has written a climbing Western, with philosophical overtones. Yosemite Valley provides the setting and much of the substance of his exciting and extravagant novel. This is not the Valley that seemed, to a member of the discovering party of 1851, to be a "fit abode for angels of light," but the tourist-ridden, climber-infested scene of the last two decades. Long knows his Valley-dwellers well. And one of the pleasures of the book is his description of their eating, smoking and sexual habits.

"Expatriate rabble with their hair in leonine disarray," they are compared to mountain men of the previous century, "outcasts from society, discontented with the world, comforting themselves in the solitude of nature by the occasional bearfight." The author also of the book *Outlaw: The Saga of Claude Dallas,* Long appears fascinated by those who live at or beyond the fringes of society. His climbers are essentially loners with shadowy backgrounds. Their social connections are fleeting, always subordinate to the big walls to which they are drawn. Long calls them "fundamentally peaceful folk," but often they are suspicious of outsiders, coarse in sensibility as well as language, rough with women and hard to like.

Although they have the energy as well as the skill to undertake the hardest routes, many of the book's subjects seem burned out—emotionally exhausted. This is particularly true of "Bullseye" Broomis, an older climber of metaphysical bent, who with his dog Elmer inhabits a wheelless VW van on the outskirts of Camp 4, where all the others live, and true also of the protagonist, John Dog Coloradas, "Grandson of a Chiricahua Indian shaman, half Indian and magician himself." John seems to come right out of *The Bear,* Faulkner's tale of a vanishing wilderness and the men who vanish with it. Haunted by the death of a climbing partner in South America, he pushes himself onto the cliffs long after his desire has lost its freshness. "All the mountains," Bullseye tells him. "They all been climbed." What John really wants is to get out of the Valley. When he and his girlfriend Liz along with the ingenuous teenage rock wizard Tucker escape to Reno, there's a brief idyll.

In view of the intrinsic interest of his subject, I regret Long's decision to propel his plot by means of a vengeful drug runner whose contraband the climbers have snatched from a cold and sinister lake, where it was submerged in a fallen aircraft. This criminal's intervention only intensifies the book's harsh and violent tone, while cluttering the action with sensational and sometimes improbable events. There was plenty going on without him, and I would have welcomed more character exploration of the climbers: of John's guilt, of Tucker's nightmares, of the motives of John's antagonist, the villainous Matt Kresinski. But Long nevertheless does some nice things with this smuggler, making him brutal without being sadistic. He is a giant of a man, who embodies a fierce retribution for the feckleness of the climbers' lives. (In a particularly ugly episode, Kresinski has led the desecration of the corpse of the smuggler's brother.) Yet "Liz had never encountered a more genuine person" than this ruffian—a dismaying insight, in view of her close relations with the Camp 4 climbers: Another outlaw, he is still, in her eyes, more human and domestic than they.

Long has a taste for the patterns and resonance of myth. The Amazonian Liz is drawn to men who are "larger than life"—an apt description of many of the book's characters. They're not always easy to believe, but they are impressive. From the first sentence they are compared to "mythical heroes." There are deliberate overtones of Greek mythology, Arthurian legend, and the

Bible—all testimony to the book's greater ambitions. "Snake Lake," the repository of the drugs that precipitate the book's many deaths, is clearly a source of evil. ("There was no escaping the lake," Long tells us toward the end.) Liz, a trusting Eve who harbors visions of life on an Oregon homestead, discovers the drugs, only to have her knowledge abused by the climbers. At the book's violent climax, John hears a rope slither across the snow with the sound of a snake. The commanding feeling has been one of *hubris,* from the very first sentence of the book: High on El Cap, John is compared to Icarus, who flew so close to the sun that his wings melted, and he fell into the sea.

Although such elements expand the novel's purposes, Long's surest touch is with the climbing scenes. There are two long ones on rock, which maintain vividness while conveying a sense both of anxiety and of exhilaration. The air is thin in these passages, the rock hard, the ground a long way down. Even better, perhaps, is a harrowing account of an ice pitch so unprotectable that the belayer simply steps to one side to make way for the unstoppable leader, should he fall.

> Using it like a carving knife, he whittled a minute notch in the verglas with the hammer's pick. Then he set a pencil point's worth of pick on the notch and pulled down on it. It held. Like a curator brushing dust from a pre-Columbian pot, Bullseye exacted an equally tiny hold from another patch of verglas with his ax.

Scenes like this are sure-fire; some of the others are too ambitious for the book's structure. But better to try too much than too little. And Long is never dull: He keeps you with him all the way to the snowy shoot-out at the end.

STEVEN JERVIS

Going Higher, the Story of Man and Altitude. Charles S. Houston, M.D. Boston, Little, Brown and Company, revised edition, 1987. 324 pages, 39 black-and-white illustrations, bibliography. Price $10.95.

This is the second revision of the book originally entitled *Going High,* which was published in 1980. The back cover states that Dr. Houston "believes strongly that medicine must be made intelligible and interesting to the general public" and the book succeeds admirably in this respect. Charlie Houston has an enviable reputation in both mountaineering and medicine. He began climbing in the European Alps in 1925, was a member of the first successful ascent of Nanda Devi in 1936 and leader of attempts on K2 in 1938 and 1953. He describes himself as an internist and long-time family doctor. Few can claim to have as much experience in the medical problems of high altitude.

The book is in three sections. The first chapters are an entertaining account of the history of man's attempts to climb (or fly) higher and higher. This is followed by four chapters introducing the reader to the physiology of respiration and circulation and how these adapt to high altitude. The remainder of the book deals with medical problems of high altitude including acute mountain sickness, high-altitude pulmonary edema, high-altitude cerebral edema, acclimatization and other problems.

The book is written in a fresh, breezy style that makes it deservedly popular among climbers. The previous editions have had a considerable influence in informing climbers about the health hazards of high altitude, and Charlie Houston has been rightly honored for his unique contributions in this area.

Perhaps it is churlish to point to errors in a book which has done so much good and which is targeted at the non-medical climber. However, Charlie Houston is a prolific, persuasive writer and it seems in order to state that the book contains some opinions not shared by other medical people interested in high altitude, and also some factual errors. In the original review of the first edition in the 1981 *AAJ*, Dr. Herbert Hultgren, another experienced physician-climber, pointed out that some of the advice was of dubious value. He noted, for example that Houston's recommendation of the careful use of the powerful diuretic "furosemide" (Lasix) in the treatment of high-altitude pulmonary edema can be dangerous. Nevertheless the same advice appears in this most recent revision.

The first edition had many factual errors and though many of these have been corrected, some persist in the present edition. For example on page 255 in a discussion of altitude and barometric pressure, the author states that the aneroid altimeter frequently used by climbers "may show the actual linear feet of elevation but only under specific conditions and in certain places, and unless corrected it does not (usually) give 'physiological' altitude". Actually the opposite is true. The barometer will give the physiological altitude because it records the barometric pressure which is what matters to the oxygen-deprived climber. However, it will not accurately give the actual elevation because the relationship between barometric pressure and altitude depends on latitude and other factors. Other errors include the statement about 2,3,DPG at the bottom of page 217, and the comment about heat loss at the top of page 73. Again it is not true that the intestines are unaffected by oxygen lack, (page 171), and this is a far more likely explanation of HAFE than Boyle's Law (page 181).

A surprising omission is any discussion of the possibility of residual impairment of brain function after return from extreme altitudes. This is a topic of great current interest and importance to modern Himalayan climbers with their alpine-style techniques. The only reference is in a disparaging comment about the possibility at the bottom of page 316 which is difficult to understand because Operation Everest II (masterminded by Houston) confirmed and extended the observations on residual brain damage made by the American Medical Research Expedition to Everest.

Does it matter whether there are errors in a book principally targeted at the non-medical climber? I think it does because the book is also read by paramedical people (for example those involved in mountain rescue) and even physicians who occasionally see patients who have been to high altitude. It is not impossible to combine scientific accuracy with clear simple writing.

But these are quibbles. No other book so entertainingly presents the basic physiology and medical problems of high altitude to the interested climber, and the book deserves its enormous popularity. I look forward to the error-free apotheosis which will presumably be called *Going Highest*.

JOHN B. WEST, M.D.

Hypothermia and Cold Injury. Evan L. Lloyd. Apen Systems, Rockville, Maryland. 1986. 397 pages. 19 figures and tables.

Although this is an excellent review of virtually all that is known today about hypothermia, the title is misleading: only seven pages are given to frostbite. Here we have a great deal of information about mechanisms of heat con-servation and loss, and of the effects of cold on every organ system and function, as well as an excellent discussion of fact and fancy in rewarming. Water deaths are usually attributed to drowning, the author points out, rather than to cold. Hypothermia is more common than suspected: though few hard data can be found (and none in this book) estimates range up to 20,000 deaths per year, mostly in the elderly, caused by cold. For the physician and physiologist particularly interested in cold, the bibliography of 1200 authors will be invaluable, but the book is not as helpful to the layman as is Wilkerson, Bangs and Hayward's small book. I recommend it strongly for cold specialists but less warmly for others.

CHARLES S. HOUSTON, M.D.

The Outdoor Athlete: Total Training for Outdoor Performance. Steve Ilg. Cordillera Press, Evergreen, Colorado, 1987. 265 pages, 95 black and white photographs, 7 drawings, appendix, glossary, bibliography. $12.95 (paper).

There is nothing new about the idea of training for climbing. Both Hans Kraus and Fritz Wiessner developed the ability to do one-arm pullups in the 1930s. Emilio Comici had the body of a gymnast, and it is unlikely that he acquired such a physique just from climbing. Hermann Buhl mentions that some of his early rock-climbing successes were attributable to well-trained hands, and Reinhold Messner describes traversing exercises that he did until exhaustion.

In the late fifties and early sixties, John Gill developed some astonishing gymnastic strengths, including one-arm one finger pullups and one-arm front levers. Gill established a standard of sheer physical strength that has rarely been equalled and has never been surpassed, although other climbers have developed higher levels of endurance. Since then, an increasing number of climbers have sought, in idiosyncratic and often unsystematic ways, to improve their performance through training.

In the eighties, continental climber have redefined the sport. Adventure and self-reliance in the face of unknown problems have been replaced by the single-minded pursuit of pure difficulty. The rock has become an elaborate piece of apparatus, the climb a routine that is rehearsed and perfected in sections until a "red point" performance is achieved. These new climbs demand a tremendous level of strength and endurance, and everyone who is serious about climbing now trains for it.

The results of all this training and hard climbing have not been encouraging. Many of the best climbers have had their careers cut short by athletic injuries, and sensible enthusiasts are beginning to look for solid information before embarking on a training regimen that could be detrimental to their primary goals.

Although there are some very extensive accounts in foreign languages about how to train for climbing, there is a dearth of information in English. Most of the available literature in English is about body-building where the goal is to develop extreme muscle mass. Even the sports-oriented material is directed at the kinds of absolute strength needed by football players and field-event competitors. Little has been written about the relative strength requirements of climbers and gymnasts.

Into this vacuum steps Steve Ilg with his book *The Outdoor Athlete*, published by the Cordillera Press. Ilg, a professional trainer and self-styled "exercise guru" from Boulder, Colorado, describes training programs for outdoor activities on land, snow, and water. His climbing prescriptions are the centerpiece of the book. They are also the most interesting to AAC members and are the only ones I feel competent to review. Others will have to decide whether he has wisdom to offer kayakers, skiers and skateboarders.

Ideally, a book on training should not only provide specific workouts, but it should also convey enough information about exercise principles to allow the reader to create personal programs, or at least sensibly modify the given routines. Ilg supplies the workouts, but when it comes to the elucidation of principles, *The Outdoor Athlete* must be judged a failure. The problem is twofold: First, Ilg is more interested in prescribing and motivating rather than educating. This may make sense for the clientele he gets as a personal trainer, but the audience he gets as an author is more likely to want to know why they should do what he says. Second, Ilg's writing and organizational abilities are utterly inadequate to the task of clear communication. Many paragraphs wander aimlessly, having only a tenuous connection to the section headings that precede them.

Ilg insists on investing every aspect of training with profound spiritual consequences. I suppose this is something gurus are obliged to do, but in places the text is almost suffocated by the weight of new-age commercials for self-actualization through workouts.

Although Ilg makes much of a lean physique, his language suffers from cellulite. Grotesque paragraphs, their meaning obscured by cascading rolls of verbal flab, lumber shamelessly through the book.

Even those hardy souls with the forbearance to plow through the writing will encounter organizational and conceptual obstacles to understanding. For example, the description of each training motion contains a section mysteriously labelled "Aspects", which lists the Latin names of the muscles affected by the motion being described. Nowhere in the book, however, is there any kind of diagram illustrating the position of these muscles in the body. Another example is the barely functional index.

Blame for a book this badly produced falls squarely with Cordillera Press. Ilg is a professional trainer, not a writer, and the editorial staff at Cordillera Press has done him a great disservice in allowing his manuscript to appear in this form.

It is particularly unfortunate that the style and organization are so incoherent, because some useful content may be overlooked. *The Outdoor Athlete* has the most varied and best thought-out weight-training routines I have ever seen. Ilg's workouts integrate most of the current knowledge about strength training: weekly variation in the exercises for enhanced stimulation and reduced chance of overuse syndromes, division of the year into distinct training periods with different exercises and levels of resistance for each period, balance of motions to prevent the kind of joint stress that results from the differential development of opposing muscle groups, the inclusion of some power work in addition to the usual strength and endurance exercises, the integration of cardiovascular and flexibility training, and the allowance for suitable rest periods.

Having said this, I have to admit to reservations, ones that are shared by virtually every climber I know who has looked at the book. It is evident that Ilg, though he climbs, is first and foremost a lifter and has allowed the demands of his primary interest to color his prescriptions for other sports. For example, in one of his transitional phase routines for climbers, he recommends a once-a-month strength day, which involves doing bench presses, squats, and full deadlifts with maximum poundages. These exercises are as dangerous as anything the adherents of climbing specificity promote, and they are of such marginal use for technical climbers as to be superfluous. If you happen to find yourself pinned under a 250 pound boulder, you will wish you had developed maximal bench pressing ability, but otherwise you are risking shoulder injuries for very minimal climbing benefit. An example of a recommended exercise that is not irrelevant but is poorly adapted to climbing is dips. Repetition mantles on a flat surface and muscle-ups on a bar are no more dangerous and far more productive for the time and effort expended. If you must do dips, performing them with the palms facing outward will enhance their usefulness considerably, but Ilg doesn't mention this variation.

In addition to the inclusion of exercises of tangential utility, there are some serious omissions. The most glaring is the lack of hand strength and endurance work. All the upper body strength in the world is going to be useless to a climber who can't hold on long enough to use it. There is no exercise topic more important to climbers than safe and effective methods of developing hand strength and endurance, and Ilg is silent on this crucial issue. After all his very sensible talk about balanced and progressive training, Ilg simply abandons ship when it comes to hand exercise, recommending some buildering on days off from the gym. It is going to be pretty difficult for modern climbers to take seriously an exercise program that neglects to train the most important single part of the climber's anatomy.

The second kind of omission has already been alluded to above. Ilg prefers weights and machines to bodyweight exercises. The result is that many of the neural pathways appropriate for climbing will not be adequately trained, and the coordination of muscles will be lacking. I know a number of climbers who have emerged from a winter of weight-training stronger than ever, but who find that they feel awkward and strained when they begin to climb. They have been training their bodies to be rigid centers around which weights are lifted and balanced, while climbing demands that the body be continually shifted to adapt to the position of the extremities and the forces they exert. For these climbers weight training has tuned an inappropriate set of neuromuscular responses, producing the experience of clumsiness and stress.

I am not suggesting that all traditional weight exercises are of little use to climbers. Some lifts, like the overhead press, are essential for strengthening muscles that oppose the pulling motions that are common in climbing. Some kinds of cable machine exercises, for example tricep pressdowns, are already quite specific to climbing. But there is a host of climbing-specific bodyweight exercises that is absent from Ilg's account. This is really the subject for another book, but a few examples will illustrate the kinds of exercise that Ilg either ignores or slights:

Rope Climbing: Rope climbing is probably the best single upper body exercise you can do for climbing. A rope is far better than a Bachar ladder or a peg board. You aren't limited to some fixed spacing in your reaches, so you have the opportunity to work on maximum extension when you are fresh and shorten your stride progressively as you tire. A long stride requires both pulling and pressing motions, thereby working and coordinating a full range of muscles. Climbing a rope for speed is one of the best power exercises for climbing. Ilg emphasizes the importance of power training in his introduction, but includes no upper body power work in his exercise routines. (Incidentally, Ilg credits Steve Wunsch with the introduction of dynamic power techniques to climbing. Pierre Allain and scores of other Fontainebleau boulderers predate Wunsch by as much as 40 years. In this country, John Gill, Dick Williams, and John Stannard also made extensive use of dynamic techniques long before Wunsch first employed them.)

Uneven grip pullups. An alternative for those who can't find a rope to climb, or who are too weak to climb a rope initially. One hand on the bar, one hand lower on a towel or piece of webbing looped over the bar. Both hands must pull; don't flip the lower elbow up and mantle. Keep working the hands further apart as you gain strength.

High Pullups: Another explosive power exercise in which you attempt to accelerate upwards as high as possible. The back is kept straight, and you don't lean over the bar as you pass it. Ultimately, you should be able to slap the bar to your thighs.

Muscle-Ups: A pullup followed by a press to straight-armed support, done slowly. A full-range motion that is much better than doing pullups and dips separately.

Front Levers: A still-ring move. The body is held parallel to the ground, facing up, arms straight. Most weight lifters can't come close to doing this, whereas most climbers can. It must be a useful climbing strength if so many climbers develop it naturally. It seems to be related to body control on overhanging walls. A particularly good combination exercise is to do repetiton front lever muscle-ups. Hold a front lever for three seconds, pull to a muscle up, drop back down to a front lever, and repeat.

One-leg Deep Knee Bends: An alternative to squats that involves more balance and body control. Best done by walking a bar or pipe and alternating one-leg deep knee bends.

Routines: These exercises can be combined to stress the body in a way more analogous to what is experienced climbing. Here is an advanced example that needs a high bar: One arm pull up on the right hand, one arm pull up on the left hand, muscle up, foot to bar, pivot, one leg deep knee bend up and down, regrasp bar, drop to front lever, hold three seconds, drop to hang, and repeat sequence, using other foot for the knee bend.

Ilg considers this kind of training "overly specific" and warns about the injuries that will result. Indeed, his position was supported by Dr. Mark Robinson's superb talk at the 1987 AAC meeting in Las Vegas. Personally, after more than twenty-five years of regular "overly specific" training, I am unconvinced. The kinds of injuries that climbers get from specific training can also be attributed to extreme overzealousness and a failure to do exercises that balance muscle groups. We don't know whether their injuries are the result of the type of training they do or the approach they take to training. There is nothing inherently safe about conventional weight-training activities, and a rational, progressive, climbing-specific program does not have to be any more dangerous. The key to effective body weight training is not to restrict yourself to body weight! The secret is to use counterweights or an elastic band system to effectively reduce body weight in a controllable, modifiable fashion.

There are two topics that Ilg doesn't omit but which are very incompletely presented. The first is flexibility training. Ilg pays lip service to it and includes an incomplete and idiosyncratic set of movements that looks as if it were appended as an afterthought because the pictures were available. These photos are accompanied by ecstatic and incoherent prose but almost no useful advice. Get *Stretching* by Bob Anderson, a book that Ilg recommends but which doesn't appear in the bibliography.

The second sketchily presented topic is nutrition. In addition to an inadequate chapter, there is an appendix on Ilg's personal eating habits. Ilg himself suggests you ignore this appendix, a judgement with which I heartily concur.

Finally, there is a psychological problem with all training that Ilg does not address. The athlete in training strives for momentary muscular failure, focusing all his efforts on exhausting his strength. The climber, at every moment, wants to do exactly the opposite, namely, to conserve strength. Long periods of training can subtly promote very bad energy management habits, and the climber needs to think about this quite consciously as he resumes climbing in the spring.

It is clear by now that *The Outdoor Athlete* is a seriously flawed book. As a source of general information and advice, it cannot begin to compare to the paradigmatic *Sports Illustrated Strength Training* by John Garhammer. Nonetheless, the actual workout descriptions in *The Outdoor Athlete* are unique and deserve the thoughtful attention of anyone planning to train for climbing. If you are new to training, Ilg's workouts are probably the best way to start. Buy the books by Anderson, Garhammer, and Ilg. Read Garhammer so you know what's going on. Skip the first sixty pages of Ilg's book, and follow his program for a year, adding full-body flexibility sessions from Anderson. Then start to branch out to more specific routines.

The primary goal of training for climbing is to increase performance, as Kraus, Wiessner, Comici, Buhl, Messner, and Gill realized years ago. A secondary goal, one understood only recently, is to prevent injury. Some very good books on training in general exist, but we still await a definitive treatment aimed specifically at the unique demands of climbing.

RICHARD GOLDSTONE

El Everest, Historia de una conquista. Conrad Blanch and Joan Massons. Ediciones Península, Barcelona. 1986. 236 pages, 174 color photographs.

This lovely, large-format book reports on the Spanish Catalan expeditions to Mount Everest, an unsuccessful attempt in 1983 and the climb to the summit on August 30, 1985. Both expeditions climbed during the monsoon period via the North Col and the Northeast Ridge. The text tells also of previous Catalan expeditions, of preparations, of China and more especially Tibet as well as the climbing activities.

The English-speaking reader will be immediately attracted to the book by the beautifully reproduced color photographs. Many are full page, a number are double-paged, measuring 11½ by 18 inches, and a few are even larger fold-outs. They illustrate this route on Everest extremely well. One which caught my eye in particular was a shot of the Second Step. There was one strange omission; in the diagram of routes on Everest there was no indication of the East-Face route climbed by Americans in 1983. This is certainly a book which will appeal to collectors of beautiful mountain books.

ADAMS CARTER

In Memoriam

NOEL EWART ODELL
1890-1987

Striding up through the sun-scented evergreens toward Nanda Devi in 1936, I remember Odell exclaiming, "God! It's good to be back." It was twelve years since his great effort on Everest had been hailed by the mountaineering world. He and three other distinguished British climbers had joined us four brash young Americans in what became a marvelous experience for all. We kept in touch thereafter; just fifty years later, I dined with him in Cambridge; he seemed unchanged. A few weeks later he died in his sleep at 97.

Noel Odell was of the old school of climbers, tweedy, casual, low key and more concerned with joy than triumph. Forever linked with Mallory and Irvine and Everest, he remains one of the great figures of mountaineering. Though he never sought fame and fortune, he was known and loved all over the world as a distinguished father figure, far more interested in others' activities than in talking of his own. Indeed he seldom spoke of himself, his family or his long and diverse record of climbing and exploration. In 1975 he charmed and delighted a mountain medicine symposium in Yosemite showing old glass slides of the 1924 Everest expedition without mentioning his own heroic role. He often spoke in many parts of the world and in his later years brought a flavor of the old world to many meetings.

He became a member of the Alpine Club in 1916, a founder of the Himalayan Club, and was made honorary member of a dozen mountain clubs around the world. He had a long and intimate connection with American climbing. He was guest of honor at the American Alpine Club's Annual Meeting on December 29, 1926. He became a member of the Club in 1928 and was made an honorary member in 1936.

His personality, strength and endurance during a sledge trip across Spitsbergen in the twenties led to his selection for Everest in 1924. We were awed by his acceptance of our invitation to Nanda Devi, where he and I shared the first summit bid. Then, paired with Bill Tilman he went to the top and held the record for the highest summit reached for the next fourteen years. Two years later, he went back to Everest with Tilman's reconnaissance, and after the Second World War he climbed in the Rockies, the Canadian Yukon, Alaska and New Zealand, his last excursion being on the occasion of the 125th anniversary of the Swiss Alpine Club, when he was 93 years old.

He was a Lecturer in Geology at Harvard University from 1928 to 1930. While there he was a great inspiration to the recently founded Harvard Mountaineering Club and inspired Harvard students to organize expeditions to the great mountains of the world. During his stay at Harvard, he climbed the

NOEL EWART ODELL
1890-1987

ice gully in Huntington Ravine on Mount Washington which bears his name and has been a touchstone for undergraduates ever since.

The record shows that he was trained as a geologist, was three times wounded during the First World War and thereafter worked in various oil and mining companies around the world. He never aspired to be and never was a great geologist but, perhaps more importantly, he inspired many by example and a voluminous correspondence. His wife Mona was a climber though not an expeditionary; his son was a geologist but not a climber.

He was a gentle man. Generous, mild, modest and seldom ruffled or angry, he was a lovely companion, never bloody minded or out of sorts even when his companions were impatient with his deliberate pace. Although he had a grand store of reminiscenses and anecdotes, he was never boring. He was a joy to be with and a loss to generations who may never know someone like him.

CHARLES S. HOUSTON, M.D.

BRADLEY BALDWIN GILMAN
1904-1987

Bradley Gilman, a long-time member of the Club's hierarchy, served it as councilor, secretary, treasurer and president over a period of four decades. He was descended from two primeval New England families, the Gilmans of New Hampshire and the Baldwins of New Haven, Connecticut. Numbered among his many prominent ancestors were a signatory of the Declaration of Independence and the Constitution of the United States and two governors of Connecticut. He was a native of Worcester, Massachusetts, the son of Warren R. Gilman and Helen Baldwin Gilman. After his father's death, when Brad was 16, the family moved back to his mother's family home in New Haven. Brad attended the traditional family college, Yale, graduating in 1925. While there, he earned a reputation as an outstanding athlete, being elected captain of the soccer team and playing lacrosse in such a manner as later to be elected to the American Lacrosse Hall of Fame.

Upon graduation from the Harvard Law School in 1928, he entered a Worcester law firm where he practiced until 1953. Subsequently he became vice-president for trusts and investments at a Worcester bank, from which he retired in 1969. Brad was a patient, tolerant and understanding listener and a thoughtful, practical counselor. He was especially effective at bringing about the resolution of problems without attendant confrontation or rancor.

Though he may have "played it safe" in his family and professional life, Brad Gilman possessed an unusually strong sense of adventure which manifested itself in his life-long passion for outdoor activities in general, and in mountaineering in particular. He was happiest in this other side of his life, whether cutting firewood at his camp in Barre, Massachusetts, or leading an Alpine Club of Canada party up Mount Hungabee. Not a daredevil, he was nonetheless a bold, skillful mountaineer, not so much in a narrowly technical sense, although he was a first-rate rock climber in his time. His particular strength lay as a route-finder, as a planner, as a leader whom people trusted.

First as a camper and then as a counselor at Camp Pemigewasset in Warren, New Hampshire, he became acquainted with the White Mountains of New Hampshire, to which he returned right to the end. Brad's first mountaineering experiences occurred in the Alps, often in the company of his cousins, Roger and Hassler Whitney, who had learned to climb while attending prep school in Switzerland. These early trips were made possible, to a degree, by grants from great-uncle George Baldwin, who resided in lonely splendor in a hotel at Vevey on Lake Geneva. Brad complained about including a tuxedo in his climbing kit for the obligatory visit with the old gentleman, then in his 90s, but a hot bath, substantial meal and decent night's sleep were not unwelcome after a stint in the mountains.

In an era when the style was to climb with guides, he and his companions flouted the convention by undertaking serious ascents without any. In 1927, with Bev Jefferson, he made the first guideless ascent of Mount Louis, near Banff. He was especially proud of his ascents in 1928 of the Grépon and of the Arête des Quatre Anes on the Dent Blanche, not the sort of things young American climbers were supposed to be doing guideless! On several occasions, Brad and his friends astonished the other inhabitants of Alpine huts by using picture postcards of the peaks as a means of working out a route, instead of utilizing a proper guidebook. In one of his letters of that period, he writes with disdain of the arrival at the hut of the well-known English climber, Fitch, with his entourage of guides, porters and manservants.

When he was at the Harvard Law School, Brad became a member of the then-fledgling Harvard Mountaineering Club, where he met Henry Hall. This contact blossomed into another life-long friendship and it was Henry who encouraged and sponsored Brad's attendance at the 1926 Alpine Club of Canada encampment at Moat Lake in the Ramparts. There, along with Bev Jefferson and Bob Cleveland, he accomplished the first ascent of Blackhorn Mountain, despite strenuous opposition to the venture from the ACC hierarchy. Brad delighted in describing how the old fogies were outwitted and their dire predictions were proven unfounded.

In 1928, Robert Underhill, the best American climber of the day, succeeded in climbing the first route on the great cliff of Cannon Mountain in Franconia, New Hampshire. Of the route, now known as the "Old Cannon," he wrote, "This appears, from all examination to date, to be the only possible route up the cliff." The next spring, before the ink was dry on Underhill's pronouncement, Brad Gilman and Hass Whitney climbed the spectacular ridge left of the prominent gash in the face. Originally called the "New Cannon," the route has since been memorialized as the "Whitney-Gilman." Indeed they enjoyed it so much that they climbed down and repeated it, so that each of them could lead every pitch! In one stroke, they had advanced the level of American climbing by a whole grade. Even today, six decades later, the Whitney-Gilman serves as the reference point for New England rock climbs.

BRADLEY BALDWIN GILMAN
1904-1987

Following his marriage in 1929, Brad's time for climbing inevitably became curtailed and his objectives became tamer. But the mountains remained a necessary ingredient for a complete life. He became active at the camps of the Alpine Club of Canada, attending eleven of them between 1931 and 1952. He earned a well-deserved reputation as a leader "who gives his party a good time." Leading large groups of mostly inexperienced people requires a kind of patience and encouraging manner that he possessed in abundance. Guiding such people through the hazards and difficulties imposed by the terrain used his consummate route-finding abilities. He often commented that the fascination of mountaineering lay principally in finding a way that would work and be enjoyable as well. He emphasized the intellectual and artistic aspects of the sport. In 1938, in company with Henry Hall and Rex Gibson, he pioneered a direct approach from the Sunwapta valley to the base of Mount Alberta, a route that can be continued either to the north end of the Columbia Icefield or to the headwaters of the Athabasca River below Mount Columbia. Although conditions prevented their making a successful attempt on Alberta, they had made forever obsolete the long, earlier approach via the Athabasca River to the very heart of the range. In recognition of his services to mountaineering in Canada, the Alpine Club of Canada awarded him in 1940 the Silver Rope, its highest honor for leadership.

During the war years, Brad participated in the training of Canadian troops in mountain techniques and he served as president of the venerable Appalachian Mountain Club, the first non-Bostonian to do so. For the next 20 years he was actively involved with the affairs of the American Alpine Club, serving in several capacities including president. Many Council meetings were convened at the Gilman's camp in the woods of Barre, Massachusetts. Everyone who attended these gatherings recalled with fondness what congenial and enjoyable occasions they were.

Brad made his last "real" climb, Mount Odaray in the Lake O'Hara region of the Canadian Rockies in 1964, fittingly with one of his earliest rope-mates, Roger Whitney, and with his daughter Harriet, who continues actively to pursue her father's avocation.

He was a reserved man who rarely revealed anything of his innermost feelings. On one matter, however, he was quietly but firmly outspoken: he had an abiding distaste for organized religion. It was in Nature that Brad seemed to find that solace and that exhaltation which most others seek in a dogma: in the forests teeming with life, on a beach strewn with seashells, in a desperate moment survived with a friend, on the frigid, lonely summit of a great peak. On his final visit last summer to our home in northern New Hampshire, he sometimes sat quietly in our yard, gazing up at the peaks of the Presidential Range rising just across the way. In his look we saw a sense of contentment and a suggestion of profound peace.

ROBERT KRUSZYNA

M. BECKETT HOWORTH
1900-1986

By the death of M. Beckett Howorth the American Alpine Club has lost one of its most distinguished members. Although Dr. Howorth spent most of his life in the New York area, he was born in West Point, Mississippi and spent his boyhood there, graduating from the University of Mississippi with a bachelor's degree in 1921 and then attending that university's two-year medical school before going to Washington University in St. Louis, where he obtained his M.D. in 1925. He served his internship at the Presbyterian Hospital in New York, and from then on his career was centered around that area. His medical interest, concentrated early on orthopedics, starting as a resident at the Orthopedic Hospital in New York and later serving as orthopedic surgeon there and at other well known New York hospitals. His teaching was mainly at Columbia's College of Physicians and Surgeons and its nursing school. He lectured on his specialty in many countries and was an honorary or corresponding member of many foreign orthopedic societies.

Dr. Howorth had an early love for the outdoors and trail walking. In 1943 he joined the Appalachian Mountain Club and showed great interest in rock climbing and later in white-water canoeing. I climbed with him on some of the local New York rock climbs. In 1936 he joined a group of us in the Wind River and Teton Mountains of Wyoming, his first experience in mountaineering. He did some extremely good climbs that year, including the north face of the Grand Teton, and every year from then on with few exceptions he spent his vacations climbing in the mountains of North America and Europe.

He was a prolific writer, both in orthopedics, where his *Textbook of Orthopedics* became the standard text in many medical schools, and in mountaineering on which he published many articles. After his marriage to Marjorie Meehan in 1946, she accompanied him on many of his mountain trips. His generosity was shown on his establishment of the M. Beckett Howorth Orthopedic Library, the Marjorie M. Howorth Education Fund and the endowment of the M. Beckett Howorth Chair in Orthopedics at the University of Mississippi, where he spent the last five years of his life until his death at his home in Jackson, Mississippi on July 16, 1986.

KENNETH A. HENDERSON

MARJORIE MAYE MEEHAN HOWORTH
1904-1987

Marjorie Maye Meehan was born in Quincy, Illinois in 1904. She attended the local schools and studied at the Chicago Academy of Art. She had a career in professional dancing in many cities of the Midwest. She married Dr. M. Beckett Howorth, whom she met after her move to New York during World War II.

She quickly acquired the necessary skills to accompany her husband on mountaineering, skiing and white-water canoeing trips. She had a fine list of ascents in the Rockies, the Sierra, the Alps and other ranges. She survived her husband by only a few months, dying at their home in Jackson, Mississippi on May 24, 1987.

KENNETH A. HENDERSON

ALDEN FRICK MEGREW
1910-1987

Alden Frick Megrew, retired chairman of the Fine Arts Department of the University of Colorado, died at his home in Boulder on September 17, 1987. A life-long mountaineer and 57-year member of the American Alpine Club, Megrew was especially active in the Canadian Rockies. In the late 1920s he shared a number of first ascents in that area with other Club members, including J.M. Thorington, O.E. Cromwell and Dyson Duncan. In 1928 he made the first winter ascent on skis of Mount Washington via Tuckerman Ravine. He spent the summer of 1929 in Switzerland, where he participated in the ascent of the Weisshorn and a "triple traverse" of the Matterhorn. His appetite for the mountain experience, technical debate and expedition news remained keen throughout his life, and long after his active climbing days were over. His enthusiasm for the sport was infectuous. He was particularly interested in the development of younger climbers, upon whom he always urged membership in the American Alpine Club. He leaves Rue French Megrew, his wife of 50 years, a daughter and two grandsons.

ROBERT H.S. FRENCH

ROGER MARSHALL
1941-1987

Roger Marshall died on May 21 while descending from an unsuccessful attempt on the Everest Superdirect. It was his second solo attempt on the route in less than a year. He is survived by two sons, Richard and Duncan.

Born in the Lake District of Great Britain, Marshall began his climbing as a British crag rat, a hard-climbing, hard-partying, hard-fighting raconteur. As he got a bit older, he worked as a newspaper reporter and feature writer, vacationing in the Alps when he had the chance. He relocated to British Columbia in 1967 and took Canadian citizenship. He recently became a member of the American Alpine Club.

In Canada, he formed his own small company, confining his climbing activity mostly to the abundant local crags. In 1977, he climbed Mount McKinley. It was about then that he conceived the idea of a Canadian Everest expedition and applied for the South Col route. Realizing that he needed someone with a bit more organizational ability, he eventually found himself dropping from leader to deputy leader and finally to climber. Meanwhile, in 1981, he made an ascent of Aconcagua with members of the Canadian Everest team and the first winter ascent of Annapurna IV with British climbers Al and Adrian Burgess. He began to have disagreements with the new leadership of the expedition. It had expanded far beyond his original concept of a good-time, hard-climbing, alpine-style trip into a million-dollar media event. When the expedition headed for Base Camp in 1982, things came rapidly to a head.

Marshall and Al Burgess walked into Base Camp ahead of the rest of the team, arousing the ire of the expedition leaders. Marshall soon found himself dismissed "for conduct likely to embarrass the sponsors" for somewhat mysterious reasons. Speculations have ranged from indiscretions on Marshall's part back in Canada, to a desire to punish him for trekking separately from the rest of the team (unlikely, since Burgess remained on the climb), to a desire among the leadership not to have a British-born climber—albeit one with Canadian citizenship—be the first to summit (chances for Marshall and his partner Burgess were considered excellent). Whatever the true reasons, they evidently weren't ones that the expedition leadership wanted to pursue. Back in Canada, Marshall demanded—and got—a formal apology from the Canadian Everest Society.

Now branded as "the Bad Boy of Canadian climbing," Marshall turned his attention to smaller expeditions, declaring that "army-style" teams removed the sport and enjoyment from climbing. The following year, his partner having dropped out, he soloed to 8000 meters on Lhotse; his solo career was born. His big breakthrough came in the fall of 1984. He summited solo and without oxygen on the normal route of Kangchenjunga. A year later, he was back, this time with the help of his companion, nutritionist Ruth DeCew, who helped him work out diet and conditioning programs to improve his performance. He went to Ama Dablam with Pete Athans, summiting alone, and then climbed high on Cho Oyu in winter with Al Burgess.

His first attempt on Everest came in the late summer of 1986. He tried unsuccessfully to forge a route from the North Col. Then, after watching Swiss climbers Loretan and Troillet on their two-day ascent of the Superdirect, he also gave that route a try. After climbing the Japanese couloir, he went offline on the enormous face that leads to the Hornbein Couloir. Unable to find a spot to bivouac, he descended.

In the spring of 1987, he was back on the Superdirect. Under powerful personal drive, perhaps also spurred by a concern for his sponsors, he started up the route on May 19, in spite of extremely dangerous ice conditions in the lower reaches of the Japanese Couloir. He remained on the face for nearly 36 hours, spending the night at the base of the Hornbein Couloir before turning around. On the descent, he cached his pack, evidently intending to try again. But 300 meters from the bottom, descending cautiously on the green and blue ice, he slipped and fell to his death. His companions found him at the base of the Japanese Couloir, his ice tools still strapped to his wrists, his rope tangled around him. Speculation is that he fell while rigging a rappel.

Marshall stirred strong emotions in segments of the climbing community. The bad blood surrounding the Canadian Everest expedition still persists. His outspoken dislike of big expeditions and his even more strident opposition to the use of Sherpas did not endear him to some people. Nor did his ability, through writing, to promote his expeditions over those of even more skilled climbers. But his writing on climbing was eloquent and his climbing record more than respectable. His advocacy of climbing by "fair means," alone or in small groups, without supplementary oxygen or support from high-altitude porters, has helped generate much discussion, a great deal of which has had a positive effect on mountaineering. His book, tentatively titled *Solo*, concerns his style of climbing and may explain a bit more of this complex mountaineer—when it is finally published.

JAMES CHASE

HANS PETER MISCH
1909-1987

Peter Misch, professor emeritus in geology at the University of Washington, passed away on July 23 in his home in Seattle. Until a week before his death he had continued to visit his rock-filled office, advising graduate students in their theses problems.

He was born in Berlin in 1909 and started doing many things early in life: painting watercolors at age 5, skiing at 6, studying geology at 10 and doing serious mountaineering at 14. His interest in geology came through Latin texts which his father, a professor of philosophy, brought home from the library at Göttingen. During the summers, Peter was sent to work on a farm, where he poked around the nearby hills, discovering fossils and geologic structures, which he pointed out to students of Professor Stille, who were mapping the area. Word of the *Wunderkind* eventually reached the great man, who summoned Peter to his office and, over the next years, directed Peter's geologic education.

Peter received his doctorate at Göttingen in 1932, at age 23, with a thesis that covered his study of geologic structures and metamorphic petrology of the central Pyrenees in northern Spain. Because of his strong combined background in geology and mountaineering, Peter was invited to join the 1932 German expedition to Nanga Parbat led by Willi Merkl. During the expedition Peter carried out extensive geologic mapping in the foothills of the massive peak and then took part in the unsuccessful efforts to reach the climbers trapped high by a severe and prolonged snowstorm.

He left Germany in 1936, soon after running afoul of the Nazi authorities, but he managed to spirit out of the country many of his valuable geologic notes, rock samples and thin sections (rocks sliced thin for microscopic analyses). He went with his wife and small daughter to China, where he taught geology at the Sun Yat Sen University in Canton. After the Japanese invasion of China, he moved with the university in 1938 to the free interior province of Yunnan. In 1940, he joined the staff of the National Peking University in Kunming, Yunnan. He did geological research and field work—and climbed—in northwestern Yunnan, at a time when much of the geology of this part of China was poorly defined. In 1939, as Japanese bombing increased, Peter's wife returned to Germany with their daughter; she died there during World War II, and he was not reunited with his daughter Hanna until nine years later, in Seattle.

Peter came to the United States on a lecture tour in 1946 and taught briefly at Stanford University before accepting a permanent post at the University of Washington in late 1947. While in California, he met and married Nicoletta ("Niki") Rosenthal (formerly of Munich). The Misch household was enlarged by the addition of sons Felix and Tony and by the arrival of Hanna from Germany in 1948.

He joined the Seattle Mountaineers in 1947 and in 1949 he was elected to membership in the American Alpine Club.

Peter Misch was one of the early proponents of the emerging—and often controversial—theory of granitization, which ascribes that much of the granite coring of the major mountain ranges is the end product of the metamorphism of sedimentary rock materials. In the North Cascades of Washington, he found his "geologic home" and spent the next 40 years in unraveling the complex geologic structures and metamorphic petrology of the range, which had been mapped only superficially prior to his arrival on the scene. Peter's work emphasized the relations between structure and metamorphism, especially the timing of deformation as it could be read from both large-scale field relations and thin sections of deformed minerals. Peter also did extensive work in the basin and range province of eastern Nevada. During the four decades of Peter Misch's presence at the University of Washington, he supervised the projects of more than 125 graduate students.

During my post-graduate summer of 1950, I was privileged to spend two months with him in the North Cascades, where he had an on-going project of mapping the range, supported by the University of Washington and the Geological Society of America. The two of us traveled together in four 2-week sessions, working out a geological cross-section of the range. We pounded the outcrops and collected rock specimens and did considerable exploratory climbing, including a few first ascents and ridge-crest traverses. We also enjoyed frequent breaks in the high alpine meadows, where we captured the scenes in watercolor.

Peter was an all-around mountain man, as is typical of his generation of climbers—and of his profession of field geologist. He was adept at fighting the lowland brush and slide alder, always with a large pack, designed for a two- to three-week stay in the high country, and he handled steep rock, snow and ice with equal ease.

Peter Misch was always very private about his fine watercolor renditions of the many places he had traveled—the Alps, China, the Cascades and the ranges of Nevada—and his paintings have been exhibited almost exclusively on the walls of his house, or are unframed in his basement "archives." His unique style of combining meticulous brushstrokes with bold and vivid colors brought out both the mountain mood and the geologic makeup of his landscapes. His only public showing was during the Alpine Art Show held in conjunction with the American Alpine Club's Annual Meeting in Seattle in December 1983.

Those of us who have had the pleasure of Peter's company through his inspiring geological teachings and field trips, or in skiing and climbing, will relive many fond memories of this unique scientist, teacher, artist and friend. We will miss most of all those wine-tasting and gab sessions with Peter and his delightful wife Niki at their home on the hill overlooking northeastern Seattle and beyond, to the North Cascades, Peter's outdoor laboratory.

DEE MOLENAAR

HANS MOLDENHAUER
1906-1987

Hans Moldenhauer, a Life Member of the American Alpine Club, died on October 19, 1987. He grew up in Mainz, where he studied music. He began climbing in the Swiss-Austrian Rätikon group, making several first ascents, and in the early 1930s he turned to the Western Alps, where he climbed, among many others, the Matterhorn, Dom, Zinal Rothorn, Monte Rosa, Mont Blanc and the Grandes Jorasses. Hans made ski ascents everywhere, winter climbs of the Mönch and Jungfrau and strenuous traverses (one in 1937 from Gressoney to Macugnaga in 2½ days via eight 4000-meter summits). He was active in the Swiss Alpine Club, the Österreichisher Alpen Klub and the elite Kletter-Gild Baderd.

In 1938, Hans left Nazi Germany for the United States, lived briefly in the East where he climbed with Fritz Wiessner and others, and then settled in Spokane. His *Tagebuch* from this period lists most of the major peaks of the Northwest, first ascents in the Cabinet Range and a proud note of January 7, 1941: "Election to the American Alpine Club." Our 1942 and 1943 *American Alpine Journals* contain articles written by Hans, who was an accomplished mountain writer. In 1943 he served briefly with the Mountain Troops at Fort Hale but was discharged with frostbite. Even after this, Hans' climbing diaries record a relentless (and successful) love of mountaineering.

His career in music was quiet but spectacular: from modest beginnings he built a vast collection of music manuscripts, the Moldenhauer Archives, now installed at Harvard, the Library of Congress and other institutions here and in Europe. With his wife Rosaleen, he wrote the definitive and acclaimed biography of the Austrian composer Anton von Webern, and for his work he was awarded medals and honors by Austria, the City of Vienna and the Federal Republic of Germany. All this with an eye condition which left him blind by the early 1960s.

Hans took me on my first climbs, walking behind me with his hand on my shoulder, his archivist's memory keeping us on course. In winters we rocketed down icy, winding roads on his old luge with me steering and Hans directing; "Watch out for the turn to the right!" Mountaineering was not only sport, but an inspiring analogue to the life well lived—full of beauty, risks, hard work and fulfillment. His motto *Excelsior!* applied to all he undertook, from a scholarly paper to a New Year's Day summit toasted with champagne in plastic cups. At my wedding, Hans recited, in his resonant accent, the Old Testament lesson: "Blessed by the Lord be His land . . . with the finest produce of the ancient mountains, and the abundance of the everlasting hills . . ." Like those mountains which mean so much to all of us, Hans gave freely of his riches, and drew our eyes to the highest summits. *Excelsior,* Hans!

DAVID K. COOMBS

CANFIELD BEATTIE
1900-1987

Dr. Canfield Beattie died on August 18, 1987 in Portland, Oregon at the age of 86. He was a long-time member of both the American Alpine Club and the Alpine Club of Canada, having joined the AAC in 1935 and the ACC in 1931. He was born in Omaha, Nebraska on December 30, 1900. His family moved to Portland in 1912 and Canfield went on to attend Stanford University and Stanford Medical School. In the early 1920s he took a graduate degree in ophthalmology at the University of Vienna. While in Austria, he became interested in the mountains and on his return to the Pacific Northwest he continued this involvement, which was to go on for the rest of his life.

Canfield attended a number of the Alpine Club of Canada's summer camps during the 1930s and he received the Silver Rope badge, given to outstanding climb leaders. He was full of interesting accounts of odd happenings on climbs, including such stories as having to bring down a climber from Mount Assiniboine with a cervical vertebra cracked in a fall, to arrange an upper body cast and then to shepherd the victim on horseback fifteen miles to the road. This was all long before the days of helicopters.

He continued his active medical practice until shortly before his death and, while he had not climbed for some twenty years, he still made regular trips to his best beloved mountains, the Canadian Rockies. He is survived by his wife Charlotte, a son and three daughters.

LEWIS L. MCARTHUR

CATHERINE M. FREER
1949-1987

"What do you mean?" I imagine Catherine saying, looking over my shoulder while I struggle with writing this. Well, I reply, I want to remind others of our memory of you. It is a fearsome responsibility. "Why do you feel that way about it?" I want to captivate them with your form of life so that they will remember. I don't know if I can do that. Also, you are intimidating subject matter. "Really. That's very interesting. I wonder why you think I am intimidating subject matter. Or even why you think of me as 'subject matter.' " You made a powerful statement, I think, disappearing in the snow and ice on a climb known for its cornices, horizontality and lack of a repeat ascent. We know that you and Dave Cheesmond chose the Hummingbird Ridge on Mount Logan in part out of dismay at the glamour antics associated with expeditions these days. It speaks of a determination, choosing climbs for the inherent difficulties rather than the popularity or public visibility. Such choices illustrate a thoroughness of yours that would seek in all corners, trying everything. It was not the sort of climb that seems real fun. "I went because I was asked to join the team. (Originally we were three.) It was important to be regarded as an equal."

"I like to think I've gone into things with my eyes open. And so, this time, as so many times before, I was afraid of dying." There are so few who could so honestly admit that fear. That admission was not a casual agreement. It was a clear view of the possibilities and, thereby, a rigorous look at and questioning of desires and actions. That questioning of yours illuminates a concern with looking at everything that comes to bear on a choice. "Well, really lighten up a little. You know, once I am there, packing loads, leading, skiing around with my camera, I am involved with what I'm doing and not fearful." But wasn't it all of a piece for you: difficult choices, possible outcomes, the attendant feelings, the joys of the activity and landscape? "You could put it that way. Those are your words, not mine. I did speak publicly about climbing being all-encompassing in its requirements; that it focuses all of one's resources. But so do many other activities. Conversation can be a complete experience, just as important as climbing.

What will make *this* conversation complete. How can the words round out the missing speaker? It's just memory filling in the loss. Memory of a living passion is what we have left.

* * *

Catherine was one of the best women alpinists in the States. She was also one of the best all-around climbers in the States.

She began climbing at nineteen in the Pacific Northwest. In 1982, she was chosen to represent the United States in the first women's rock-climbing meet held in Britain. For many years she did rock climbing at a high standard, leading many difficult climbs throughout the western United States. She did various difficult alpine routes in North America. She climbed Zenyatta

CATHERINE M. FREER
1949-1987

Mendata on El Capitan in 1983, alternating leads on one of the most difficult aid climbs in Yosemite. In 1984, she climbed the north face of Cholatse in Nepal with a team of three others, a new and difficult alpine-style ascent. She participated in attempts on K2 and Everest in 1986.

Catherine loved rock climbing more than anything. She also loved being on a river. She worked as a climbing guide for the University of Washington and for Lute Jerstad. She also guided river expeditions for Jerstad and Oregon River Expeditions.

Catherine's schooling and an abiding interest was in psychology. She wrote volumes of a personal journal which was not so much a diary as a dissertation on her ideas, observations, interpersonal relationships, emotional life. Her letters and conversations reflected her passion for poetry and interest in a variety of authors. She loved the arts. Photography and bird-watching were other facets to her involvement with and observation of landscape. She loved cookies.

Catherine will be remembered by those who knew her as deeply engaging and caring. Her concerns about the human condition will not be forgotten soon.

CARLA FIREY

DAVID CHEESMOND
1952-1987

David Cheesmond was so well described by Michael Kennedy in *Climbing* of October 1987 that I quote extensively from that issue. "By the time we met on the Kahiltna Glacier below Mount McKinley on a May afternoon in 1981, David had already traveled all over the world, almost always accompanied by his wife Gillian. Born in South Africa, he had been a driving force in the climbing scene there, doing numerous new rock climbs, as well as an early ascent of Mount Kenya's Diamond Couloir and a new route on Kilimanjaro's Breach Wall. Not content with distinguishing himself solely in the climbing world, he had excelled academically, graduating at age 19 from Durban University with an honors degree in engineering. Difficult classics in the Alps and an extended honeymoon—which included an ascent of FitzRoy—rounded out his early climbing experience.

"Weary of the political climate in their homeland, David and Gillian decided to move and western Canada seemed a logical choice. David rapidly established himself as one of Canada's leading lights, starting with the second ascent of the Emperor Face on Mount Robson (by a new line, no less). He also made ascents of several big Yosemite routes that fall, including the Shield on El Cap, but, in retrospect, 1981 seemed merely a warmup for climbs to come.

"Just a few hours from home in Calgary, the Canadian Rockies provided a fertile crucible for David's energetic approach and he managed rapid ascents of notable routes. In the fall of 1982, he climbed a new route on the east face of Mount Assiniboine with Tony Dick; it was a jump ahead in Canadian technical standards and the first of David's trilogy of modern desperates in the Rockies. The second was another plum, the 6000-foot north face of Mount Goodsir, which David and Kevin Doyle plucked in April 1983. After this, David journeyed once more to Alaska to make the first ascent of the east ridge of Mount Deborah. He and Carl Tobin rounded out that trip with yet another new route, the west face of Mount Hayes, and rather than flying out, floated down the Susitna River in a rubber raft to Denali Highway.

"The Himalaya beckoned, and that fall David joined the American team that made the first ascent of the east face of Everest. Although he didn't make the summit, it didn't slow him down. David continued at an astonishing pace in the Rockies, and the following spring, he led an all-star Canadian team on the north face of Rakaposhi in Pakistan. They first tried unsuccessfully to make the second ascent of the difficult Japanese route. In a typical display of tenacity, they returned to the mountain when the weather turned good after they had packed up Base Camp and started out with the porters. They finally succeeded.

"Adept at hard rock, David turned his attention to the limestone of Yamnuska and other nearby crags in the summer of 1985, producing a number of hard routes and first free ascents. But as always, the mountains drew him back and led to the last and most significant of David's Canadian Rockies trilogy, the north pillar of North Twin. Climbed over a five-day period with Barry Blanchard, the route follows a stunning, direct line on the right side of the north face. Despite many attempts, this huge wall had been climbed only once before, by George Lowe and Chris Jones; its second ascent, by a very difficult new route was a major breakthrough in Canadian Rockies climbing.

"David was a dreamer, and one of the most energetic and enthusiastic climbers I've ever known. He bubbled over with ideas, and it often seemed as though he had a plan for every season of every year. Not content to climb just for himself, he shared his passion far and wide, through his writing, his photography and his work with *The Polar Circus*, which he helped start and largely financed. Never one to take himself or his reputation too seriously, David encouraged and inspired those around him, regardless of the standard they climbed at.

"But David's energies weren't directed solely at climbing. A respected professional, he succeeded in building a solid career in engineering; more recently, he had opened a climbing shop in Calgary and designed and manufactured equipment. He was also devoted to his family and placed tremendous importance on spending time with his wife Gillian and their four-year-old daughter Sarah. He had friends all over the world and managed to keep in touch with all of them.

"David was disappointed with his back-to-back trips to K2 and Everest in 1986. Both had been characterized by poor weather, and despite his best efforts, success was elusive. He had been thinking of the Hummingbird Ridge on Mount Logan for several years and Catherine Freer, another veteran of the K2 and Everest expeditions, was also keen on the route. They started up with ten days of food and reached the start of the mile-long corniced ridge at 13,500 feet. Here, at the crux of the route, they disappeared. Two helicopter searches revealed no sign of life—just their packs, a small yellow tent hanging from an ice axe and, a short distance away, a bit of fixed rope stretched over the gap left by a huge broken-off cornice."

How well Mike Kennedy has expressed all that. I shall add a few personal insights of my own.

Losing Dave and Catherine Freer on the Hummingbird Ridge of Mount Logan in June of 1987 has caused a sobering reevaluation of my own goals. I had planned to be on the route with him two years previously, and Catherine tried to convince me to go this year. How hard can we push the odds when someone as good as Dave disappears?

I can remember being in the lead on the north ridge of K2 with Dave on the crux section between Camps I and II. As he zoomed up the hardest mixed section, I thought to myself that there was no one I would trust or enjoy more in the situation. It was one of those days with a great companion when you feel as if you are really climbing, laying out thousands of feet of fixed rope, in contrast to the usual expedition tedium of waiting on a big mountain.

Dave's enthusiasms and skills made him a driving force on any trip. On our Everest east face climb, he had volunteered to do a double carry to establish the high camp, Camp III, just prior to his scheduled first attempt on the summit. Reading from my journal at Camp II of the next morning, I see, "Cheese announces his cough has turned wet; his lungs don't feel right and he's going down. Can't be! Can't be Dave! He'd seemed the strongest of all and had probably contributed the most to the trip. Good judgment though. Better to come back again than to chance going to High Camp with HAPE. I admire his ability to make a difficult decision."

Dave went back down, recovered, came back up and was headed for the top before the last summit team was stopped by a snowstorm. Dave's contributions on Everest were more than just physical. His analytic engineering skills had helped with the design of the gravity winch, in my mind the key to our success. He never seemed to have a psychological let-down and really helped to carry the team. His infectious enthusiasm about the larger-than-life goals will be something I shall always treasure. I wish his daughter had had more time to share that.

GEORGE H. LOWE, III

Club Activities

EDITED BY FREDERICK O. JOHNSON

A.A.C., Blue Ridge Section. The Section continued its resurrection in style during 1987. Section Chairman Randy Starrett hosted a meeting/cookout at his home early in the year. Attendees were treated to a multitude of gastronomic delights, and the entertainment provided was on a similar level. We viewed some smoothly edited rough cuts from William Garner's upcoming film on his and Randy's social and climbing achievements in the Soviet Union.

At the fall meeting, the Section elected new officers for 1988. The meeting was enlivened by the presence of Fred Beckey, who is rumored to have located a new mountain range in Washington, D.C. Unfortunately, Fred wouldn't tell anyone where this new alpine playground was until he's done all the quality routes.

Climbingwise, several members travelled to the Greater Ranges (in our neighborhood, anything over 3,000 feet constitutes a Great Range!). The most popular destination was the Cordillera Blanca for alpine pursuits. Rock enthusiasts were busy, some travelling extensively in their quest for new rock.

The Blue Ridge Section recruited some new members during the past year and plans to emphasize membership during the coming year. Other plans include quarterly meetings, a slide show or two, and lots of climbing. Other AAC members and climbers are invited to get in touch with the Section when they are in town, and to remember that we are located in an advantageous (not necessarily envious) position in terms of access to the Federal government—if you have climbing-related lobbying to do, we can help. Contact the Section Secretary: Stuart Pregnall, 214 13th St., SE, #2, Washington, D.C. 20003, daytime phone number 202-225-1225.

RANDY STARRETT, *Chairman*

A.A.C., Cascade Section. 1987 marked another glorious year of mountaineering in the Pacific Northwest. Yakima, east of the Cascade crest, recorded 100 days without rain. Had it not been for the serious implications of the fine, stable weather, i.e. extreme forest fire hazard and a negative impact on our water resources, our summer would have been totally carefree! Leaving the rain gear at home, our members compiled an impressive list of new routes and ascents in our local mountains. In addition, Cascade Section members participated on expeditions to nearly every continent on the globe.

Our 1987 activities started with our annual banquet, attended by 150 members and guests. This capacity crowd enjoyed a wonderful presentation on the American K2 North Ridge Expedition by former Cascade Section Chairman, Steve Swenson. Additional programs in 1987 included participation in

The Mountain Summit held at Mount Rainier, 33 Years of World Mountaineering by Doug Scott, the Seattle/Tashkent Mountaineering Exchange presented by Bill Sumner and Matt Kearns, and an 80th Birthday Celebration potluck for mountaineering legend and Honorary A.A.C. member Ome Daiber.

The Section co-sponsored the Seattle/Tashkent Mountaineering Exchange that climbed in the Tien Shan and Sindon Ranges of the U.S.S.R. during June and July. This team of Northwest climbers included Cascade Section members Bill Sumner, Matt Kearns and Jim Phillips. They made ascents of many summits in these ranges including Ak-su and Mount Sindon. Many of these peaks were basically unexplored by Westerners. This was the only exchange having A.A.C. involvement that actually went to the Soviet Union in 1987. The Section is proud to have been a part of this activity and is heavily involved with the hosting of Tashkent climbers in the Pacific Northwest in 1988.

Other Section activities centered around access problems associated with lowland rock-climbing areas in the state, conservation issues, and volunteer trail maintenance projects. The Peshastin Pinnacles, a popular sandstone area near Leavenworth, remains closed to climbing. The Section is working with a local Congressman to introduce a bill next year to acquire the Pinnacles and turn the properties over to the Forest Service. Several Section members testified on behalf of the Section at a local hearing on the long-term management of the North Cascades National Park. The Section continued its maintenance of the Mount Pugh trail, which had been abandoned by the Forest Service a couple of years ago. This trail is a popular conditioner and viewpoint in the Central Cascades. Nearly 100 man-hours were spent on it in 1987. Eight newsletters were published in an effort to maintain a high level of communication within the Section and with Club headquarters. The Section added 20 new members in 1987.

Our goals for 1988 are to continue our high level of communication within the Section; maintain our number of annual Section activities, both social and project-oriented; and to continue to solicit support from and improve our relationship with the national Club.

DONALD J. GOODMAN, *Chairman*

A.A.C., New York Section. The New York Section offers its 200-odd members a diversity of activities including lectures, outings, an annual dinner and other social events. In 1987 members received invitations to six lectures followed by a social hour. Topics covered a wide range of subjects including Sacred Mountains of the World by Edwin Bernbaum; Adventure Skiing by John Harlin, III; a High Altitude Medical Symposium featuring Charles Houston, M.D., Drummond Rennie, M.D., and moderated by Samuel Silverstein, M.D.; the First Winter Ascent of Ama Dablam's Northeast Face by Carlos Buhler; Skiing the Haute Route by Fred Selby; and a documentary on the yeti by Tony Wooldridge, a British physicist and mountain runner.

The 1987 Annual Dinner, a gala black-tie benefit for the Library attended by 150 members and guests, featured Bob Bates as the after-dinner speaker discussing "Fifty Years of Mountain Exploration" in the Yukon, Karakoram and China. The inaugural John Case Award for accomplishment by a New York Section Member was presented at the Dinner to Lynn Hill for her first place finish in the women's division of this year's European Rock Climbing Competitions and to Girard Bloch for his ascent, at age 68½, of the Nose Route on El Capitan, beating the previous age record by 20 years. The award, a gold carabiner appropriately mounted and inscribed, commemorates the late AAC President, Section member and pioneer Adirondack climber and skier. Proceeds from the Dinner are being used to fund the country's largest climbing video collection, which will be housed at the Clubhouse and available to the membership on a circulating basis, as well as funding rare book restoration and preservation.

A climbing outing in the Adirondacks attracted 20 members to the Ausable Club on the weekend after Memorial Day. Despite torrid weather and a Sunday afternoon thunderstorm, numerous routes up to 5.11 were completed in the area. A cocktail party and dinner at the Lake Placid Club golf house, with slide shows by Don Mellor and Olaf Sööt, topped off the festivities. In June, the Section co-sponsored a buffet dinner and award ceremony with the Explorers Club and The Society of Woman Geographers featuring the first award of the Tenzing Norgay Trophy to the Professional Mountaineer of the Year. The 1987 recipient was Sharon Wood of Banff, Alberta, for the first ascent of Everest by a North American woman; the presenter was Sir Edmund Hillary.

During the year Section members distinguished themselves in numerous climbs and expeditions in Alaska, South America and the Himalayas. Particularly noteworthy was a successful pre-monsoon ascent of Ama Dablam's southwest ridge by John Iacovino and Chip Kamin, their first major Himalayan expedition.

PHILIP ERARD, *Chairman*

A.A.C., Oregon Section. Our annual Smith Rock trail work party took place April 4. Smith Rock has become "The" place to rock climb in Oregon and is also attracting many foreign climbers to its beautiful walls. Because of this increase in use, Smith is experiencing damage to its environment and trails. The Oregon Section is working with the Oregon State Parks Department and the climbing community to find solutions to these problems. In March at the evening get-together we were given an exciting slide show by photographer/climber Avery Tichenor, featuring several ascents of El Cap. Our annual trip to the Snow Shoe Club Cabin on the north side of Mount Hood took place in December.

TIM C. CARPENTER, *Chairman*

A.A.C., Sierra Nevada Section. During 1987, Section members were involved in the resolution of several access disputes. In both cases, climbing was permitted to continue. In crags on top of Mount Tamalpais, a traditional learning area in a spectacular setting overlooking San Francisco Bay, was the center of dispute in May. The local water district was concerned with liability and proposed banning climbing. A ban on climbing at the Stanford University campus (a haven for "buildering") was averted by negotiating some reasonable ground rules.

Section leadership met with Yosemite Park management this spring and found that the current regime is much more attuned to the climbing community than some in the past. They actually think that climbing is a legitimate activity in a National Park. Superintendent Morehead recalled climbing the Royal Arches with Al Steck some time in the misty past!

A project to preserve and document invaluable old climbing films from the pioneer climbing days in California finally got off the ground this year. The films have been transferred to studio-quality video tape and interviews with the participants are being done to record an irreplaceable bit of history. Tax-deductible donations payable to the A.A.C. can be sent to Armando Menocal at 820 The Alameda, Berkeley, CA 94707.

The Section played host in California to a 13-member climbing team from the Czechoslovak Mountaineering Association. The group, led by Vladimír Weigner, accomplished some fine climbs in Yosemite Valley during their September visit.

Section members opened their homes to host a political delegation from Lhasa, Tibet, in October. The timing was interesting, as the Mayor, Vice Mayor, and others were in this country during the "troubles" in Lhasa. It was certainly an interesting experience for the hosts, and hopefully, the source of useful contacts for A.A.C. members heading to Tibet. Our involvement was at the suggestion of Bob Craig, who helped host this "sister city" delegation in Boulder, Colorado.

Other Section activities included the annual ski tour, hot springs soak, and gourmet meal near Lake Tahoe and the Section Banquet, which featured a view of the Yosemite Valley speed-climbing scene presented by Steve Schneider.

KARL GERDES, *Chairman*

Harvard Mountaineering Club. The year saw an upswing in climbing activity as well as increased social gatherings. Furthermore, we expect to publish Issue 23 of the *Harvard Mountaineering Club Journal* next year.

In January, members Lou Derry, Alex Green and Peter Green were joined by Charlie Mace for a climb of Aconcagua. They all made an ascent of the standard route. Lou and Charlie then went to the south side of the mountain and climbed the south face via the French Route with the Messner finish. Alex and Peter returned to South America in June to climb Nevados Pisco and Huascarán in Peru's Cordillera Blanca.

In North America three members, Carl Gable, Bryan Kriens and Steve Perlman, were joined by Pat Gallagher, Dick McDougald and Alasdair Street for a traverse of the northern Picket Range in the North Cascades. The area lived up to its reputation for rugged terrain.

Local activities included climbing at local crags, with instruction for beginning climbers. Trips to the Gunks in New York and to Cannon and the North Conway area in New Hampshire were common weekend excursions. The club sponsored three slide shows: Fred Beckey drawing on his vast background talked about mountaineering in North America; Pat Clark described his trip to Baffin Island; and Sam Streibert reviewed his experiences over 25 years of climbing.

The H.M.C. cabin in Huntington Ravine, New Hampshire, which is open to the public, continues to serve as a base of ice climbing on Mount Washington. There have been some improvements such as propane lights and burners to reduce the fire hazard and to increase comfort. The cabin and its caretaker also serve to increase the safety of climbing by providing initial response to accidents. Last year when two climbers fell out of the Pinnacle Gully in −20° F weather, the presence of caretaker John Jackson in Huntington Ravine was critical to a rapid evacuation of the injured climbers. There is discussion this year of improving the first-aid and rescue cache at the cabin.

We encourage climbers visiting the Cambridge area to look us up and drop by our Thursday night meetings, if not to talk shop, then to join us for happy hour or to try our workout area.

This year's officers include President Nathan Faulkner; Secretary Alex Green; and Treasurer Carl Gable. Our address is H.M.C., 4 University Hall, Harvard University, Cambridge, MA 02138.

CARL GABLE, *Treasurer*

Iowa Mountaineers. The club completed another active year in 1987. Nearly 1260 members participated in one of the many instructional courses, the mountaineering camps, or the foreign expeditions. The courses and mountain camps were again offered for University of Iowa credit. Under the instruction of Jim Ebert 105 members finished the concentrated one-week basic rock climbing courses held at Devils Lake State Park, Wisconsin, and 630 members completed the weekend rock climbing courses offered to University of Iowa students. Three general weekend outings were held at Devils Lake with an average attendance of 50.

Jim Ebert planned, led, or instructed members on the following mountaineering camps and courses during 1987: During December, 20 members participated on a seven-day cross-country skiing trip to the Collegiate range of Colorado. Members built and lived in snow shelters at 11,300 feet near West Tennessee Lakes. During January, 70 members participated in two weekend cross-country ski courses at Devils Lake State Park. In early January, 14 members hiked to the bottom of the Grand Canyon for five days of hiking and backpacking. During March, over 40 members participated on a five-day Grand Canyon Havasupai backpacking trip to Arizona.

The club's annual banquet was held May 9 and featured the Alaskan film made by John and Jim Ebert. John Ebert presented the film. Over 100 people attended.

In June a four-day intermediate rock-climbing course was sponsored to Devils Tower in Wyoming. Over 54 manned ascents were made to the top of Devils Tower via four different routes (5.7 to 5.9) by a group of 22 members.

During July 21-31 the club held a 10-day mountaineering camp in the northern Wind Rivers of Wyoming. Fourteen members participated in two groups. Four people ascended Gannett Peak, Wyoming's highest, and 12 ascended Fremont Peak. Three other peaks were also ascended.

During early August a 10-day mountaineering camp was held in the Sawtooths of Idaho. Thirty-four members participated. Twenty-eight manned ascents were made on Warbonnet via four different routes rated from 5.6 to 5.9; 28 manned ascents were made on the Finger of Fate via four routes rated from 5.7 to 5.9; and eight people ascended Mount Heyburn via the Sturr Chimney rated 5.5. Four other peaks were ascended by members.

From August 17-21, 15 members participated on our annual Grand Teton Outing. Six members climbed the Grand via the Owen-Spalding route while seven other members climbed the Grand via the Exum Ridge. Four members climbed Teepe's Pillar and Glenco Spire. Three members traversed the Middle Teton via the north ridge and then climbed the South Teton via the northwest couloir.

In 1988 the club will again sponsor six one-week basic rock climbing courses at Devils Lake State Park during May, June and August. Devils Tower will again be ascended during the intermediate rock-climbing course from May 29-June 2. The main 12-day summer mountaineering camp will be held in the Purcell Mountain Range in British Columbia, Canada, from August 2-12.

The main 1988 foreign expedition will be to East Africa to ascend Kilimanjaro and Mount Kenya from June 25-July 24. The club will then go to New Zealand from January 14-February 20, 1989, to ascend peaks on both the North and South Islands and to hike the Milford and Routeburn Tracks; to the Peruvian Andes from June 24-July 22, 1989, to climb in the Quebrada Shallup and later ascend Nevado Huantsán and Nevado Huascarán; and finally the European Alpine Outing from June 29-July 22, 1990, to ascend the highest and most famous peaks in six Alpine countries.

JIM EBERT, *Vice President*

The Mazamas. The Mazamas of Portland, Oregon, ended their fiscal year with 2718 members. Climbing activities of the year included 157 climbs for the May-through-September summer season, four of which were cancelled because of bad weather. Twenty-seven ascents were unsuccessful, leaving 130 Mazama parties which actually reached their intended summits, a total of 1,240 individual ascents. About 20 climbs were scheduled for the winter season, and as usual, most were stormed off.

Dick Weisbaum led a winter ski outing of 28 people to Austria and Italy in February. Martin Snoey joined a successful ascent of Alpamayo in Peru in June. Nate Rathbone led a hiking group to Machu Picchu in Peru and Chimborazo in Ecuador. Jim Miller and Jack Samper took a group over the Chilkoot Trail in Alaska. Jack Grauer led a climbing group through the North Cascades. Two expeditions found disappointment on Mount McKinley in Alaska. Bob Breivogel, Richard Denker, Scott South, Barry Bell, and Don Cosgro attempted the South Buttress. Dennis Olmstead, Chris and Barry Evenson, Tom Gordon, Evan Jones, and Ed Strohmaier gave the West Rib a good try. Cosmo Palomba and Gary Barnes led a hiking group to Havasu Canyon, Arizona, in March. Ray Mosser led a party of nine down the Main Fork of Idaho's Salmon River, and John McAnulty took another nine down the Green River in Utah. George and Sue Stonecliffe took a group of nine climbers into the Goat Rocks area in Washington.

The Trail Trips Committee scheduled 198 hikes, with four cancelled. Almost all were within easy driving distance of Portland. This amounted to 2,525 individual trips. Hikes varied through a range of easy "A" grade trips to difficult "C" trips. Snowshoe hikes and overnight snow bivouacs were included.

Don Burnet yielded his position of presidency in October to the new president, Paula Beers-Klee. The club has continued with an active conservation program under chairmanship of Greg Parsons. The Research Committee awarded six grants for mountain-oriented scientific study during the past year. Mountain-book expert, John Pollock of Seattle, evaluated the Mazama library, and computerized control of the Mazama book collection has been instituted.

JACK GRAUER

Memphis Mountaineers, Inc. In 1987, the Memphis Mountaineers enjoyed a productive year. The total membership of 55 included 35 regular members residing in the Memphis, Tennessee area, seven honorary members, and 13 associate members scattered throughout the United States. The club sponsored two domestic expeditions involving nine participants at Zion National Park, Utah, and 14 participants at Rocky Mountain National Park, Colorado. In addition to ascents of numerous trade routes, new routes were established on the Organ and Deer Ridge Buttress at Zion and Rocky Mountain, respectively, by the expeditions. The Memphis Mountaineers also assisted the National Park Service with two rescues while visiting Rocky Mountain. The club also sponsored 22 shorter outings to Mid-South bluffs, the Carolinas, Texas, and New England. Individual members were active afield, and their successes included a variety of activities from trekking in Napal to paragliding in the French Alps.

The Memphis Mountaineers met monthly on second Mondays at seven P.M. in the Highland Branch of the Memphis Public Library. Informative programs presented at 1987 meetings included a variety of subjects such as glacier travel in the Cascades, oil painting mountain scenes, and a Steve Matous video. Other club functions included social events, programs on mountaineering for other local organizations, and the unanimous formulation of a public statement denouncing the placement of fixed protection on Mid-South cliffs, a very limited resource. Club members also assisted the National Park Service and Memphis State University in the production of two videos demonstrating rock climbing and rescue techniques. Members were notified of club activities through the monthly newsletter *Memphis Mountain News.*

Club officers included Jim Detterline, President; Robin Daniels, Vice President; Richard Bennett and Cynthia McKinnon, Treasurers; Jay Tomlinson, Secretary; Larry Mallory, Zion expedition leader; and Skip Daniel, Rocky Mountain expedition leader.

The Memphis Mountaineers will celebrate their 10th anniversary in 1988 with numerous activities including a banquet with special guest speaker in September. Anyone with an interest in promoting climbing in the Mid-South is encouraged to join Memphis Mountaineers. For more information, write Memphis Mountaineers, Inc., P.O. Box 11124, Memphis, TN 38111.

JIM DETTERLINE, *President*

Mountaineering Club of Alaska. Membership in the club slipped below 300 this year as the state lost more population, but we were still an active group. The club conducted its popular ice-climbing school in September and several other classes during the year to help others enjoy the outdoors during the long winters. It also sponsored various hikes and climbs locally, including the fourth annual Harding Icefield crossing, and the club also did much work on its remote glacier huts.

Members reported on several climbs of note this year. Todd Miner and two others made the second ascent to the summit of Amulet Peak, Chugach Range, in February. Mike Miller, Charlie Sassara, Karl Swanson and Brian Cannard made the first ascent of a Grade V waterfall, Mitre Might, in the Chugach in March. Leo Americus made the first winter ascent of Mount Palmer, a solo. Members also made the second ascent of Paradise Peak, Kenai Range, first ascents of Icicle Peak, Benevolent Peak and Sunlight Mountain in the Chugach, and new routes on Bellicose Peak and Benign Peak, the latter an impressive climb considering the nature of the rock in the Chugach.

WILLY HERSMAN, *President*

Potomac Appalachian Trail Club. The PATC's Mountaineering Section again had a big year during 1987. Climbing, access, and conservation were the three major activities. Climbing was really good. Over the winter of 1986-87 members climbed in New England (Lake Willoughby and the White Mountains) and locally, rock when weather permitted and ice when it was too beastly cold to contemplate rock. Skiing, with emphasis on mountain technique, was also very popular. Spring unleashed rock-hungry hordes, and the Section spread its members from Stone Mountain, North Carolina, north to Maine and west to California over the course of the year. A big trip to Peru was highly successful, and other members climbed in the Bolivian Andes as well.

Access work continued at Bull Run Mountain in Virginia. The Mountaineering Section now manages a trail easement to the climbing area. We ask that climbers interested in climbing there either a) climb at Bull Run during one of the Section trips or b) join the Section to help cover the administrative costs of managing the property. The Section also worked with local climbing activist John Gregory to persuade the National Park Service to permit a volunteer work project at Carderock, one of our local crags It took six months, but we were finally successful! Work will begin in 1989. Other projects included climbing instruction to nearly 200 people during the year. Several Boy Scout Troops also requested and received instruction in various climbing and rope-handling techniques. The Carderock guidebook neared completion, with publication scheduled for early 1989.

One project was started in response to an alarming number of local climbing accidents (none of them on Section trips, fortunately). An ad hoc group was formed to develop a three-part response: 1) provide, through local retailers, climbing seminars with an emphasis on safety; 2) develop and distribute an analysis of local climbing accidents, similar to the A.A.C.'s *Accidents in North American Mountaineering*, and 3) coordinate our instruction program with other local groups and national groups to ensure that climbing safety measures are being emphasized and taught properly.

The coming year should be fun—a film festival is scheduled for February 1989, climbing plans are shaping up with lots of different objectives being listed, and who knows what else the year will bring. Climbers interested in participating in Section activities are encouraged to contact us: PATC Mountaineering Section, 202-638-5306, 7-10 P.M. weekdays.

STUART PREGNALL, *Chairman*

AAC BOOKS

THE AMERICAN ALPINE JOURNAL, edited by H. Adams Carter.

THE AMERICAN ALPINE JOURNAL INDEX
1929-1976, Edited by Earlyn Church.
1977-1986, Edited by Patricia A. Fletcher.

ACCIDENTS IN NORTH AMERICAN MOUNTAINEERING, edited by John E. Williamson.

ACONCAGUA, Topographic map by Jerzy Wala. Text by Carles Capellas and Josep Paytubi.

CLIMBING ICE, by Yvon Chouinard.

CLIMBING IN NORTH AMERICA, by Chris Jones.

THE COLUMBIA MOUNTAINS OF CANADA—CENTRAL (The Interior Ranges of B.C.), by Earle R. Whipple, John Kevin Fox, Roger Laurilla and William L. Putnam.

THE COLUMBIA MOUNTAINS OF CANADA—WEST (The Interior Ranges of B.C.), Earle R. Whipple and William L. Putnam.

THE GREAT GLACIER AND ITS HOUSE, by William L. Putnam.

HIGH ALASKA, by Jonathan Waterman.

THE INTERIOR RANGES OF BRITISH COLUMBIA—SOUTH, by Robert Kruszyna and William L. Putnam.

MOUNTAIN SICKNESS, by Peter Hackett, M.D.

THE MOUNTAINS OF NORTH AMERICA, by Fred Beckey.

MOUNTAINS OF THE MIDDLE KINGDOM, by Galen Rowell.

THE RED ROCKS OF SOUTHERN NEVADA, by Joanne Urioste.

THE ROCKY MOUNTAINS OF CANADA—NORTH, by Robert Kruszyna and William L. Putnam.

THE ROCKY MOUNTAINS OF CANADA—SOUTH, by Glen W. Boles, with Robert Kruszyna and William L. Putnam.

SHAWANGUNK ROCK CLIMBS, by Richard C. Williams.

SURVIVING DENALI, by Jonathan Waterman.

TAHQUITZ AND SUICIDE ROCKS, by Chuck Wilts.

TOUCH THE SKY: The Black Hills in the Needles of South Dakota, by Paul Piana.

TRAPROCK: Rock Climbing in Central Connecticut, by Ken Nichols.

A WALK IN THE SKY, by Nicholas Clinch.

WASATCH ROCK CLIMBS, by Les Ellison and Brian Smoot.

WHERE THE CLOUDS CAN GO, by Conrad Kain.

YURAQ JANKA: The Cordilleras Blanca and Rosko, by John Ricker.

Prices and order information on request from The American Alpine Club, 113 East 90th Street, New York, NY 10128-1589.

INDEX
Volume 30 ● Issue 62 ● 1988
Compiled by Patricia A. Fletcher
This issue comprises all of Volume 30

V

Vaid, A. K., 228
Valdez (Alaska), 120-21
Valhaltinde (Greenland), 102
Valley of the Gods (Utah), 139
Vallunaraju Norte (Cordillera Blanca, Peru), 158
Vallunaraju Sur (Cordillera Blanca, Peru), 156
van Gelder, James, 187
Van Meter, Steve, 269
van Nieuwkerk, Edewin, 193
van Sprang, Gerard C., 191
"Vanishing Pinnacle" (Revelation Mountains, Alaska), 119
Veiga González, Constancio, 97
Venables, Stephen, 258, 282-83
Venkatesh, T., 228
Vest Fjord (Greenland), 98
Vidette, East (Sierra Nevada, California), 137
Vidmar, Lado, 37-40
Vidoni, Tullio, 262-63
Vigouroux Vidal, Iván, 169-70
Voll, Herbert, 97

W

Wada, Seichi, 256
Waddington, Mount (Coast Mountains, British Columbia), 146
Wade, Mount (Saint Elias Mountains, Alaska), 123
Wahlund, Ebbe, 266
Waillani (Cordillera Quimsa Cruz, Bolivia), 168
Waitman, Randy, 109, 117
Wallaby Peak (Cascade Mountains, Washington), 129
Walter, Thomas, 119
Walter, Tom, 15-20
Warburton, Michael, 126-28
Washington, 128-34
Washington Column (Yosemite California), 128
Waterfall Wall (Yosemite, California), *art.*, 1-14
Watkins, Mount (Yosemite, California), 128
Watkins Mountains (Greenland), 153
Watters, Robert, 209-10
Wegener Peninsula (Greenland), 102-3
Weigand, Geoff, 63, 66
Weigner, Vladimír, 128
Welsh, David A., 106
West, John B., 312-14
Westmacott, Michael, 186
Wheeler, Simon, 229
White, Greg, 131
White Needle (Kashmir), 239
Whitehouse, Annie, 199
Whitney, Mount (Sierra Nevada, California), 136

Whitton, Louis A., 272
Wickersham, Mount (Chugach Mountains, Alaska), 120
Wielicki, Krzysztof, 201-2
Wila Llojeta (Cordillera Real, Bolivia), 165
Wila Wilani (Cordillera Real, Bolivia), 164-65
Wildspitze (Greenland), 100
Wind River Range (Wyoming), 143
Wind Tower (Eldorado Springs Canyon, Colorado), 87
Winstone, Mount (Coast Mountains, British Columbia), 147
Witches Tower (Cascade Mountains, Washington), 130
Wolf, François, 154
Wolf, Hermann, 166-69
Wood, Mount (Saint Elias Mountains, Yukon Territory), 145
Woolley, Stan, 153
Wörner, Stefan, 280
Wrangell, Mount (Wrangell Mountains, Alaska), 120
Wrangell Mountains (Alaska), 120, 121-22
Wrangell Mountains: Peak 8880, 122, Peak 9008, 122; Peak 9105, 122; Peak 9110, 122; Peak 9124, 122; Peak 10565, 121
Wumkes, Mark, 118
Wyoming, 143

Y

Yackulic, Charles F. (Fred), 130
Yadev, M. P., 238
Yalung Kang (Sikkim Himalaya), 188-90
Yamagata, Masami, 221
Yamamoto, Munehiko, 256
Yamamoto, Ryozo, 286
Yamanaka, Yoshiki, 229
Yazghil Sar (Karakoram Range, Pakistan), 260
Yerupajá (Cordillera Huayhuash, Peru), 161-63
Yokomizo, Takehiko, 243-44
Yosemite (Sierra Nevada, California), *art.*, 1-14; 128, 135-36
Yukon Territory, *art.*, 76-79; 145-46
Yulong Shan (Yunnan Province, China), 265

Z

Zagdoun, André, 97
Zanetti, Mount (Wrangell Mountains, Alaska), 120
Zappelli, Cosimo, 109, 118
Zawada, Andrzej, 246
Ziel, Frederick, 198
Zimmermann, Ralf, 149-51
Zion National Park (Utah), 142
Zmurko, Waldemar, 166